Hakibbutz Ha'artzi, Mapam, and the
Demise of the Israeli Labor Movement

Modern Intellectual and Political History of the Middle East

Fred H. Lawson, *Series Editor*

For a full list of titles in this series, visit
https://press.syr.edu/supressbook-series/modern
-intellectual-and-political-history-of-the-middle-east/.

HAKIBBUTZ HA'ARTZI, MAPAM, AND THE DEMISE OF THE ISRAELI LABOR MOVEMENT

Tal Elmaliach

Translated from the Hebrew by
HAIM WATZMAN

SYRACUSE UNIVERSITY PRESS

First Edition 2020

20 21 22 23 24 25   6 5 4 3 2 1

∞ The paper used in this publication meets the minimum requirements of the American
National Standard for Information Sciences—Permanence of Paper for Printed Library Materials,
ANSI Z39.48-1992.

For a listing of books published and distributed by Syracuse University Press,
visit https://press.syr.edu.

ISBN: 978-0-8156-3658-8 (hardcover)
　　　978-0-8156-3664-9 (paperback)
　　　978-0-8156-5488-9 (e-book)

Library of Congress Cataloging-in-Publication Data

Names: Elmaliach, Tal, author. | Watzman, Haim, translator.

Title: Hakibbutz ha'artzi, Mapam, and the demise of the Israeli Labor movement / Tal Elmaliach ;
　　　translated from the Hebrew by Haim Watzman.

Description: First edition. | Syracuse : Syracuse University Press, 2020. | Series: Modern intellectual
　　　and political history of the Middle East | Revised version of the author's doctoral dissertation
　　　submitted to the University of Haifa, Israel, 2013. | Includes bibliographical references and index. |
　　　Summary: "'Hakibbutz Ha'artzi, Mapam, and the Demise of the Israeli Labor Movement' tells the
　　　story of Israel's political transformation between the 1950s and the 1970s. It asks how the Israeli
　　　Labor movement, which played a leading role in building the country, lost its hegemony to the
　　　political Right in the 1977 elections and analyzes the historical origins of this dramatic event,
　　　known as the 'upheaval' (mahapach). Elmaliach argues that the political upheaval was the result
　　　of a long-term internal crisis in the Labor movement, beginning in the mid-1950s, during which
　　　its public support gradually collapsed until it reached the low point of the 1977 elections. In so
　　　doing, he seeks to offer an innovative analysis, suggesting that the crisis that led to the collapse of
　　　the Labor movement was the outcome of the manner in which its power had been built, and that
　　　it was rooted in the economic, social, political, and cultural processes that were at the foundation
　　　of its hegemony—in other words, that the sources of the Labor movement's strength were also the
　　　causes of its weakness"—Provided by publisher.

Identifiers: LCCN 2019037233 (print) | LCCN 2019037234 (ebook) | ISBN 9780815636588
　　　(hardcover) | ISBN 9780815636649 (paperback) | ISBN 9780815654889 (epub)

Subjects: LCSH: Ḳibuts ha-artsi ha-shomer ha-tsa'ir (Israel) | Shomer ha-tsa'ir (Organization : Israel) |
　　　Mifleget ha-po'alim ha-me'uḥedet (Israel) | Israel—Politics and government—20th century.

Classification: LCC HX742.2.A3 E45 2020 (print) | LCC HX742.2.A3 (ebook) | DDC 956.9405—dc23

LC record available at https://lccn.loc.gov/2019037233

LC ebook record available at https://lccn.loc.gov/2019037234

Manufactured in the United States of America

Contents

Acknowledgments

THE PUBLICATION of this book gives me an opportunity to thank a number of people and institutions I cherish. Daniel Gutwein (University of Haifa) and Aviva Halamish (Open University) have guided me over many years. I am greatly in their debt for their investment of time and energy and hope that they will be proud of the result. Thanks are also due to my mentors in my postdoctoral fellowships, Tony Michels (University of Wisconsin–Madison) and Avi Bareli (Ben-Gurion University) for their ideas and advice, which contributed a great deal to my research. Further gratitude goes to Tom Navon, a friend and colleague, who read the manuscript and provided me with his insights; to my translator, Haim Watzman, whose comments and suggestions improved the book significantly; and to the staff of Syracuse University Press for their professional and kind treatment. I am also grateful to the Israel Institute, which provided the fellowship that enabled me to produce the book, and to the Havatzelet Group—Education and Culture Institutions of Hashomer Hatza'ir, the Yad Yaari Research Center of Hashomer Hatza'ir, the Faculty of Humanities at the University of Haifa, and the Ben-Gurion Research Institute for the Study of Israel and Zionism for their general support of my work and especially for the financial help they have provided for the translation of my manuscript into English.

Hakibbutz Ha'artzi, Mapam, and the
Demise of the Israeli Labor Movement

Introduction

SOCIALISM, which arose as a political and social current in the mid-nineteenth century and became a major force during the first part of the twentieth, went into decline—indeed, collapse—in the last quarter of that century. By some accounts, its economic, social, and ideological principles had been tried and found wanting. In the early 1980s, a tide of conservative neoliberalism eroded the welfare state, most notably in the United States and Great Britain. The Socialist parties of France and Sweden and the German Social Democratic Party suffered electoral defeats during this decade, and the Communist bloc dissolved in 1989.[1] In Israel, the change came at the time of the political upset of 1977. That year's election saw the defeat of HaMa'arakh (the Alignment), a slate that united virtually all the parties of the country's socialist–Zionist Left, collectively referred to in Israeli parlance simply as "the labor movement."[2] Government passed into the hands of the right-wing nationalist party Likud (Consolidation) after forty years in which the labor movement had enjoyed hegemonic status in the Zionist movement and Israel. It had come to power in the Zionist movement in 1933, when it emerged as the largest force in the Zionist Congress; after the founding of Israel in 1948, it held the reins of government for twenty-nine years.[3]

The labor movement's ejection from power in Israel had two immediate results, which were evident by the beginning of the 1980s. The first was a spurt of construction of Israeli settlements in the territories Israel had occupied since the Six-Day War of 1967.[4] Israel first established civilian outposts in these territories while the labor movement was in power, but the numbers were small, and their locations limited, in keeping with the movement's hope of achieving a territorial compromise in the future. The second result was economic liberalization, aimed at reducing state over-sight of the economy and empowering free enterprise.[5] A major reform program was implemented in 1985, ironically under a national unity gov-ernment led by Shimon Peres of the Labor Party, in which he and Likud leader Yitzhak Shamir held the prime minister's post for two years each in rotation. The Economic Stabilization Program, as it was called, was neoliberal in spirit and demonstrated that a significant segment of the Israeli labor movement had adopted the economic views of the Right and was prepared to put them into practice.[6] In the second half of the 1980s, crisis hit the Histadrut (General Organization of Workers in Israel), the labor movement's economic base. The Histadrut was both a national labor union and a concern that owned and ran a large range of factories, busi-nesses, and social services. In 1995, it was finally dismantled—during the tenure of a government led by Yitzhak Rabin and the Labor Party, leaving only its labor-union core intact.[7] At the same time, the kibbutzim, one of the labor movement's most important emblems, sank into a severe debt crisis, and over the course of the 1990s many of them began to privatize and to adapt their way of life to the capitalist environment in which they found themselves.[8] The crisis of the kibbutzim, the dismantling of the His-tadrut, and the Likud's rise to power epitomized the collapse of the Israeli labor movement, at least as the public saw it.

This book claims that the roots of this collapse are to be found in the economic, social, political, and cultural transformations the labor move-ment underwent in the two decades from 1956 to 1977. I begin in 1956, a year marking the beginning of the crisis of the Left, not just in Israel but around the world. A new Israeli economic era began during the second half of the 1950s, marking the transition from emergency and austerity to accelerated growth.[9] The same happened in other Western countries as a result of the economic boom of the post–World War II era. The boom set off a strident debate in Israel and around the world about the future of socialism in the era of the capitalist welfare state.[10] But 1956 was not just an economic turning point; it was also a year of ideological crisis in the socialist world. The text of Nikita Khrushchev's secret speech to the Twentieth Communist Party Congress was published in the West in June, and at the end of October labor-led Israel invaded the Sinai Peninsula with the support of Britain and a French government headed by a Socialist, Guy Mollet. The worldwide socialist Left viewed the Sinai Campaign as a patently colonialist and imperialist military operation.[11] In Israel, the late 1950s were also the years of a crisis in the pioneering ethos of the socialist Zionist Left, when the labor movement's leaders began to find it difficult to mobilize younger members of the movement to carry out national and movement missions.[12] In 1977, the labor movement lost power to the Right. Following that, the Left in Israel and the rest of the world faced the series of other crises mentioned earlier.

A systematic, comprehensive, and in-depth examination of the history of Hakibbutz Ha'artzi (Kibbutz Movement) and Mapam (United Workers Party) contributes to the understanding of the decline of the Israeli labor movement. These two names refer collectively to a *movement* in the sociopolitical meaning of that term. In this sense (as opposed to the more general use of the term *movement* to designate any group of people acting together), it refers to an amalgamation of linked organizations and institutions that together constitute a self-contained environment that provides a specific public with everything from ideology, political representation, housing, health care, and employment to entertainment, newspapers, books, theater, and sports leagues. Although such movements could be nationalist and right-wing populist in nature, they were especially prominent on the socialist left.

Hakibbutz Ha'artzi and Mapam were two interlinked organizations— the settlement movement, Hakibbutz Ha'artzi, and its associated political party, Mapam, along with a number of subsidiary and allied social and cultural institutions.[13] Hakibbutz Ha'artzi was one of three major large kibbutz settlement movements in the 1950s, the other two being Hakibbutz Hameuhad (United Kibbutz) and the Ihud Hakevutzot Vehakibbutzim (Union of the Kvutzot and the Kibbutzim), which was allied with Mapai (Workers Party). At the end of 1955, Hakibbutz Ha'artzi had sixty member kibbutzim with a total population of 25,000, of which about 15,000 were members of the commune and the rest children, candidates for membership, or nonmember residents. Mapam was the Zionist party farthest to the left on the Israeli political spectrum and an inseparable part of the labor-movement hegemony. The name "Mapam" originally designated an alliance of Hakibbutz Ha'artzi and its allies in the cities (which together founded the party Hashomer Hatza'ir [Young Guard] in 1946) with Ahdut Ha'avodah (Unity of Labor) and Hakibbutz Hameuhad. But in 1954 the latter two split away from the united party. From then on, Mapam constituted the political arm of Hakibbutz Ha'artzi. It first contested elections in that incarnation in 1955, receiving 62,402 votes and winning 9 seats in the 120-member Knesset. For the first time, it joined the government. Mapam and Hakibbutz Ha'artzi were controlled by their "historical leadership": Meir Ya'ari and Ya'akov Hazan, graduates of Hashomer Hatza'ir youth movement in Poland who arrived in Palestine in the 1920s. They founded Hakibbutz Ha'artzi and Mapam and led them in the decades that followed.

The crisis that Hakibbutz Ha'artzi and Mapam experienced as a socialist Zionist movement of the Left was the result of changes the movement underwent from the mid-1950s to mid-1970s. During Israel's early years, they had a clear ideological identity, and the movement structure operated with great effectiveness. The membership obeyed the leadership's directives and displayed social cohesion, ideological unity, and a high capacity for working together. But the structure came apart during the crisis years. Serious ideological differences arose; members began to complain about and blame the historical leadership for the movement's ills, as a result of which Ya'ari and Hazan's power waned; the movement's loyalists split into warring factions; its cultural and ideological organs ceased to serve it and the party apparatus; and some of its members even began to act against it. Throughout this period, Hakibbutz Ha'artzi and Mapam also had difficulty defining their politics—from 1956 to 1977 (with the exception of 1961–66) Mapam was a member of Israel's governing coalitions, and in 1959 it ran on a joint slate with the Labor Party, called HaMa'arakh, the Alignment. Yet it behaved like an opposition party in conflict with the other parts of the labor movement. At the end of the 1960s, members began to leave Mapam to join rival political organizations. All this was accompanied by steady decline in the number of seats it held in the Knesset, from nine in 1955 to seven in 1973 (as part of HaMa'arakh). In the elections of 1977, in which it again ran as part of HaMa'arakh with the Labor party, it received only four seats.

The crisis of Hakibbutz Ha'artzi and Mapam coincided in large measure with a crisis in the rest of the labor movement. In general, the Six-Day War of 1967 and the Yom Kippur War of 1973 are seen as turning points in the stability of the Israeli labor movement's hegemony.[14] But this historiographic consensus does not correspond to reality because severe cracks in the labor hegemony were already evident in the 1950s.[15] In fact, between the mid-1950s and the mid-1970s both Hakibbutz Ha'artzi and Mapam in particular and the labor movement as a whole found themselves increasingly riven by ideological debates, social disintegration, political debilitation, and cultural protest.[16] Whatever the case, it is not self-evident that the years 1956–77 should be defined as the crisis period, both for the larger labor movement and the case at hand. In fact, during this time the State of Israel experienced impressive development. Much of its population grew increasingly prosperous, especially that part associated with the labor movement.[17] The kibbutzim continued to expand; once debt ridden and plagued by economic distress, they grew increasingly wealthy, and their members became part of the Israeli middle class that emerged following the early years of austerity and mass immigration.[18] By all appearances, these years were the height of the labor movement's cultural might, especially following the Six-Day War, which burnished its prestige.[19] Not many believed that the labor movement was so close to losing power in 1977 or could conceive that the Histadrut and kibbutzim would implode just two decades after that. Indeed, the crisis of the Israeli labor movement and of Hakibbutz Ha'artzi and Mapam within it in the last quarter of the twentieth century came largely as a surprise. It caught the members of the movement off guard, precisely because of the sense of power that the movement's components felt during the country's initial decades. What can explain this contradiction, a crisis that befell the movement just as it was at its zenith?

Studies of Hakibbutz Ha'artzi and Mapam have paid little attention to the connection between economics, politics, and culture, by which I mean their mounting economic strength, the process of social and political change that this prosperity brought on, and contemporary events in the movement and party cultural and ideological establishment.[20] This lack of attention is somewhat surprising because the connections between economics, society, politics, and culture were fundamental to these bodies' Marxist ideological foundations and were integral to the way they enhanced their power and conducted themselves as a movement. A consequence of how the historical debate has addressed these elements separately has been a contradiction in the attempt to explain the circumstances and reasons for Hakibbutz Ha'artzi and Mapam's decline. On the one hand, scholarship that has focused on the ideological and political aspect of Hakibbutz Ha'artzi and Mapam has stressed the alternative that they offered to the type of regime and society promoted by the other parts of the labor movement, Mapai most of all.[21] Such studies have deduced that Hakibbutz Ha'artzi and Mapam represent the "road not taken" by the labor movement as a whole. The corollary is that this movement stood outside the labor-movement crisis, which occurred despite them.

In contrast, another line of research, focusing on the labor movement's economic and social structure, argues that Hakibbutz Ha'artzi and Mapam had much in common with Mapai and that the contention between them was a result of the way they constituted their political power.[22] In other words, Hakibbutz Ha'artzi and Mapam participated in the labor-movement crisis, which was caused *by* and not *despite* the path the movement offered. In the history of Hakibbutz Ha'artzi and Mapam, the separation between economics and society on the one hand and politics and culture on the other have also created a further lack of clarity regarding the history of the crisis in these organizations. From an ideological and political point of view, the kibbutz movements suffered heavy blows when the state was established. In political terms, Hakibbutz Ha'artzi and Mapam lost any influence they might have had on setting the agenda and molding the shape of the Israeli state and society when Mapam was not included in the first government and then suffered an additional blow when Ahdut Ha'avodah split away from it in 1954. Yet the economic and social picture was the precise opposite: during these years the kibbutz movements grew economically secure and developed a rich and wide-ranging cultural infrastructure. These contradictions suggest that scholars need to take a new look at Hakibbutz Ha'artzi and Mapam that will include the entire range of economic, social, political, and cultural events connected to them, not as separate spheres but as an integrated whole, so as to offer a complete historical picture. In other words, these organizations need to be examined as a *movement*, and in considering them as such the research program may also contribute to the study of the labor movement as a whole.

The larger field of the study of the labor movement indeed has noted the contradiction between increasing power and disintegration, but up until now the process has been seen only from a bird's-eye view.[23] Most of the effort to explain the contradiction has taken place in the general sociological discourse about Israeli society. According to some accounts, the focal point of the crisis was the "overload" experienced by the political system established by the labor movement in response to the myriad demands made by new groups that emerged in Israeli society.[24] Others have challenged this "overload hypothesis," not agreeing with its implicit assumption that the political system was fundamentally sound but simply could not withstand the pressure placed on it. This challenge produced what has been called the Critical School of Israeli sociology.[25] The Critical School sociologists challenged the existing analysis of the labor-movement crisis, arguing that it disregards the movement's internal failures. In their view, the labor movement was a power structure that combined economic, political, and cultural elements that during the state period based itself on an asymmetrical division of power in relation to the public it addressed.[26] They depicted the emergence of social tensions within the milieu established by the labor movement and the inability of its leaders, the heirs of the founding generation, to cope with them successfully.[27] Some linked the unrest that accompanied the asymmetrical division of power to the labor movement's declining power, which manifested itself primarily in the "ballot-box rebellion" of voters whose origins lay in the Islamic world (Mizrahim) in the elections in 1977, who switched loyalties to Likud, and in the casting of protest votes by members of the middle class who had previously voted for one of the labor parties and now supported a new center party, the Tnu'a Demokratit LeShinui (Democratic Movement for Change), founded just before that election.[28] The claims made by the Critical School remained largely on the theoretical level, and the school was widely criticized both for its misstatement of the facts and for its fundamental assumptions.[29] Nevertheless, it offered an important interpretive framework for understanding the decline of the labor movement, which

I adopt here in analyzing the case of Hakibbutz Ha'artzi and Mapam. Its most important contribution is the view that the labor movement lost power not only because of events beyond its control, such as the multiplying demands of a variety of social groups, or factors such as the rise of a new generation, the rise of the political Right, and the inception of the age of neoliberalism, but also because the process by which the labor movement aggregated power created internal structural contradictions that played a decisive role in weakening it.

Historians who have directly addressed different aspects of the history of Israel's labor movement from the mid-1950s on have in large measure confirmed the sociologists' claims about the mutual relations between the movement's economic rise, its social dissolution, and its political decline. They also see a connection between these processes and contemporary cultural developments.[30] Their work has supplemented the sociologists' account of the social unrest that led voters to abandon the labor movement. They have chronicled the emergence of the Israeli New Left, part of which was linked to Hakibbutz Ha'artzi and Mapam; the young kibbutz generation's (including in Hakibbutz Ha'artzi) cultural rebellion against the kibbutz-movement establishment; the emergence of a "pioneering bourgeois" culture in the 1960s, which began to turn against the labor movement when that culture exhausted the opportunities for social mobility that the movement offered; the development of neoliberal leanings in the Israeli Left, which found expression in cultural rebellion; and the development of the Israeli Left's liberal-dovish ideology in a class context. Some historians have focused in particular on the cultural manifestations of the political orientations and linked them to economic and social processes. In doing so, they have carried forward the broad scholarly discourse that has analyzed the decline of the Left and the rise of the neoliberal Right throughout the world in the context of the interaction of economics, politics, and culture.[31] They have adopted that discourse's starting assumptions and applied them to the case of the Israeli labor movement in a way that serves as a foundation for the analysis I pursue here.

Historical and sociological research on the Israeli labor movement and the broader discussion of the links between economics, politics, and culture thus provide a framework for analyzing the movement's decline.

Such a framework connects the economic and social stabilization of Israeli society both to the internal unrest that found expression in the cultural sphere as well as to declining support for the labor movement. Yet current scholarship on the labor movement has a gaping hole in it—part of it has remained on the theoretical level, while another part has addressed the relatively narrow bounds of historical events, but no study has yet examined the decline of the Israeli labor movement as a long-term process at the nexus of economics, politics, and culture, taking a specific case as its subject.

My central argument in this book is that in the case of Hakibbutz Ha'artzi and Mapam there was a dialectical interrelationship between their socioeconomic development and their political and ideological crisis. This makes it possible to explain how the movement's rising power was connected to its dissolution. I develop this claim in two stages. First, in the book's background section, using the general theoretical analytical framework for the study of the labor movement that I have described, I offer a new view of Hakibbutz Ha'artzi and Mapam in the years from 1927 to 1956. During this period, the movement paradoxically drew its power from the difficulties of the Yishuv (prestate) period. The movement's leadership gained power because of its ability to organize frameworks that offered effective solutions in every area of life for the graduates of Hashomer Hatza'ir youth movement. The larger labor movement built up its power with a similar system of mediation between the immigrants who arrived in Palestine and organized themselves in the Histadrut and workers' parties.[32] But Hakibbutz Ha'artzi sought to preserve its separate identity within the labor movement, maintaining political and social independence by operating its own separate mediating apparatus. The members of Hakibbutz Ha'artzi kibbutzim established a social structure that perpetuated its youth-movement ethos, centered on a communal way of life enabled by the guidance and assistance of the movement's institutions. Cooperation between the public and the leadership was an important element in founding the movement's institutionalized indoctrination apparatus, which operated within its sophisticated cultural establishment. This set of institutions was meant also to mobilize political support for the movement from the broader public, people who were not members of kibbutzim. As such, the movement's cultural instruments were divided in accordance with this dual purpose between (voluntary) internal indoctrination and external mobilization. On the eve of the founding of the State of Israel and during its initial years, Hakibbutz Ha'artzi and Mapam thus constituted a power structure with internal cohesion that had a high capacity for action based on the congruence of three elements: the public's economic and social needs, a political system centered on the need for an apparatus with a mediating role, and a sophisticated cultural establishment that provided the supporters and members of the movement with justification, meaning, and the capacity for interpreting events. Yet the cultural establishment also served as a way of mobilizing a certain level of support from parts of the public that had no direct connection to the power structure.

The book's central section, consisting of parts one, two, and three, addresses the second stage of the economics, politics, and culture nexus in Hakibbutz Ha'artzi and Mapam during the years 1956–77. Part one presents the economic and social revolution that Hakibbutz Ha'artzi and Mapam's public underwent from the mid-1950s to mid-1970s as part of the high growth enjoyed by the Israeli economy as well as by Western countries following World War II. As Israel transformed from a developing to a developed society, prosperity came first and foremost to the veteran population, meaning those who had lived in the country prior to the mass immigration that followed independence. Most supporters of the labor movement belonged to this cohort. The kibbutzim transformed from agricultural communities living in austerity to affluent industrialized societies. Part two follows developments that accompanied this process of economic and social stabilization. One consequence is that the mediating apparatus became superfluous. Alongside this consequence, new internal political orientations emerged in Hakibbutz Ha'artzi and Mapam. These changes sought to update the structure and character of the movement for the new age it had entered. These new political orientations contended with each other at the same time that they allied against the movement's traditional leadership. The outcome was a conservative counterreaction from the leadership, which opposed change in a way that further weakened the existing movement structure. Part three recounts how these internal tensions made their way into the cultural establishment, partly out of their need for a platform and partly so as to distance them from the political arena. The result was that the cultural establishment developed rapidly, eventually gaining a fair amount of independence in the context of the rise of the protest culture in Israel. This independence further exacerbated the pressures on Hakibbutz Ha'artzi and Mapam's traditional power structure and hastened its dissolution.

The book's conclusion offers the process by which Hakibbutz Ha'artzi and Mapam disintegrated as a model for understanding the history of other socialist movements. During the first half of the twentieth century, these movements also established an apparatus that played economic, political, and cultural roles, and in their cases, too, this apparatus disintegrated during the second half of the twentieth century as a result of changing relationships within the movements. In this sense, as Anita Shapira has written, the Israeli labor movement, like other socialist movements, "changed the world, and as it did so, it became the victim of its own success."[33] Despite the deterministic elements inherent in every structural explanation, this book looks not only at these internal pressures and the subsequent attempts to avert the waning of the movement but also at the political alternatives proposed for Hakibbutz Ha'artzi and Mapam during the period in question. The question of whether things could have turned out otherwise remains unanswered, as it must in any historical study.

Background

Economics, Politics, and Culture in
Hakibbutz Ha'artzi and Mapam, 1927–1956

I

The Emergence of the Kibbutz Movement
and the Rise of the Mediating Mechanism

HASHOMER HATZA'IR, founded in Galicia in 1913, was the first Zionist youth movement and served as a model for subsequent Zionist labor youth organizations, all of which saw themselves as the vanguard of the Jewish nation and of settlement in the homeland. Hashomer Hatza'ir founded its first chapters in Palestine in 1929. By the beginning of World War II, it had chapters all over the world. In the 1930s, it and two dozen other Zionist youth movements together claimed more than 100,000 active members across the globe. It was these young people who formed the backbone of the labor movement in the Yishuv and later in the State of Israel.[1]

The first graduates of Hashomer Hatza'ir and the other pioneering movements arrived in Palestine in 1920 as part of the Third Aliyah of 1919–23. The earliest Hashomer Hatza'ir immigrants organized themselves in two communes, Beitaniya and Shomriya. Hashomer Hatza'ir graduates established other such cooperatives in the early 1920s. These first cooperatives operated in temporary locations around the country, after which they established permanent settlements on land assigned to them by the Zionist movement's institutions in Palestine.

The kibbutzim founded by Hashomer Hatza'ir graduates deliberated on the creation of a national organization in 1927 and subsequently established Hakibbutz Ha'artzi–Hashomer Hatza'ir (Nationwide Kibbutz) as a network of ostensibly autonomous kibbutzim that in fact owed fealty to a central leadership and depended on the larger organization for financial, organizational, and political support. Young members and graduates of Hashomer Hatza'ir who had received pioneer training and sought to carry out the movement's ideals joined these existing kibbutzim or founded new ones with the help of the larger organization.[2] Another kibbutz movement took form the same year. Hakibbutz Hameuhad comprised the kibbutzim that split off from the Joseph Trumpeldor Labor Battalion (a pioneer organization that in the years 1920–28 consisted of communes of workers who engaged in manual labor, such as road construction and swamp drainage) and those that had been left without any larger framework after the battalion disbanded. A third grouping was Hever Hakevutzot (Federation of Communes), founded in 1929 and composed of communes that did not want to be tightly affiliated to a larger movement. Six years later, a handful of kibbutzim associated with Hapoel Hamizrahi (Mizrahi Workers), a labor party made up of religiously observant Jews who opposed the rejection of traditional Judaism by the kibbutz mainstream, founded what would later become the Religious Kibbutz Movement. Because of its small size, unique profile, and political affiliation, however, this movement does not figure in the current study.

The division into these three separate currents had three main causes. One was the differences in the nuances of ideology in the Zionist youth movements. Youth-movement members who planned to settle in Palestine as pioneers underwent pioneer training (*hakhsharah*) in Europe under the aegis of Hehalutz (Pioneer), an umbrella organization of all the pioneering youth movements that had been founded in Russia in 1917. But because of nuances of ideology, the members of different movements tended to train in separate frameworks and to seek to maintain their specific identities in Palestine. A second reason for the division was that in the Yishuv the pioneers affiliated themselves with rival Zionist parties, which vied for supporters and maintained separate institutions, such as schools and newspapers. A third factor was different views about the nature of communal life in Palestine. Despite these differences, the kibbutz movements were much alike. They all were founded by pioneers from eastern Europe; most of their members had been members of youth movements, shared a socialist Zionist orientation, and had similar views about Yishuv society. Their differences remained institutionalized because they constituted separate social and economic power structures, shaped directly by the political pressures within the Yishuv's labor movement.

In the 1930s, Hakibbutz Hameuhad emerged as a force that opposed the Mapai leadership in the party's internal power struggles. It cooperated with urban factions to oppose David Ben-Gurion and the party machine. Hever Hakevutzot supported Ben-Gurion and viewed itself as a pluralistic organization that advocated for communal settlements without taking a position on political or ideological issues. Hashomer Hatza'ir, with its roots in and under the influence of its youth movement, refused to give up its autonomy to form a single united kibbutz movement. It jealously guarded its independence and to every extent possible sought to provide the services and institutions its members needed. When that was not possible, it cooperated with Mapai reluctantly and on an ad hoc basis. It participated in Yishuv, Histadrut, and Zionist institutions, such as administrative and representative bodies, by participating in common slates with other movements. It also received social and economic services from these institutions, the Histadrut in particular—for example, from the Kupat Holim Clalit (Histadrut Health Services). The kibbutzim of the different movements nevertheless had much in common, no matter their alliances, and thus developed in similar ways. Although the fine differences between them were of huge importance to their members, in the big picture they closely resembled each other in their economic and organizational structures, social composition, cultural activities, population size, and physical layout.

Following the establishment of the kibbutz movements, the graduates of pioneering youth movements in the Diaspora continued to immigrate to Palestine, joining existing kibbutzim or establishing new ones. At the birth of the state, the kibbutzim altogether had a population of about 50,000. At the end of 1955, close to 80,000 people lived in kibbutzim belonging to all three movements, constituting about 4.5 percent of the Jewish population.

The movements' main concern during their initial decades was to ensure both the physical survival of their member kibbutzim and their capacity to take in new members. The kibbutz economy was based on labor-intensive agriculture, which meant that the kibbutzim needed an influx of new members to provide additional working hands. The Zionist movement as a whole also saw the kibbutzim as essential to the establishment of a Jewish commonwealth in Palestine and thus provided considerable assistance to the communes. For most Zionists, the kibbutzim were the embodiment of the Jewish return to and connection with the land, a cure for the physical and mental ills that Zionists believed plagued the Jews of the Diaspora, and a vanguard for creating a normal Jewish society based, as were other nations, on a firm and large foundation of farmers. Furthermore, the communal life of labor that the kibbutzim exemplified was a natural continuation of the fellowship of young people created in the pioneering Zionist youth movements, which were an essential source of highly motivated young immigrants willing to sacrifice personal comfort and welfare for the national cause. Experience had shown that the nature of the available land and the circumstances of the Yishuv were not amenable to the success of individual farmers. Cooperative farming seemed to be the only solution. As such, the ideals of agricultural settlement and the commune were intimately linked, to the point that later writers on the kibbutz institution still debate what came first, the communal idea or the settlement enterprise.[3] The two were inseparably linked in the pioneers' experience and consciousness.

The social and political development of the kibbutzim was tied closely to their economic structure, agriculture first and foremost. Any change in the way the commune provided for itself would inevitably lead to changes in other aspects of kibbutz life. In this regard, the kibbutzim remained in a more or less steady state until the mid-1950s. Farming methods in the 1920s were fairly primitive, but in the 1930s, as the Yishuv as a whole advanced economically, some mechanization and advanced agronomic methods were introduced, including the use of tractors and combines, improved crop strains, pest and disease control, and improved irrigation techniques. Even with these labor-saving improvements, however, the kibbutz economy was highly dependent on physical labor. After independence, further technical improvements were quickly made in what was termed a second technical revolution. They included the importation of state-of-the-art machinery and advanced methods of cultivation. The technical improvements and a huge increase in the amount of available farmland after independence led to an increase in productivity and agricultural production as well as a jump in profits. Yet none of this brought much improvement in the quality of life at kibbutzim because new kibbutzim were constantly being founded and the populations of the existing ones expanded. The dramatic increase in available farmland and production also meant that mechanization did not have a significant effect on the structure of the kibbutz economy. Agriculture continued to be the major occupation, and machines did not completely replace working hands at most farming tasks.[4]

Although farming remained relatively simple and appropriate for communal settlement, it suffered from seasonal instability and frequent crises. The kibbutzim had no choice but to diversify into manufacturing and industry. From 1936 to 1939, the Yishuv as a whole faced an economic depression. During these years, factories of various kinds were built in kibbutzim. They were mostly local initiatives and included metal working, sandal making, textiles, and machine shops. In 1936, Hakibbutz Ha'artzi established Hashomer Hatza'ir Fund to provide assistance for the economic development of the kibbutzim, and in 1952 the company Techen was set up to establish kibbutz industries and in particular to help communes transform their workshops into modern plants. The other kibbutz movements set up similar bodies. Nevertheless, kibbutzim and their members took a guarded approach to industrialization and placed many limits on it. The kibbutz leadership feared its effect on communal life.[5] Agriculture remained the preferred field of occupation both because of its interrelationship with the cultural aspects of the Zionist revolution and because farm settlements were an important way of establishing a Jewish presence on the land, thus bolstering the claim for Jewish sovereignty.

Because kibbutzim were based on a labor-intensive agricultural economy, along with a bit of low-profit small manufacturing, kibbutz life during the Yishuv period and the early years of the state was typified by constant "pioneering tension," meaning a very frugal and even Spartan quality of life. Housing data bring this home. In the 1930s and 1940s, members of Hakibbutz Ha'artzi kibbutzim were allotted an average of 4.5 square meters per person (less than 50 square feet) of living space. But even this space was not private in many cases. Couples often had to share their rooms with a third single member (called the "primus," after the three-legged kerosene stove in common use at the time). In 1949, housing density—people per room—was higher in kibbutzim than in any other type of community in the country. Common conveniences and advanced hygienic conditions were also lacking—there was one latrine for every twenty-one adults, and 32 percent of the latrines were not flushable. The situation did not improve in the years that followed. In 1954, a full 71 percent of kibbutz couples had homes of 12–15 square meters (130–60 square feet), and sometimes a room of this size was occupied by four members. Only 29 percent of rooms had attached toilets (apartments were without toilets until the 1950s), and kibbutz members were able to eat in permanent structures (as opposed to improvised shacks) in only 53 out of 212 kibbutzim.[6]

The starkness of kibbutz life imbued the kibbutz movement with tremendous power during the prestate period. The movements directed kibbutz settlement and development because funds from the national institutions and Histadrut were funneled through the movements rather than given directly to individual kibbutzim. Immigration permits and land allocations, valuable assets in the Yishuv period, were also apportioned to the movements. Furthermore, most of the capital invested in the kibbutzim came from private sources; most kibbutzim lacked the capacity to raise funds from investors on their own. The movements also set up their own financial loan-granting institutions, without which the kibbutzim were helpless. Kibbutz members, most of whom were immigrants who had no personal property, were completely dependent on the kibbutz organization that took them in and saw to all their needs. The member placed himself at the service of the organization and in exchange received cradle-to-grave sustenance and care. The system defined him as an organic part of the kibbutz and movement collectives.

The establishment of the state weakened the kibbutz movements. Following independence, the kibbutz movements ceased to take voluntary lead in national missions as they had during the Yishuv period, and their contribution to society declined. In 1949, on the cusp of a massive wave of immigration, the kibbutzim accounted for 7 percent of the country's Jewish population. That peak was never matched after that point. A few years later, their numbers declined to less than 5 percent of the population, where they remained for a long time. Furthermore, during the 1950s the kibbutz ceased to be the preferred form of settlement. It was replaced by the moshav (village) cooperative, where families farmed separately but shared some equipment and marketed their produce together. The kibbutzim also played only a marginal role in that decade's major national enterprise, the absorption of huge numbers of immigrants. Many kibbutz members also left the settlements, a phenomenon that eroded the communes' image of themselves and increasingly made them feel marginal. Hakibbutz Ha'artzi's affiliation with a political party in opposition from 1949 to 1955 also rendered the movement less able to obtain resources for its members. Furthermore, the flow of capital also changed, with most investment now coming from sources that were under state control and to which the kibbutz-movement investment funds had no access. These sources included grants and loans from the US government and the Export–Import Bank of the United States, the reparations payments from Germany, the Israel Bonds, and the United Jewish Appeal.

Although independence turned out to be a crisis for the kibbutz movements, it actually strengthened the movements' leadership of their member kibbutzim, at least for a time. In addition to the crisis of morale, the kibbutzim found themselves in severe economic straits following independence. One cause of these economic problems was that the rapid growth in their economies and populations in the previous decade had made them highly dependent on major sources of credit. The Zionist Organization was unable to fully supply this need, forcing the kibbutzim to take loans from other sources at high interest rates. Many of them sank into debt. A second cause was that after independence major investments were made in response to kibbutz members' demand for a higher standard of living. Such investments, beginning in the early 1950s, were made despite the communes' difficult economic plight. The kibbutzim consequently incurred more debt, making them ever more dependent on aid from the movements. Thus, by the 1950s, as the indispensable mediators between the kibbutzim and the government (and Histadrut), the kibbutz movement leadership exercised huge power over individual kibbutzim and their members.

The kibbutz movements wielded much the same power over kibbutz members that Mapai, the leading force in the state's absorption operations in its early years, wielded with regard to Israel's citizens. Government ministries—most of them controlled by Mapai—and the Histadrut provided new immigrants with housing, schools, medical care, and employment, meaning that the immigrants were entirely dependent on the party. This dependence enhanced Mapai's political strength, which was organized by party representatives in immigrant camps, development towns, and immigrant moshavim. These representatives served as the directors of the local branch of the Histadrut Employment Bureau service, immigrant camps, the committees responsible for the establishment of new settlements or housing projects, and the local Kupat Holim Clalit clinics. Mapai representatives also served as secretary of the local Workers' Council and mayor.[7] Mapai's role as go-between was a significant source of power during the state's first decade. For the same reason, from a sociopolitical point of view, the kibbutz movements enjoyed the same kind of power. Even if they wielded it over a smaller number of people, they based themselves on a system that apportioned services and benefits that tied the kibbutz public to them.

With Mapam's political clout dependent both on its role as mediator between the kibbutzim and national institutions and on the role the kibbutzim and their members played as party activists who could campaign for the party and gain it voters in the cities, its interests lay in opposing Ben-Gurion's policy of strengthening the state at the expense of voluntary institutions, a policy he called *mamlakhtiyut*. At the time, for those involved, this debate was understood as being between *halutziyut*, pioneering Zionism, and *mamlakhtiyut*, statism. But studies examining the phenomenon from a historical perspective have found that Mapam actually supported what has been termed "consociational *mamlakhtiyut*," meaning the parallel operation of multiple sources of power that observe arrangements among them regarding their purview and authority. In such a situation, Mapam and its kibbutz movement would retain, within the state-building process, their roles as mediators between their publics and national institutions. Ben-Gurion, for his part, sought "majoritarian *mamlakhtiyut*," in which the political force that receives the majority of votes assumes all power. Under this model, citizens theoretically need no mediator because they are to receive services directly from the state on an equal footing. In practice, however, the majority party, because of the power it holds, serves as the sole such mediator, to the exclusion of all other parties, movements, and institutions.[8] This being the case, there was no fundamental difference between the way Ben-Gurion built up Mapai's power and Mapam's ambitions. Both used similar means of mobilization based on their position as mediating institutions. Grounding itself on its prestige as part of a pioneering movement, Mapam acted largely in favor of the kibbutzim and enlisted supporters outside them by creating a cultural front that stressed the values of the brotherhood of nations and class radicalism. Mapai brought the veteran population into the Histadrut and state bureaucracies and recruited new supporters, especially among the immigrants, by means of the idea of *mamlakhtiyut* and Ben-Gurion's personal prestige. In contrast with Mapam, which had to form its cultural front on its own, Mapai's ideological work was carried out by means of the educational and cultural operations of the state and the Histadrut, which functioned as Mapai's own cultural front. Both parties thus used similar structures of power based on a defined public's commitment in the framework of a bifurcated distributional system. Majoritarian *mamlakhtiyut* granted Mapai the same mediating role that Mapam sought as part of its consociational *mamlakhtiyut*. But it was precisely this similarity between the parties that formed the background to their rivalry.

2

The Politicization of Hakibbutz Ha'artzi

Mapam as a Mass Party

THE YISHUV'S POLITICAL SYSTEM was a direct product of its being an immigrant society that sought to establish a sovereign nation-state. Its political parties took on roles far greater than those in established states. Each party and its membership constituted a distinct sector and subculture within the larger Jewish society in Palestine. Parties provided their members with health care, education, and job placement and engaged in immigrant absorption and settlement. Because the Jewish population enjoyed a large measure of autonomy under the British Mandate, these parties were a major force in shaping life in the Yishuv. This status also meant that anyone who wanted to have an influence on Yishuv life in both the present and the future had to act within the framework of a political party. Hakibbutz Ha'artzi's decision to engage in political activity thus had two causes: it sought to absorb and settle the graduates of Hashomer Hatza'ir under its aegis, and it sought to play a role in decision making in the Yishuv and in the establishment of the Jewish national home.

The central question faced by the movement's leaders was the choice of political framework. Over the course of the 1930s, Hakibbutz Ha'artzi and Mapai discussed the possibility of the kibbutz movement joining forces with Mapai, but the movement's leaders were more inclined to avoid identifying with an existing faction and to set up their own independent political arm within the larger Yishuv labor movement. This preference grew out of the heritage of Hashomer Hatza'ir youth movement, which saw its organizational independence as essential to its identity and its role as a social force. Its standing as an independent movement whose ideas and program were an outgrowth of an organic process of communal deliberation was an even more important part of its ethos than its official ideology.[1] The last serious attempt to bring Hakibbutz Ha'artzi into Mapai was made in 1939, on the eve of World War II. Despite the gravity of the historical hour, which seemed to mandate cooperation, the effort was unsuccessful. Hakibbutz Ha'artzi wanted to remain a discrete and separate faction within the party, a condition Ben-Gurion refused to accept. Another obstacle was the movement's radical socialist platform, which included planks that Mapai found hard to stomach. Among them were Hashomer Hatza'ir's commitment to class struggle, equal rights for Arab workers within the party, Marxism–Leninism, and a hardline pro-Soviet orientation (all to be elaborated later).[2]

The youth movement's ethos served as the foundation on which Hakibbutz Ha'artzi's internal political structure was built, and it was carried over to the political party it founded. It shared parts of this set of principles with other branches of the labor movement. Both Hakibbutz Ha'artzi and Mapam were headed by what was called the "historic leadership." It consisted of two men, Meir Ya'ari and Ya'akov Hazan, whose standing was modeled on that of the youth-movement counselor, granting them broad powers.[3] Ya'ari and Hazan, who immigrated (separately) during the Third Aliyah and began to work together in 1923, emerged as leaders when they together oversaw the reorganization of Hashomer Hatza'ir's graduates and the establishment of Hakibbutz Ha'artzi. Their role, as they saw it, was to serve as ideological, social, and political mentors for their protégés, while maintaining the movement's graduates as a distinct and separate social cadre. Beyond their charisma, Hazan and Ya'ari owed their standing to their strengths in the areas of organization (Hazan in particular) and ideology (Ya'ari's expertise).[4] In combination, these two aptitudes met a need among the membership for counselor-like figures who could mediate between them and the rest of the Yishuv.

The relationship between the historic leadership and the membership was a total one, voluntarily entered into and excluding all other affiliations and loyalties. Because of the kibbutz movement's stress on absolute loyalty to leaders who laid down rules for all areas of life, outsiders often compared the movement to a Hasidic court. But this leadership style,

combining charisma, organizational ability, and ideology, also characterized other labor-movement leaders, among them Yitzhak Tabenkin, the
leader of Hakibbutz Hameuhad (and later of its party Ahdut Ha'avodah),
and Berl Katznelson, the moving force behind the creation of Mapai and
the Histadrut. Although these figures led different currents within the
labor movement and often clashed bitterly with each other, their power-
building practices were erected on the same sociological foundation. They
also entered into a counselor–protégé relationship with a public organized
in communal frameworks of one sort or another. Like Ya'ari and Hazan,
they advocated a version of socialist Zionism, a mobilizing ideology inter-
twined with the Yishuv's experience of austerity and crisis.[5] This common
legacy was important because the Zionists who emerged from the pioneering ideology of settlement and manual labor and the youth groups it
inspired served as the nucleus of the Yishuv labor movement. This public
accepted the need for a strong party apparatus that effectively combined
economics, politics, and ideology to create a total fabric of life.

The stress on social intimacy, part of the total character of the labor
movement's pioneering branch, was especially potent in Hakibbutz
Ha'artzi. For that reason, fearing that political activity might create dissension, the leadership avoided establishing a party during its early years.
The turning point came after a number of years of soul-searching and internal discussions. It was catalyzed by the awareness that the movement
had many political allies in the cities and that it was imperative to take advantage of this electoral power. In 1935, the movement decided to encourage sympathizers among the urban working public to establish a party
that would initially not include kibbutz members. In 1936, these sympathizers organized as Ha-Liga ha-Socialistit (Socialist League), a protoparty
of urban workers and intellectuals that for all intents and purposes followed the lead of Hakibbutz Ha'artzi. The kibbutz movement handled the
league cautiously, avoiding any formal organizational link, but guided and
oversaw it to suppress its radicals, who veered leftward from the movement's socialist-Zionist identity. Only in 1941, when the talks about uniting with Mapai reached a dead end, did the movement's leaders come out
publicly in support of establishing an independent party. This decision
was preceded by a "trial balloon" during the Histadrut elections in which

Hakibbutz Ha'artzi ran for the first time on a joint slate with the Socialist League as a way of seeing how an alliance would be received in both the cities and the kibbutzim. The results were very promising. In 1932, when Hashomer Hatza'ir's slate represented only kibbutz members, it received 8 percent of the vote in the Histadrut elections. In 1941, the joint slate won 19.2 percent of the votes, comprising 5,800 votes of kibbutz members and 11,000 votes from urban workers. The potential was clear to the kibbutz leadership. They took advantage of the momentum, and in the years 1942–46 the party, although not yet officially established, was already functioning in many respects. In 1943, a party newspaper, *Mishmar* (Guard, renamed *Al Hamishmar* [On Guard], in 1948), was founded, and Hakibbutz Ha'artzi was represented in the Histadrut, municipal councils, the Va'ad Le'umi (National Council, the Yishuv's governing body), the Zionist Executive, and the Haganah, the Yishuv's self-defense force.[6]

In 1946, as the leadership of Hakibbutz Ha'artzi came to the realization that Hashomer Hatza'ir's membership in Europe had been decimated by the war and could not muster votes in Zionist Organization elections, it decided to establish a Hashomer Hatza'ir party that would unite Socialist League supporters in the city with the members of the movement's kibbutzim. It was a significant concession as a common political framework stamped a moral seal of approval on city-dwellers who had not fulfilled the pioneering dream in the fullest sense by joining a kibbutz. Nevertheless, the party established a clear internal hierarchy in which the kibbutzim members ranked higher than the urban members. The latter benefited from the alliance, however, because the kibbutzim were able to provide the new party with organizational capacity and financial support. Hakibbutz Ha'artzi also brought with it a mobilized and aggressive youth movement fully obedient to the kibbutz and party leadership, which could provide manpower for political and other campaigns.

While the decision to found a party followed a soul-searching process dating back to 1927, the events of 1947 brought a new development. Following the establishment of Hashomer Hatza'ir party, another new labor-movement party came into being. Ahdut Ha'avodah–Poalei Tzion (Unity of Labor–Workers of Zion) was founded by Hakibbutz Hameuhad, Faction B (which had split away from Mapai in 1944), and a small Zionist

Marxist faction called Poalei Tzion Smol (Leftist Workers of Zion). The two new parties gradually grew closer; in January 1948, at the beginning of the War of Independence, they joined to form Mapam. The new united party expected a major success in the elections to the First Knesset in 1949. But these hopes were dashed when the results gave it only 19 of the Knesset's 120 seats. Although it was the second-largest party, it lagged far behind Mapai, which received 46 seats, and it remained outside the coalition that Ben-Gurion formed. In the elections to the Second Knesset, in 1951, its results declined to 15 seats, proving that its self-confidence about enjoying wide public support was an illusion.[7] The two groups that came together to form Mapam decided to retain their separate identities as factions within the party, with the hope that in time they would fully unite. But the lack of political success ignited sharp conflict between them. It was not long before the crisis became so acute that a rift was inevitable. In the summer of 1954, it finally happened. Ahdut Ha'avodah formed a new party with that name, which included Hakibbutz Hameuhad. Hashomer Hatza'ir and Hakibbutz Ha'artzi's party retained the name "Mapam."[8]

The nature and structure of Mapam following the split was influenced by the spirit of its central component, Hakibbutz Ha'artzi. The kibbutz movement's two guiding political principles had already been enshrined in Hashomer Hatza'ir Party from the start. First, it would maintain internal political uniformity in accordance with the principle of ideological collectivism—namely ideological consistency inculcated and supervised by the leadership. Second, it would make decisions by means of democratic centralism, meaning that decision making would be directed by the historic leadership, which the party apparatus was obligated to accept. Both principles were taken from the Soviet Communist Party, which served as an inspiration to Mapam, just as it did, in varying degrees, to other parts of the Zionist labor movement.

The Soviet Union's influence on the thinking and political organization of the parties composing the Yishuv labor movement stemmed from the impression left by the ideological and political arena from which the movement's leaders hailed. Most had been born and raised in eastern Europe, and some, before arriving in Palestine, had been active in revolutionary socialist movements. As Anita Shapira has written, their attitude to the October Revolution reflected their affinity to socialist philosophy and to the world socialist movement (of which they considered themselves an integral part) as well as their yearning for the land of their birth. It was a land at once remote and terribly much their own.[9] During the labor movement's formative years, all of its currents had a connection of some sort to the Soviet "world of tomorrow." Some became unbounded enthusiasts for it, whereas others at an early stage discerned the gap between the myth and the reality of the Soviet regime and distanced themselves from it. The connection was expressed in three central ways. The first was identification with socialist values, whether revolutionary or reformist, which shaped the platforms of labor-movement parties (in a form adapted to the special conditions of the Yishuv). The second was profound cultural influence in areas such as literature, poetry, music, and the clothing worn by pioneers. The third was the influence of Soviet organizational concepts and methods.

The Israeli labor movement and the pioneering movements within it inherited from the Russian revolutionaries the vertical structure of the Soviet revolutionary avant-garde party, which distinguished between the elite and the masses they were to lead.[10] This structure was part of the form of political action preferred by all political movements that emerged in the industrial age and sought to gain the support of a large public— that of the mass party. The mass-party model had several components that differentiated it from the elite or caucus-party system of the eighteenth and nineteenth centuries, such as regular members, branches, a party congress, and a party press.[11] However, another characteristic of the mass party, opposed to its democratic and inclusive aspiration, was that, like the avant-garde party, it consisted of a leadership composed of professional revolutionaries. They led a highly developed party apparatus that was responsible for recruiting voters. This hierarchical model meant that political inequality was built into the mass-party membership. Women and some kinds of professional workers were not accepted as members in these parties in the early decades. Party activity was highly centralized, and there was no participatory democracy.[12]

The inequality in the labor mass party also derived from different levels of commitment to the party. The structure of the mass party required absolute devotion from its members, while its voting public was passive and not viewed as an organic part of the party. In the case of the Soviet revolutionary movement, for example, this structure included the consolidation of a new social class, the nomenklatura, which constituted the party machine. This group included all the senior figures in the party, army, security agencies, economy, school and university systems, culture, medicine, state bureaucracy, press, and more. It had a client relationship to the party leadership and received many benefits in exchange for its service to the party, especially in the form of housing and consumer goods, thus granting it a much higher standard of living than that of the average citizen. This class also existed in the Soviet client states in eastern Europe.[13] In Western socialist and social democratic movements, the nomenklatura phenomenon was less extreme but still prominent, as it was in the Yishuv.[14]

The mass party's leadership and officials had a functional relationship to each other, aimed at giving its members an economic, social, and cultural framework. In the case of Mapam, this meant principally the establishment of kibbutzim. In contrast, the connection between the officials and the public was founded on ideology by means of the party's cultural front. The term *cultural front* was used to designate the ideological and educational environment in which a political party, especially a socialist one, acted. The target audience for the cultural front were those members of the population who were sympathetic to the ideas of the Left but were not members of Communist or Socialist parties—that is, fellow travelers. The party's connection with this public was not directly functional in nature. Rather, it was made through mediums such as newspapers, educational and cultural centers, and books.[15] This public owed nothing to the party in its daily life, and the party owed nothing to the public. The ideological appeal was meant to gain support in advance of elections, and the voters trusted the party to exert its influence in the larger political system to implement its principles.

The mass-party model was also taken up by the Yishuv's other political movements in the transition to the state. All of them consisted of a small elite, a fixed coterie of activists, and a broad public mobilized to vote in elections. In Mapam's case, the model grew out of its development as an independent political force that allied kibbutz members with urban voters. After the split with the Ahdut Ha'avodah Party, however, Mapam abandoned its explicit hope of constituting an alternative governing party to Mapai. Led by Hashomer Hatza'ir, Mapam became small and relatively marginal. Nevertheless, its organizational structure changed only slightly. It continued to depend on its kibbutz base and the sympathy of a larger public. The connection between the kibbutz movement and its urban supporters, dating from the establishment of Hashomer Hatza'ir Party in 1946, dictated the mass-party structure. The same was true of its sister kibbutz-led party, Ahdut Ha'avodah.[16]

The three concentric circles that together make up a mass party were clearly evident in Mapam after 1954. The party was headed by an unchanging small leadership, with Ya'ari and Hazan at the top, supplemented by several dozen of their acolytes. The most central of these acolytes served as members of the Knesset and as government ministers (that is, when Mapam participated in the governing coalition).[17] Ya'ari and Hazan exercised almost absolute discretion over appointments to important party positions, vetoing anyone who opposed their ideas. The party leadership continued to exercise nearly untrammeled power until the beginning of the 1970s. Mapam formally operated along democratic lines, with its members electing a party council and other institutions, but the latter were virtually powerless.[18]

The kibbutzim, another circle of the mass party, served as Mapam's organizational base and the infrastructure of its party apparatus. Their members made up more than half of the party membership. Following the split, Mapam had 13,500 kibbutz members out of a total membership of approximately 25,000. They gave the party its capacity for action, among other things, by running the party's branches in the cities (which were funded by Hakibbutz Ha'artzi), recruiting supporters, organizing demonstrations, and providing an audience for political and cultural activities.[19] The functional relationship between the party and the kibbutzim was mutual in that Mapam served as a mediator between the kibbutzim and the suppliers of the resources they needed for their survival and for the establishment of new settlements. In this symbiosis, the kibbutzim were fully committed to the party and in return directly benefitted from its power. They enjoyed preferential status. Kibbutz members always made up about two-thirds of the party's Knesset members, even though they constituted only one-third of its voters.[20] Mapam also focused principally on promoting the interests of the kibbutzim and their economic needs.

Mapam's supporters outside the kibbutzim composed two groups—party members and nonmember voters. Nonmembers were fellow travelers, but that term applies just as well to the party's urban members, given that their actual power in the party was nil. In fact, the party had more urban than kibbutz members; most of its city adherents had been, at some point in their lives, members of the youth movement Hakibbutz Ha'artzi or of the Socialist League. A smaller number were Arab citizens of Israel. Most of the Arab party members participated in a variety of social and cultural organizations that Mapam operated in their community, in particular Ha-Noar ha-Aravi ha-Chalutzi (Pioneering Arab Youth Movement), founded in the mid-1950s. Following the split, Mapam had some 11,500 members outside the kibbutzim, of which about 1,000 were Arabs. At that time, Mapam received the votes of about 35,000 Israelis who were not party members; at its height, it garnered some 50,000–60,000 such votes.[21] Because Mapam provided significant tangible benefits only via its kibbutzim, its connection with these two groups was for the most part not functional. It was, rather, based for the most part on ideology in the framework of a cultural front.[22]

Mapam promulgated an ideological gospel—not a very popular one—that set it apart from its political and social environment. It combined pioneering Zionism, class-based radicalism, and moderation in the conflict with the Arabs, all summed up in its slogan "For Zionism, socialism, and the brotherhood of nations." The slogan, which appeared on the banner of its print arm *Al Hamishmar,* proclaimed these principles and the order of their importance. Its Zionism distinguished it from the non-Zionist socialist and Marxist parties of the Left, while its moderate stance on the Arab question distinguished it from Ahdut Ha'avodah and Mapai (under Ben-Gurion), both of which were hawkish in comparison to Mapam.

The origins of Mapam's position on the Arabs lay in Hakibbutz Ha'artzi's ideological principles. Hakibbutz Ha'artzi's founding congress in 1927 accepted the idea of a socialist binational regime in Palestine, in which the Jews would constitute a majority (in its insistence on a Jewish

majority, Hakibbutz Ha'artzi differed from other Yishuv organizations
that advocated binationalism, such as Brit Shalom). The idea of a shared
society manifested itself in the daily life of the kibbutzim, which maintained friendly relationships and cooperated with their Arab neighbors.[23]
In the wake of the Arab revolt of 1936–39 and subsequently during World
War II, the binational idea metamorphosed into a more detailed plan for
separate entities for Jews and Arabs, with a shared federal regime, to be put
into place in stages under the aegis of a supportive international force (that
is, not under the British Mandate, which was perceived as hostile to fostering a shared Jewish–Arab society). During the years 1942–45, Hakibbutz
Ha'artzi opposed Ben-Gurion's line of establishing a Jewish state under a
partition settlement, as laid out in the Biltmore program of 1942. After the
world war, it continued to promote the binational idea in forums on the
future of Palestine. Yet the binational solution began to look increasingly
impracticable and faded into irrelevance after the United Nations decision
in 1947 to establish separate Jewish and Arab states.[24] After the establishment of the State of Israel, Mapam advocated accommodation with the
Arabs, including by territorial compromise. It also called for the abolition
of the military government imposed on Arab-populated areas between
1948 and 1966.[25]

Mapam stood out from other parts of the labor movement also in its
explicit and enthusiastic support for the Soviet Union. Hakibbutz Ha'artzi
and Mapam's orientation toward the Soviet "world of tomorrow" reached
the point of nearly blind adulation during World War II and the first years
of the Jewish state. But it took a heavy blow during the 1950s as events
revealed the darker side of the Soviet regime. Mapam was eventually
forced to disassociate itself publicly from this aspect of its heritage, a story
recounted in chapter 11. Mapam nevertheless maintained its identity as a
revolutionary party for many years thereafter, and Marxism continued to
have an important place in its ideology, alongside pioneering Zionism. The
theoretical solution adopted in this regard, called the "theory of stages,"
was included (like the binational idea) in Hakibbutz Ha'artzi's manifesto
of 1927. It declared that Hashomer Hatza'ir was to work in the short range
to build the Hebrew national home in Palestine and in the long run, at a
second stage, to work for class revolution.[26] Support for the Soviet Union

thus did not carry with it any practical implications. Hakibbutz Ha'artzi and Mapam were entirely committed to Zionism. Their Marxism played the instrumental role of internal ideological mobilization, with their leaders asserting this dogma all the more forcefully as the party lost ever more popularity with the public.

The attempt to be both revolutionary and radical while remaining within the Zionist political consensus was one of several contradicting trends in Hakibbutz Ha'artzi and Mapam's politics and ideology. Others were their sectoral character as a settlement movement (located in the frontier and focused, first and foremost, in the settlements' own survival and well-being), the aspiration to lead masses of city workers (who were preoccupied with very different problems), and their will to be part of the broad Zionist labor movement and its intimate and "organic" character, which pushed Hakibbutz Ha'artzi and Mapam to separate self-definition. The moral purity that was part of the kibbutz's utopian socialism was also in tension with political life—its power struggles, manipulations, and cynicism. In addition, there was tension between the democratic and even anarchic ideology of the kibbutz and the reality of the hierarchic and even oligarchic structure that developed within Hakibbutz Ha'artzi and Mapam.[27]

Rifts between reality and utopia were a significant element in the life of the Zionist labor movement in general since the movement's role in building a new society involved, naturally, a constant encounter between ideas and their fulfillment. However, in Hakibbutz Ha'artzi and Mapam these rifts were even more notable, following the strong influence of the youth-movement heritage on them. This heritage affected Hakibbutz Ha'artzi and Mapam in many ways, but regarding their ideological and political life it had one main implication: it pushed Hakibbutz Ha'artzi and Mapam to create an organizing theoretical framework that touched almost every aspect of life, from erotic relationships to global affairs, with an attempt to find a logical connection between these aspects. This need for thorough explanations was part of the idealistic nature of the youth movement, which demanded reasons for everything. Only in this way could the members of the movement agree on the fundamentals of life and build an ideological collective. However, a total ideology always includes elements that do not easily fit together. Such dissonance energized ideological life in Hakibbutz Ha'artzi and Mapam, involving an ongoing effort to reconcile different and sometimes contradicting ideas into a single worldview.[28]

Hakibbutz Ha'artzi and Mapam's complex ideology and intellectual nature attracted mostly people from the intelligentsia. This fact led to further tension because it contradicted the aspiration to be a workers' movement. One of Mapam's urban leaders put it succinctly when he complained that the party's ideology was so complex that "it's impossible to explain to the masses."[29] However, the need for constant mediation between reality and ideas required developed intellectual tools that would operate under a well-supervised ideological establishment. This was a significant factor in the foundation of Hakibbutz Ha'artzi and Mapam's cultural front.

3

Founding Hakibbutz Ha'artzi
and Mapam's Cultural Front

THE POLITICIZATION of Hakibbutz Ha'artzi was accompanied by the establishment of a cultural institution with a goal and structure that were meant to meet two needs. First, it pursued the classic cultural-front type of activity offered by all labor movements around the world, aimed at influencing a broad public and gaining its support. Second, it sought to serve the kibbutz movement, particularly to provide a way to ameliorate internal pressures brought on by the movement's transformation into a political party. The second function was specific to the special case of Israeli settlements in general and to those of Hakibbutz Ha'artzi and Mapam in particular, with their roots in a youth movement. The first, however, was universal. The combination of culture and politics had been part and parcel of workers movements from the end of the nineteenth century as they fashioned a working-class culture. In the 1930s, as European democratic movements faced off against Nazism and fascism, the line along which this political struggle was carried out with the help of mobilized culture was called the "cultural front." Communicating with the public by means of newspapers, plays, films, and books was fundamental to the struggle for support and identification, and the cultural front's task was to prove that democratic governments were no less successful than totalitarian regimes, which also manufactured mass culture for the purpose of mobilizing the masses.[1]

In the Israeli case, institutions that fostered "labor culture" first appeared in the framework of the labor movement in the early 1920s. They were meant to garner political support and to meet the needs of workers and were influenced by the European model. But they differed in important ways from the European institutions because of the unique conditions created by the Zionist movement's national revolution, which sought to create a new culture. For example, the Histadrut founded the daily newspaper *Davar* (Speech) in 1925 to provide immigrant workers with news, opinions, and cultural content from a socialist point of view. It was meant to serve as part of the spiritual and intellectual foundation for the national revival and to serve as a means of enlisting support for the labor parties. Similarly, in 1942 the Histadrut founded the publishing house Am Oved (Working People) so as to participate in the Hebrew literary revival and to provide workers and their families with books for their home libraries. It also aimed to educate the public in pioneer values, to foster awareness of the labor movement's historic role, and to translate both of the former into political support. Between *Davar* and Am Oved, the Histadrut founded two organizations that enhanced the labor movement's capacity for contributing to the national-cultural revival, to give it a popular-labor cast, and to vie for the hearts of the public. One was the popular sports organization Hapoel (the Worker), the other a theater, Ha'ohel (the Tent). On top of all of these efforts, the Histadrut operated many other cultural institutions, such as a school for activists, adult education, lectures, organized vacations, study days, and more.[2]

Prior to independence, most of Mapai's cultural activity was pursued in the framework of the Histadrut, which the party controlled. After the founding of the state, however, Mapai had the state apparatus and budget at its disposal, enabling it to expand its cultural activity beyond the boundaries of the labor organization and to set cultural policy for the entire country. Education and culture were combined into a single government ministry, and the portfolio was always held by Mapai (or its successor, the Labor Party, until Labor lost the election of 1977). During the state's first two decades, the Ministry of Education and Culture, headed by Ben-Zion Dinur and Zalman Aran, promoted *mamlakhtiyut* as well as the concept of Israel as a melting pot in which Jewish immigrants from all over the world would be absorbed into a single Israeli culture. The policy of *mamlakhtiyut* was aimed at gaining support for Mapai and for Ben-Gurion as the ultimate representatives of the ingathering of the exiles and the rebirth of the Jewish people in their sovereign state.[3] In 1954, the ministry established a unified national school system and abolished the Labor Stream, the school system run by the Histadrut, which had aimed to instill labor-movement values. Although this change might seem counterproductive to the dissemination of labor ideals, from Mapai's point of view it simply meant that the new national school system would further the same values.[4] Mapai's control of Histadrut and of the state's cultural front impelled other parts of the labor movement to establish their own individual cultural fronts so as to enlist supporters for their parties. Hakibbutz Hameuhad founded its own eponymous publishing house in 1939 and its own teacher-training college at Efal in 1949, and the Ahdut Ha'avodah party weekly, *Lamerhav* (To the Open), became a daily in 1954.[5] Hakibbutz Ha'artzi/Mapam cultural institutions were born out of the same need: to serve the members of Hakibbutz Ha'artzi and its urban political supporters.

Credit for the establishment of the cultural front of Hakibbutz Ha'artzi and Mapam goes largely to the special connection that emerged at the end of the 1930s between the movement's leadership and the poet, translator, and editor Avraham Shlonsky.[6] It was not unusual at that time for a leading intellectual and writer such as Shlonsky to work as part of a partisan cultural front. On the contrary, this relationship was just one instance of intellectuals' involvement in working-class culture in general and in the cultural life of the Yishuv labor movement in particular. For Hakibbutz Ha'artzi, the connection with Shlonsky was part of its process of eschewing alliances and establishing itself as an independent political force, in part by establishing its own independent cultural front. To do so and to gain influence over the public, the movement needed the help of well-known intellectuals, writers, and artists, especially urban ones. Shlonsky took on this role not because he agreed with Hakibbutz Ha'artzi and Mapam's ideology, but rather because, after unsuccessfully trying to gain entry into the cultural system of Mapai and the Histadrut, he sought a position that would enable him to work and make a living. Despite his ideological differences with Hakibbutz Ha'artzi movement's leaders, Ya'ari and Hazan, the partnership turned out to be beneficial to both sides and lasted for many years.[7]

By the end of the 1920s, Hakibbutz Ha'artzi was already considering the need for cultural programming to supplement the movement's work in education, settlement, and politics. In 1930, the leaders called on the movement's governing council to address the subject.[8] But that didn't happen until five years later, culture being the last subject to be taken up as part of Hakibbutz Ha'artzi's organizational process. According to a report on cultural activity in the kibbutzim that was prepared for the council when it met in September 1935, "the first years were devoted to laying the foundations—and only upon development and internal fortification is culture also demanding its share." The reason given for addressing culture at this particular time was that

> in the meantime, our society is expanding, new kibbutzim are being added, our children are growing, and a new generation has arisen, for whom our kibbutzim constitute their only social and cultural environment, in which they will be educated and from which they will draw their cultural experiences, and within which their spiritual profile will be shaped. The question of culture thus requires immediate clarification and illumination.[9]

Aside from these internal needs, the development of the cultural sphere supplemented the movement's move into politics. The first cultural institution the movement established, a year before the cultural council was established, was an organization of kibbutz artists and sculptors who pursued creative projects both in their communities and outside the kibbutzim. The organization was aimed at providing a platform for the creation of political art expressing the particular ideas of Hakibbutz Ha'artzi against the background of the political rivalries of the Yishuv period. The recognition that kibbutz life "necessitates culture" fit in with the need for visual elements to serve as background for kibbutz holiday celebrations and other ceremonies as well as for use in posters and political publications. Marxist–Leninist ideology pervaded both the art organization and the cultural council.[10]

In 1939, the movement founded a publishing house, Sifriyat Poalim (Workers' Library), which also integrated the movement's political and educational requirements with the need for a home for kibbutz writers. The feeling among members of the kibbutz community in the late 1930s was that their lives had been revolutionized, and they sought to depict in literary form the new man and new society created in the kibbutzim. In their view, literature's calling was not just to describe but also to help shape the new generation. The books published by Sifriyat Poalim from the beginning of the 1940s reflected the mood of the socialist-Zionist Left in general and of Hakibbutz Ha'artzi in particular, with its increasing admiration of the Soviet Union and adherence to strict Marxist doctrine. The publishing house was seen to have a specifically ideological mission, and so the movement's involvement in it increased. The establishment of Hashomer Hatza'ir Party in 1946 made Sifriyat Poalim's role as a means of enlisting public support all the more crucial. The publisher opened stores in the cities, and cooperation between the movement and sympathetic intellectuals was broadened to other areas of culture and art. A mission statement composed for Sifriyat Poalim in 1954 declared that it aimed "to place the good socialist book within the ranks of the workers and working intelligentsia."[11] Until 1956, the house did all it could to be part of the world of the Communist bloc's socialist revolution.

Another cultural organ of Hakibbutz Ha'artzi was its newspaper *Mishmar*, which published its first issue in July 1943 and was renamed *Al Hamishmar* when Mapam was founded in 1948. The decision to launch a daily newspaper (the movement had previously published a weekly, *Hashomer Hatza'ir*) grew out of a combination of the need to gain supporters and sympathizers for the projected political party and the aspiration to engage in ideological and socialist education within the party. Furthermore, even if a movement preferred not to publish a newspaper or lacked funds to do so, it found itself impelled in that direction. Most of the newspapers published in the Yishuv were party affiliated, so their pages were closed to members of other parties. The direct impetus for the founding of *Mishmar* was the Histadrut daily *Davar*, which for all intents and purposes served as a mouthpiece for Mapai. *Mishmar* was a means of attacking Mapai and the parties of the Right but was also used by the movement's leaders to shape Hashomer Hatza'ir Party from within. The newspaper was entirely controlled by the leadership. No opposition opinions were allowed, in accordance with the principle of ideological collectivism. On the outside, the newspaper sought to enhance Mapam's avant-garde image by using high and heroic language to extol the movement's achievements.

Events of importance to the party were covered extensively. The staff also produced ideological issues addressed to subjects such as the celebration of May Day, the observation of the anniversaries of the deaths of Marx and Lenin, and the commemoration of the October Revolution. In keeping with this approach, the newspaper's reporters viewed themselves as emissaries enlisted by virtue of their membership in the movement and the party. There was sometimes dissonance between the newspaper's reporting of the facts and its presentation of the party's positions. But until the 1960s such dilemmas were decided in favor of the party and movement leadership.

In February 1946, soon after Hashomer Hatza'ir Party was founded, Shlonsky agreed to the party leadership's request that he enlist friends and associates from the literary and artistic world to form a cultural cadre. In July, he organized a conference at Kibbutz Merhavia. The participants held lengthy discussions about culture and its social role and agreed that there was a need for a progressive culture that would shoulder public and social responsibility. Art had to take part in the political and class struggle. The conference led to the founding of Ha-Merkaz le-Tarbut Mitkatemet (Center for Progressive Culture), which was to bring the culture of Hakibbutz Ha'artzi to the city.[12] In its early years, the center took the form of a respected but relatively marginal social club in Tel Aviv. Most of its participants were Tel Aviv intellectuals who numbered among Shlonsky's admirers as well as kibbutz members who happened to be in the city. They met once or twice a week to listen to talks given by leading Hebrew literary and artistic figures as well as political and military leaders. In July 1955, the group leased a relatively large hall on Dizengoff Street and moved its meetings there. The club was also given a new and catchy name, Tzavta (Circle of Friends). In 1957, the group drafted an official statement of purpose: Tzavta was aimed at "establishing a home for artists that would disseminate the values of Hashomer Hatza'ir to the broad public."[13]

Another area addressed by Hakibbutz Ha'artzi and Mapam's cultural front, growing jointly out of needs coming from below and organization from above, was sports. Members of Hakibbutz Ha'artzi engaged in sports at their kibbutzim under the aegis of Hapoel, the Histadrut sports organization. Hapoel made no distinction between the different kibbutz

movements or parties and sponsored a variety of amateur and professional teams and activities. Each kibbutz movement, however, had a sport
that it specialized in and sought to excel in and that served as a source of
pride and movement solidarity. Ihud Hakevutzot Vehakibbutzim focused
on water polo (its team Hapoel Givat Hayim Ihud led the national league
and won the national championship each year from 1967 to 1992). Hakibbutz Hameuhad put its efforts into basketball (its top team, Hapoel Gvat/
Yagur, played in the national league beginning in 1965 and became the top
team in the 1970s; in 1976, it won the state cup, the first time a team other
than Hapoel Tel Aviv or Maccabi Tel Aviv won any basketball tournament
in Israel). The sport associated with Hakibbutz Ha'artzi more than any
other was volleyball.

The Yishuv began organizing volleyball tournaments at the beginning
of the 1930s. Most of the teams came from Hakibbutz Ha'artzi. In 1942, a
national tournament held in Sheikh Abreik awarded the Zaïd Cup. Most of
the participating teams represented kibbutzim, as did the winners.[14] From
the time the National Volleyball League was founded in 1956 until 1976,
nearly all the teams competing for the men's championship and all the
winners came from Hakibbutz Ha'artzi. A women's league was founded
in 1961, and its championship was won by a kibbutz team—usually from
Hakibbutz Ha'artzi—for twenty-six years running.

Volleyball would seem to have been an especially appropriate game
for a socialist movement with views about the educational and political
role of sports. Whereas the nonsocialist sports organizations, Maccabi
and Betar, exalted the idea of "muscular Judaism," the display of force
and strength, the socialists insisted that sports should serve as a force for
society building, education, and solidarity, while also contributing to its
participants' health. As such, the socialists opposed professional sports
in principle. They also opposed sports such as weightlifting and boxing,
which emphasized strength and bodybuilding, as well as soccer because
of the relative violence involved in the encounter between players on the
field. However, these views were not imposed in practice, and such sports
were pursued in the socialist clubs. The socialists also fostered champions,
although they placed most emphasis on popular sports.[15]

The investment in sports by the labor movement among the kibbutzim was based on the view of the role of "workers' sports" in the building of social awareness.[16] Like the rest of the labor movement's institutionalized cultural activity, "workers' sports" were meant to foster the class consciousness of the masses and to prepare them for the struggle against the bourgeoisie. In the context of Hakibbutz Ha'artzi, the argument was that the centrality of volleyball in the movement and the purpose of developing it to the level of professionalism grew out of the movement's ideological orientation toward the Soviet bloc, where volleyball was a central game.[17] The movement's adoption of the game was thus an effort to emulate the "world of tomorrow" and to draw cultural inspiration from it. The same was true in music, painting, sculpture, literature, and other fields.[18] Volleyball was also considered a socialist sport because of its particular characteristics. It was believed to encourage cooperation because it does not involve competition between members of the team. Unlike soccer and basketball, it does not depend on star players. It is a game both men and women can play, and there is no physical contact or violence. Audiences do not get too worked up, and the game needs only simple gear (a ball and a net), requiring neither a concrete court nor a lawn. Because of its high net, players need to stretch their spines and lift their heads, which is good for improving posture and especially important for people who work in agriculture and factories, where they spend much of their time sitting or bending over. Here, too, Hakibbutz Ha'artzi followed the lead of the Soviet Union, where the Communist Party Central Committee declared volleyball to be a game that makes a national educational-pedagogical contribution. Furthermore, the game was believed to enhance solidarity.

Hakibbutz Ha'artzi and Mapam's cultural front included another institution that provided cultural content and political education for kibbutz members. Established in 1947, it was called the Department of Culture and Propaganda of Hakibbutz Ha'artzi, which oversaw a variety of ideological education programs. Most of its activity took place at the movement's educational and ideological center, Givat Haviva (Haviva's Hill, named after Haviva Reik [1914–44], a Hakibbutz Ha'artzi member who was one of the parachutists sent by the Jewish Agency and Britain's Special

Operations Executive on military missions in Nazi-occupied Europe), founded in 1949. The college's mission statement spoke of "deepening kibbutz consciousness," "understanding Hashomer Hatza'ir's mission in the nation and class," and "understanding the nature of the world's progressive forces." It defined its target audience as new immigrants, members of the youth movement, and members of kibbutzim.[19] The curriculum included subjects such as Marxism–Leninism, Zionism, Borochovism, the Jewish labor movement in the Diaspora and Israel, the kibbutz movement, Hashomer Hatza'ir, and Mapam. The relative number of hours devoted to the different subjects indicated the importance attributed to them: Marxism–Leninism and the kibbutz were at the top of the list, security and the military at the bottom. Many study hours were devoted to talks with movement and party leaders.[20]

During Givat Haviva's first years, most members of Hakibbutz Ha'artzi and Mapam enrolled in its ideological training program, which became very popular.[21] The success indicated that the members of the movement and party were ideologically committed, but even more so it testified to the fact that the party's and the movement's officials mediated between the outside world and the movement's members in the cultural sphere as well. The lack of other communications media at the time, the distance between the kibbutzim and centers of culture and intellectual dialogue, and the fact that kibbutz members could not educate themselves on their own because they lived on the country's frontiers in an austere agricultural society granted Givat Haviva as well as the party-affiliated daily newspaper, publishing house, and other activities sponsored by Hakibbutz Ha'artzi and Mapam's Department of Culture and Propaganda a strong position because they provided information about and interpretation of events in Israel and the world. Furthermore, the studies in the college were a form of entertainment and leisure. While the college schedules and quantity of material covered were demanding, the students enjoyed the social contact with members of other kibbutzim and the cultural enrichment. As demanding as the ideological courses were, they were a needed respite from everyday labors and the drab routine of kibbutz life. The movement, for its part, gained an opportunity to reinforce ideological collectivism. This package, which had economic, social, and political aspects, was thus successful for both sides. It demonstrated the efficacy of the method by which Hakibbutz Ha'artzi and Mapam mobilized sympathy and support and the way in which the interplay of economics, politics, and culture became the secret of the movement's and the party's strength. However, from the mid-1950s on, a series of economic, social, ideological, and political developments in Israel and the rest of the Western world posed new challenges to Hakibbutz Ha'artzi and Mapam as well as to other parts of the labor movement. These developments marked the beginning of a new era in the movements' and parties' power structures as well as the beginning of the crisis of the Left in Israel and the rest of the world.

PART ONE

The Economic Turn

From Agricultural Austerity to Postindustrial Prosperity

ISRAEL EXPERIENCED both booms and recessions over the course of the two decades between 1956 and 1977, but the long-term trend was one of increasing prosperity and emergence from agricultural austerity to one of postindustrial abundance.[1] During the first part of this period, from the mid-1950s to the mid-1960s, Israel, or more precisely a large swathe of it, moved from being a developing agrarian society living with relative scarcity to being a developed society with a manufacturing-based economy. During the second part of the period, beginning after the Six-Day War of 1967, the country moved into postmaterial abundance, sharing many characteristics with the most developed countries of the West. Each stage confronted the labor movement with new circumstances that challenged its hegemony in Israeli society.

4

From a Developing
to a Developed Society

AN UPSWING beginning in the mid-1950s produced accelerated growth
enjoyed by all sectors of Israeli society.[2] Before that, following independence, the government had pursued an austerity policy aimed at coping
with a huge influx of immigrants. As a result, Israelis of all walks of life
had to cope with several years of scarcity. The approximately 700,000 newcomers who arrived during the state's first three years more than doubled
the size of Israel's Jewish population, which numbered about 650,000 at
independence. Furthermore, the country needed time to recover from the
costs and effects of its long War of Independence and, in a larger sense,
from ongoing hostilities dating back to the Arab Revolt of 1936.[3] It also
needed to establish sovereign and independent governing institutions. The
first indications of recovery appeared in 1954; by 1956, Israel had entered
an era of dramatic growth. The immigrants had been absorbed, and housing had been built for them. At the same time, the country enjoyed a
period of relative security on and beyond its borders as well as political
stability. Life in the new country changed fundamentally as the state of
emergency of the country's early years gave way to a new era of normalization and entrenchment.

Israel's economic growth was part of a global phenomenon directly
attributable to the policies pursued by the strongest power in the West in
the postwar period—the United States. US gross national product (GNP)
doubled during the war, and in the spring of 1945 the United States held
half the world's manufacturing capacity, most of its food reserves, and
most of its foreign-currency reserves. It was the world's leading economic

power, with the Soviet Union in second place, making both of them essential to the recovery of those countries that had been ravaged by the war. The two superpowers divided the world into spheres of influence that were agreed on during the final stages of the war, creating an East–West divide that would last for decades to come. The United States assumed responsibility for rehabilitating large parts of Europe, Asia, and the Middle East and thus shaped the economies of many countries, Israel among them.

The United States was the moving force behind two programs for rehabilitating the world economy in the postwar period. One was the establishment of international institutions to provide funding for development of and commerce in and among the affected countries. The United Nations Monetary and Financial Conference, convened in July 1944 at Breton Woods, New Hampshire, was attended by delegates from forty-four countries. It founded both the World Bank, charged with providing credit on easy terms to developing countries, and the International Monetary Fund, which established a new monetary order based on fixed exchange rates that was aimed at encouraging and facilitating international transactions. The major architects of the new regime were the British economist John Maynard Keynes and Harry Dexter White of the US Treasury. World currencies were pegged to the American dollar, backed by gold, which became the new international reserve currency. It provided an institutional imprimatur for the standing of the United States as the world's leading economic power.[4]

The second program was a set of economic-development initiatives in which the United States granted massive direct aid and advice to war-torn and underdeveloped nations. By offering loans, grants, and debt relief, and by sending American expert advisers for the development of local industry, the United States wielded enormous influence. These initiatives were organized under the Marshall Plan, officially called the European Recovery Program, launched in 1948 at the initiative of Secretary of State George Marshall. By 1952, the United States had provided $13 billion in aid to Britain, France, Italy, Poland, Denmark, Greece, and other countries. The program also brought thousands of European managers, technicians, and labor-union activists to the United States to learn American-style business administration. American experts were also sent to Europe, where they became deeply embedded in the continent's economic recovery.[5]

In the process of encouraging the economic development of the countries it aided, the United States taught them American ways of working as well as its values and beliefs. The result was an economic regime that coupled massive government involvement with an emphasis on individual initiative, efficiency, and productivity. This combination grew out of the American Progressive movement of the late nineteenth and early twentieth centuries, which found its ultimate expression in President Franklin Roosevelt's New Deal of the 1930s. Progressivism, a form of modified capitalism, was foreign to most European leaders, especially those of the socialist persuasion. They thus opposed the American approach, which fundamentally contradicted their ideology. Over time, however, the huge power wielded by the United States, the demands it made in exchange for its aid, and the huge success engendered by its programs wore down opposition, and these countries opened themselves to large-scale Americanization.[6]

American involvement proved effective, spurring rapid development in the countries under US influence. A stable platform for international trade, technological development, industrial expansion, and the growth in manufacturing productivity were combined with the availability of low-cost credit. These policies were intended to promote economic expansion and full employment. The old capitalist doctrine that the state should not seek to influence economic trends was replaced by the new concept of the welfare state, in which Western democracies offered their citizens a safety net to help them through hard times, sickness, and old age. Large and strong labor unions ensured that workers enjoyed a rising standard of living, creating what came to be called the "affluent society." Some countries displayed exceptional capacities for development, earning them the label *economic miracles*. West Germany and Austria were two such instances in the initial period following the war, and they were joined in the 1950s by the "Asian tigers" South Korea, Taiwan, Hong Kong, and Japan. Israel was another economic miracle.[7]

As in these other cases, Israel owed its economic development in large part to the United States. From 1951 on, Israel received American economic aid in the sum of tens of millions of dollars per annum, granted as part of the US policy of assisting developing nations. This aid came in the form of development loans at low rates of interest and in the sale of food surpluses.[8] In addition, American progressive capitalism was exported to Israel in an organized way by means of massive transfers of knowledge as part of cooperation between the two governments. A total of 198 American business and industrial experts came to Israel during the 1950s, and 525 Israelis were sent for training in those fields in the United States. The Institute for Labor Productivity was established in Israel under American sponsorship, as was the Department of Industrial Engineering at the Israel Institute of Technology (Technion) in Haifa, a business administration program at the Hebrew University of Jerusalem, and the Israeli Center for Management. All of these institutions sought to inculcate American business methods in Israelis. As was the case elsewhere, however, American progressive capitalism clashed with local political ideologies. American experts complained about the effect of Israel's socialist past, which they saw as countervailing the values they sought to promote. US technological aid came to an end in 1962, but America's intensive involvement in Israel's initial decade of growth left its mark on the young country.[9]

Israel's economic development was also funded by sources that were unique to it. One source was a reparations agreement with West Germany, signed in 1952. Over more than a decade, these reparations injected hundreds of millions of dollars into the Israeli economy. The money was used to buy ships, raw materials, and machinery that allowed Israel to upgrade its electrical grid, exploit its natural resources, and build water and transportation networks.[10] Another source was the Israel Bonds program, started in 1951, which in the 1950s and 1960s raised hundreds of millions of dollars from the Jewish Diaspora, especially American Jewry. This money boosted economic development, investment, and consumption.[11] The huge population boost Israel enjoyed in the 1950s as a result of immigration, when combined with this capital, enabled an industrial expansion program led by Pinhas Sapir, who assumed the position of trade and industry minister in 1956 and turned his office into the Israeli economy's major engine of growth.[12] Taken together, all these factors brought about rapid growth and full employment. At the beginning of the 1960s, the

Israeli economy boomed; in December 1965, national annual per capita income crossed the $1,000 line, marking the country's move from the status of a developing country to a developed country.[13]

The kibbutz movements followed a trajectory similar to that of the Israeli economy at large and serve as excellent examples of how Israel's economic development played out. When Israel's spurt began in the mid-1950s, the kibbutz movements were in severe economic crisis, having built up large amounts of debt. But following the establishment of Israel's Seventh Knesset in November 1955, the parties with which the kibbutzim were affiliated were members of the coalition and exerted their political clout to press for government aid. In 1956 and 1957, the government reached several economic arrangements with the kibbutzim under which they rescheduled their debts and received special development funds.[14] These arrangements were growth oriented, aimed at providing the kibbutzim with a stronger economic base in the long term. They were grounded in the progressive paradigm that now prevailed in Israel and the rest of the West, according to which the involvement of government and international agencies was essential to bringing about exploitation of the economy's full potential and these agencies working together would bring about growth. As production-oriented entities, the kibbutzim were effective at taking advantage of the good terms provided by the government to develop both of their main industries, farming and manufacturing.

Until the mid-1960s, agriculture was the most important occupation at kibbutzim. As a result of the changes that took place in the 1950s, it also was an important money earner. Agricultural productivity rose at first thanks to the introduction of new technologies, a sharp rise in the demand for food products by the Jewish population (which more than tripled between 1948 and 1966), the expansion of exports, and government policies aimed at creating jobs for immigrants and settling them in sparsely inhabited areas. To fully exploit the economic promise of agriculture, the kibbutzim of the three movements—Hakibbutz Ha'artzi, Hakibbutz Hameuhad, and Ihud Hakevutzot Vehakibbutzim—set up regional cooperatives to enable cooperative efforts to streamline production and processing. Heavy equipment, such as combines, and essential materials, such as fertilizer and pesticides, were purchased jointly, and huge regional warehouses and processing plants—for example, cotton-carding plants and slaughterhouses—were established as common ventures.[15] The growth of alfalfa, a foundation crop in kibbutz farming, was revolutionized when it was coordinated by the regional organization. The individual kibbutzim were responsible only for watering the field, and the regional cooperative assumed responsibility for planting, fertilizing, reaping, harvesting, and transporting the crop.[16] This efficient method was pioneered by individual kibbutzim but soon received the sanction of the kibbutz movements, Hakibbutz Ha'artzi included, which in March 1956 decided to encourage it.[17] The regional organizations burgeoned, and by the middle of the 1960s the great majority of kibbutzim were members of a regional organization.[18]

In 1969, kibbutzim supplied 28.6 percent of Israel's agricultural production, almost five times as much as their population would warrant. Hakibbutz Ha'artzi kibbutzim were more productive than those of the other two movements, producing a bit more than a third of total kibbutz production and 9.9 percent of the country's agricultural output. This movement's kibbutzim cultivated more land (37.2 percent) than the other two movements, and it led in central fields: dairy cattle, beef cattle, chickens both for slaughter and for egg production, fish farming, and field crops.[19]

Even though agricultural productivity increased during this period thanks to technological improvements, profitability began to decline at the beginning of the 1960s. The Israeli economy was saturated with farm products, causing prices to drop; the government reduced its aid for agriculture, and production quotas were imposed. The rate of growth of agricultural production at kibbutzim declined from 25.2 percent in the years 1951–55 to 12 percent in the years 1955–60 and 4.9 percent in 1960–65.[20] Because farming was a major source of income, this decline in agricultural production led to a decline in kibbutz profits as a whole. Furthermore, a move into more-intensive crops and the adoption of state-of-the-art methods of cultivation led to a rise in productivity per unit of land, meaning that ever fewer workers were needed in the farming sector. Despite all this, however, in the 1960s the economies of individual kibbutzim continued to be based largely on farming, which provided more than 70 percent of their gross product and employed more than half of kibbutz members in the production of goods at the kibbutzim.[21]

These changes required kibbutzim to seek new profit centers. Overwhelmingly, they turned to manufacturing, which had been practiced on a small scale in some communities for a number of years already.[22] To a great extent, kibbutzim industrialized despite their movements' reluctance to endorse this trend. Movement leaders did not encourage the change; in fact, they imposed a variety of constraints on it. For example, they forbade or limited the number of outside workers who could be employed at kibbutz factories and placed strict limits on the investment of private capital in these enterprises.[23] Kibbutz factories were for the most part local initiatives, encouraged directly by the government under Sapir's direction. Seeking to bring down the national unemployment rate and raise per capita product and income, he encouraged industrialization by offering public grants and loans.[24] Further encouragements were the establishment of the Industrial Development Bank in 1957 and the amendment in 1959 of the Encouragement of Capital Investments Law of 1950 to provide more incentives for potential investors.

Kibbutzim moved increasingly into manufacturing for other reasons as well. Factories answered a need to provide employment for aging members who could no longer work in the fields. Industrialization also answered the need to provide productive employment for the kibbutzim's excess labor because there were often more workers at a kibbutz than were needed for farming. This was particularly true as these communities became homes to a second generation of young people who had been raised there and needed to be employed when they returned home after completing their military service. The fact that kibbutzim had engaged in manufacturing on some level for two decades already meant manufacturing had been tried and tested, which overcame some of the objections to it.[25] By 1961, there were thirty-nine factories in Hakibbutz Ha'artzi; close to half of the movement's kibbutzim had one. Kibbutz industries together increased production by 333 percent in the years 1950–60.[26]

The development of kibbutz industry, an outgrowth of the progressive capitalist era in the Israeli economy, ran counter to the founding principles of the pioneering socialist kibbutz, which viewed working the land not just as a job but as a spiritual and patriotic endeavor, essential to the creation of a new and just Jewish society. Rapid development, however, created a demand for labor as well as economic opportunities that were difficult to refuse. All of these factors overcame the principle of self-labor, which is that all kibbutz labor be performed by the commune's members themselves. According to classic kibbutz ideology, a commune that employed laborers who were not members of the commune crossed the line from being a community of workers to being the very bosses whom socialism so decried. However, industrialization inevitably impelled the kibbutzim to bring in manpower from outside. The huge immigration wave of the early 1950s presented the kibbutzim with a dilemma. Ben-Gurion called on the kibbutzim to take part in immigrant absorption by operating factories to provide jobs to the newcomers. Hakibbutz Hameuhad and Ihud Hakevutzot Vehakibbutzim rose to the challenge and founded a number of large factories that provided employment to residents of nearby villages and towns. Because these movements also had ideological reservations about employing hired labor, however, they tried as much as possible to employ outsiders at regional factories and plants that were not located on the grounds of the kibbutzim themselves.

Yet Hakibbutz Ha'artzi refused. To answer Ben-Gurion's call would be to sacrifice its principles, its leaders claimed.[27] But the movement could not stand on principle for long—Hakibbutz Ha'artzi kibbutzim needed to go into manufacturing to survive, and once factories were built, they required more working hands than the kibbutz members could or wished to provide. Furthermore, outside laborers were plentiful and proximate, living in the development towns and moshavim built by the government for new immigrants on the country's margins, where the kibbutzim were located. In 1966, kibbutz industries from all movements employed 4,130 outside workers as against only 2,850 kibbutz members, a situation of great concern to the leaders of all three movements.[28] The result was a dissonance between ideals and practice that Hakibbutz Ha'artzi had a hard time resolving. In the years 1962–64, for example, its Executive Committee convened five times to discuss the issue of hired labor and to seek practical decisions. Each time, the Executive Committee resolved to give the phenomenon no quarter. Whether it won the fight is a matter of interpretation—between 1961 and 1964, the number of hired laborers working at Hakibbutz Ha'artzi kibbutzim declined from 840 to 521 (this does not include regional plants, where there was no decline and where most of the hired labor was employed). Hakibbutz Ha'artzi could not pretend that the phenomenon did not exist but refused to grant it legitimacy. The movement's official policy was that its kibbutzim were employing outside labor only as a temporary stop-gap measure until the members could run the factories on their own.

The industrialization drive in the kibbutz movement went into high gear at the beginning of the 1960s as part of a large-scale process that the Israeli economy as a whole and the economies of other countries were undergoing. This process amounted to a comprehensive industrial revolution. Manufacturing output's relative weight in the kibbutz economy rose from 7 percent in 1958 to 16 percent in 1965 and then to close to 30 percent in 1969. Sales of manufactured products were also steadily rising.[29] In the second half of the 1960s, the rate of kibbutz industrialization picked up even more, greater than that of Israeli industry as a whole. Between 1960 and 1968, the number of people employed in kibbutz factories more than doubled, but the number employed in factories in the country as a whole rose only 45 percent. Similarly, the proportion of kibbutz members employed in manufacturing was in 1965 higher per 1,000 inhabitants than in the country's cities. Especially prominent in the kibbutz economy were lumber and wood products, making up 13.2 percent of the national total, more than four times greater than the percentage of kibbutz members in the population. The kibbutzim also held 12.5 percent of the Israeli machinery sector, 6.1 percent of the rubber and plastic sector, and 5.8 percent of the metalworking sector, in all cases higher than these sectors' share in Israeli industry as a whole, 4.7 percent. In 1967, the annual output per worker in kibbutz industries was 32,000 Israeli pounds (IL) ($9,142), as opposed to IL 28,000 ($8,000) per worker nationally.[30] In the latter half of the 1960s, the rate of industrial development in Hakibbutz Ha'artzi was the highest in all three kibbutz movements, as was the growth in the number of factories.[31] Hakibbutz Ha'artzi's economic success was a product of its own efforts but also owed much to the conditions the state presented it with.[32]

Kibbutz society's economic foundation was also connected to aid from external sources of the same sort enjoyed by the Israeli government. The principal ones were the reparations from West Germany and donations from American Jewry. The irony is that even though the economic development enjoyed by the kibbutzim was brought about by Western methods and with Western funds, Mapam and Hakibbutz Ha'artzi continued to declare fealty to the Soviet Union and revolutionary socialism and to oppose all ties with what they said was the capitalism and imperialism of the United States and western Europe.[33] But their rhetoric was belied by their actions. Mapam may have been a leader of the campaign against signing the reparations agreement with West Germany, but after the agreement was signed, it happily accepted the money. Similarly, despite seeing the United States as tainted, Mapam and its kibbutzim established strong relations with well-off American Jewish business figures, who provided considerable support for their development.

German reparations reached the kibbutzim in two ways. One was procurements made on the basis of reparations granted to the Israeli government, which the government then allotted to the kibbutzim. The second way was through the West German government's payment to kibbutz members who had survived the Holocaust or had fled Europe before the Holocaust but had left property behind. The reparations made it possible to buy large quantities of manufacturing equipment from Germany. A survey conducted by a committee set up by Hakibbutz Ha'artzi's Executive Committee in 1965, toward the end of the reparations agreement's term, showed this capability. The committee examined thirty kibbutz factories and found that in eight of them more than a third of the equipment came from Germany. Furthermore, four factories had knowledge ties with Germany, five factories were planning to import equipment from there, one exported directly to Germany, seven imported German raw products, six imported Germany spare parts, and two planned to bring in expert consultants from Germany.[34] In parallel and in the continued implementation of the reparations agreement between the two countries, the West German Parliament enacted in 1953 a law granting those persecuted by the Nazis to receive personal compensation. Acting on behalf of their members, kibbutzim applied to Germany under the terms of this law and received hundreds of German Marks per month for each qualifying member. Hakibbutz Ha'artzi alone had 1,600 members eligible for compensation, amounting to more than 10 percent of the movement's membership in the mid-1950s. The total sum received by these members thus amounted to millions of Marks per year. The payments were received in a number of ways, one of the most important of which was rehabilitation loans. Although these loans were designated for individual members, the kibbutzim reached a special agreement with Germany providing that this money could be invested in the kibbutz economy. Such rehabilitation loans were received during the 1960s at a very low interest rate of 2 to 3 percent, to be repaid over twelve years. They were very beneficial to the kibbutzim and were paid off early because of changes in the economic conditions in Israel and significant discounts offered by the Germans.[35]

Hakibbutz Ha'artzi also enjoyed economic-development assistance from American Jewish businessmen and industrialists who were committed to the pioneer settlement enterprise in Israel and viewed Hakibbutz Ha'artzi and Mapam as promoting their vision of a progressive Israel. American admiration for the figure of the Israeli pioneer dated back to the days of Hashomer (the Guard), the self-defense organization founded in 1909, with its mounted defenders so reminiscent of the Wild West. In the 1920s, the image of the lone guard was replaced by that of the kibbutz pioneer. From the 1930s on, as the kibbutz model became well founded and the kibbutz movements began to operate, progressive American Jews enthused over kibbutz society, the efficiency of the communal economy, and the spirit of economic initiative that they saw there. In addition, in a way that resonated with the American ethos of individual initiative, efficiency, and productivity, pioneering Zionism was all about personal metamorphosis and the redemption of the individual soul. Israel's communes also showed that the Jewish interest in Israel was not just particularist but universalist.[36]

Although pioneer youth groups, Hashomer Hatza'ir among them, had been active in large American Jewish communities since the 1920s, few American Jews immigrated to Palestine. For the youth groups, aliyah, as immigration to Israel was called, was an ideological and national duty, but they enabled their members to feel like Zionist pioneers even if they did not make the move by fostering organizations that supported the pioneer idea in their communities and by raising money for the youth movements. For these American youth-movement graduates, the social element of these organizations quickly became marginal, and their ranks filled with activists who identified with the progressive ideas of the kibbutz enterprise. Movement emissaries who came to the United States from the Yishuv to raise money spent most of their time and energy establishing contacts with sympathizers and developing organizations to support the kibbutz movements. The American Jewish community became more of an economic than a human resource for the pioneer movements.

When it came to kibbutzim, Jewish progressives focused on Hakibbutz Ha'artzi, which in their minds most fully realized the Zionist-progressive ideal. This embodiment was due in part to the particular impact that progressive educational ideas had on that movement's educational system and in part to the movement's vision of Jewish–Arab coexistence in a binational state. In the 1930s, an American Zionist faction led by Supreme Court justice Louis Brandeis was especially active in supporting Hakibbutz Ha'artzi and Hashomer Hatza'ir youth movement; its representative in Palestine was Irma Lindheim (president of Hadassa [Women's Zionist Organization of America] in 1926–28). In 1922, this group, which included leading American Jews such as Julian Mack, Robert Szold, and Steven S. Wise, founded the Palestine Endowment Fund (now the Israel Endowment Fund) to promote scientific and educational projects in Palestine in the spirit of the fund's progressive founders, and in this way they became patrons of the movement.[37] The group funded the establishment of a Hashomer Hatza'ir training farm in the United States, the establishment of the first kibbutzim in which American pioneers settled, the development of kibbutz industry, and kibbutz education.

Hashomer Hatza'ir's success in enlisting broad public interest in the American Jewish community and its connections with that community's opinion leaders and political and economic elite led in 1946 to the establishment of the Progressive Zionist League. The organization sought to promote the cause of a Jewish state founded on progressive values in the American Jewish community and the American public as a whole. Its inner circle of activists included Americans who had been members of Hashomer Hatza'ir during their school years. Most of its members, however, had no direct connection to the movement and were recruited on the basis of their identification with its political ideas. In 1947, American Hashomer Hatza'ir graduates established another organization in cooperation with the movement in Palestine: Progressive Israel Projects. It offered wealthy American Jews investment opportunities in kibbutzim and raised philanthropic money for the economic development of Hashomer Hatza'ir kibbutzim. In 1954, the Progressive Zionist League and Progressive Israel Projects merged to become Americans for Progressive Israel.[38]

Another example of progressive American Jewish involvement in providing economic support for Hakibbutz Ha'artzi could be seen in the promotion of kibbutz industry by Leon Mohill. Mohill was a businessman from Pittsfield, Massachusetts, and a labor leader who was involved in American national politics.[39] As a member of the Brandeis group's social circle, he was involved in a number of projects in Israel. Deciding that this level of involvement was not enough, in 1950 he sold some of his property in the United States, immigrated to Israel with his wife and two daughters, and settled at Kibbutz Ein Hashofet, "the Judge's Spring," named in honor of Brandeis. His home there, luxurious by the standards of the time and place, was built specially for him. Mohill became a central figure in the development of kibbutz industry and headed Hakibbutz Ha'artzi's investment company. Following several intensive years at the kibbutz, he moved to Tel Aviv but retained his home at Ein Hashofet for visits and vacations. He spent the rest of his life traveling between Israel and the United States, managing his business interests in Pittsfield alongside extensive involvement in the kibbutz movement's affairs. There is no sign that he saw any contradiction between his life as a wealthy American businessman and his membership in a pioneering socialist community in Israel. He personified the enigmatic link between the Israeli labor movement and American capitalism.

In short, Hakibbutz Ha'artzi of the 1950s and 1960s was an industrialized society operating, with the state's backing, within the market economy and according to enlightened capitalist principles. It traded with West Germany and fostered warm relations with wealthy American Jews. This relationship did not jibe well with Mapam's Marxist ideology. The economic ventures the kibbutzim engaged in fostered an atmosphere of capitalist entrepreneurship that stood in contradiction to the fact that the

political party that represented the kibbutzim adhered to its Soviet orientation and promoted revolutionary socialism. The consequence of this
incongruity between ideology and practice was an incoherence between
the image kibbutz members and leaders had of themselves and the lives
they actually led, which were by this time to a large extent bourgeois and
capitalist.[40] The party and movement leadership simply disregarded the
contradiction, however, so long as it did not clash too visibly with kibbutz principles and as long as it served the purpose of strengthening and
developing kibbutz communities. Issues such as membership in regional
economic initiatives, hired labor, and relations with financiers outside the
kibbutz were brought up for discussion in a number of forums, but these
discussions produced only desultory declarations. In these early years, no
real effort was made to avoid or forbid such capitalist practices because
it was clear that they were essential for kibbutz development.[41] However, these contradictions reflected a larger process of a transition from
ideas, values, and patterns of action that had emerged from the European
revolutionary labor movements to American ones. The economies of the
kibbutzim, of Israel, and of the Western world as a whole underwent a
dramatic transformation. The question was how political movements and
social structures founded before this change occurred would respond.

The Rise of the New Middle Class

The kibbutz economic surge that began in the second half of the 1950s had
produced visible social results by the first half of the 1960s. During the
first five years of this economic spurt, from 1954 to 1961, the annual average per capita income of kibbutz members in all movements rose from IL
1,630 ($905 at the official exchange rate of the time) to IL 3,030 ($1,683). In
1963, for the first time ever, all Hakibbutz Ha'artzi kibbutzim operated in
the black, with more income than outlays.[42] In the years that followed, economic growth in the kibbutzim surprised the movement's leaders—to the
point that they became concerned. A survey of the state of the movement
issued by its leadership in 1966, in advance of a meeting of the movement's
Lamed-Vav (Thirty-Six) Council to be devoted to economics, warned
that "this stabilization may blind us. . . . [A] consumerist consciousness
is ensconcing itself, the standing of labor is under challenge, and, even

worse than all this, the different kibbutzim are stratifying according to their earnings." The council debated what should be done with kibbutz profits to ensure that they did not become deleterious to the communities' traditional way of life.[43]

By the midpoint of the 1960s, kibbutz society had transformed from an ascetic society to one that was for all intents and purposes middle class. That is, its standard of living, as measured by annual per capita disposable income, placed it in the sixth decile of that measure in Israeli society as a whole.[44] Lifestyles also changed. Most kibbutzim found industry to be more profitable than agriculture, which was undergoing an industrial revolution in its production methods that made it less labor intensive. The rising productivity in both sectors brought higher profits. Kibbutz members no longer needed to work from "sunrise to exhaustion" to achieve minimal sustenance. They now had leisure time. In an eight-hour day, they earned their keep and more and could thus devote afternoons and evenings to other activities. Living conditions were also transformed. At the beginning of the 1950s, most members lived in shacks, ate in ramshackle structures, bathed in common showers, and shared bathrooms with dozens of others. Within a decade, the kibbutzim had built permanent dwellings, well-appointed dining halls, theaters, swimming pools, and rooms for social and cultural activities. Furnishings also improved. In the 1950s, members were first allotted refrigerators, transistor radios, record players, and even electric kettles—not as personal property but rather purchased and allocated by the kibbutz on a strictly egalitarian basis. But little by little members gained increasing freedom in fitting out their homes. Despite a vehement campaign against the use of consumer products, they became increasingly common as the standard of living rose. The pioneers were quite clearly turning bourgeois.[45]

The increasing wealth and financial stability of the kibbutzim were part of a process that large swathes of Israeli society experienced during this period of rapid economic growth. Between 1956 and 1963, the average annual wage in Israel rose from IL 3,277 to IL 5,304, and by 1964 families of wage earners had an average gross monthly income of IL 615.70, a rise of more than 50 percent since 1959, when the average monthly income per family was IL 377.90.[46] At the same time, real consumption outlays per

working family rose by 28 percent. The average monthly wage throughout the Israeli economy rose from IL 295 to IL 605 in the years 1961–68,
an increase in real terms of 38.5 percent.[47] This increase created a large
middle class that enjoyed relative comfort. In 1966, a full 83.1 percent of
Israeli families owned a gas stove or oven; 80.1 percent owned a refrigera-
tor; and 79.2 percent owned a radio.[48] The middle class began to develop a
new consumption culture, influenced by Western fashions in the area of
culture and lifestyle.[49]

Economic development also created a new professional class in Israel,
as it did in other countries. This class had two central characteristics.
First, the members of this group were variously termed "professionals,"
"technocrats," or "white-collar workers." They were, for example, engineers, teachers, physicians, nurses, economists, bookkeepers, social workers, university faculty, government officials, managers in government and
public companies, and personnel in the standing army and other security
agencies. Second, most of them were employed by government agencies
or other parts of the public sector (which in the Israeli case included the
Histadrut) or by private companies that maintained manifold connections with the establishment (in particular via the Ministry of Trade and
Industry when that portfolio was held by Pinhas Sapir).[50] The state's position as the major employer of such professional workers or as the pro-
vider of subsidies and support for private companies that employed them
grew out of the expansion of the public sector's responsibilities beyond
education, immigrant absorption, law, the military, and the economy. In
this expansion, Israel was no different than many other countries, which
did the same (at American instigation) during the era of development and
rehabilitation that followed World War II. But in Israel the government's
growth also occurred because of the requirements of a new state. The public sector thus grew from 20,000 workers on the eve of independence to
197,000 in 1962 (out of 777,000 workers in the entire economy). Along with
the Histadrut sector, which included the officials in its bureaucracy as well
as the employees of its service subsidiaries, such as Kupat Holim, and of
the factories, enterprises, and projects owned by its business subsidiary,
Hevrat Ha'ovdim (Society of Workers), the public sector accounted for
half of the country's employees (close to 400,000). In parallel, the private

sector shrank during this same period, from 1949 to 1962, from providing the livelihoods of 70 percent of all workers to providing just 50 percent.[51]

Government and Histadrut employees enjoyed job security and good conditions (forty to forty-five hours per week, with thirty to forty-five vacation days per year). During the 1950s, gaps in wages and conditions gradually widened within this group (discussed more fully later), but in general these people were on solid economic ground, as were the proprietors of private businesses that enjoyed government support.[52] This class and kibbutz members were alike in that they benefitted from their close association with political power centers. In both cases, their interests were seen to by the political machine to which they belonged. Like kibbutz members, employees of the government and Histadrut sector constituted the power base of the political machine. The party took them under its wing, and in return they voted for the party. The symbiosis produced an efficient, sophisticated, and mutually beneficial sociopolitical mechanism. The result was what has been termed the "pioneering bourgeoisie," created and maintained by the state.[53] Kibbutz members continued to see themselves and to be seen by those outside the state as frugal farmers, but they were in fact the backbone of Israel's new middle class.[54]

In other countries, middle-class groups connected to the state also led development. They had parallels in social democratic countries, but the classic, if extreme, example is the nomenklatura of the Soviet Union and its client states, which ran these countries in exchange for material benefits. The Israeli model was very much like the Soviet one on a number of counts. First, both countries were led by revolutionary movements that had assumed broad powers as part of a process of bringing about comprehensive social and political transformations. Second, these movements took it upon themselves to bring about dramatic economic growth, including industrialization and the settlement of marginal lands. Third, the socioeconomic regime that emerged in the 1950s in both Israel and the Communist world was that of state socialism, a regime that establishes economic enterprises that belong directly or indirectly to the state.[55] Nevertheless, in the 1950s, when Israel established wide-ranging and close ties with the West and emulated American economic behavior, it embarked on a transition from state socialism to state capitalism. In other words, the state established an economy under its ownership and control and then gradually turned it into a private sector.[56]

Apart from the kibbutzim, the Israeli university system also brought into being a political middle class produced by the party machines in cooperation with the state. Here, too, strong functional relations served as a means by which the labor movement enhanced its power.[57] Three institutions of higher education were established during the Yishuv years—the Hebrew University, the Technion, and the Weizmann Institute of Science. In the 1950s and 1960s, they were joined by Tel Aviv University, Bar-Ilan University, Ben-Gurion University, and the University of Haifa. The number of students rose close to twentyfold between 1948 and 1968, from 1,635 to 32,389. In the 1970s, Israel's system of higher education comprised six universities, employing 17,000 academic and administrative staff members and serving 17,000 students. The state, led by Mapai, oversaw the founding, development, and promotion of the higher-education system as part of its project of making Israel into a modern Western country. State sponsorship had clear political dimensions. The academy constituted a power center for Ben-Gurion's *mamlakhtiyut* project and was thus allied with Mapai (while preserving its own autonomy and independence). It produced young people who joined other parts of the professional class. Having grown up within the system, they were loyal to it.[58]

Alongside the institutionalized academic system, with its close ties to Mapai, the pioneering parts of the labor movement established their own institutions of higher education, where, in an unusual turn, the kibbutz movements cooperated. Kibbutzim College, which focused on training preschool teachers, was founded in 1939. It was followed in 1949 by Ruppin College, which offered training in agriculture and other trades and skills required by the kibbutzim. Oranim College, opened in 1951, trained teachers. These separate institutions were ostensibly a product of the contemporary ideological debate within the labor movement between pioneering values and *mamlakhtiyut*. The universities, as the kibbutzim saw them, were producing a bourgeois, technocratic, achievement-oriented elite, which ran counter to the pioneering ideal and the principles of cooperative society.[59] In practice, however, the kibbutzim themselves were metamorphosing into bourgeois communities that fostered competitive values. As they gained economic security, they became an arena for the development of a "normal," materialistic Western society.[60] There was no real contradiction in terms of values between *mamlakhtiyut* and the kibbutzim. Rather, the two competed to promote a middle class produced by the system, one that would serve their political interests. In this area, as in other manifestations of the socioeconomic activities of the labor movement, the struggles between different parts of the movement derived more from the similarities than from the differences between them.

From Political to Economic Inequality

The Israeli economy's dramatic progress led to a situation in which the practical meaning of the special sponsorship that the labor movement's political system provided to the social groups that served as its power base underwent a dramatic transformation and took on a new form. True, during the Yishuv period the political parties served as agencies that distributed a variety of goods and services, and in the state's early years those who were affiliated with Mapai and kibbutz members affiliated with the kibbutz movements enjoyed high economic and social security relative to the rest of the population, which grappled with austerity and emergencies. But the economic growth that began in the mid-1950s produced much more for the parties to hand out. Political strength (that is, closeness to a party machine) translated into considerable economic power, which magnified the hierarchical structure of political parties that adopted the mass-party model. The result was that political inequality translated into economic inequality along fault lines that shaped Israeli society in the years that followed.

The major beneficiaries of this privileged access to jobs and social services were party members in the case of Mapai and kibbutz members in the case of Mapam and Ahdut Ha'avodah. The advantages that came with political affiliation to Mapai differed somewhat from those provided by the kibbutz parties, but their material significance was fairly similar. Mapai was able to offer better public housing in new projects in the country's center, with low rent payments or purchase prices that made becoming a homeowner relatively easy. It could also offer careers in the civil service, in management positions, in high-earning professions, generally in one of the Histadrut's subsidiaries—Hevrat Ha'ovdim, Kupat Holim, or the trade unions, for example—or in state institutions, such as the educational and security systems. Mapai could also ensure that a family's children attended an academic high school, which was the entry ticket to a college (as opposed to vocational school, which channeled young people into technical jobs), as well as wage protection via membership in the Histadrut, health services via membership in Kupat Holim Clalit, and job training and experience that enabled a transition into the growing private sector.[61] The pioneering parties, for their part, relied on the kibbutzim as providers of comprehensive and high-quality social services, such as education, health care, culture, physical space, and high-quality food, which even Mapai members could envy. Of course, to enjoy such benefits, one had to join a kibbutz, which required ideological and social allegiance to the collective, its principles, and its permanent leadership, but this requirement bothered only a few kibbutz members. For purely functional reasons, they found themselves ever more tightly tied to their communities as the kibbutz transformed from a chosen way of life into simply home.[62] Kibbutz and Mapai members together constituted the well-off middle class that the labor-movement apparatuses produced.

The economic benefits offered by the labor movement made it attractive to outsiders. It is hardly surprising, then, that increasing numbers of Israelis took out membership in Mapai and the Histadrut. Likewise, once the kibbutzim recovered from their economic crisis, more and more Israelis sought to join them. Between 1946 and 1953, Mapai membership rose from 29,947 to 132,472, and by the mid-1960s it had reached 200,000.[63] The Histadrut expanded in the state's first decade, 1949 to 1959, from 170,000 members, or 43.5 percent of the population, to 1.1 million, or 59 percent of the population. From the founding of the state through the end of the 1960s, the kibbutz population doubled, from 47,500 in 1948 to 98,000 in 1969, about a third of that consisting of adult members. The percentage of kibbutz members and candidates for membership in the Israeli population grew steadily; after 1967, the ratio of new members as against those who left the kibbutzim improved considerably.[64] At the end of the 1960s, Hakibbutz Ha'artzi was the largest kibbutz movement, numbering 18,000 members and candidates on seventy-five kibbutzim (4,500 more people and fifteen more kibbutzim than in 1956).[65] The profile of those who joined the kibbutzim from the outside showed what made them attractive. For example, in 1973 some 10 percent of new members were youth-movement graduates, and 30 percent were young people born on the kibbutzim. But a full 60 percent had not been members of Hashomer Hatza'ir. This group included spouses who married people in the first two groups, graduates of Hebrew-language programs for immigrants sponsored by kibbutzim, and soldiers from the Nahal Corps (Noar Halutzi Lohem, Fighting Pioneer Youth), a branch of the army in which soldiers combined military service with periods of work on kibbutzim and the establishment of new ones— all of whom joined despite lacking a youth-movement background.[66]

The party structure, which created a situation in which benefits and services were granted only to party members and kibbutzim, meant that a much larger group of people who voted for the labor parties did not receive anything in exchange. In the 1950s, about half of Mapai's voters were not party members, and about three-quarters of Mapam's and Ahdut Ha'avodah's voters were not kibbutz members. During the state's early years, this larger group consisted largely of new immigrants. They had no functional relationship to the parties and supported them rather for ideological reasons—because of promises the parties made to them or because they were the victims of manipulations during their absorption process. Many voted for Mapai because they admired Ben-Gurion, whom they saw as the founder of the country. Mapai also gained support because it was able to instill its ideology and reinforce its image as the country's natural and indispensable party of government through the influence it wielded over the school system and national culture. Furthermore, its melting-pot concept of immigrant absorption created an atmosphere in which voting for Mapai was a badge of being truly Israeli, whereas those who voted for religious parties or parties of the center or Right were portrayed as still having one foot in the Diaspora.[67] For similar, largely emotional reasons, Mapam won the support of voters in the cities who did not enjoy the benefits it provided to kibbutz members. Israelis who had grown up in Hashomer Hatza'ir but who did not settle on kibbutzim remained loyal to the movement that had forged their personalities. Furthermore, Mapam enjoyed considerable prestige as a pioneering party that represented a kibbutz movement whose members had displayed self-sacrifice and played a critical role in settling the land, defending the Yishuv, and bringing about independence. On top of that, its class radicalism attracted a small group of intellectuals and certain parts of the working class. Ahdut Ha'avodah, a kibbutz party, attracted primarily urban voters with its ideology and the identification it offered with the history of Hakibbutz Hameuhad, the founding of the state, and, in particular, the Palmach (Strike Forces), the elite combat force of the War of Independence that grew out of this kibbutz movement.[68] As against the prestige the figure of Ben-Gurion provided for Mapai, the pioneering party could offer World War II partisans and ghetto fighters, commanders in the Palmach and the Israel Defense Forces (IDF), and other such exemplary figures. All parties recognized that the state's founding myths were good for getting out the vote and made unabashed use of them during election campaigns for the Knesset and the Histadrut.

Israel's socioeconomic inequality, the product of a political hierarchy created by the labor movement during a period of high growth, increased as the country progressed. The result was a seemingly paradoxical situation: when the era of austerity came to an end, the expectation had been that poverty would be eliminated, but inequality grew instead. True, in the mid-1960s this growth led to a situation in which Israel's income distribution placed most of the population in the middle. But disparities of income and living conditions steadily widened. At the beginning of the 1960s, the wages of senior officials and college graduates were three times those of laborers. By mid-decade, the average wage of an unskilled laborer was less than a quarter of the average salary of a manager. At that time, the poorest half of the population earned only 24 percent of the nation's income. In 1964, one-quarter of wage-earning families made less than IL 400 per month at a time when the average salary was IL 600 and the median IL 500, so these families could not make ends meet. A full 61.3 percent of families earned less than the average income.[69]

Economic inequality correlated strongly with seniority in the country and ethnic origin. Yet those factors did not cause inequality directly. Rather, they were surrogates for how close people were to political power.

True, some new immigrants joined labor-movement parties (Mapai for the most part) because of the benefits such membership offered. (Few new immigrants joined kibbutzim because they were not attracted to communal life and the secular culture that prevailed there.) However, most immigrants remained outside the party circle. The profile of those immigrants who did join the party shows a clear ethnic bias. Between 1948 and 1950, Mapai membership was taken out by 26,591 immigrants, more than half of them of European origin. Mapai remained a fundamentally Ashkenazi party even after the huge wave of immigration from North Africa and Asia. The situation was much worse for Mapam—in 1956, a survey of about 2,000 of the party's 11,000 nonkibbutz members found that only a quarter were of North African or Asian origin (Mizrahim) and that the party's activity among this sector of the population had been largely a failure.[70] Ahdut Ha'avodah had a bit more success with these immigrants—in 1955, a third of its voters (a little more than 20,000) were from the transit camps, where some 90,000 immigrants, the vast majority of them Mizrahim, lived. Support for Mapai in the camps declined in the mid-1950s, in part because of disappointment at the party's failure to live up to its ideology and its promises to improve the daily lives of these new Israelis.[71] Hakibbutz Hameuhad benefitted from controlling the Hehalutz movement, which was active in the Jewish communities of North Africa and Asia. Like the other two kibbutz movements, it also took groups of young immigrants into its kibbutzim, where they went to school and experienced kibbutz life. Although many of them did not settle in kibbutzim, they continued to identify with the movement politically.[72] It was not that Ahdut Ha'avodah evinced a fundamentally different attitude toward the Mizrahim than did the other two movements; it was simply more successful organizationally at bringing immigrants into its socialization frameworks.

Immigrants who did join any one of these three parties were not, however, successful in advancing and gaining within them.[73] The general view in these parties was that immigrants were not capable of taking on leadership roles in Israeli society because they needed to undergo acculturation and acclimatization. This paternalistic attitude was all the more pronounced with regard to Mizrahim, who were considered backward. It was easier for veteran Israelis and European immigrants to join and move up in parties (and kibbutzim), thanks to their shared cultural and ideological background, language, and connections with established Israelis.

The immigrants', especially the Mizrahim's, restricted access to political power, which was the key to economic power, kept them out of the state and movement-crafted middle class. The outcome was pronounced discrepancies in the quality of life between them, on the one side, and the veteran population, native-born Israelis, and—amounting to much the same thing—Israelis of European and North American origin, on the other. In the mid-1960s, the income of Israelis who arrived in the country after 1948 was 27 percent less than those who had lived in the Yishuv prior to independence. Mizrahim earned 30 percent less than Ashkenazim. Income in the new towns where many immigrants were settled was much lower than the income of residents in general in the major cities; 93 percent of the families supported by the welfare system arrived after 1948.[74] Consumption outlays per capita (on food, clothing, housing, health, education, and culture) were highest among the veteran Ashkenazi population (IL 205 per month) and lowest among Mizrahi immigrants who arrived after 1948 (IL 103).[75] This ethnic gap was exacerbated by the personal compensation payments paid out by West Germany. In the years 1957–64, about a third of Israeli households, almost all of them Ashkenazim, received one-off compensation payments, which averaged IL 2,400 per family. The average annual income of those who received ongoing payments was IL 5,518, much higher than average.[76] These stipends, received by 3.6 percent of urban families, nearly doubled their annual incomes and provided direct access to the middle class.[77]

The emergence of this ethnically skewed economic hierarchy under labor-movement rule constitutes the basis of the claim that the Mapai regime was founded on favoritism. The Critical School of sociologists and some historians charge that the ethnic discrimination was intentional, a product of the corruption of Mapai, Israel's ruling party. But this claim does not accord with the facts that current historical studies have emphasized.[78] Mapai was not unique in establishing a bifurcated system of handing out benefits, thus creating a social hierarchy. A comparison with Mapam and Ahdut Ha'avodah shows that they also produced political and economic inequality, even though they were not as central and strong as Mapai. Similarly, a broader perspective shows that after World War II inequality increased in other Western countries as a result of the emergence of a bifurcated labor market that treated citizens differently in accordance with their ethnic affiliation and immigrant status.[79]

Furthermore, the provision of material benefits in exchange for political support was not unique to the labor movement or socialist parties. For example, studies of Shas (Shomeri Torah Sfaradim, or Torah-Observant Sephardim, an ultra-Orthodox Mizrahi party that emerged in the 1980s) and of Israeli right-wing parties have shown that these parties have also provided benefits in exchange for political support. Shas established a network of nonprofit organizations that provided assistance to Mizrahi families while encouraging them to vote for the party. The Likud and other right-wing parties have together created a "welfare state" in Israeli settlements in the territories. Both these systems emerged as a result of the dismantling and privatization of the institutions and services founded by the labor movement.[80] The central factor in the establishment of the economic and social hierarchy that emerged under the labor movement was the combination of a concentric political structure in accordance with the mass-party model; the power wielded by state institutions, the Histadrut, and the kibbutz movements during the state's first decade; and the accelerated economic growth and development that Israel enjoyed beginning in the mid-1950s. Although discrimination against the immigrants was political in nature, its principal impact was economic. In this sense, the social structure that emerged under the labor movement was the product of an unexpected concurrence between a traditional political model and an entirely new economic situation.

The Recession

Alongside increasing social inequality, the economic policies that Western countries followed after the end of World War II were shaken during the first half of the 1960s. Steady growth in output and full employment had greatly enhanced organized labor's bargaining power. In most countries, labor demanded and obtained significant salary increases. Wage increases raised consumption, which in turn drove prices up. The price rises lowered the value of the currency, causing inflation. Inflation destabilized the economy, made life difficult for unorganized workers whose salaries remained stagnant, and lowered the value of savings, hurting those who had been able to put money aside. In Israel, this problem was compounded because the major rise in demand for consumer products, many of which came from overseas, caused a trade deficit, draining the country's foreign-currency reserves. The government's solution was to deliberately initiate a recession to cool down the economy and relieve inflationary pressures. The government also saw an opportunity to take care of the balance of payments by integrating the Israeli economy more fully into the global economy, with an emphasis on exports. This change required increasing worker productivity, avoiding pressure for pay increases, exposing the economy to imports (so as to provide local industry with an incentive to produce goods of a quality and price that would gain buyers outside the country), and cutting losses due to strikes. All these goals were to be achieved by implementing an economic program put together during 1964. Among the program's major points were lower demand, budgetary and monetary restraint, a wage freeze, the elimination of subsidies, and a tax increase.[81] Administrative and financial restrictions limited new building so as to dampen down the construction sector.

The program's impact was gradual. The balance of payments improved, and inflation was brought down, but at the beginning of 1966 it became clear that the program had brought on a more severe crisis than had been intended. This outcome was due to a number of factors, some that had been anticipated and others that came as surprises. Reparations payments from Germany ended, the sale of Israel Bonds declined, and the US government reduced its economic support. On top of these things, the number of immigrants plunged. Taken together, these factors exacerbated the recession and turned it into a major economic crisis. Economic growth diminished to between 1 and 2 percent, and the unemployment rate shot up.

Israel's social divisions and the economic benefits enjoyed by the labor movement's core supporters in the cities and the kibbutzim became increasingly apparent as the recession grew worse. Unemployment hit worst those parts of the population that were not part of the labor movement's economic system, especially nonprofessional and nonorganized workers in the development towns, which had been built on the country's periphery to house immigrants and disperse the population away from the country's center. The national unemployment rate in mid-1966 was a reasonable 4.2 percent, but in the development towns it ranged from 16 to 20 percent.[82] The recession brought the full extent of political equality into sharp and unfavorable contrast. From 1956 to 1965, wages and living standards had risen for all, even if the improvement was skewed toward a largely Ashkenazi and established class of party insiders. In 1966 and 1967, however, wages, employment, and living standards stagnated or fell, with the brunt born almost entirely by the politically unconnected, a large proportion of whom were Mizrahim.[83] The result: during the recession, inequality among wage-earning Israeli families, as measured by the Gini index, reached unprecedented proportions.[84]

The central reason for worsening inequality during the recession was the bifurcated structure of the labor market and social services system. The jobs that the labor-movement machines provided for their members were secure because most of them were in the civil service—the Histadrut and other public organizations—and in the kibbutzim. These jobs were protected even in times of economic downturn. The working class, a large proportion of which was employed in construction trades and private industry, lived outside the world of civil service perks and benefits and at the mercy of the free market. Furthermore, a large proportion of public services were provided by the Histadrut (and the kibbutzim). For example, the state had no national unemployment insurance program. The Histadrut did, but membership in the Histadrut cost money that workers often could not spare. Furthermore, many workers perceived the labor organization, not without cause, to be a closed club that did not particularly welcome unconnected newcomers. And some workers wanted no part of its socialist ideology, which they associated with the countries of the Soviet bloc and their oppression of Judaism and Zionism. No matter what reason they had for not belonging to the Histadrut, nonmembers who lost their jobs, especially those who lived in development towns, suffered a drastic drop in their standard of living. The lack of a national welfare policy for all citizens was one of the unique features of the Israeli case.

The suffering endured by the underprivileged in the parallel economic crises occurring in other countries that followed full-employment policies was mitigated by the fact that these countries had national unemployment insurance and social support programs.[85]

As long as the recession did not hurt the middle class, policy makers were little concerned about the fact that the standard of living of workers was declining. Minister of Labor Yigal Allon referred to the crisis as "transitory spasms" and opposed instituting a national unemployment insurance program on the grounds—which had deep roots in pioneering Zionist ideology—that it would encourage idleness. Finance Minister Pinhas Sapir also argued that unemployment helped bolster the work ethic and said that the unemployment rate was not extreme.[86] In the summer of 1966, the government did take steps to relieve working-class unemployment via direct job creation by the state, budgetary expansion, and cash grants to the jobless. But in the final months of that year, unemployment spread to the center of the country, and college-educated workers began losing their jobs as well. At the beginning of 1967, the national unemployment rate zoomed to a record high of 12 percent of the labor force. It was only when unemployment spread from the development towns and began to affect the middle class, white-collar workers, professionals, and, in particular, new university graduates who refused to take make-work manual-labor jobs and began to leave the country that the government and economic leadership ceased to oppose unemployment benefits. These benefits were instituted in April 1967.[87] Indications that the recession was easing appeared in mid-1967, and the economy was soon growing again.

5

A Postmaterial Society

Boom

The effects of the recession disappeared when the Israeli economy boomed following the Six-Day War of June 1967. The war, which had been preceded by a tense waiting period of several weeks during which the Arab countries threatened Israel and war seemed imminent, resulted in unprecedented levels of support for Israel in the Jewish Diaspora. The Israeli government conducted an emergency fund-raising campaign overseas, collecting about $165 million, which covered the costs of the war. At the same time, the economy's external sources of income (primarily US aid) reached $240 million, more than the country had received in the 1950s from the United States and Germany together.[1] The sympathy the war aroused in the Jewish world also led for the first time to a wave of immigration from the West. More than 30,000 such immigrants arrived in 1968, with 40,000 immigrating in each of the two following years. Furthermore, about 100,000 immigrants arrived from the Soviet Union in the period between 1967 and 1973. Tourism also skyrocketed after the war, with the number of visitors to the country growing by 30 percent.[2]

One of the reasons the economy recovered after the war was a significant rise in military expenditures. This rise was largely the result of ongoing hostilities with Jordan and the Palestinian guerrilla organizations, military construction in the territories occupied during the war, and the need to balance massive Soviet military investments in Egypt and Syria. The army purchased huge quantities of locally produced products, such as food, textiles, pharmaceuticals, motor vehicles, and electronics—all provided by the country's rapidly expanding factories. With the help of an expansionary economic policy, the economy returned to full employment at the beginning of 1969.[3] Imports began to rise in 1968, much of them capital goods and inputs. Exports, which had begun to grow at the beginning of 1967 and then plummeted during the war, grew by 5 percent in the second half of 1967 and by 20 percent in 1968. One factor in the increase in exports was the establishment around the world and primarily by Jews of organizations to encourage the purchase of Israeli-made products.[4] The territories taken in the war also had an effect on the Israeli economy. Of particular importance were the oil fields in the captured Sinai Peninsula, which in 1968 produced $30 million worth of oil.[5] In addition, the Palestinian Arabs who lived in the territories captured by Israel provided the economy with cheap labor. Unorganized and willing to work for much less than Israelis, the Palestinians provided the growing economy with the working hands it needed. Furthermore, as they filled the ranks of the working class, they enabled Israeli workers to advance into management positions and to open small businesses of their own.

The boom also owed much to a government decision to invest in and expand Israel's military industries, which led to a huge change in Israel's export profile and in the economy as a whole. Israel joined the relatively exclusive club of countries with a high per capita GNP. Between 1968 and 1972, electronics moved into second place among Israel's export products; prior to that, it had not made the list of the six leading exports.[6] Beginning in 1968, Israeli manufacturing grew by leaps and bounds. It underwent major structural changes, the most important being the rise in exports as Israel entered world markets. A gap opened between the rate of growth of advanced industries and the rate of growth of traditional industries. Between 1968 and 1972, industrial output grew by an average of 15 percent per year, productivity grew by 7 percent, and exports grew by 16.6 percent in real terms, more than any time before or since. The growing role of exports in GNP was accompanied by rapid technological advancements in production and marketing.[7] This momentum was evident in kibbutz industries as well. In 1968, manufacturing provided 35 percent of the income of the entire kibbutz economy, and 7 percent of the country's manufacturing products were produced in kibbutz plants, even at a time when kibbutz members made up only 4 percent of the country's Jewish population.[8]

Within four years alone, between 1969 and 1973, the number of kibbutz factories grew by 47.7 percent, from 157 to 232.[9] In comparison, their number had grown by 57 percent (from 100 to 157) over the entire decade of the 1960s.[10] The boom continued until the Yom Kippur War of 1973.

The boom strengthened Israel's middle class. Between 1968 and 1973, wages rose by an annual average of 12.3 percent, while per capita consumption rose by 5.2 percent a year.[11] The standard of living rose significantly for a large part of the population. The number of car-owning families doubled, from 10 to 20 percent; the proportion that owned washing machines rose from 29.5 to 55.2 percent. Television ownership rose from 3.4 to 74.4 percent; telephone ownership rose from zero to 44.3 percent.[12] Home ownership increased from 54 percent at the end of the 1950s to 71 percent in the mid-1970s.[13] The comfort enjoyed by the new middle class was evident in the kibbutzim as well. In 1976, kibbutzim enjoyed an annual per capita income that placed them in the country's eighth income decile, two deciles higher than it had been a decade earlier. The kibbutzim were now firmly ensconced in the middle class.[14]

At the end of the 1960s, the standard of living enjoyed by Israel's established middle class was much like that of the middle classes in western Europe and the United States. Israel now met the definition of a "postmaterial society":[15] a society with strata that have reached a new developmental level in which their central concern is no longer physical security (obtaining food, clothing, and housing) but rather the meeting of new needs (self-fulfillment, freedom of expression and thought, opposition to the oppression and injustices suffered by weaker groups, the development of an alternative culture). In fact, this universal phenomenon did not tally with what could be seen in the new middle class and the kibbutzim. Israel's and the kibbutzim's unique conditions, even in this age of wealth, were still different from conditions in the West. But the things that preoccupied Israel's new bourgeoisie, especially its young people, became more and more like the things that preoccupied their counterparts in Europe and North America. This similarity prepared the ground for further cultural and political developments that I take up later.

But the boom did not end economic inequality. Some classes benefitted more from economic growth than others did. At the beginning of 1971, for example, salaried workers in the free professions, sciences, and technological fields earned IL 207.40 per week, half again as much as artisans and manufacturing workers, who made only IL 138 per week. The number of years a person had lived in the country no longer correlated with economic success, but country of origin did. Jews of North African and Asian origin were still at the bottom of the labor market in terms of the kinds of jobs they did or could get. Most Mizrahi families still lived in much more crowded conditions than did Ashkenazim. At the beginning of 1970, the average weekly wage for Jews of European and American origin was IL 183.80, whereas those of North African or Asian origin earned on average IL 132.30 per week, or 28 percent less. The gap was even more pronounced in the second generation. Israeli-born children of fathers who had immigrated from North Africa or Asia earned IL 113.60, nearly 39 percent less than those born to fathers from Europe or America, who earned IL 185. The gap also had a geographic dimension: the economy's lowest wages were paid to textile and clothing workers, a branch that employed many inhabitants of the development towns on Israel's periphery, most of whom were Mizrahim.[16] In February 1971, the National Insurance Institute published its first report on poverty in Israel. It reported that 68,400 urban families, out of a total of 614,000 families in the nation, lived under the poverty line. This number translated into 253,000 poor individuals, 11 percent of the population. The report found that economic distress was a broad phenomenon because beyond those under the poverty line another 63,400, constituting 10.3 percent of the population, lived on the edge of poverty. This meant that there were altogether 519,200 low-income Israelis.[17]

From a Bifurcated State to a Universal Welfare State

The Yom Kippur War brought the boom years to an end. When the fighting ended, it was clear that the Israeli economy stood before a difficult period.[18] The cost of the war and the absence of tens of thousands of men from their workplaces after they were called up as reservists and continued to serve for months after the war ended caused major economic damage, the equivalent of the loss of an entire year's GNP during this short period.[19] Growth declined from 10 percent in 1973 to 7.5 percent in 1974; on top of that came the energy crisis that followed the war when oil-producing Arab states refused to export oil to Western countries that had supported Israel during the war. The result was that at the end of 1973 oil prices jumped by hundreds of percent. At the beginning of 1974, the prices of gasoline, electricity, and basic food products went up by about half, and inflation took off. For the first time in two decades, Israel suffered from an economic downturn that lasted for an extended period.[20] The war hit Israeli manufacturing especially hard. Immediately following the war, manufacturing sales declined by 50 percent, and average production declined by 70 percent.[21] The picture for kibbutz factories was similar, with production declining by half.[22]

The Israeli government also faced the challenge of operating under these new conditions in addition to under the crisis brought on by the war. A new government, headed by Yitzhak Rabin, came to power in June 1974, and a month later the new finance minister, Yehoshua Rabinowitz, announced a new economic program to address the crisis. Rabin and Rabinowitz chose not to hurt the weaker classes. The program included measures such as government budget cuts, a purchase tax, a capital-gains tax, a mandatory bond imposed on all citizens, and the postponement of a cost-of-living wage increase that workers were slated to receive. Interest rates were also raised moderately in an effort to dampen inflation without holding back the productive sector. In November 1974, the government also decided to devalue the currency in order to improve the balance of payments. Government subsidies of various sorts were also eliminated. In September, a value-added tax was proclaimed at a rate of 8 percent (it went into effect in July 1976).[23]

The economic program hit the well-off disproportionately, infuriating industrialists and company owners—including the kibbutzim.[24] The government also provided expanded services to the less well-off. It instituted an unemployment insurance program in 1973 and a general disability insurance program the following year. In 1975, it embarked on a comprehensive reform of the child allowance and throughout this period gradually implemented other national insurance reforms to make it easier to qualify for pensions and payments.[25] The government also set up a commission to study the tax system. The commission issued its findings in March 1975, recommending an end to nearly all exemptions from income tax that had hitherto applied to a variety of wage components (for example, reimbursements for car and phone expenses), a rise in the income cutoff point at which tax was levied, and a system of tax credits according to criteria that would benefit the less well-off. Yeruham Meshel, director-general of the Histadrut, led a campaign against the economic program, which imposed serious burdens on employers, apartment owners, and small businessmen, but much lesser burdens on wage earners.[26]

The central goal of the Rabin government's economic program was to avert a severe recession by tamping down growth in a limited way while granting relief to the disadvantaged. In fact, Rabin carried on the approach taken by his predecessor, Golda Meir, who had also sought to mitigate the economic inequality that had emerged during the previous two decades of labor-movement rule.[27] The change in approach was an outgrowth of the trauma caused by the previous recession as well as by Ha-Panterim ha-Shchorim (Black Panther) social protest movement among second-generation Mizrahim and Sephardim and by the findings of government commissions established in the wake of the protests. Particularly influential was a report on poverty that demonstrated just how severe inequality had become. By this point, the labor movement had already suffered irreparable damage to its reputation, and its attempt to change direction angered its traditional supporters among the well-off.

PART TWO

The Political Turn

From Socialism to Radicalism and Sectoralism

THE EXACERBATION of economic inequality in Israel from the first half of the 1950s through the mid-1970s was bound up with a number of social and political developments in the labor movement. One, itself a product of the country's economic advancement, was a decline in the standing of mediating apparatuses (party machines, the kibbutz movements, and the economic organizations they controlled). Another, growing out of the unequal distribution of the benefits of prosperity, was the subdivision of the movement into a number of different currents, each of which criticized this inequality from a different angle. Yet counterintuitively, perhaps, an additional phenomenon was that these currents banded together, despite their large differences, to fight the labor-movement machine. Finally, in response to the crisis and to the attempts to weaken the machine, the labor-movement establishments sought to avert change and preserve their power and the structures that supported it. This conservative reaction paralyzed the labor movement, further opening it to attacks from its internal critics and thus exacerbating its crisis.

6

The Decline of the Mediating Mechanism

THE ECONOMIC DEVELOPMENT Israel enjoyed from the mid-1950s to the mid-1970s weakened the mediating role of the party machine in the labor movement. The machine lost power as a consequence of the social mobility experienced by the middle class that the machine itself created. With their incomes rising and their jobs secure, the members of this new middle class grew less dependent on the labor movement's economic organizations and thus less committed to the movement. Economic development also engendered new institutions that replaced the old mediating system, further weakening it. The result was that the movement lost support, and so its power waned.[1]

In the case of Mapam and Hakibbutz Ha'artzi, the kibbutzim slowly freed themselves from their yoke; kibbutz members gained increasingly more independence within the tight communal structure in which they lived. The control that members of Hakibbutz Ha'artzi kibbutzim gained over their own lives paralleled a similar process in the cities, where as people moved into the middle class, they enjoyed more personal freedom. The causes were much the same in both cases. Another key factor was a new social atmosphere created by massive industrialization, expanding higher education, and changes in the quality of life, especially in communications and transport.

The establishment of the State of Israel had dealt a heavy blow to the sectoral system. In the case of Mapai, it had led, at the end of the 1950s, to a conflict between Ben-Gurion, who sought to expand state authority at the expense of sectoral bodies such as the Histadrut, and a faction, led by Pinhas Lavon, that wanted the Histadrut to retain and expand its independence and its control over large swathes of the economy and society.[2]

In the case of the kibbutzim, the emergence of the state had impinged on the economic mediating function of the kibbutz movements, which during the Yishuv had served as an intermediary between kibbutz members and the national institutions. Furthermore, the debt settlements that the kibbutzim signed with the government in the mid-1950s shored up their finances and made them less dependent on funding from the movements to which they belonged. While the movements continued to serve as the pipelines through which the state transferred funds to the kibbutzim, the equity the kibbutzim were able to accumulate after moving from loss into profit provided them with alternative sources of capital. Prior to the refinancing of their debts, they had been almost entirely dependent on the movements to fund their manufacturing ventures. But by 1965 the movements were providing only 30 percent of the investment in new kibbutz factories, with the rest coming from the state and the equity held by kibbutzim.[3] Furthermore, government ministries and banks handled the kibbutzim's credit arrangements, negotiating directly with each individual kibbutz. Even though a movement representative sat on the government committee that oversaw the arrangements for each kibbutz, the new system constituted a sea change from the previous era's system. The movements lost control of the affairs of individual kibbutzim. With this newfound autonomy, kibbutzim were able to pursue independent economic policies.

The emergence of regional economic enterprises, held and operated in common by a group of kibbutzim in a given area, gave the individual communities further clout in their dealings with the kibbutz movements. As these enterprises expanded, they became power centers in their own right. Kibbutzim invested some of their profits in these operations, which turned out to be highly profitable, in part because they were less subject than the kibbutzim to the control and oversight of the movements and were thus free to maneuver in the free market. The regional enterprises also served as financing bodies—they could plow back some of the profits of their manufacturing and commercial ventures into investments in individual kibbutzim. Furthermore, the regional enterprises developed norms far different from those that prevailed within the kibbutzim—such as the employment of wage labor, a cohort of permanent managers who received privileges and perquisites, and hierarchical structures. All of these changes undermined the model kibbutz society that the movement leaderships sought to inculcate.[4]

Industrialization mitigated the mediating apparatus's power throughout the Israeli economy in two ways. First, it produced a cohort of private industrialists who, although they received considerable state assistance in establishing their firms, in time began making profits that turned them into power centers independent of the state. Second, it created a large class of workers who were employed by factories owned by the Histadrut and the government. These workers enjoyed higher wages and benefits than did their counterparts in private industry, providing them with economic independence.

In the case of the kibbutzim, the effect of industrialization was clear and visible: the profits the kibbutzim earned from their manufacturing initiatives made them less dependent on the kibbutz movements because they could now use these profits for investments and projects for which they would previously have required financing from the movements.[5] Industrialization also overturned the frugal and insular agricultural way of life that had formed the fabric of kibbutz life. The kibbutz factories entered the larger free market, where industrial products were traded and priced largely in response to the forces of supply and demand. The factories made deals with financiers and employed outside labor. They operated as units separate from the rest of the kibbutz. Agriculture, in contrast, operated as a planned economy, with government and public agencies setting production quotas, while regional enterprises, the movements, and producer and marketing monopolies or cartels developed technologies and centrally marketed produce. Kibbutz manufacturing was so independent that there were even conflicts between different kibbutzim in the same movement whose factories were competitors.[6] Industrialization thus constituted a counterforce to the highly centralized authority exerted by the movements at that time in the areas of ideology, society, and politics. While the effects of industrialization on daily life were most notable in kibbutz society, they could be seen in other parts of the labor movement as well. They brought in new mores and served as the channel through which American capitalism made its way into Israel.[7]

The reparations agreement with Germany also gave some Israelis more economic independence, and it did the same for kibbutzim. In the latter case, it enhanced the autonomy of the individual kibbutz both because it provided funds that could be invested in the community and because the reparations paid by Germany to kibbutz members went straight to the kibbutzim themselves and not to the kibbutz movements. Furthermore, the movement decided that compensation payments, as opposed to rehabilitation loans, would not be placed in the individual kibbutz's general budget. They would be devoted instead to special projects at the discretion of each kibbutz—for example, the construction of theaters, dining halls, and swimming pools, all of which improved the quality of life and mitigated the austerity that had previously been a trademark of kibbutz life. A not insignificant number of kibbutz members refused to hand over all their compensation payments to their kibbutzim; they spent the money on themselves, raising their own standard of living.[8] As we have seen, German reparations also constituted a major source of income for families in other parts of Israeli society, providing them with economic security and opportunities that made them less dependent on the labor movement's institutions.

The expansion of Israel's higher-education system further weakened the mediating apparatuses. New universities opened their doors in the 1950s and 1960s, creating spaces for individual thinking and attracting tens of thousands of young people each year. The effect on the kibbutzim was quite visible. In ever-growing numbers, members of Hakibbutz Ha'artzi began to pursue higher education outside the movement's own academic institutions. About 1,000 members of Hakibbutz Ha'artzi were enrolled in universities and colleges around the country at the beginning of the 1970s, most of them disregarding the movement's strictures by pursuing fields of study that were not required by their kibbutzim, such as social sciences and humanities.[9] The movement leadership had almost no power to impose ideological collectivism on these people. The experience opened new horizons for these members, exposing them to new ideas and political views. They became politically involved and expressed independent ideas, to the leadership's chagrin.[10]

7

Internal Divisions
in the Labor Movement

Economics and Politics

THE ECONOMIC DEVELOPMENTS enumerated in the previous chapters led to the rise of groups within the labor movement stridently opposed to each other. Their disputes directly or indirectly addressed the social consequences of the activities of party and movement apparatuses. This criticism had three notable aspects. First, it was internal—that is, it came out of groups that were connected to some or all of the labor movement's social, economic, or political institutions. Second, it came from the grass roots, groups that were not orchestrated by any part of the establishment. Third, it was directed at and opposed to the movement machine.

Internecine divisions and rivalries within the labor movement were nothing new. From its inception, the global labor movement displayed radicalizing and moderate tendencies that pitted revolutionaries against reformers and socialists against social democrats, dividing the movement into "right" and "left" wings.[1] These same divisions could be seen in the Israeli labor movement, dividing it into different ideological factions. But the divisions that appeared in the Israeli labor movement in the mid-1950s were of a new kind. These new fissures ran between the leadership and the public as well as among the working class, the middle class, and the white-collar workers who had emerged from within the labor movement. In the past, as the labor movement was on the rise, different streams had argued over questions of ideology and tactics. They disagreed about how to bring about social change—by means of revolution or reform? The new dissenters charged the party's and movement's institutions and leaders with corruption, incompetence, and ossification. The underlying causes of these attacks were fading class solidarity and the labor movement's failure to bring about the changes it had aspired to. In the previous era, when the labor movement was enjoying relative political success, none of the factions had any doubt that they belonged to a larger movement with shared values and political goals. Some of the new factions that emerged out of the crisis of the Left positioned themselves on the outside.

Although these new political orientations were responses to the same economic changes, the criticisms they leveled at the machines differed in ideology. Some of the critics emerged from those groups that had benefitted from the unequally distributed economic growth of the previous two decades. They declared that the system was in fact overly egalitarian and invoked arguments being put forward in capitalist societies by neoliberals, who had emerged as the standard-bearers of a new doctrine. Any attempt to distribute income equally was inherently unfair, they charged, and created perverse incentives. A thriving economy, they declared, should reward those who work hard and take risks rather than coddle the indolent. Another political orientation, also emerging from those who were better off, critiqued inequality in an ostensibly socialist spirit. They drew their ideas from two sources—the Old Left, to which some members of the labor parties remained loyal, and the New Left, which in the 1960s proposed a broad critique of capitalist society. A third orientation emerged from those who had not enjoyed the benefits of the power-distributing apparatus—for the most part, indigent workers. In the Israeli case, this group consisted largely of Mizrahim who had immigrated after the founding of the state. They accused the labor movement of creating an unequal society along ethnic lines.

This political division is central to explaining the labor movement's crisis and its loss of votes between the 1950s and the 1970s.[2] The contemporary discourse tended to depict this division in terms of the traditional ideological battles between the movement's right and left wings, but that is not really the case. The division took place in a new socioeconomic context, as a look at Hakibbutz Ha'artzi and Mapam demonstrates. The combination of internal divisions and the increasing redundancy of the movement and party machines heralded the movement's dissolution.

Technocrats and Meshekists: The Rise of Sectoralism in the Labor Movement

From the time the Israeli economy began to prosper, white-collar professionals, who were also closer to state, Histadrut, and party power-distributing apparatuses, began to demand higher wages, more extensive benefits, and higher status than less-educated and less-skilled workers.[3] At the beginning of the 1950s, managers and professionals employed by the Histadrut pressed that organization to do away with the standard family salary that had been paid equally to all of the labor organization's employees since 1924. They were successful. Mapai's representatives on the Histadrut Executive Committee pushed through a new pay scale in 1954 according to which different salary levels were paid to members of different professions, such as doctors, teachers, and carpenters. The decision increased competition in the economy as professional unions and associations organized and sought to gain more state resources for their members. These organizations staged a series of strikes at the end of the 1950s and the beginning of the 1960s.

For example, in 1954, following an across-the-board wage freeze imposed in 1952, workers with college degrees demanded that their salaries be raised. In 1955, Prime Minister Moshe Sharett adopted the recommendations of a commission set up to study the issue, but at the beginning of 1956, when David Ben-Gurion returned to the post of prime minister, he decided not to honor the agreement Sharett had reached with the unions. As a result, workers with college degrees, including engineers and physicians, went on strike in February that year. In 1957, the country's engineers, who had hitherto been members of a union that represented nonacademic technicians as well, left that organization and established their own on the grounds that they deserved better conditions than workers who did not have degrees. At the same time, high school teachers also sought to set up their own union separate from the elementary school teachers.[4]

The situation grew more acute in the 1960s. The combination of a fast-growing economy, overemployment, and rising prices had a serious impact on the labor market. Workers' committees at places of employment, which had heretofore largely toed the line set by the Histadrut's sectoral labor-union branches, realized that they were in a position of power and began to negotiate with their employers independently. If they did not get what they wanted, they staged wildcat strikes unapproved by the Histadrut and protesting against that organization. Employers, facing a burgeoning labor shortage and competing for workers, began to give in to wage demands. Wage hikes followed, increasing salaries by double-digit percentages in 1964 and 1965; prices rose steeply in their wake. Strikes grew more and more frequent as workers came to believe that they could get more without the Histadrut than through it. At the same time, white-collar professionals sought to preserve their advantage over other sectors, so that every salary increase for workers led to a parallel rise in white-collar wages.[5]

In 1962, seeking to ward off inflation, the Israeli government announced a devaluation of the currency by two-thirds and imposed a wage freeze. Workers responded with more strikes and protests. Action committees including members from Mapam, Ahdut Ha'avodah, Maki (Ha-Miflega ha-Komunistit ha-Yisraelit, Israeli Communist Party), and Herut (Liberty) exhorted workers to take militant stances, and the Histadrut began to lose control of the situation. To preserve the value of wages in the face of the devaluation, workers demanded a semiannual cost-of-living increase tied to the inflation rate, but the government refused. In response, the action committees declared a general strike in December 1962. The strike was for the most part confined to the Tel Aviv metropolitan area. In the meantime, the annual number of striking workers rose continuously and sharply, from 13,000 in 1960 to 86,000 in 1963.[6] Employers had to give in to these demands despite the official wage freeze—wages rose 30 percent in 1962. In 1964, wage increases were supposed to be limited to 3 percent but reached 10–14 percent. The Histadrut complained that it was losing control of the workers' committees, which were taking advantage of the labor shortage to continue to demand wage hikes.[7] In 1960–65, the number of workers' committees shot up by 150 percent. Wildcat strikes rose from 25 percent of all strikes in 1960 to an average of 60 percent in the five subsequent years.[8] In 1965, there were twice as many strikes as in each of the two previous years, a total of 284.[9] In that year, the proportion of strikes devoted to gaining better benefits peaked, comprising 78.4 percent of all strikes.[10]

Sectoral orientation fit in with a similar trend that had begun to develop in the kibbutz movements in the mid-1950s. As their economies expanded, kibbutzim saw the rise of a new social group that their own residents called—with no little derision—the "meshekists." The label derived from the word *meshek*, which means both "economy" and "farm." For the meshekists, the kibbutz was a community with primarily economic interests, and it should pursue those interests and those of the kibbutz sector as a whole unabashedly and without too many ideological compunctions.[11] The meshekists (sometimes called "technocrats" in kibbutz studies in view of their status as part of a larger professional class in Israel's developed industrial society) were kibbutz directors, treasurers, factory managers and senior staff, economists, personnel coordinators, accountants, managers of tourism operations, and the managers of agricultural production branches and those of the large service units (dining hall, laundry, auto shop, and so on). Their numbers varied according to the size of a kibbutz and its concerns, ranging between about twenty and twenty-five in each community. In other words, it was a class of several thousand people among all the kibbutzim in Israel.[12] Some kibbutz movements, individual kibbutzim, and regional councils had more of a meshekist orientation than others. For example, the kibbutzim of the Jordan Valley, especially those of Ihud Hakevutzot Vehakibbutzim movement, were seen as a stronghold of the meshekist outlook. But the phenomenon spanned all three movements. The meshekists were especially notable in the regional factories situated outside the grounds of the kibbutzim and in the cooperatives located in Tel Aviv and owned by the large federations of kibbutzim and moshavim or by the Histadrut—for example, the Tnuva dairy; Hamashbir Hamerkazi (a purchasing cooperative that served agricultural settlements and other projects in the periphery); and government companies such as the Israel Dairy Board, the Egg and Poultry Board, and agriculture cooperatives that oversaw agricultural production and pricing. In these places, the meshekists could operate as capitalists in the fullest sense.

The meshekists developed attitudes much like those of urban professionals. Some of them were, like their counterparts in the cities, dissatisfied by the fact that they did not receive "suitable compensation" for their
work and achievements.[13] They strove to maximize kibbutz profits and
thus to build up the power of the kibbutz sector even if this accrued power
came at the expense of others (such as the hired laborers the kibbutzim
employed, most of whom lived in nearby development towns). Kibbutz
members with drive and competitive instincts generally found their way
into this professional and managerial class because it was virtually the only
path for personal advancement available to them within the kibbutz system. Political careers were not really an option, given the centralized and
hierarchical nature of the parties that represented the kibbutzim (as well
as of Mapai and other Israeli parties). Furthermore, the dramatic growth
of the kibbutz economies meant that there were always new projects that
needed to be set up and old ones that needed to be managed. Talented
young men returning to the kibbutzim after their military service were
quickly swept into managerial positions in agricultural and manufacturing operations, where they could realize their ambitions. In such jobs, they
absorbed the practical, methodical, and nonideological values of meshekism as well as its economic logic, an outlook that fit in well with the larger
atmosphere of Israeli economic development. They were the kibbutzim's
"field command" and led a metamorphosis of kibbutz life that turned it
into something entirely different from the cooperative socialism that had
been the communes' founding ideology. Furthermore, they owed no fealty
to the kibbutz movements' political and ideological leaderships. This lack
of loyalty created a huge dissonance between the kibbutz as an idea and
the kibbutzim on the ground, between the ideological and political leadership and the public, and between consciousness and lived experience. That
dissonance started a series of tremors that shook the foundations of the
kibbutzim in later years. The reverberations spread through the rest of the
labor movement and led in the end to its collapse.

The first indication of the rise of meshekism in Hakibbutz Ha'artzi
appeared in January 1956. The kibbutzim were at the nadir of their economic crisis; the recovery program had not yet been signed with the government. The economic plight the kibbutzim were facing exacerbated

tensions between the individual settlements and the movement, and a fierce altercation broke out between Meir Ya'ari and several kibbutz managers who had acted against his instructions on an issue that was slated to come up for discussion in the movement council meeting scheduled for April. These managers—kibbutz economic coordinators, treasurers, and others—sought to end one of the movement's most hallowed institutions, the traditional seminar for high school seniors that was held each year at the movement's Givat Haviva college. At this month-long seminar, these young people were indoctrinated in the movement's philosophy, hearing dozens of lectures given by the movement's leaders and ideologists. Ya'ari wanted an even longer seminar—he said that if he could, he would have it last a year. The managers, for their part, wanted to revise and shorten the program and run it on a regional rather than a national basis. Their reasons were primarily economic. First, the kibbutzim were reliant on the high school seniors as a workforce. Second, the national seminar was costly, and the bill was divided among the kibbutzim. For Ya'ari, ideological education was an important means of creating ideological collectivism and was thus essential to the stability of the movement's social and political structure. He had agreed to cut the seminar from a full month to three weeks, but the managers' demands were more than he could stomach. He raged against what he termed "distressing manifestations" and charged that the managerial attack on the national seminar was a warning sign that individual kibbutzim were building up local power at the expense of the movement.[14]

The managers, who wanted to strengthen their kibbutzim economically and opposed what they saw as Ya'ari's attempt to subordinate the interests of individual kibbutzim to those of the movement, acted as a bloc on other issues as well. That same year, Hakibbutz Ha'artzi Secretariat told kibbutzim to send members to help out Kibbutz Harel, which urgently needed working hands (Harel had been reconstituted after being dismantled by the movement leadership because of its leftward political deviation). The managers responded with a defiant, even provocative counterproposal—the needed workers, they suggested, should be taken from the movement's national offices. Ya'ari was furious, warning against meshekism, which would, "if it is allowed, destroy everything spiritual about the kibbutz."[15] One kibbutz treasurer responded to Ya'ari's tirade in the kibbutz movement's weekly newspaper. The movement had developed a huge bureaucracy free of all external oversight, he charged.[16] Ya'ari volleyed back with his own long and sharply worded article. "The community does not breathe because of its treasurers," he declared. He stressed that the movement staff provided great support for the kibbutzim and, compared to the other movements, took little manpower from the kibbutzim themselves.[17] It was the first time that the movement leadership had ever had to justify the movement's operations and was an important milestone in the decline of the mediating apparatus and the rise of the sectoral trend.

Meshekism gained more and more strength in the late 1950s and early 1960s, the years in which the kibbutzim rapidly industrialized and sectoral loyalties grew in other parts of the new middle class created by the party and movement machines. In the case of the kibbutzim, rapid development reinforced the meshekist mindset and was of great significance in determining the character and needs of kibbutz society, which in turn affected its political orientation. The managers responsible for the well-being of their kibbutzim were pragmatists; their immediate concerns were things such as manpower, investment funds, land, reasonably priced irrigation water, and low interest rates on loans. Seeking to obtain benefits and advantages for their kibbutzim, they fostered close relationships with decision makers in government offices, especially the ministries of Finance and Agriculture. The kibbutz economy was highly dependent on the government for easy credit, subsidies, and protection against imports, which dictated the meshekists' political orientation. Those responsible for ensuring that their communities had food on the table and clothes to wear needed to focus on the practical means of making money rather than on ideological purity and political separatism. They were willing to compromise on ideals and to cooperate and ally with other political forces if by doing so they could obtain immediate economic gains. As far as the managers were concerned, it was vital for the kibbutz parties to be members of the governing coalition and to maximize cooperation with the ruling party, Mapai. At that time, in the context of socialist politics this orientation was called "rightist."

Hakibbutz Ha'artzi meshekists also sought cooperation with the other kibbutz movements, Ihud Hakevutzot Vehakibbutzim and Hakibbutz Hameuhad. One of the manifestations of this cooperation was the proposal to establish a regional commune—a new kind of kibbutz based on hired labor and the merging of the production operations of several kibbutzim in the same area. This idea was first proposed in Sha'ar Hanegev, a small regional council in southwestern Israel in which there were ten kibbutzim belonging to Ihud Hakevutzot Vehakibbutzim and one to Hakibbutz Ha'artzi. The individual settlements were in chronic deficit and were losing members. By joining forces, they hoped to become self-sustaining and financially independent.[18] The level of cooperation gradually increased in accordance with economic logic. In the 1950s, the Sha'ar Hanegev settlements established regional projects of the kind that were also being founded elsewhere—alfalfa cultivation, a slaughterhouse, a cotton-ginning factory, warehouses for sorting farm products, a refrigeration plant, a gas station, a weighing facility, a regional garage, to name a few. At the beginning of the 1950s, cooperation entered a new stage as the kibbutzim began to work together in branches that had previously been the preserve of individual communities, such as grain and cotton harvesting, sugar beet cultivation, fertilization, the harvesting of manure from barns and poultry coops and its use as organic fertilizer for crops, and the harvesting and sorting of potatoes. The next stage was the idea of managing all agricultural activities jointly and the creation of a regional cooperative that would unite the production of all the branches of all the kibbutzim. Under this scheme, the individual kibbutz would be a consumer managed by a regional organization.[19]

The regional cooperative idea never got off the ground because Hakibbutz Ha'artzi's leadership rejected it. It was, however, the ultimate manifestation of sectoralism because it involved cooperation between kibbutzim so as to achieve greater efficiency and economies of scale, while accepting the need for compromise on principles, both in terms of the different kibbutz movements' ideologies and the employment of outside workers. Although the plan was not implemented, it set off an internal debate showing that the requirements of economic development had created two opposing orientations in Hakibbutz Ha'artzi. Supporters of the regional coopera-tive offered pragmatic arguments. Kibbutz autonomy and the distinctions between the kibbutz movements, they maintained, should make way for a larger body with greater economic advantages. Opponents warned against "the emergence of new theories" about the kibbutz. Hakibbutz Ha'artzi's secretary, Shlomo Rosen, said that these views represented two schools of thought—what he called the "developmentalists" and the "guardians of principle."[20]

Despite the critique leveled by the meshekists, like that coming from the urban professional class, the fact was that in the 1950s and 1960s they bowed to the dictates of their political movements and did not challenge them head to head, for a number of reasons. First, the generation of the new technocrats had nevertheless been brought up in labor-movement socialization frameworks during the period of the movement's unchal-lenged hegemony. They were thus relatively conservative about pushing the boundaries of acceptable behavior.[21] Second, until the mid-1960s this coterie did not achieve a level of independence that enabled it to thrive outside the labor movement, and at this time it had not yet fully exploited all the advantages and benefits it received from the mediating apparatus. Third, the nature of this coterie's economic activity was not avowedly pathbreaking and subversive. It was more of an ethos than an explicit ideology. As such, the normative system developed by the technocrats brought about a profound and long-term evolution rather than a revolu-tion in Israeli society.

The second half of the 1960s marked a new stage in the development of the sectoral element in the labor movement. In Hakibbutz Ha'artzi and Mapam, this stage meant the rise of the "Right," which led in the end to Mapam running on a joint slate, the Alignment, with the Labor Party in the Histadrut and Knesset elections of 1969. Mapai's right wing also grew stronger, but with the opposite result—a split. In 1965, a faction led by David Ben-Gurion broke away from Mapai to form Rafi, a party that, although paying lip service to socialist ideals (the party's name was an acronym for Reshimat Poalei Yisrael, the Israel Workers List), was in fact composed of the leaders of the sectoral tendency. It placed Ben-Gurion's principle of *mamlakhtiyut*, rather than socialism, front and center. In the

Knesset elections that year, Rafi won ten seats, a disappointment for its leaders, but their willingness to break with the labor movement and found a rival party evidenced a new sense of independence and audaciousness on the part of the new middle class. Rafi was clearly a direct creation of the socioeconomic milieu of the economic boom of the early 1960s, which strengthened the middle class. Thanks to rapid economic growth, the new middle class was no longer dependent on the mediating apparatus of Mapai. Their newfound independence meant they could reject and seek to replace it.

After the Six-Day War in 1967, the sectoral struggle calmed. The boom that lasted until the Yom Kippur War of 1973 provided the new middle class with what it wanted, so it and the kibbutzim flourished and made no new demands. The catalyst for the renewal of the class conflict was the economic crisis that followed the latter war. The Rabin government's strategy for addressing the crisis, which placed most of the burden on the middle and upper classes, led to furious protests from sectoral interests and made the government and the labor-movement establishment into the enemy. The Israeli case was part of a larger phenomenon throughout the West in which the professional class and white-collar workers turned against the welfare state.[22] Israel's sectoral interests took up the banner of Western neoliberalism, which declared that the principles of the era of high growth of the 1950s and 1960s were dead letters and so sought to fashion an alternative economic and social order. In Israel, this tendency was reinforced by the crisis of legitimacy that the Israeli leadership faced following the bloody and costly war. Israel had prevailed in the end, but its sense of security was shattered, and its enemies gained new confidence. As a result, during the years after the war the new sectoral interests turned away from the labor movement and allied with the center-right opposition, which now, for the first time in Israeli history, was in striking distance of shattering labor hegemony. Its time had come.

When the Yom Kippur War came to an end, the middle class began to form new political frameworks. In the national election held at the end of 1973, a new party, Ratz (HaTnua'a le-Zkhuyot ha-Ezrah ve-la-Shalom, or the Movement for Civil Rights and Peace), won 35,023 votes and three Knesset seats. Its leader, Shulamit Aloni, had bolted from the Labor Party.

Its platform stressed issues and values—such as separation of church and state as well as territorial compromise with the Arabs—that appealed to well-off Israelis who had formerly voted for the parties of the labor movement. Centering on issues of individual rights rather than on economic and social issues, Ratz embodied the liberal-dovish worldview of many members of the new middle class.[23]

In the early days of the protest movement that followed the Yom Kippur War, another political movement also began to organize. With ambitions and pretentions much greater than Ratz's, it sought to take advantage of the crisis in the labor movement and to unify all those who opposed it. Shinui (Change) was led by Amnon Rubinstein, dean of the Tel Aviv University Law School, and other members of the academic, business, and public elites, which had traditionally been associated with the labor movement. Although Shinui began as an extraparliamentary movement, it soon gained considerable support among better-off Israelis, and its leaders and supporters transformed it into a political party. In 1976, it announced its merger with another new political force led by Yigal Yadin. Yadin, a well-known archaeologist, had also served as the IDF chief of staff and enjoyed considerable public prestige. The merged movement was called Dash, an acronym for Tnu'a Demokratit LeShinui (Democratic Movement for Change).[24] Polls soon showed Dash garnering more public support than any new party had ever achieved in Israel. It began to look as if it could pose a serious threat to the labor-led Alignment in the next election.

The Democrats: Fighting for Peace, Equality, and Social Justice

From the late 1950s through the mid-1960s, Israel's and the kibbutzim's first period of intensive growth engendered a materialist society as well as the technocrats and meshekists of the new Israeli middle class. The second period of expansion, from the mid-1960s to the early 1970s, saw the rise of a new group within the middle class. In economic terms, the first group, the technocrats and meshekists, emerged as they moved into the sixth decile of Israel's income distribution. The second group emerged as it moved into the eighth decile. The two groups also had different ideological groundings. The first group, which critiqued the labor movement from the right, had its genesis in the revelations about the Soviet Union that became public in the 1950s, and it took advantage of this blow to social-ism's foundational beliefs to seek to reform the labor movement. But a different, left-wing critique of the labor movement also emerged in the 1960s, growing out of dissatisfaction with the welfare state that the movement had created. These critics, reinforced by the theoretical crisis of Keynes-ian economics brought on by the era of inflation and recession that many Western societies experienced, attacked the labor movement and party establishment in a pincer movement, and although their ideologies were different, the two groups emerged from the crisis of the Left and sought to reform the labor movement.

The roots of the "democratic" critique of the labor-movement machine's inequitable allocation of power lay in the early 1950s, but at first it focused on internal affairs, in particular the institutionalization of party hierar-chies and organizations as well as indications that democracy was not being practiced and power was being misapplied. A Mapai young guard arose in 1950–53, calling itself Hame'orer (Awakener). Its members demanded that the party be democratized and built on a larger social base. Another group, Shurat Hamitnadvim (Circle of Volunteers), founded by student support-ers of Mapai and active between 1951 and 1956, called for reform of the government and Histadrut to ensure sound and honest administration. A wildcat seamen's strike broke out in 1952, the strikers charging that their labor union, part of the Histadrut, was not run democratically. In 1952–53, the leadership of the still united Mapam battled an opposition composed of members of both of the party's components (Hakibbutz Hameuhad and Hakibbutz Ha'artzi). In part, this battle took the form of an ideological purge of what the leadership saw as left-wing extremism, but in actual fact it was much more a fight over control of the party.

The democratic critique of the labor-movement machine intensi-fied at the end of the 1950s and beginning of the 1960s in response to its increasingly institutionalized hierarchy. And the critique was no lon-ger restricted to the young. People of all ages fought this trend. One such group, Min Hayesod (From the Foundations), was led by prominent intel-lectuals and professors, most of whom were members of Mapai, but also encompassed activists from all parts of the labor movement and kibbutz movements. They protested what they saw as Ben-Gurion's authoritarian leadership.[25] The immediate trigger for the foundation of Min Hayesod was the Lavon Affair, a convoluted scandal in which Ben-Gurion accused Pinhas Lavon, a prominent Mapai leader who had briefly served as defense minister in 1954–55, of botching an espionage operation in Egypt.[26] But Lavon, it will be recalled, was also the leader of the anti-*mamlakhti* camp in Mapai and an advocate of the independence of the Histadrut, which he headed in 1949–50 and 1956–61. Min Hayesod supported Lavon against Ben-Gurion. The group split away from Mapai in 1965, hoping to establish an independent political force. In advance of that year's national election, Mapam proposed to Min Hayesod and Ahdut Ha'avodah that the three groups form a new united party, but the latter two rejected the idea. In the end, most of these movements' members returned to their original parties and sought to achieve their goals within those frameworks. Their reasons for doing so were much the same as those of the meshekists and sectoral interests who prior to the mid-1960s refrained from breaking with the labor movement.

A democratic tendency also emerged within Hakibbutz Ha'artzi and Mapam, which charged the historic leadership with authoritarianism. In 1958, the Mapam leadership got word of a small group of young people who were meeting regularly. These young people described themselves as an independent ideological circle and later came to be called Hug ha-Achad-Asar (Group of Eleven).[27] Their leader was Efrayim Reiner, at that time Hashomer Hatza'ir's youth-movement leadership coordinator. Reiner was an up-and-coming figure in the movement who seemed likely to rise to the head of Hakibbutz Ha'artzi and Mapam.[28] The Group of Eleven convened every few weeks at one of the kibbutzim or in Tel Aviv to discuss movement, national, and world affairs, while seeking to further its members' influence over events. In violation of Hakibbutz Ha'artzi's sacred principle of democratic centralism, the group's meetings were held without the movement leadership's sanction or knowledge. Although the group's members were not cut of one cloth—they held a range of views on the issues, a fact that would later be an obstacle to their work together—they shared a common interest in challenging the historic leadership.

Reiner and his colleagues were part of a broader cohort in Hakibbutz Ha'artzi and Mapam that was dissatisfied with the movement and party's hierarchical governance. The concept of ideological collectivism was the subject of particular discontent. A dispute over this issue broke out in the summer of 1962 after a group of young people from Kibbutz Mishmar Ha'emek, without getting clearance from above, invited a lecturer from Mapai to speak about his views. The kibbutz-movement leadership issued a severe formal reprimand of the offenders, a decision that outraged many members of the movement's kibbutzim.[29] The issue was sharply debated in an unprecedented fashion in Hakibbutz Ha'artzi newspapers and journals. As a result, the principle of ideological collectivism came up for discussion in two successive meetings of Hakibbutz Ha'artzi Executive Committee at the end of 1962.[30] These meetings made it clear that the public was extremely disgruntled about the movement's political structure. But the historic leadership asserted itself, and in the end the Executive Committee resolved that, despite the criticism, ideological collectivism should be reinforced. This resolution only intensified the anger at the leadership.[31] At the Tenth Hakibbutz Ha'artzi Council, held in April 1964, many participants spoke on the issue and protested the movement's leadership style and decision-making procedures.[32]

Another manifestation of the democratic orientation that appeared in the other kibbutz movements in the mid-1960s was the "discourse culture."[33] This new phenomenon had its base in the Ihud Hakevutzot Vehakibbutzim journal *Shdemot* (Fields), edited by Avraham "Pachi" Shapira, an educator and later professor of philosophy at Tel Aviv University. Shapira brought together a group of kibbutz writers and intellectuals, most of them young, and gave them broad scope to express their opinions without censorship and to publish essays and articles that editors of other kibbutz publications rejected. *Shdemot* fashioned a distinct identity for the young kibbutz generation in opposition to the founders' generation. It served as a platform for initiatives that brought together young members of the different kibbutz movements, a matter of great significance given the developments of the early 1960s. The connections made in *Shdemot* led to the founding of a new group in February 1966, Hahug Habein-Kibbutzi (Interkibbutz Circle). The group held eleven meetings, at which members of all the kibbutz movements discussed subjects such as Jewish identity, self-fulfillment at the kibbutz, and the quest to formulate a specifically generational identity in the face of pressure from the founders.[34] That same year also saw the formation of Tzavta (a branch of Mapam's cultural club in Tel Aviv) in Emek Hefer (a region near the town of Netanya that includes many kibbutzim), another ideological circle with the same goals. Similar groups came together in other areas. Such gatherings leveled incisive but not fiery criticism at the founding generation and rebelled against the leadership. They incidentally also served as evidence that Israel had entered a postrevolutionary age in which the ideological distinctions that had once separated the kibbutz movements faded; young kibbutz members no longer found them relevant. On the contrary, they found that their counterparts at kibbutzim of other movements shared many of their ideas and commitments. The younger generation thus wanted to remove the barriers that separated them. They also sensed that Israeli society and kibbutz society were growing ever more ideologically distant from each other, which created a feeling of solidarity among the young members of all the kibbutz movements. The desire to sit together and trade ideas grew out of this experience of commonality. Although the people involved were unaware of the fact, this change of consciousness was a product of the economic changes the kibbutzim had undergone. The activity of the *Shdemot* group ran ideologically counter to the sectoral phenomenon. Both grew on the same substrate, but the former sought democratization, and the latter was willing to allow inequality to grow.

The Six-Day War was a watershed for the democratic orientation in the labor movement. It brought two new developments in its wake. The first was integration into the global New Left, and the second a shift in priorities, with security and foreign-policy issues, in particular rule over and the fate of the territories Israel occupied during the war, taking center stage and shunting economic and social issues to the side. Security and the Occupied Territories soon became the central dividing line of Israeli politics. These changes were not just a result of the war itself; they also grew out of economic developments in Israel. The country's entry into the global cultural and political scene grew out of the increasing similarity between the standard of living of parts of the Israeli population and the populations of other Western countries, which opened up Israel to their influence. Security and foreign-policy issues could move to the center because the country was now economically strong enough to enable Israelis to turn their attention from economic development to injustices and the plight of the other and thus to proffer democratic critique of Israeli settlement in the territories.

The label *New Left* entered international parlance in the mid-1960s. It named a global phenomenon among socialist intellectuals and young people in the West. Contrasting itself with what it called the "Old Left," by which it meant both bureaucratic Stalinism and labor-union-based social democracy, the New Left called for a reengagement with social issues. It rebelled against established socialist and labor parties and movements rather than seeking to reform them. Among other things, it focused the attention of citizens, many of them young people, on postmaterial values such as freedom of expression and thought, opposition to oppression, and the battle against injustices suffered by distant publics. In Israel, the New Left inspired a protest movement with mostly cultural manifestations. It could be seen in all the reaches of the labor movement, but especially in the kibbutz movements and most visibly in Hakibbutz Ha'artzi.[35] The culture of protest is surveyed in the next chapter, but here I focus on the political aspect of the New Left as a part of the broader democratic tendency.

Following the Six-Day War, the Israeli labor movement saw the rise of a struggle against the occupation, marking a new stage in democratic orientation's development. It was not an entirely new phenomenon—prior to the war, groups in the labor movement, such as the Va'ad ha-Shalom ha-Israeli (Israeli Committee for Peace) and Ha-Liga le-Meniat Kfia Datit (League against Religious Coercion), charged that the government was denying full democratic rights and equality to Israel's non-Jewish citizens and that it was caving in to Jewish religious parties' efforts to control the country's public space. But these groups did not garner broad public support, nor did they seek to delegitimize the regime.[36] During the boom that followed the war, as the new middle class grew stronger both economically and socially, this critique, formerly focused within the labor movement, now began to be voiced with regard to Israeli society as a whole. It was not only a part of the postmaterial agenda but also a response to the postwar foreign and security situation. The middle class also realized that they had gained as much social mobility as the labor-movement machines could provide. No longer dependent on the system, they could turn against the movement and its institutions. The democratic protest movement grew stronger as it confronted Israel's rule over the Palestinians in the territories conquered in the war; the long War of Attrition that, so many of the protestors believed, was caused by Israel's unwillingness to make peace with its neighbors; and, a few years later, the disillusionment with the traditional leadership and what was perceived as its failure to prepare for and properly conduct the Yom Kippur War.

The protest against the occupation emerged immediately following the war. The democrats turned from critique of the ossification of the labor-movement hierarchy to critique of the government's treatment of the Palestinian population in the territories. The two central movements that took up this issue were Ha-Tnua le-Shalom ve-Lebitachon (Movement for Peace and Security) and Siah (Smol Israeli Hadash, or Israeli New Left), both of them founded by a combination of Hakibbutz Ha'artzi members and urban activists. The Movement for Peace and Security was founded in the autumn of 1967 by kibbutz members and left-wing intellectuals such as Yeshayahu Leibowitz, Yehoshua Arieli, Dan Ben-Amotz, and Amos Kenan. It launched its activity in 1968 with protests, public statements, and petitions. In 1969, it changed its strategy and character, moving from a position of cooperation with the establishment to open opposition. In the period preceding the elections in 1969, it even considered fielding an independent slate for the Knesset, but most of its kibbutz adherents did not want to compete with Mapam. In the end, such a slate was put together by a small minority of the movement's supporters, but it failed to win enough votes to gain a Knesset seat. In 1970, the movement took a radical turn, and some of its founding members left it, reducing its influence.[37]

Siah, founded in 1969, was more antiestablishment than the Movement for Peace and Security. Its members were young kibbutz members who left Mapam after the party entered the Alignment with the Labor Party. They were joined by students and faculty members from Tel Aviv University and the Hebrew University. Their activity in subsequent years largely took the form of demonstrations calling for Israeli withdrawal from the Occupied Territories and equal rights for Palestinians, both those living in the territories and those who were citizens of Israel.[38] Siah and the

Movement for Peace and Security were critical of the infringements of human rights and democratic values that they saw as inevitable consequences of military rule over another people. They eventually lost all hope of influencing government policy and turned their efforts toward forming a democratic and humanistic political force. In 1972, Siah joined members of the Movement for Peace and Security to form Tehelet Adom (Blue Red), which in 1973 formed Moked (Center) by merging with what remained of Maki, the Israel Communist Party, after its Arab wing and hard-core Soviet loyalists broke away to form Rakah (Reshima Komunistit Hadasha, New Communist Left). In the elections of 1973, Moked, led by Meir Pa'il, won a single seat in the Knesset. In 1977, Moked united with several other small groups: the Meri (acronym for Machane Radicali Israeli, Israeli Radical Wing) list led by Knesset member Uri Avneri, editor and publisher of the dissident and antiestablishment weekly magazine *Ha'olam Hazeh* (This World); an independent socialist faction led by a prominent former top Mapai leader, Arieh (Luva) Eliav; and a faction of the Black Panthers, a Mizrahi protest movement. Their joint slate was called Sheli (Shalom le-Israel, Peace for Israel). The move from protest and its cultural manifestations to parliamentary activity marked a crossing of the boundary from a politics of legitimization to a politics of delegitimization of the political hegemony.[39] Like those members of the new middle class who broke away to form a right-wing rival to the labor movement, the left-wing democratic trend now entered the lists against the ruling labor machine.

Another line of the democratic critique of the labor movement emerged out of despair that peace had not arrived and anger at what was seen as the government's insincerity about its attempts to conclude a peace treaty. This anger was exacerbated by the increase in the numbers of victims claimed by the Arab–Israeli conflict, which reached their height during the War of Attrition (March 1969–August 1970).[40] The most notable expression of this position during the War of Attrition was known as the "Letter of the Twelfth Graders," written and signed by high school seniors from central Israel who had read in the press that the government had refused to sanction a meeting between Nahum Goldmann, president of the World Jewish Congress, and Egyptian president Gamal Abdul Nasser.[41] They declared that they, standing on the verge of risking their lives as soldiers, wanted to be sure before they had to enlist that the government was doing all it could to achieve peace. The letter made waves because of the social group from which the signatories came. Their leader was Shmuel Shem-Tov, whose father, Victor, was a cabinet minister for Mapam; the other signatories came from families belonging to the Israeli elite. Right-wingers charged that the group came from Hashomer Hatza'ir, which was not far from the truth.[42] Although the letter was critical of government policy, it did not go beyond declarations made by the democratic camp. These young citizens wrote of a crisis of faith between them and the government and asked whether the country's leaders were really making every possible effort to ensure that they, young people who were soon to enlist in the IDF, would not die needlessly in a war. They did not challenge the need for the War of Attrition but protested what they saw as the government's arrogance, which they believed came at their expense. After meeting with Minister of Education Yigal Allon, they were persuaded that the pursuit of the war was being coupled with efforts to achieve peace, and so they enlisted.[43] Less well known is a similar letter sent to Defense Minister Moshe Dayan about four months later. This second letter was much more extreme and blunt. Its signatories were a group of teenagers from Kibbutz Kerem Shalom of Hakibbutz Ha'artzi who were preparing to enlist together in the Nahal Corps. Yet they, too, did not protest the war itself. They only demanded government honesty about its peace efforts and condemned any effort to mislead the public.[44]

Another manifestation of the democratic tendency in the labor movement came in the context of what was seen as government violations of the basic rights of Arabs, both those who were citizens of Israel and those who lived in the territories. In one case, Bedouin living in the northern Sinai Peninsula were removed to enable the construction of an Israeli settlement. A second case involved the government's refusal to allow Arab citizens of Israel who had been expelled from two villages along the Lebanese border, Biram and Ikrit, to return to their homes. In a third case, farmland belonging to the residents of Akraba village in the northern West Bank, captured in the Six-Day War, was confiscated, and the crops being grown there were destroyed. The leaders of this protest came from Hakibbutz Ha'artzi and Mapam, but they were joined by members of the other kibbutz movements and urban Israelis. The confrontation between these protestors and the government testified to the rise of the democratic tendency and to the weakness of the existing labor-movement power struggle and the internal rebellion it faced.

At the beginning of March 1972, members of Hakibbutz Ha'artzi kibbutzim along the border with the southern Gaza Strip, close to the city of Rafiah (an area called *pitchat* Rafiah, salient of Rafiah), noticed that army bulldozers were knocking down the dwellings of the Bedouin who lived there and expelling their inhabitants. The government had decided to build an Israeli settlement there. The action set off a storm, and members of thirteen of the nearby kibbutzim organized a public meeting to protest the damage the planned new settlement would cause to the local Arabs. The secretary of Hakibbutz Ha'artzi, Haim (Jumes) Oron, a member of Kibbutz Lahav in the Negev and a close associate of the leaders of the protest, informed the Mapam Central Committee of the events and conveyed the protestors' demand that Mapam take action.[45] A few days later representatives of the southern kibbutzim attended a meeting of the party secretariat and made it clear that they were serious about pursuing their campaign. They informed the secretariat about their efforts and demanded an official party response.

But the leadership of Hakibbutz Ha'artzi and Mapam had reasons for concern. First, the southern kibbutzim were made up of young people, most of whom had grown up in urban chapters of Hashomer Hatza'ir during the 1960s. They were very much under the influence of the New Left and were thus rebellious and undisciplined. Second, many of them had bolted from Mapam and had helped found Siah in 1969, when the party joined the Alignment with the Labor Party. Yet despite the leaders' reservations about the struggle, they decided to embrace it. They hoped to avert a head-on confrontation with the democratic tendency and to neutralize the threat it presented. The Central Committee condemned the new settlement and resolved to lead a public campaign against it. It was also decided that Hazan and Ya'ari would bring the issue up at their next meeting with Prime Minister Golda Meir.[46]

The Mapam leadership's greatest concern was keeping the protestors under control. In an effort to cool down the dissent, the secretariat formed a team to take the initiative in responding to the issue while, via Hakibbutz Ha'artzi, denying the protestors the freedom to represent themselves.[47] On this team's recommendation, the secretary of the Mapam Political Committee, Naftali Feder, called a press conference with the members of Kibbutz Nir Oz, where they declared that they expected that the displaced Bedouin would be allowed to return to their land. Feder stated that Mapam supported the people of Nir Oz but opposed "marginal groups of an anti-Zionist character who are taking advantage of this outcry to make gains for their separatist activity." The aim was to make a clear distinction between Mapam, on the one hand, and Siah, Matzpen (Compass, the anti-Zionist Israel Socialist Organization, founded in 1962), and other radical organizations, on the other. Feder stressed that Mapam did not wish to leave the government and that its platform supported the construction of settlements in the territories for "security" purposes, a vague term that did not precisely define what defense considerations would justify such settlements. A tense meeting of the Alignment's Knesset delegation discussed the Rafiah salient affair.[48] Mapam's parliamentarians did their best to meet the demands of their associates in Hakibbutz Ha'artzi, even traveling to Rafiah salient to study the events and demonstrate that the party was absolutely serious about its involvement.

Despite the Mapam Knesset members' efforts, construction work on the new settlement, slated to be home to 350 Israeli families, continued. After the cabinet officially approved the plan, the kibbutz activists called their own wildcat press conference along with representatives of the Bedouin, where they presented proof that the Bedouin had been forced into leaving by a campaign of intimidation and threats. Mapam's Knesset delegation rushed to calm the flames, acceding to the protestors' demand that Mapam insist on an urgent meeting of the Alignment leadership to discuss the issue.[49] Mapam's leadership was being pressured from the outside as well—the party found itself fighting alone, without any assistance from its partners in the government. Prime Minister Meir made it clear that she was extremely displeased with the Mapam faction, which in this case was opposing the government in which it served. Other cabinet ministers also condemned Mapam. Even worse for the party was the widespread public rejection of its position.[50]

Hakibbutz Ha'artzi and Mapam were trapped. On the one side, Knesset members from the right-wing parties saw an opportunity. They fired up public opposition to the "left-wingers" and questioned the movement's commitment to Zionism. On the other side, the democratic current in Hakibbutz Ha'artzi and Mapam continued to demand that the party achieve real results in its fight against the evacuation. Some communities were riven by the issue. In April 1972, a group of members of Mizra, one of the oldest Hakibbutz Ha'artzi kibbutzim, published a petition in support of the construction of the Rafiah salient settlement in the movement newspaper *Al Hamishmar*. Other members of the same kibbutz sent a letter to the newspaper stating that not all members of the kibbutz agreed and that it would be best for the two factions not to fight out their differences in public.[51] Mapam's institutions also split along these lines. When Latif Dori, coordinator of Mapam's young guard, organized the Rafiah Bedouin residents' signing of a petition to Israel's Supreme Court, the party organization denied any connection to his initiative.[52]

Mapam's leaders, feeling that they were losing control, ended its embrace of the protestors and began working to suppress them. Ya'akov Hazan led the campaign. "We must first of all imbue our hearts with concern for the Jewish people, and after that try to be more just," he declared. He said that he favored Israeli settlement in the Rafiah salient but opposed the way it had been accomplished.[53] Had the protestors restricted themselves to opposing the confiscation of Arab land, he claimed, Mapam would have garnered much public support. But they had sabotaged the effort when they also came out against the entire concept of Israeli settlements in the territories.[54] At a meeting of Hakibbutz Ha'artzi Executive Committee, Hazan went so far as to say to his colleagues that he could not understand how the members of a nation that was fighting its ultimate battle for survival could care more about Arabs than about their own kind. Many in the movement subsequently denounced him, charging that he was insensitive to the fate of the Bedouin refugees.[55] The government sought to defuse the protest by gaining the consent of the evacuees to resettle them in another location, but when no agreement was reached, the protests continued. Hazan declared that the protests were detrimental to the Bedouin's cause.[56] He later even expressed doubt whether there was any truth to the claim that the Bedouin had been deprived of their land and homes.[57] Ya'ari also condemned the angry young people who had organized the protests. When one of the activists appeared at a meeting of Mapam's Rikuz, its highest forum, and argued that not enough had been done for the Bedouin, Ya'ari responded angrily that he was wrong.[58] Hazan and Ya'ari were able to stymie an initiative by Hakibbutz Ha'artzi's Youth Division to organize a gathering of representatives of the Bedouin who had been affected by the expropriation.[59] The two historic leaders of the movement ranged themselves against the left-wing faction for reasons of principle, but there were also political considerations. The "right-wing" old guard no longer dominated Hakibbutz Ha'artzi and Mapam. The radical New Left young guard, inspired by the democratic zeitgeist, constituted a real threat to the movement and party leadership.

In the meantime, the country was rocked by another controversy. In April 1972, a group of Arab citizens of Israel who had been evacuated from two Galilean villages, Ikrit and Biram, during the War of Independence submitted a petition to Prime Minister Meir, demanding to be allowed to return to their villages. Although they were hardly the only Arabs who had been displaced during the war, their case was unique because the two villages had been inhabited by Christian Arabs who had consented in 1948 to a request made by the minister of defense, in accordance with a Supreme Court injunction, that they move out of their homes for a two-week period. They were promised that they would be allowed to return. When the two weeks expired, the government did not honor the agreement and prevented the Arabs from returning, despite the fact that there was no apparent military reason for not allowing them to do so. The cabinet once again turned down the villagers' request to return. It took up the issue once again in July 1972 in response to pressure from Rakah but again voted to reject the request. "Ikrit and Biram are a dangerous precedent," Prime Minister Meir declared, arguing that other Arabs who had been expelled from their homes during the War of Independence would also demand the right to return to their original villages—the sites of which were now in many cases occupied by Israeli kibbutzim, moshavim, and towns.[60]

That same month demonstrations in support of the villagers were staged in front of the Knesset building, and rallies were held at the villages. The campaign won much sympathy from part of the Israeli public and especially in Hakibbutz Ha'artzi. This support was a complex matter because 350 of the 12,000 dunams (3,000 acres) of Biram farmland had been given to Kibbutz Baram of Hakibbutz Ha'artzi, founded in 1949. Nevertheless, the leadership of the kibbutz movement and Mapam supported the evacuees. In opposition to the government position, the Mapam cabinet ministers voted in favor of allowing them to return, but that vote was not enough action for the party's democratic faction.[61] The young guard vociferously insisted that the struggle had to continue, and so they organized vigils, demonstrations, and rallies. Mapam waged a parliamentary battle as well—it demanded that the Israeli cabinet reconsider its position. The issue rose to the top of the agenda of the party secretariat. As a result of Mapam's campaign, the Knesset took up the issue. But the draft law to allow the villagers to return was voted down.

As far as Mapam's leaders were concerned, they had done all they could. Ya'ari said that he did not want to open up the subject again,[62] but the party's activists in the field refused to let the subject die. Worried that the young guard was growing ever more extreme, the Rikuz decided to shut it down. Rikuz members resolved to prevent a protest rally slated to take place at the Tzavta club in Tel Aviv or at least to block the organizers' intention of inviting the Maronite bishop who represented the villages to participate in the rally. In the end, the rally was held at Tzavta Jerusalem—but outside, in the yard, because the protesters were not allowed to enter the building.[63] A few months later the young guard issued a notice about a rally in support of the evacuees. The Rikuz cited them on a disciplinary violation and discussed whether to oust Latif Dori, the coordinator of the young guard, from his position because of his refusal to obey the party leadership's dictates. "I cannot accept that we have a person around here who assumes autonomy for himself and flouts the party," Ya'ari declared. "We have a problem with an opposition, and we cannot ignore that."[64] But the leadership had no way of imposing its will, and Dori remained in his post. But just when the protest over Ikrit and Biram was at its height, a new controversy broke out over the spraying of Akraba's farmland.

Akraba is located near Nablus; in 1972, it had a population of about 3,000. After the Six-Day War, the IDF declared some of the Akraba farmland, which lay close to the border between the West Bank and Israel (the Green Line), a closed military area. The army fenced off the land and prevented the villagers from entering and cultivating it but offered them no compensation. In January 1972, the army sought to expand the closed area and offered the villagers compensation for the additional land to be confiscated. The villagers refused; the army seized the area anyway. At the beginning of April, the military governor announced that the crops in this newly confiscated area would be destroyed, and a few days later the land was sprayed with herbicides. The villagers were informed that a Jewish settlement would be built on the confiscated land. Akraba's *mukhtar* (village leader) told Eliezer Be'eri of Kibbutz Hazorea, who headed Mapam's Arab Department, how angry the villagers were. Be'eri contacted Defense Minister Dayan, who informed him that the IDF officers involved in the decision had erred in their judgment. Prime Minister Meir also acknowledged that "there were painful irregularities" in the affair.[65] In the months that followed, Israelis, a large proportion of them from Hakibbutz Ha'artzi kibbutzim, protested the army's action. When protestors staged a demonstration near the village without receiving permission from the military government, five of them were arrested, among them a member of Kibbutz Gan Shmuel. A few weeks later kibbutz and Siah members staged another unauthorized demonstration in the same location.[66] The campaign did not succeed. Two Jewish settlements, Gitit and Mekhora, were erected on the confiscated land, which only intensified the protest movement.[67]

In the meantime, another sign of the increasing potency of the democratic orientation (in the labor movement as a whole) and the growing dissension between it and the labor-movement establishment was the rise of the radical faction Yesh (There Is), which in 1972 ran a slate in the University of Haifa's Student Association elections. Yesh was an alliance of a number of left-wing groups, unmistakably part of the democratic protest movement, which cooperated with the campus's Arab Student Association. A number of its activists were new immigrants who brought with them the attitudes and practices of the New Left from North America and Latin America. It was highly critical of both the university administration and the national government. One of its innovations was a feminist caucus; another was an alliance of students and faculty members who called for structural reforms at the university; a third was the formation of a "free university" aimed at fostering critical thinking and active involvement in solving social problems. Yesh met hostility from the university administration, the national media, and the large-party organizations both because of its radical politics and anxiety about the rise of a broader student protest movement.[68] Israeli students tended not to get involved in politics, but in 1972 students and university administrations clashed over tuition and the curriculum, which led to a national student strike.[69] Yesh fought back against attempts by the university and opposing factions to prevent it from running in the student elections and ended up winning by a landslide, soundly defeating student factions associated with the large national parties. Following this triumph, the faction joined forces with Tehelet Adom, reinforcing the democratic protest movement's influence over Israelis who had broken away from the labor movement. In response, in 1973 the Labor Party made the unusual decision of forming a pact with the right-wing faction Gahal (Gush Herut-Liberalim, or Herut-Liberals Bloc), the alliance of Menahem Begin's right-wing party Herut and the free-market party Miflega Libralit Yisraelit (Liberal Party), to end Yesh's control of the student association and to contest the student elections the following year. At the end of 1973, Yesh fell apart.[70]

Members of Hakibbutz Ha'artzi and, to a somewhat lesser extent, the other kibbutz organizations were prominent in all these protest movements. That involvement was a direct result of socioeconomic developments in the kibbutzim as well as in the cities, from which the rest of the democratic orientation's activists came. Israel's increasingly affluent society provided people, young people in particular, with free time as well as public and private transportation; the expansion of the university system created a larger student body, and these students, many of whom had their tuition, room, and board expenses covered by their parents or by kibbutzim, were able to devote time to public causes. New young faculty members, many of whom had studied overseas and absorbed radical ideas there, helped create an atmosphere of lively debate on campus and challenged accepted ideas about Israel's society, history, and the Arab world. Students who had grown up reading party and movement newspapers and journals such as *Al Hamishmar* and *Davar* were exposed to other publications. These young people thus had far more freedom to think and act than had been available in the kibbutzim and in the country as a whole up until the mid-1960s. Kibbutz members who were interested in these issues enjoyed a much freer flow of information and could travel and participate in whatever demonstrations they wanted. More sophisticated communications (telephones did not enter Israeli homes until the beginning of the 1970s) made it much easier to plan protest activities. As a result, Hakibbutz Ha'artzi and Mapam organizations lost much of the power they had previously enjoyed to impose discipline on their radical members. In the contention between the protestors on the one hand and the movement and party establishment on the other, the latter lost. The leadership was caught by surprise by the boldness and audacity of the young militants, who, in the spirit of the times, no longer had much respect for the established leadership. The combination of New Left ideas and the situation in Israel at the beginning of the 1970s fueled a political and cultural brushfire. The young generation at the kibbutzim as well as elsewhere in the labor movement broke free of the consensus and turned against the political and social framework within which it had grown up.

The Yom Kippur War of 1973 was another watershed in the rise of the democratic critique. It ignited a public debate over why Israel's political and military leadership had not anticipated and prepared for it better and why the country's losses had been so high. Citizens asked why Israel's position had been so dire during the war's initial stages. At the beginning of 1974, Motti Ashkenazi, a reserve officer who had fought in the war and seen close up just how unprepared the IDF had been, staged a one-man vigil in front of the prime minister's office in Jerusalem. He was soon joined by tens of thousands of others. Ashkenazi and his fellow protestors demanded that Prime Minister Meir and Defense Minister Dayan accept ministerial responsibility for the war and resign. At the beginning of April, the Agranat Commission, set up to conduct an inquiry into the war, released its interim report. The commission cleared the political leadership of responsibility and placed all of the blame on the IDF command. The protestors were infuriated. Soon afterward Meir resigned and was replaced by Yitzhak Rabin.

Ashkenazi had focused on toppling the government, and a variety of organizations and a variegated public joined the protest movement he led. The demonstrators protested more than just the war. They also spoke of the "nature of democracy."[71] Ashkenazi felt that the government was treating individual citizens unjustly because of a "culture of lies" that had infected the Israeli establishment. "For decades the historic Mapai leadership, the leading political elite, has ignored public opinion and the acute problems of developing Israeli society," he charged.[72] He was particularly affected by a meeting he had had with Dayan when his vigil had just begun. Dayan had given Ashkenazi the impression that the leadership was not prepared to listen to the people. Meir also declared that "the street will not dictate the [government's] actions." In response, Ashkenazi intensified his protest.[73] He declared that his movement was a continuation of prewar movements that had protested the government's insensitivity toward, for example, Shurat Hamitnadvim, the Wadi Salib rebels (addressed later), and the Black Panthers. In essence, Ashkenazi was an incarnation of the democratic axis. He declared that he represented a large public that was fed up with the establishment. Israel, he maintained, needed to address phenomena and processes that were unconnected to the war and that needed to be analyzed as part of a long-term project of rectifying relations between the citizens and the government.[74]

After the Yom Kippur War, the democratic struggle continued to address the occupation and hopes for peace. In December 1973, more than 10,000 Israelis signed a petition, organized by several university faculty members, calling for "peace now."[75] At the end of July 1974, a large national demonstration was held to protest the building of Israeli settlements in the territories.[76] At the end of October, the secretaries of the three kibbutz movements held a joint press conference to condemn the settlements.[77] In February 1975, Hava'ad le-Shalom Tzodek bein Israel ve-ha-Shchenot ha-Araviot (Committee for a Just Peace between Israel and Its Arab Neighbors) held a seminar where current and past members of Mapam's left wing lectured on the Palestinian problem.[78] In December 1975, an antisettlement demonstration was staged outside the Shikmim Farm, the home of Ariel Sharon, then an adviser on military affairs to Prime Minister Rabin and a promoter of the settlement project.[79] Early in January 1976, the Mapam and Hakibbutz Ha'artzi young guard staged a protest in front of the Knesset building against the construction of a settlement at Sebastia.[80] At the end of that month, they also distributed flyers against Gush Emunim (Bloc of the Faithful), an organization that promoted the settlement enterprise and opposed returning any of the territories captured in 1967.[81] The debacle of the Yom Kippur War reinforced the democratic opposition to the Israeli establishment. Three wars in six years had brought much of the Israeli public to the brink of despair. The occupation and the crisis in the labor movement turned the democratic trend in a more radical direction. Although most of those involved in the protest movements considered themselves Zionists, they were highly critical of the labor movement, the government, and Israeli society as a whole. A large part of the radical Zionist Left was connected to one or another branch of Hashomer Hatza'ir youth movement, Hakibbutz Ha'artzi, and Mapam, but it had representatives also in other parts of the labor movement, especially young members who had been influenced by the zeitgeist and the New Left. Left-wing radicalism ostensibly ran counter to the sectoralism that had emerged alongside it, but the two phenomena shared common roots in the postmaterial era of the labor movement. Each represented a different way that the public responded to changes in their living conditions.

The Underprivileged: The Second Israel versus the Labor Movement

Another reason for the decline in support for the parties of the labor movement was their steady and ongoing loss of working-class voters, especially those of North African and Asian origin. During the 1950s, most of these citizens cast their votes for Mapai, with much smaller numbers preferring Ahdut Ha'avodah and even fewer Mapam. They cast their votes both in the hope of gaining perquisites and preferences and because they felt ideological sympathy for Ben-Gurion and respected the prestige of the pioneering movements. By the end of the 1950s, however, many Mizrahim were losing faith with the labor movement, a loss of faith expressed in what the literature calls the "rebellion at the polls." Many of these voters migrated to the parties of the Right and the alliance of those parties that eventually became Likud. Studies of this phenomenon have generally seen this voter migration as a manifestation of identity politics, with voters who felt discriminated against because of their origins moving to a party that enabled them to take pride in their ethnic identity.[82] But it was not only identity that caused these voters to grow disappointed with the labor movement, and making identity a central explanation obscures some important facts. First, the labor movement initially welcomed Mizrahi voters. There was initially no conflict between the party and this community; the two only later grew estranged. Second, most of those who abandoned the labor parties were voters who lay outside the circle that received advantages and benefits through their association with the movement. Their economic weakness in comparison with the new middle class created by the party apparatuses was a significant factor in the social unrest directed at the labor movement. Third, Mapai was not the only party that lost working-class Mizrahi voters. So did Ahdut Ha'avodah and Mapam, both of which were opposition parties during part of this period and had different ideological identities. That the economic inequality that prevailed under labor-movement rule ran along ethnic lines is beyond doubt. The debate is not over the existence of inequality but rather over what caused it. As I have shown, to a large extent this economic disparity was a product of political inequality and was built in to the model of the mass party adopted by all the labor-movement political groupings. The economic plight of the Mizrahim resulted from restricted access to the labor movement's centers of political power. The people who were left out—ironically making up the bulk of the working class as veteran Ashkenazi workers moved up into the new middle class that the party machines created—thus directed their grievances at the labor movement and gradually switched their support to the Right.

Although Mapam, as an elitist kibbutz party, attracted relatively few Mizrahi supporters compared to the much more inclusive Mapai, looking at it in particular can nevertheless offer insights into how the labor movement lost such working-class voters. In the country's early years, the party enjoyed a certain amount of support from this demographic. In 1956, a survey carried out in Mapam's urban branches showed that although most of their members were veteran Israelis of Ashkenazi origin, the party enjoyed not inconsiderable support from immigrants, Mizrahim, and working-class citizens.[83] About a quarter of the party's urban members were day laborers without fixed jobs. These people were employed largely in government make-work jobs at a low salary, and a solid majority of them were Mizrahim. But a report written in the wake of the survey shows that despite the fact that these economically weak voters were sympathetic to Mapam, the party did not do much to keep them. The secretariat termed its work among them "dismal." The urban branches were dependent largely on the kibbutzim for manpower to run their operations; the party did not manage to create a cadre of activists in the cities. The urban branches complained that the party did not give them the budgets they needed. Sometimes they claimed that the branches were essentially dormant except at election time.[84] The situation was similar in Ahdut Ha'avodah.[85]

From the mid-1950s on, as I have shown, distance from the sources of political power became a source of economic inequality. It in effect divided Mapam's supporters into two groups—one, comprising the members of Hakibbutz Ha'artzi, that received the economic privileges that came with political power and another consisting of all the party's other sympathizers and voters, both those who were party members and those who were not. (Because the pioneering parties were small, they could offer only a small number of jobs in the party organization and a few in the Histadrut and government, given that the latter were largely the preserve of Mapai; as such, party membership did not in and of itself bring any economic advantages.) Although Mapam was in theory supposed to fight inequality in the government sector, it was largely paralyzed politically because of its internal conflicts. As a result, it did not fulfill its class mission. Mapai and Ahdut Ha'avodah also had supporters who lay outside the circle of political power, but these supporters were also largely neglected for the same reasons. The parties fostered their inner circles (party members in Mapai's case, kibbutz members in Ahdut Ha'avodah's case), in keeping with the mass-party concentric structure. The resulting inequality was ethnically skewed, a fact that aroused the ire of Mizrahi immigrants, which broke out in protest movements.

The roots of the economic and social protest movement were evident as early as 1950, sparked by the unequal manner in which the labor movement apportioned its benefits. In that year, unrest swept through the immigrant camps where many Mizrahim had been settled after arriving in the country. Two years later riots broke out, first in the Emek Hefer camp. Symbolically, the match that ignited the protests that year was friction between the Emek Hefer camp and nearby kibbutzim. The immigrants were in great distress and lacked sufficient food. Some of them stole crops from the fields of the nearby kibbutzim, so the kibbutzim stationed guards in the fields. One day a guard apprehended a woman from the camp who was picking oranges. She was hurt when he set his dog on her. A few days later her son, a soldier, and some of his friends took revenge by beating up the guard. Police came to the camp to search for the avengers and were attacked, after which they fled. They called in reinforcements, and when the reinforcements arrived and entered the camp, a riot broke out. It took hundreds of police officers applying severe force to quell the disturbance.[86]

The economic surge that began in the mid-1950s improved the lives of the entire population and made it possible for the government to dismantle the immigrant camps and move their inhabitants into permanent housing in newly built urban neighborhoods, development towns, and farming villages (moshavim). Yet growth also exacerbated inequality. As the economy expanded, immigrants, mostly of Mizrahi origin, moved into skilled and unskilled labor positions once occupied by the veteran, mostly Ashkenazi working class, while the latter moved up into managerial, government, and white-collar jobs. During the years of scarcity, the difference between the poor and the better-off had been narrow; no one had much of anything. The boom created a much greater range of possibilities, significantly differentiating the life of the emerging new middle class from that of unskilled and semiskilled workers. The underclass grew ever more resentful of this lifestyle gap. Unrest among Mizrahi immigrants soared between 1956 and 1958, with protests and riots breaking out all over the country.[87] In parallel, election results began to show that these voters were abandoning Mapai. In the national election of the summer of 1955, support for Mapai in the immigrant camps plunged to half of its former level, with many of these disappointed voters turning to Menachem Begin's party Herut.[88]

Mizrahi discontent grew in tandem with the widening income and lifestyle gap. In 1959, it broke out in the worst disturbances the country had seen since independence. Although the protest grew mainly out of economic and social grievances, it bore a salient ethnic profile. The focal point was the Wadi Salib neighborhood in the lower, old part of Haifa, not far from the port. During the war in 1948, the Arabs who lived there left the neighborhood and then were replaced by North African immigrants, who were settled in the formerly Arab homes during the 1950s. Unemployment was high, and the quality of the housing and infrastructure low, so the usual consequences were not long in following—delinquency, crime, and prostitution. In July 1959, a fight broke out at a café. Police arrived; during the subsequent altercation a drunken customer went berserk, and the police shot and seriously wounded him. A rumor that the police had killed a man quickly spread through the neighborhood. Angry residents attacked nearby Mapai and Histadrut offices and then began to march up toward the middle-class neighborhoods on the slopes of Mt. Carmel. They threw stones, burned tires, shattered windows, and blocked roads. In attempting to quell the riots, the police wounded and arrested dozens of protestors. Over the next few days, the riots spread to other towns and urban neighborhoods inhabited by Mizrahim, such as Migdal Ha'emek, Be'ersheva, and Tiberias.[89]

A national election was held four months after the riots, in November 1959, and Mapai made an impressive showing, winning forty-seven seats in the Knesset, a significant gain from the forty garnered in the previous election. But the main reason for this upwelling of support for the ruling party was the return of David Ben-Gurion to the party leadership and prime minister's seat instead of the less popular and much less charismatic Moshe Sharett, who had led the party in the previous election. The Mapai campaign had coupled the prestige of Ben-Gurion, the "old man," with the popularity of a number of young and popular figures. The most prominent was Moshe Dayan, a former IDF chief of staff who had led the army in the Sinai Campaign of 1956. Ahdut Ha'avodah lost three seats, however, largely owing to a sharp decline in support of it in Mizrahi neighborhoods.

Mizrahi activists in this party reported that their public was losing faith in the party and that many complained that Ahdut Ha'avodah treated immigrants paternalistically.[90]

The next elections were held in 1965. The labor-movement parties lost support in the development towns, and many of these votes went to the Right and improved its showing. This was the first election contested by Gahal, the alliance of Herut and the free-market Liberal Party that would later become Likud. A similar trend was evident in the housing projects on the margins of the big cities as well as in the *moshavot*, farming villages that had urbanized after immigrants were settled there. For the first time, the parties composing Gahal actually received more votes in some of these places than labor-movement parties.[91] When the country sank into recession the following year, disillusionment with the labor movement mushroomed. Protests staged by unemployed workers broke out in April, and the traditional May Day parade in two development towns, Ashdod and Dimona, turned into riots by recently laid-off workers, who burned the Histadrut's red flag. Similar incidents became increasingly frequent throughout the country.[92]

The labor-movement parties' urban adherents were well aware of the loss of support for the parties among the working class, especially Mizrahim. At the beginning of 1960s, some Ahdut Ha'avodah Mizrahi urban activists tried to gain more power within the party, but the party's triumvirate, Yisrael Galili, Yigal Allon, and Yitzhak Ben-Aharon, quashed the initiative. By this point, the party had only a handful of working-class members, who did their best to preserve something of its working-class character.[93] In 1966, these activists clashed with Allon, who was minister of labor, over the government's recessionary policy. Among other things, they opposed a law Allon was promoting that would have instituted a cooling-off period before workers could go out on strike. The law, the urban members claimed, ran counter to the Ahdut Ha'avodah Party's socialist principles.[94] As the party set aside its socialist ideals, working-class voters abandoned it, and its support base in the cities was reduced to some white-collar workers and Histadrut members.

Mapam had a similar experience. Between the mid-1950s and mid-1960s, its larger circle of urban supporters virtually disappeared. Each city branch office had a list of thousands of "sympathizers," meaning people who had voted for the party but were not members, yet these people were gradually moving elsewhere. "Where are the party's supporters from the card file? Why don't they appear at branch meetings?" asked Zalman Livneh of Kibbutz Ein Hashofet, coordinator of Mapam's Haifa operations in 1967.[95] From his list of 20,000 "sympathizers," he could turn out only a few hundred for meetings. In 1975, the secretary of the party's Jerusalem branch, Avraham Koblanov, complained that the count of hundreds of sympathizers on the rosters was a fabrication. The party branches actually had no members, he said. "The branch council is clearly a fiction. There are seventy-five members. Who has seen them?"[96] A party report found that "no Mizrahim" came to the party's May Day demonstration in 1967.[97] The Labor Party's disengagement from its proletarian identity was an established fact. The term *socialism* was not even mentioned at the party's founding congress in 1968.[98]

Mapam's leaders felt helpless and confused by their failure to make inroads among working-class voters. In 1958, Ya'akov Vilan, coordinator of Mapam's Trades Department, searched for a way for the party to recruit urban supporters. He said that in factories he encountered many workers who had warm feelings about the movement because they had once worked at kibbutzim, but the only idea he could come up with to enlist their political support was to organize them into work details to help out on kibbutzim during the intensive seasons.[99] At the beginning of the 1960s, the proposal for a regional commune composed of kibbutzim in the South included a provision about employing workers from the nearby development towns, but it was rejected. Vilan's successor as head of the Trades Department, Naftali Ben-Moshe, submitted an incisive report to the party leadership in 1963. He argued that Mapam was not taking advantage of its potential among the working class and that it was deliberately missing the opportunity to gain their support.[100]

Mapam's lack of investment in its urban branches was in part a result of friction between the kibbutzim, which operated as independent economic entities with sectoral interests, and the requirements of the party, which needed people for ideological activity that went beyond the kibbutzim's direct short-term interests. The kibbutzim were not eager to send funds and members to support the party's urban activities. Some party branches were paralyzed, even during periods when they were active, because of the lack of a kibbutz member prepared to lead them.[101] The party could not enlist enough volunteers to run even the most important urban branches, such as the one in Tel Aviv.[102] The tension between the kibbutzim's needs and party activism came up, for example, when urban activists sought to circumvent the party machinery that had neglected them. They contacted the kibbutzim directly, asking for contributions to set up a branch office in Wadi Salib. The goal was to enlist support for Mapam from the residents of the neighborhood, who were suffering from the recession. Most of the kibbutzim disregarded the request, while others complained to the party leadership and asked that it put an end to the solicitations. This case clearly showed the disparate orientations within the party.[103]

Mizrahi agitation against the labor movement grew after the Six-Day War. In the midst of the prosperity that followed the war, pockets of inequality were still quite evident. In 1971, riots again broke out over economic discrimination of an ethnic cast. The flames flared up this time in Jerusalem's Musrara neighborhood, which before the war had stood on the uneasy cease-fire line that separated Jewish and Arab Jerusalem and lay adjacent to the city's downtown. After independence, the neighborhood had filled up with immigrants, most of them from the Islamic world. They suffered from overcrowding, unemployment, inferior housing and infrastructure, and all the social ills that plague poor neighborhoods. The motivation for the riots there was much the same as in Wadi Salib, where the Mizrahim had resented the better-off residents of the Carmel neighborhoods. The residents of Musrara were angry that other neighborhoods in the city were thriving, in part thanks to state and municipal investment in them, while their own neighborhood remained neglected and poor.[104] In the early days of March 1971, young people in the neighborhood began to organize to demand "equalization of conditions." The immediate catalyst for this organizing came from outside in the form of encouragement provided by street counselors that the Jerusalem municipality had sent into the neighborhood as well as by radical-left activists. The timing of this protest was important because with the end of the War of Attrition in 1970 the Israeli public was able to turn its attention to other issues.

Left-wing activists helped the young people organize a protest movement in the spirit of the New Left. In May 1971, the neighborhood activists, who called themselves Ha-Panterim ha-Shchorim, the Black Panthers, set up their first demonstration. Several thousand people took part. They staged an even larger demonstration in July and yet another in August, the latter ending in violent clashes with the police, who put down the disturbance forcefully. The facts that the demonstrations took place in the center of Jerusalem, shutting down the country's political center for hours at a time, and that the police response was harsh encouraged the activists and turned their movement from a local to a national one. Black Panthers demonstrated across the country and made newspaper headlines.[105]

The Black Panthers voiced the anger, despair, and disappointment with the state felt by members of the Mizrahi second generation, who had not experienced significant social mobility during Israel's years of prosperity. They aimed their resentment at the labor movement and switched their votes to the Right. In the national elections of 1969, 30 percent of Mizrahim voted for Gahal. In 1973, Likud—formed when Gahal allied with a few smaller political parties—received 50 percent of the Mizrahi vote. (The smaller parties that allied with Gahal included a faction of former Mapai activists and Ben-Gurion loyalists as well as Ha-Tnua le-Eretz Israel ha-Shlema [Movement for a Greater Israel], which opposed any compromise on the territories Israel had occupied in the Six-Day War.) In 1977, Likud's support among Mizrahim zoomed to 70 percent.[106] At the same time, the power of the labor-movement parties declined. In 1969, all the labor parties ran together on the Alignment slate and won 56 out of 120 seats in the Knesset. In 1973, that number declined to 51 seats, and in 1977 it plunged to just 32 seats. The same trend was evident in elections to the Histadrut. In 1959, Mapai, Ahdut Ha'avodah, and Mapam together received 87 percent of the vote; in 1965, when Gahal ran a slate for the Histadrut for the first time, support for the labor parties declined to 77 percent, then to 62 percent in 1973. In 1977, only 57 percent of the members of the Histadrut voted for the Alignment slate.[107]

8

The Rebellion Within

Cracks in the Hegemony

THE LABOR-MOVEMENT establishment found itself under attack from multiple directions—from the new middle class with its sectoral interests, from radical-democratic ideology that emphasized human rights and equality, and from those ethnic and socioeconomic groups that had been left behind as Israel achieved prosperity. These three dissenting groups leveled different critiques of the movement and called for different sets of reforms, but they all were united by opposition to the existing apparatus. Under their attack on the existing political order, the labor hegemony cracked. These groups were part of the larger zeitgeist, a phenomena much broader than the dissenting factions, parties, and protest movements themselves. They all had emerged in one form or another from the grass roots of the labor movement itself and now cooperated to topple it.

Mapam and Hakibbutz Ha'artzi were microcosms of this larger phenomenon. In them, the first stirrings of it could be seen in a move to change the rules for electing the kibbutz movement's Executive Committee, its most important governing institution. The issue first came up for debate at a meeting of the movement's council in 1958, after many years of submissive obedience to the leadership. The delegates debated two proposals for changing the way in which the Executive Committee's members were chosen. Up to this point, they had been elected by the party's council from a list of candidates composed by a committee controlled by the leadership. One proposal stipulated that the Executive Committee would be chosen by the council, while the other mandated that the council would continue to elect some of the committee's members, but the others would be chosen through a mechanism that gave kibbutz members a role. The second proposal was accepted. It was a major victory for the kibbutzim over the leadership.[1] The selection of the Executive Committee members came before the council once again in 1964, and again the kibbutzim demonstrated that they had the upper hand. Although the council this time agreed to change the balance in favor of the leadership, it did not undo the vote of 1958.[2]

Another significant milestone in the decline of the traditional leadership's power came in 1965 as Mapam prepared itself for the national elections that year. A new method of choosing the party's slate of candidates was put into effect. Previously, a nominating committee directed by Hazan and Ya'ari had proposed a slate of candidates, which was then voted up or down *en bloc* by the party Central Committee (needless to say, the slate was always approved). Under the new method, the nominating committee would propose twenty candidates, and the Central Committee would add seven candidates of its own. The first two places on the slate would be reserved for Hazan and Ya'ari (who would be officially approved in a public vote), but the rest would then be chosen by secret ballot. Up to this point, the two senior leaders had held unchallenged power over such decisions; now, clearly, their power had waned.

After the Six-Day War, internal opposition to the traditional leadership grew even stronger. The opposition now had a clearly defined, if not formal, leadership, which made it more effective.[3] The war had unleashed sharp dissent among the residents of the kibbutzim and other members of Mapam over political and foreign-policy questions, in particular over the issue of the future of the Occupied Territories. Nevertheless, both sides to this debate united in their opposition to the historic leadership. In advance of Hakibbutz Ha'artzi's Eleventh Congress, held in February 1969, young members of the nominating committee secretly agreed to mark the ballots of all young candidates for the Executive Committee so that their peers would know who to vote for. The gambit was a success—all the young candidates on the national slate were elected, and together with young candidates among the kibbutz representatives the young guard captured 70 of the 175 seats on the Executive Committee, giving it 40 percent of its seats, doubling its strength. Many members of the party's senior leadership, loyalists of Ya'ari and Hazan, found themselves ousted from this top body. This young people's rebellion made a huge impression and was trumpeted by the Israeli media.[4]

Another harbinger of the decline of the traditional leadership was the election in July 1970 of Naftali Ben-Moshe to the post of secretary of Mapam's Central Committee over the objections of the historic leadership. Ben-Moshe, a field operative of Mapam's urban wing, had served for several years and with much success as coordinator of the party's Trades Department, but the historic leadership did not want to see him promoted because he was not among the leaders' supporters. Ya'ari and Hazan ran a candidate of their own against him. Nevertheless, the Central Committee chose Ben-Moshe by a vote of sixty to forty, with the opponents of the establishment bridging over their ideological differences to defeat the traditional leadership.[5]

Criticism of the historic leadership increased with the approach of Mapam's Sixth Congress in 1972. Ya'ari, who was seventy-four years old, and Hazan, who was seventy-two, had headed Hakibbutz Ha'artzi for forty-five years; their disciples in the traditional leadership were not that much younger. The generation gap between them and the young guard was huge, and the young guard focused its attack on the two elders. Ya'ari had been a target of the young guard since the early 1960s, but in the summer of 1971 the attacks on him in the movement press intensified. They accused him of acting like a dictator whose major concern was staying in power. His behavior, they charged, had damaged the party and had pushed it into the margins of Israeli politics. For the first time ever, the dissenters explicitly demanded that Ya'ari be relieved of his post as secretary-general and leader of Mapam.[6] In October 1971, Ya'ari told internal party forums that he would not seek another term as party leader, blaming the vilification he had been subject to in the kibbutz movement and party press.[7] He remained in office for another year, however, resigning prior to the party congress, declaring that he was not willing to continue to work for the party when he was being undermined within Hakibbutz Ha'artzi.[8]

The next stage in the collapse of the established leadership came as the party prepared for the national election of October 1973. At a meeting of Hakibbutz Ha'artzi's council in October 1972, young kibbutz members proposed for the first time that Mapam should no longer enjoy a special and exclusive status in Hakibbutz Ha'artzi, as it had in accordance with the principle of ideological collectivism. Other parties should be allowed to campaign at the kibbutzim. The proposal was voted down by a wide margin, but the very fact that it was tabled and the notion that all members of Hakibbutz Ha'artzi should not have to belong to the same political framework were an innovation. In practice, ideological collectivism no longer existed, and everyone knew it; the proposal simply pointed out that the emperor had no clothes—the historic leadership was no longer able to impose its will on the movement's members. The fact was that, despite the refusal to sanction the activities of other parties at the kibbutzim, many kibbutz members had long since stopped supporting Mapam—in the 1970s close to 20 percent of the members of Hakibbutz Ha'artzi kibbutzim voted for other parties.[9] At the same council meeting, the young guard sought again to end the block vote by which two-thirds of the delegates to the council were elected. The block vote enabled the historic leadership to control the membership of the council and thus to determine its decisions in that the slate presented for the vote was outlined by a nominating committee that was itself chosen by the Mapam Secretariat, a body that Ya'ari and Hazan held sway over. Hazan confronted the sponsors of the proposal and succeeded in defeating it—but only after a difficult battle.[10]

Ya'ari and Hazan's long reign reached an end in September 1973. The Mapam Central Committee met then to choose the slate it would run (as part of the Alignment) in the national election scheduled for the following month, and for the first time since independence Hazan and Ya'ari were not included. Although the two elders ostensibly retired of their own volition, they had actually been forced out. Mapam's secretary-general Meir Talmi declared that, unlike ever before, the two would have to face the same secret ballot by which all the other candidates were chosen. The decline in the historic leaders' power and the demands that they be replaced had reached the point that they were to be treated like everyone else. Hazan decided not to run for a Knesset seat, and Ya'ari, who had intended to, realized that if he ran without Hazan, he was liable to suffer a humiliating defeat.[11] This shift did not end their public careers. As the "last of the Mohicans" in the movement's founding generation in Israel, they continued to serve in the Mapam and Hakibbutz Ha'artzi leadership, but with much limited power.

Ya'ari and Hazan were not the only traditional leaders to be eased out at this time. Both David Ben-Gurion and Yitzhak Tabenkin reached the end of their roads during these years and not of their own volition.[12] They lost the last shreds of their formal power and became expendable to the parties they had founded, Mapai and Rafi in Ben-Gurion's case and Ahdut Ha'avodah in Tabenkin's. Their attempts to hold on to power showed that they did not understand the changes that had taken place around them and that they were also unable to refashion themselves to suit these new conditions. Beyond their advanced age, they were the victims of a phenomenon common to many socialist movements in the late capitalist age, which also underwent generational transformations.[13] The exit of such historic leaders and the accession of a younger leadership were among the roots of the labor movement's decline.

9

The Leadership's Response

Revolutionary Conservatism

THE LEADERSHIPS of the different components of the labor movement found themselves in defensive mode against ongoing attacks on their authority. As I have shown, that rebellion was a product of the improving economic and social position of Israelis who had been part of the labor camp. The leadership's defensive campaign thus had a conservative cast—they sought to hold back or reverse the new affluence or at least to mitigate its impact. Paradoxically, however, the prosperity they feared would turn the hearts and minds of their erstwhile supporters against them had resulted from the efficient operation of the movement machines they themselves had led. They were thus in a bind. They could not halt the new affluence; at most, they could regulate it. The leaders' defensive posture was a response to this general threat; they responded in different ways, according to the different directions from which the threat to their authority came—sectoral interests, democratic agitation, and demands from the working class.

The leadership first took on the sectoral interests of the professional part of the new middle class when members of this group demanded differential salaries at a level that reflected their professional qualifications. The Mapai leadership, addressing these demands via the Histadrut Executive Committee, offered a variety of arguments—economic, security, and moral—for refusing and maintaining the egalitarian pay scales then in force, with partial success.[1] The government, worried that the full employment that prosperity brought with it was creating severe upward pressure on wages, decided on drastic measures. It deliberately induced a recession meant to cool down the economy. Although it did not say so publicly, the thinking was that the recession would cause unemployment and that unemployment would put an end to demands for higher wages. The government was aware, however, that the brunt of the recession and its consequent loss of jobs would hit the working class, not the professionals whose wage demands it sought to counter.[2] In March 1966, Minister of Labor Yigal Allon also proposed a law to restrict the right to strike because strikes were the most powerful means the professional and white-collar sector had to assert its demands. The provisions required a cooling-off period before a strike could begin, classified work slowdowns as strikes, granted legal force to collective-bargaining agreements, and set up a system of labor courts. The law came into effect in 1968.

Sectoral interests were clearly evident in the kibbutzim and worried the leaderships of the kibbutz movements. As early as the beginning of the 1950s, the leaderships of all three kibbutz movements found themselves contending with kibbutz members' desire to raise their standards of living, following long years of self-denial and sacrifice. But once the kibbutzim began to flourish at the end of the 1950s, kibbutz members were able to do just that, no matter what the leadership said. Trying to preserve what they saw as the traditional kibbutz way of life, the leaders then fought a rearguard crusade against the "harmful" influence of material prosperity. Their campaign took the form of detailed sets of bylaws governing what forms of individual consumption were permitted and what forms were forbidden, imbuing appliances such as electric kettles and refrigerators with almost demonic powers.[3] The anxiety aroused by such devices grew out of the assumption that allowing them into the homes of kibbutz members would fundamentally change kibbutz society. They were right.

The leaders of Hakibbutz Ha'artzi also took exception to industrialization on the grounds that it would have deleterious social effects. When they realized that the kibbutzim could not survive without factories and that kibbutzim were taking their own initiative in establishing them, the leaders tried to lay out strict rules to govern and regulate the process.[4] They instituted strictures against private capital, competition between the movement's kibbutzim, an egalitarian organizational structure providing for nonhierarchical relations between workers and managers, the subordination of industrial norms to kibbutz principles, as well as other measures intended to channel the industrialization process and keep kibbutz society from changing.[5] The principal measure used by the movement leaders to regulate factories was the limitation on the number of outside wage laborers, which they justified on ideological grounds. Indeed, whenever the leaders tried to slow down industrialization, they invoked the claim that the expansion of hired labor that would inevitably be required would threaten, endanger, and destroy the kibbutzim. They also put the brakes on the development of regional plants out of fear of the effect the plants would have on kibbutz society. Hakibbutz Ha'artzi's Executive Committee ruled that with regard to labor practices, the employment of outside labor in place of kibbutz members, and cooperative decision making, all kibbutz principles and norms had to be enforced at regional plants located outside the kibbutzim.[6] It also forbade the establishment of plants beyond those needed to process the kibbutzim's own farm products, and even in those cases another condition was imposed to prevent the plants from expanding too much—they were required to employ only kibbutz members. But this rule was impossible to enforce.[7]

The movement leadership was concerned about the social milieu of industrialized kibbutzim. As early as 1961, Ya'ari expressed concern about what he considered the emergency of a technocratic or scientific ethos instead of a worker ethos being followed and countered the claim that kibbutzim ought to be home to highly technological industries. "The de-proletarianizing and technocraticizing trend must not be fostered by hallucinations," he said.[8] In 1968, a strident debate over industrial automation was fought out in the pages of *Al Hamishmar*'s weekend supplement. Opponents of automation claimed that kibbutz factories ought to be aimed at fully exploiting kibbutz labor rather than at introducing technology that made the employment of kibbutz members redundant. Automation, they argued, created a problematic social milieu—it was detrimental to the worker's identification with his workplace, estranged kibbutz members from each other, and alienated labor from product. Those who advocated automation argued, for their part, that it would help solve the problem of inadequate manpower as well as attract more young people because it offered technical challenges. Furthermore, bringing in advanced technologies actually strengthened the connection between the worker and his job because he could see the entire process of producing the final product.[9] The conservativism of the opponents of automation was criticized by Eliezer Hacohen, one of the movement's industrial pioneers, who was a major booster of advanced technological industry at the kibbutzim. He argued on the pages of *Al Hamishmar* that holding back from building large factories was liable to turn the kibbutzim into what he called "economic ghettoes." The kibbutzim of different movements could gain efficiency by pooling their labor—a revolutionary idea at the time. He also wrote that the lack of a systematic industrialization plan that would include job training was liable to be detrimental to the kibbutzim's capacity for realizing their economic potential. Hacohen's concern was well justified because in the area of industrial development the kibbutzim suffered from many disadvantages that grew out of their ideology—the issues of foreign workers, of training kibbutz members to fill management positions, and of outside investment. As a result of this debate, in 1969 most (about 80 percent) of Hakibbutz Ha'artzi factories were of simple and conventional types.[10] But, despite the efforts to limit industrialization, in particular of the technological type, the conservatives were not able to contain the social consequences of the establishment of kibbutz factories. Social problems such as permanent managers, status differentials between different posts, fixed divisions between hired blue-collar labor and white-collar kibbutz member managers, and even commercial competition between Hakibbutz Ha'artzi kibbutzim resulted from the gap between rapid development and the limited capacity for pointing it in a particular direction.[11] The conservative method of coping with the problem proved ineffective; industry developed nevertheless, and it had social consequences. The 1970s saw the emergence of extreme situations such as "a factory that has a kibbutz" when a factory became so large and so economically powerful that it overshadowed the community that established it. The factory had more employees than the kibbutz had members, and its kibbutz managers, the meshekists, gained huge power to mold kibbutz society.

Hakibbutz Ha'artzi leaders' conservatism regarding economic development was also evident when it came to a number of initiatives to set up cooperative projects between kibbutzim of different movements during the 1960s. From the leadership's point of view, this cooperation was a threat to the delicate balance that it sought to fashion between economic development and the established social structure. In one case, the leadership quashed the proposal for a regional commune. Government officials saw the economic and social logic in regional cooperation among neighboring kibbutzim of different movements, but the movement's leadership categorically rejected the idea.[12] Following this initial attempt, the leadership issued instructions to the kibbutzim: partnerships in regional factories and concerns were prohibited from becoming too powerful, and they were not to bring about overly close relationships between kibbutzim, especially not between Hakibbutz Ha'artzi kibbutzim and those of other movements. The practical significance of these instructions was that Hakibbutz Ha'artzi kibbutzim were not to enter into joint farming agreements with other kibbutzim—that is, they were not to farm crops together, although they were permitted to cooperate in the processing and marketing of produce.[13] This rule severely crippled the kibbutzim's ability to pursue their sectoral interest.

Two other cases in which the leadership restricted cooperation between Hakibbutz Ha'artzi and its sister movements grew out of the demand made by the different movements' kibbutzim that they be allowed to enter into economic cooperation so as to maximize development. Each of the kibbutz movements responded to this demand in a different way. Ihud Hakevutzot Vehakibbutzim and part of Hakibbutz Hameuhad sought to promote such cooperation, in part because the meshekists had a great deal of influence in these movements. But Hakibbutz Ha'artzi rejected the initiative, fearing that a common organization would threaten its independence.[14] Nevertheless, representatives of the three movements commenced negotiations at the beginning of 1963 over forming an umbrella institution that would oversee kibbutz industry. These negotiations led to the establishment of Igud ha-Ta'asia ha-Kibbutzit (Kibbutz Industries Association). Hakibbutz Ha'artzi accepted the body as a necessary evil, given that its kibbutzim had already been running factories for two decades with nearly no support from the leadership. In allowing its kibbutzim to operate through the association, the leadership was not expressing any desire to industrialize more. It simply wanted control over the process and its social and political consequences. Evidence that this was the case can be found in the establishment in October 1963 of another economic umbrella organization, Brit ha-Tnu'a ha-Kibbutzit (Kibbutz Movement Alliance). Pressures from the other two movements to increase cooperation among them, with an eye to eventual full union, compelled Hakibbutz Ha'artzi to agree to this partnership, but it made sure that this cooperation would pose no threat to its own and Mapam's social and political independence. The alliance was meant to exploit the economies of scale and the potential for cooperation in many areas of the kibbutz economy, purchasing goods and services the kibbutzim needed and making administration more efficient. But because of the limitations that Hakibbutz Ha'artzi imposed, the alliance did not move beyond that. From the movement leadership's point of view, these two umbrella organizations served mostly as a means of controlling the economic development of its kibbutzim and, most important, of preventing social and political cooperation with the other movements.[15]

Alongside its attempts to counter the influence of sectoral interests, the labor-movement leadership combatted the democratic critics of the party and movement machines. This second campaign employed two opposing but complementary tactics: co-option and suppression. These tactics were applied selectively to different manifestations of the democratic critique in keeping with the danger that the leadership thought the critics presented to the consensus. When the critics were well-spoken people from good families who simply raised questions—for example, the twelfth graders who wrote the letter asking whether the government had done enough to pursue peace initiatives or the protest movement over the conduct of the Yom Kippur War—the establishment was forbearing and accepting. The protestors were invited to meet with political leaders to "clear the air" and resolve their differences "at home."[16] When protestors went a little further, transgressing the accepted boundaries of public discourse, but not by much, the authorities let the critics sound off. This strategy was followed in cases such as the protests over the issues of the Rafiah salient, Ikrit and Biram, and Akraba as well as regarding the critiques voiced in *Shdemot*.[17] But when a critique of the labor establishment was seen as a real threat, which happened mostly when the protestors refused to control themselves and show respect, as was the case with Siah or Yesh members, the response was harsh to the point of hysteria. Although this graduated scale of responses was aimed at not losing control of the moderate elements among the democratic dissenters, the leadership also feared that any accommodation would send them down a slippery slope. This concern applied principally to the younger generation, which the establishment feared would descend into radicalism. At the beginning of 1969, Golda Meir voiced this concern when she warned that Israel's youth protests were liable to lead to the outbreak of a student rebellion like those seen in Europe and the United States.[18]

Mapam and Hakibbutz Ha'artzi's leaders' response to the democratic protests within their fold took similar forms. They alternated between co-option and suppression, while fearing a plunge down a slippery slope. The first attempt to address a democratic initiative by co-opting it was the reaction to the Group of Eleven. When Ya'ari heard of the group, he wanted to forbid it to meet. Hazan agreed that the group's activity should be restricted, but he offered a more original response to these opinionated and ambitious young people. Instead of a head-to-head confrontation, he proposed welcoming the group and allowing it to continue its activities within the framework of the movement and under its oversight. He made one condition, however—that the group expand its ranks. Its leader Efrayim Reiner agreed, and the Group of Eleven became the Group of Seventeen, with Hazan and Ya'ari choosing most of the new members. The broader forum was more ideologically heterogeneous, and, as a result, it turned into a debating society focused more on ideas and theories than on action. It lasted a few years before falling apart in 1964 because of internal differences and declining activity. The co-option of Reiner and his fellow critics neutralized for a time the threat posed by a young-guard opposition to the movement's traditional leadership.[19]

When it came to the New Left, however, Hakibbutz Ha'artzi and Mapam brooked no dissent. A formal decision was made to battle this tendency.[20] The means were varied—the leadership exploited the fact that New Left groups such as Siah and the Black Panthers were associated in the public mind with explicitly anti-Zionist forces such as Rakah and Matzpen.[21] The leadership sought to extend the aversion that most of the movement's members felt toward the latter groups to radical New Left forces that nevertheless claimed to remain in the Zionist camp. *Al Hamishmar* writers devoted their columns and sections to castigating the New Left, accusing its members of antisemitism and of ties with Arab terror organizations. They argued that the New Left movements were futile, powerless, unrealistic, and detached from reality. Some writers depicted New Left activists as harmless, spaced-out kids whose youthful radicalism would pass as they matured.[22] The newspaper also voiced considerable hysteria about the student rebellions of the late 1960s, focusing particularly on the most prominent global New Left theoretician, Herbert Marcuse, who was the subject of dozens of articles in Hakibbutz Ha'artzi and Mapam's press.[23] Older kibbutz members also enlisted in the fight against the new radicalism. In 1970, Daniel Cohn-Bendit (Danny the Red), the leader of the French student rebellion of 1968, arrived in Israel as a guest of Matzpen. He was invited to speak at Gan Shmuel by some young members of that kibbutz who were active in Matzpen, but older kibbutz members tried unsuccessfully to prevent his appearance. To their chagrin, he lectured before the kibbutz's young people for several hours. During his talk, one of the opponents of his appearance cut off the electricity to the room where he spoke in an attempt to disrupt the event. The next issue of the kibbutz's weekly newsletter was replete with condemnations of the decision to allow this European revolutionary to enter the kibbutz.[24]

Meir Ya'ari accused New Leftists in Hakibbutz Ha'artzi of "hopping between two opinions," thus using the same language with which Elijah the prophet chastised the Israelites, who worshipped both their own god and pagan deities. Those who lent their support to a small left-wing faction that ran in the Knesset elections were wasting their votes and weakening the Left, he charged. The trend of small factions and political groupings, so common in the New Left, was crucially different from the mass-party politics to which the old leftist Ya'ari remained committed. In other words, his opposition to New Left initiatives was not only a matter of substance but also of the model of activism involved. Again invoking biblical language, in this case from the book of Joshua, Ya'ari said that these people would have to decide whether they "are of us or of our enemies."[25] Hazan, for his part, said, "I warned against Siah and argued that it was a cancer on the back of Hakibbutz Ha'artzi. Now that has proved to be true."²⁶ The passion with which the leadership fought the New Left evinced a sense of moral panic, which Tali Lev and Yehuda Shenhav define as an "over-reaction by the media, public figures, politicians, and the legal authorities to the actions of a person, a number of people, or a specific social group that is perceived as a threat to the [prevailing] system of values and public order."²⁷ This moral panic could be seen in the fact that the response to the New Left was manifested not just in opposition to radical ideas that ran counter to the spirit of the established Zionist movement but also in anxiety that the New Left was a menace to the stability of the movement and party themselves.

Another way Hakibbutz Ha'artzi responded to the demands the dem-ocrats were making of the movement was to seek to enforce ideological collectivism. One means of doing this was to prevent kibbutz members from pursuing higher education outside kibbutz frameworks. For many years, members of Hakibbutz Ha'artzi kibbutzim could not attend Israeli universities because the movement forbade not just higher studies but also the administration of the country's high school diploma exams, the *bagrut*, at kibbutz high schools.²⁸ As the kibbutzim grew economically stable and wealthier, however, more and more members wanted to "see the world" and pursue their education outside the three kibbutz colleges, which provided only training in education, teaching, and professions needed by the kibbutz economy.²⁹ The movement leadership sought a solu-tion that would answer the younger generation's wishes for broader study and personal development and at the same time shore up the movement's own colleges. It wanted to ensure that young people received ideological educations in the spirit of the movement and to preserve what remained of ideological collectivism.³⁰ In 1969, Hakibbutz Ha'artzi convened a meeting of representatives of all three kibbutz movements to discuss the establishment of a kibbutz university that would "serve as a center for the promotion of kibbutz ideology and spiritual values." The new institution would enable Hakibbutz Ha'artzi and the other movements to maintain the academic isolation of its members.³¹ But by this time the members no longer wanted to go to a kibbutz school. They argued that a separate kibbutz college would isolate the kibbutzim academically and engage in ideological indoctrination.[32] The most vociferous opponents were kibbutz students who wanted to continue their studies at the existing universities and not in an isolated kibbutz institution.[33] So the idea of a kibbutz university was shelved in 1971.

The labor movement's response to its loss of support among the working class, especially from that part of it made up of Mizrahi immigrants, was less direct and was divided into two major stages. At first, in the years 1963–69 the movement attempted top-down solutions. The parties reorganized and founded the Alignment but did not break free of their traditional sociology. They sought, rather, to reinforce the existing hegemony. During the second stage, from 1969 to 1977, the movement fundamentally revised its economic and social policy. This bottom-up effort was made to fashion a new apparatus of political mobilization by establishing a welfare state that would mitigate social inequalities.

In January 1963, Yitzhak Ben-Aharon of Ahdut Ha'avodah published an article that would quickly become a classic, "The Courage to Change before Catastrophe."[34] He proposed that all the labor parties unite. It was hardly a new idea, but now the timing was right. The labor movement as a whole was aware that it was losing its electoral base, in particular because it was losing the votes of the working class and the Mizrahim.[35] Given that the labor parties as currently constituted and operated had not succeeded in gaining working-class and Mizrahi support, their leaderships needed a new organizational approach. Ben-Aharon's proposal fell on ready ears.[36] Although Ben-Aharon was simply advocating better organization, not a fundamental change in the party's approach or attitude toward these groups, his idea nevertheless aroused considerable opposition as well. Among those who decried it were the three traditional leaders of the different wings of the labor movement—Ben-Gurion, Tabenkin, and Ya'ari. But Ben-Gurion resigned from the prime minister's post shortly thereafter, in June 1963. Tabenkin had already lost authority in Ahdut Ha'avodah and thereafter focused mostly on teaching. Their replacements, Levi Eshkol in Mapai and Yigal Allon in Ahdut Ha'avodah, supported and advanced the idea of an alliance. At a Mapai congress in October 1963, Eshkol proposed that the three labor-movement parties run joint slates for the Knesset, Histadrut, and local political positions. Negotiations went into high gear at the end of 1964 and early 1965, but Mapam decided not to join. The agreement establishing the Alignment, made up of Mapai and Ahdut Ha'avodah, was signed on May 19, 1965, but a month later Ben-Gurion and his supporters bolted Mapai and founded Rafi. In the national election held that November, the Alignment won forty-five seats.

The idea that uniting the labor parties could counter its loss of votes gained more support in the wake of the Six-Day War. All three parties had incentives to unite. Rafi was eager to return to power, and its star, Moshe Dayan, the architect of Israel's victory, was hugely popular but also being sought after by Gahal. Mapai wanted to rope him in, and Ahdut Ha'avodah wanted to prevent a Rafi takeover of Mapai. In 1968, they merged to form the Labor Party, and in 1969 Labor formed a new Alignment, a joint slate with Mapam. But unification, it turned out, did not stanch the drain on the labor movement's political power.[37] In the elections of 1969, the Alignment won fifty-six seats, seven less than the parties comprising it had held separately after the election of 1965. Unification provided the labor movement with breathing space for a few more years, but it could not put off the upheaval for long.

The labor movement took a different tack beginning in 1969 under the Meir and Rabin governments. It revised its economic policies and refashioned its sociopolitical methods. The movement realized that its bifurcated political, economic, and social strategy had lost it support, a realization brought on by three seminal events. The first was the government-initiated recession of 1966, the second the Black Panther protests, and the third the publication of the National Insurance Institute's first poverty report in February 1971. All three jolted the leadership into rethinking policy. The practice of granting services and rights preferentially to party and Histadrut members was replaced with a universal-welfare system.[38] The most significant reform was in the area of social insurance—the government instituted unemployment and disability stipends, reformed the system of child allowances, and gradually broadened eligibility for national insurance assistance, making it easier to receive pensions.[39]

This universal-welfare policy was especially evident under the Rabin government of 1974–77. Despite the economic crisis that followed the Yom Kippur War and the global energy crisis, Rabin's government significantly increased funding for social services. Between 1973 and 1977, the Social Insurance Institute's outlays for pensions increased from 3.1 to 5.6 percent of the country's GNP, an 80 percent increase. Social spending increased from 16.1 to 19.6 percent of GNP, a rise of 21.7 percent.[40] A Social Insurance Institute study of changes in the nature of poverty among Israeli wage earners from 1969 to 1975 found a decline in inequality on the Gini index. In 1975, the number of poor families declined as a result of pensions and transfer payments.[41] Housing was another area in which major reforms were made. From 1974 to 1977, there was a significant increase in public-housing construction for the poor and young couples and in new communities.[42] But this revision of economic and social policy did not stop working-class voters from continuing to abandon the labor movement. Two decades of discrimination had alienated them from it.

10

Political Paralysis

THE LABOR MOVEMENT was torn from within between, on the one hand, its working-class, sectoral, and democratic currents and, on the other, the leaderships of component parties and movements. This situation led the leaderships to engage in internal maneuvering so as to shore up their positions. The labor movement was as a consequence largely paralyzed politically from the mid-1950s on and presented the country with no clear agenda for facing the economic, social, and political changes taking place in and around it. As Anita Shapira has put it, in the years following independence and the mass immigration

> the creative impulse that had characterized the Israeli labor movement, manifested in original thinking and the organizational structures it built, in the innovative social and economic forms that had emerged within it, suddenly began to perish. After the "mobilized training" of the Palmach, it did not succeed in producing any new framework that was unique to it or an original solution to social and economic problems. Enthusiastic experimentalism was replaced by conservative and bureaucratic thinking.[1]

Shmuel Eisenstadt, an Israeli sociologist, writes that "Israeli society was dynamic, worked hard on economic development and education, on immigrant absorption and more, but, unlike in the past, it did not found innovative institutions like the kibbutz, moshav, moshavah, Histadrut, and professional unions, nor did it produce innovative revolutionary cultural works as it had in earlier generations."[2] The Israeli case was part of the larger ideological and political ossification that was the salient symptom of the crisis of the Left around the world.[3] In other cases as well, the British

Labour Party being one example, this rigidity resulted from the attempt to maintain a common political front despite the many internal splits and turns within the movement and to extend its life as much as possible even as it was falling apart.[4] The conservative reaction to challenges evident in the Israeli labor movement was, in other words, a structural phenomenon, an attempt to maintain traditional political frameworks in the face of huge changes in the economy, society, and culture.[5]

A very influential factor in the paralysis of the Israeli labor movement, as of other socialist movements, was that it had simply not anticipated the changes that were taking place all around it or their political implications. At the midpoint of the twentieth century, the entire world was in a state of chaos. Could anyone have predicted then the coming American-led economic miracle that occurred in many countries or the internal conflicts that the capitalist welfare state brought forth? When what has been called "embedded liberalism"[6] proved able to modify itself and provide citizens with many of the benefits and protections that the Left had long claimed only a socialist state could put into place and maintain, it shuffled the deck and left socialists unable to explain how this had happened and what their movement's calling was. Marxist theory and the socialist idea, which were the ideological foundation of the labor movement, found themselves facing a world they could not diagnose. A number of Western socialist movements that had developed as mass parties found it difficult in the 1960s and 1970s to recast themselves structurally for the age of affluence. Many of them found themselves homes to different currents that contradicted each other in ideology and policy. The debate between these factions reflected the parties' confusion and their desire to find a new organizing principle for themselves. In the meantime, they worked to stay alive and to put out brush fires. Managing the internal tensions produced by late capitalism became the labor movement's new agenda, much more than building up its political strength, but all that could do was put off the inevitable.

All three Israeli labor-movement parties found themselves paralyzed by internal conflicts during the period between the mid-1950s and mid-1970s. Mapai was split between two factions along generational, social, and ideological lines. One, called the Tze'irim (Young People), led by Shimon Peres and Moshe Dayan, were adherents of Ben-Gurion's doctrine of *mamlakhtiyut*, according to which the state rather than political parties or movements should be the central force in society and provide the services that parties had provided in the prestate period. They were allied with sectoral interests and the technocrats. Min Hayesod coalesced at the beginning of the 1960s, representing the democratic tendency and identified with the pioneering, movement-oriented part of the labor movement. It was supported by intellectuals, students, and young kibbutz members. The skirmishing between these two groups at the beginning of the 1960s, especially around the Lavon Affair, kept the labor movement focused inward and sapped its standing among the Israeli public as a whole. To maintain Mapai's unity, its leadership had to maneuver between these factions, but it had only limited success. In 1965, the Tze'irim and Ben-Gurion's loyalists broke away to form Rafi, which opposed Mapai in the elections that year. Min Hayesod also walked out of Mapai that year. The group dissolved some years later, and its members individually joined the Labor Party after its formation in 1968. Rafi also incorporated itself into Labor, although it continued to maintain a separate identity as a faction within the party.

A new cleft opened in the unified Labor Party following the Six-Day War, dividing the hawks, led by Moshe Dayan, from the doves, led by Yigal Allon. These two groups disagreed in particular over the question of the future of Israeli rule over the territories captured during the war and over what kinds of concessions, if any, Israel should be willing to make to the Arab countries and the Palestinian population in order to achieve peace. Rafi and the sectoralists aligned mostly on the side of the hawks, and the members of Min Hayesod found their place largely among the doves. Although both Dayan and Allon saw themselves as future party leaders and prime ministers, their position at the apex of the two rival wings of the Labor Party made them for all intents and purposes ineligible for that role because it was feared that a victory for either would split Labor in two. When Prime Minister Levi Eshkol died in 1969, the party leadership instead preferred to promote a figure acceptable to both sides—Golda Meir, a longtime cabinet minister and party stalwart who had been instrumental in the unification efforts. She and Yisrael Galili assumed the role of mediators between the two camps.[7] Their success in this role bolstered the power of the party leadership after the blows it had suffered from recent economic and social developments. But the need for constant maneuvering between the two camps rendered the Meir government and the Rabin government that succeeded it unable to move forward significantly on the pressing issues of the territories and negotiations with the Arab states.[8]

In a way similar to Mapai, Ahdut Ha'avodah also responded to its own political paralysis and the resurgence of a leadership that mediated between factions. From its inception as an independent party in 1955, it had lacked a clear identity and ideological justification, other than being Hakibbutz Hameuhad's party. Yet its internal struggles left it powerless to make decisions about its future.[9] It was riven by conflict between those who supported partnership with Mapai and those who opposed it. Most of the opponents came from the democratic current and wanted to refashion the party as the voice of the working class and weakest parts of Israeli society. This platform, they maintained, would reinforce the party's ideological identity as a manifestly socialist party that, unlike Mapai and Mapam, was not dedicated simply to defending the interests of its own, increasingly bourgeois camp. (Party leader Yitzhak Tabenkin and his loyalists supported this approach, but they represented a radical pioneering ideology that was anachronistic by the 1960s, oblivious as it was to the economic and social developments that had taken place since independence.) The supporters of cooperation with Mapai were sectoralists who believed that the party should, first and foremost, look after the needs of its kibbutz movement.[10] The conflict split the party leadership as well.[11] In 1965, the supporters of an alliance with Mapai gained the upper hand, so Ahdut Ha'avodah entered the Alignment, and in 1968 the two parties formally merged into the Labor Party. But the internal divisions continued within Hakibbutz Hameuhad, where the old party leadership refused to budge, even though it had nothing new to offer.[12] Yisrael Galili emerged as the conciliator between the movement's factions, making him its leading figure from the 1960s on.[13]

Mapam also found itself politically paralyzed as a result of factional conflict. On the one hand, it needed either to join the governing coalition or to maintain close ties with it in order to serve its sectoral kibbutz power base. On the other hand, it often had to oppose the government's policies to demonstrate fealty to its socialist ideology if it wanted to maintain its support among the working class and the allegiance of its democratic current. When it faced voters for the first time after the split with Ahdut Ha'avodah in July 1955, it had spent six long years in the opposition, largely against its will. Now the election halved the strength it had displayed in the country's first national election. It won 62,401 votes, 7.3 percent of the total, gaining only nine seats in the Knesset. Its internal tensions were evident during the subsequent coalition negotiations. On the one hand, Mapam had attacked Mapai in the election campaign and continued while in government to take an adversarial stance; on the other hand, it very much wanted to influence government policy from the inside. It also needed to be in government to obtain financial assistance for its kibbutzim, which were facing a serious debt crisis. The fact that Ahdut Ha'avodah was also seeking to enter the government was another consideration; if that party, a former partner with a very similar socialist ideology, could see its way into sitting at the cabinet table with Mapai, it would be difficult for Mapam to explain to its kibbutz voters why it could not do the same. Immediately following the election, Mapam sent clear signals that it was interested in coalition talks with Mapai. The negotiations took four months, but in November 1955 Israel's seventh government took office, and Mapam was in it.

In the cabinet, Mapam was able to achieve a debt arrangement for its kibbutzim and take an active role in government. But membership in the coalition created a new problem. Given the ideological crisis triggered by the events of 1956 and the rightward tilt of its meshekists, the party was liable to be perceived as weak because it had cast aside its core values. That perception would alienate both its growing democratic current and its old-guard left wing. Its leaders were able to reestablish balance with a new political strategy in which it took part in government while opposing many of the government's policies. This strategy was called "partnership while in conflict." It was evident in particular in Mapam's ongoing opposition—in word but not in deed—to the government's foreign, security, and economic policies.

Mapam's positions on foreign and security policy offered an alternative to those taken by Ahdut Ha'avodah and Ben-Gurion, but the party was not willing to risk its place in government by asserting itself too strongly. Its pronouncements were aimed mostly at asserting its political independence and justifying its existence as a separate party, as its democratic current demanded. In the period prior to the Sinai Campaign of 1956, for example, Mapam attacked the government frequently and declared its opposition to war.[14] Membership in the government was explained as natural to a party like Mapam. After all, members of Hakibbutz Ha'artzi kibbutzim, who had grown up with their movement's long-standing pioneer and military tradition, were disproportionately represented in the IDF's officer corps and elite combat units. The party thus needed to share in the responsibility for dealing with the security challenges that Israel faced. For that reason, when the decision to go to war was finally made in 1956, Mapam supported it.[15] Ya'ari rose in the Knesset to congratulate the army on its victory, and the party's Central Committee passed a resolution to call the campaign a shining military success, while at the same time decrying the difficult political position Israel found itself in as a result of the war.[16] Mapam took the same ambivalent positon with regard to postwar diplomacy. It supported the official nonalignment of Israel and the rest of the Middle Eastern countries between the two superpowers, but it also advocated annexation of the Gaza Strip, a position that allied it with Ahdut Ha'avodah and was the territorial maximalist line that Mapam had consistently criticized. Mapam also took the opportunity to castigate the government's foreign policy by declaring its opposition to the Eisenhower Doctrine of January 1957, aimed at curbing Soviet influence in the Middle East;[17] declaring support for the anti-Western regime that came to power in Iraq following a military coup;[18] and condemning Israel's opposition in the United Nations to Algerian independence.[19] The height of Mapam's opposition to a government it served in came in 1959, when it (along with Ahdut Ha'avodah) voted in the cabinet against an arms deal with West Germany and demanded Ben-Gurion's resignation.[20] The cabinet and the Knesset approved the deal over the two parties' objections, but Ben-Gurion, who would have liked to send the two parties' ministers packing, had no alternative coalition given the makeup of the Knesset at the time. He thus resigned, turning the government into a transitional one that served until after the national election that was held in November 1959.

Mapam maintained its strength in the elections of 1959, again receiving nine seats with 69,468 votes (7.1 percent). During the coalition negotiations, the party's Central Committee was split into two camps. On the one side were those who advocated making the compromises necessary for membership in the government. The party should not issue ultimatums that would force it into opposition if Mapai did not accede. On the other side were those who opposed joining the coalition. They argued that Mapai had not respected the previous coalition agreement and that there was no basis for partnership with the larger party. This division largely marked out the party's right and left wings and forced the leadership to perform a balancing act. The solution was that Mapam would join the government but oppose its policies when, in practical terms, it could fight for its positions from the inside by abstaining if policies it opposed came before the Knesset. This decision led the party to demand that the coalition agreement stipulate that Mapam's Knesset members could abstain on votes regarding the sale of arms to Germany, the extension of the military government over Israel's Arab citizens, and the ban on pioneering youth-movement activity in state schools.[21] At the beginning of December 1959, Mapai agreed to this provision, and the final obstacle to Mapam's participation was removed.[22] The Mapam Central Committee approved the coalition agreement a few days later by a relatively large margin, but a considerable number of opponents to the agreement still viewed the abstention ploy as an act of political passivity and a betrayal of Mapam's mission.[23] Apparent proof that they were right arrived immediately after the new government took office. In January 1960, Mapam abstained in a Knesset vote on the arms deal with Germany, the very issue that had caused the previous government to collapse. Mapam further announced that it would work to ensure that the Knesset would reject the deal.[24] But at the beginning of February, Mapam and Ahdut Ha'avodah failed to push through a Knesset resolution calling on the government not to approve the deal. It seemed clear that Mapam was ineffective.

Mapam's positions on economic policy also reflected its strategy of partnership while in conflict, with all its built-in contradictions. Throughout the course of 1957, Mapam staked out a position that was the opposite of the government's policy on all central issues—for example, it supported the strikers at the Ata textile factory, whom the government was trying to force back to work; it opposed a proposal by Finance Minister Levi Eshkol to allow private investors to buy government-owned factories; it opposed the Finance Ministry's market-based investment policy; and it opposed the incentives that Industry and Commerce Minister Sapir provided to private industry. Eshkol and Sapir were in fact boosters of the manufacturing sector and the kibbutzim, the development of outlying regions, and the establishment of large government-owned factories. That being the case, Mapam sought to highlight the differences between its economic views and the government's policies, even as Hakibbutz Ha'artzi benefitted from those same policies. Mapam avoided brinksmanship in the economic area as well, fearing that taking an uncompromising stand on such issues would compel it to leave the government.[25] To compensate, it employed hard-hitting rhetoric. The representatives of urban areas and the working class in the party were outraged by the disparity between the positions Mapam trumpeted and its actual actions in government.[26]

At the end of 1958, Mapam's ministers voted against the national budget for 1959.[27] The vote was a sign of increasing tension with Mapai. Mapam declared that the government's economic program was right wing and liberal, and it made a series of demands to help the working class.[28] Two months later Mapam's criticism of the government was brought home when riots broke out in Wadi Salib and other poor neighborhoods around the country in protest against ethnic, social, and economic discrimination. *Al Hamishmar*'s coverage of the riots echoed Mapam's critique of the government's policy and the party's demands.[29] Mapam had to pay lip service to its ideology because of its position within the government. A few months later, at the end of 1959, it also joined the next government, despite its antigovernment rhetoric. The budget for 1961 reopened the dissension between Mapam and Mapai. Mapam abstained in the Knesset vote on the budget on the grounds that, despite its protests, the development budget had been cut and tax policy revised.[30] Yet Mapam remained in the government, leaving its urban members disappointed that its campaign for workers' rights was not receiving priority in the party's political activity.[31]

Ben-Gurion resigned on January 31, 1961, following Pinhas Lavon's acquittal on charges related to a botched espionage plan in Egypt. The subsequent coalition negotiations were not comfortable for Mapam. On the one hand, it wanted to remain in the government on the same terms under which it had entered Ben-Gurion's government a year earlier. On the other hand, the party's leadership was unanimous in its opinion that Ben-Gurion's obsessive and ugly conduct in the Lavon Affair would not permit it to join another government headed by him.[32] At the end of February, the Mapam Council passed a unanimous resolution stating that Mapam was interested in joining a new government to be constituted along the lines of the outgoing one, but on condition that Ben-Gurion not stand at its head.[33] The resolution was to no avail—the Mapai Secretariat insisted that Ben-Gurion was its candidate. A new election seemed inevitable. In March, the Mapai Central Committee decided on a new election, to be held in August. Mapam received 75,654 votes, 7.5 percent of the total, again winning nine seats in the Knesset.[34]

Following a short-lived attempt by Mapam to negotiate a coalition agreement as part of a block including Ahdut Ha'avodah, the Liberal Party, and the Mafdal (Miflaga Datit Leumit, National Religious Party), with the aim of weakening Mapai's position in the government, Mapam entered into its own independent negotiations with Levi Eshkol, whom Ben-Gurion had appointed to run the building of the coalition. Mapam demanded an end to the arms trade with Germany, an end to the military government over Israel's Arab population, a revocation of the ban on youth-movement activities in public schools, greater external oversight of the security system so as to prevent another scandal along the lines of the Lavon Affair, and a continuation of the status quo on matters of religion and the state. It also made a list of economic demands, largely in two areas: aid for agriculture and wage increases for workers.[35] Mapai agreed to allow Mapam to vote its conscience on the military government and arms trade with Germany and to end the ban on youth movements in the schools. It would not, however, agree to Mapam's demands regarding oversight of the security system, religious affairs, the arms trade with Germany, an end to the military government, or economic and social policies. Although Mapai had agreed to the demands that the Mapam Rikuz had declared essential in the negotiations for the party's entry into the previous government,[36] a strident debate broke out in Mapam forums over whether to join the new government. Again, there were two groups, each pushing in a different direction. One wanted to pursue the negotiations and display a willingness to compromise. It argued that what had already been achieved in the coalition negotiations was sufficient and that sitting in the opposition would be costly for Mapam because it would lose its ability to influence policy and its public support. The opposing group wanted to cut off negotiations on the grounds that serving in the government would do great damage to Mapam's public image because it would be seen as a spineless surrender to Ben-Gurion's dictates.

The concrete question faced by the Mapam Central Committee and Secretariat was whether to present Mapai with an ultimatum. Drawing a red line would be tantamount to not entering the government, given that, at this late stage in the negotiations, it was already clear what Mapai would agree to and what it would reject. Following a debate, the secretariat voted to present such an ultimatum.[37] Hazan led the Central Committee in approving a resolution laying out Mapam's nonnegotiable demands, consisting largely of conditions that Mapai had already rejected.[38] When the Knesset ratified the new government in November 1961, it did not include Mapam.

Although the debates within Mapam are well documented, it is not easy to fathom the real reasons behind the decision not to join the government. Displeasure with Ben-Gurion's conduct in the Lavon Affair clearly angered many in Mapam. True, that did not necessarily translate into opposition to joining the government. On the contrary, many members of the party's right wing argued that Mapam could not sit on its hands when Mapai was on the verge of rupture. Joining the government and cooperating closely with the larger party would actually weaken Ben-Gurion, they said.[39] But the Lavon Affair had molded Mapam's internal contours beyond the scope of the specific issues at stake in the scandal. Several commissions of inquiry had cleared Lavon's name, and he led Mapai's internal opposition to Ben-Gurion. So when Lavon set out to prove his innocence in the face of his vilification by Ben-Gurion, many in Mapam lined up behind him. Intellectuals protested against Ben-Gurion, and in 1961 they organized a series of rallies in support of Lavon. During these months, the protest movement coalesced into the Min Hayesod movement, in which many young members of Mapam were involved. This coalescence threatened the balance between the party's right and left wings.[40] The question was whether Lavon's supporters would leave Mapai and make common cause with Mapam and Ahdut Ha'avodah; there was talk that the three movements might even run a joint slate in the elections of 1961. But Min Hayesod decided at this juncture to remain within Mapai, and Ahdut Ha'avodah declared that it had no interest in a partnership with only a part of Mapai. After the election, Mapam thus found itself facing two options: it could join the Mapai government and sit alongside Ahdut Ha'avodah, where it could lend support to Lavon's supporters in their struggle against Ben-Gurion within Mapai, or it could look out for itself, in particular its need to shore up the delicate balance between its right and left wings. Mapam preferred the latter choice. It had been shaken by the experience of government from 1955 to 1961. The fact that prominent members of the party's young guard had aligned with the party's right wing by pursuing closer cooperation with their counterparts in Mapai and Ahdut Ha'avodah necessitated an internal rebalance. In other words, Mapam went into opposition in 1961 in order to demonstrate to the public and in particular to its own members and supporters that it was truly independent and distinct from the other two parties.[41] The question of whether to remain in the opposition served as a convenient platform for doing so. In particular, it distinguished Mapam clearly from Ahdut Ha'avodah, which joined the government. Mapam could now accuse its sister party of having betrayed its principles for political advantage and power, of caring more for cabinet portfolios than ideology. Ya'ari proudly declared that his party had remained true to itself.[42]

In opposition, Mapam stepped up its attacks on the government. In February 1962, it took aim at the Ministry of Finance, which had significantly devalued the currency, severely shaking the economy.[43] Not in the government now, Mapam did not have to cope with the inflationary pressures created by the large wage hikes granted during the period of full employment. It demanded that wages be linked to the cost of living, thus compensating workers for the loss of buying power caused by the devaluation, and so framed its position in socialist terms.[44] In mid-May 1962, Mapam introduced a no-confidence motion decrying the government's economic policies, and in the months that followed it organized three mass rallies calling for a united struggle against the government's antiworker policies.[45] At the end of the year, Mapam opened a front in the Histadrut against that organization's intention of instituting a wage freeze in the firms and factories it owned. Mapam declared that it would support mass resistance to this policy and organized strident protests at workplaces. Despite these protests, the Histadrut Executive Committee approved the wage freeze, which was supported only by the Mapai representatives, who were in the majority. Both Ahdut Ha'avodah and Mapam voted against it. Mapam claimed that 100,000 Israelis attended a demonstration it had organized against the move.[46] It reaped the benefits of this campaign in the Histadrut elections of 1965, when it received 95,000 votes as opposed to the 80,000 votes for it in the Knesset elections held that same year.

The decision to go into opposition in 1961 seemed, within Mapam, to have put an end, at least for the time being, to the idea of an alliance with Ahdut Ha'avodah and Min Hayesod. To many of Mapam's members, the party seemed to have reached a state of ideological unity.[47] But in January 1963, just as Mapam was asserting its independence, Yitzhak Ben-Aharon published his manifesto "The Courage to Change before Catastrophe," which restarted the negotiations for a united labor front. Mapam's leaders had no choice but to take part in the initial talks over the establishment of the Alignment; refusing to do so would have opened them up to attack from the party's right wing. But they did so reluctantly, repeatedly voicing their lack of enthusiasm for an alliance.[48] To prevent the talks from progressing, Mapam's leaders kept insisting that the three parties first had to agree on a joint program. In such discussions, Mapam could always present some issue or other as a nonnegotiable condition for its cooperation.[49]

In mid-June 1963, at the climax of Mapam's efforts to keep itself out of the impending alliance, another threat to its internal balance suddenly presented itself. Ben-Gurion unexpectedly resigned the prime minister's post and was replaced by Levi Eshkol.[50] This resignation seemingly opened the way for Mapam to join a new government under Eshkol; he had close relations with Mapam and was much more popular in the party than Ben-Gurion. But Eshkol lost no time in declaring that his government would be a direct continuation of the previous one and that he had no intention of reopening coalition negotiations. Because Mapam had refused to accept the previous government's program just two years earlier, that seemed to be the end of the matter. A debate between the party's right and left wings nevertheless broke out. Immediately following Ben-Gurion's resignation, Ahdut Ha'avodah submitted an alliance proposal to Mapam, the practical consequence of which would be that the three labor parties would field a joint slate in the next national election. The alliance's election platform would serve as the program for the government to be founded after the poll. Mapam's reaction was chilly, to say the least, but talks nevertheless continued.[51] In the meantime, Prime Minister Eshkol lent his support to the plan. In early October 1963, he paid a visit to Ya'ari at his home at Kibbutz Merhaviah to discuss the proposal, but to no avail.[52] At the Mapai congress that convened in the middle of that month, Eshkol proposed that the three parties run together in the coming national, Histadrut, and local elections. Ya'ari, who was invited to give a welcoming speech, paid lip service to cooperation, but no more than that. He instead led the campaign in Mapam against an alliance, fearing that such an arrangement would push Mapam down a slippery slope toward a full merger.[53]

At the beginning of 1964, the negotiations over Mapam's accession to the government picked up speed and approached a point of decision. Mapam's Political Committee resolved that the party was willing to consider entering the government, but that its entrance involved no commitment to joining an electoral alliance.[54] This resolution highlighted Mapam's real concern—that joining the government would put the party on the path to a united labor front, which would put an end to Mapam's special calling. Furthermore, it would upset the balance that Mapam had maintained during its previous stint in government, with its policy of "partnership while in conflict." In January 1964, Mapam appointed a delegation to negotiate its entry into the government. In the meantime, Eshkol asked the Mafdal to consent to Mapam's participation. Mapam sent out pessimistic signals, declaring that negotiations were not progressing because Eshkol refused to accede to the party's demands in the area of religion–state affairs.[55] In January 1964, Mapam's governing bodies resolved that the party would oppose Mafdal's demands that violated the religion–state status quo, which would give Mapam an official reason to remain in the opposition. They also resolved that the final authority to decide whether to join the government or not would be made by the party council, which would vote on the program that would emerge from the coalition talks when it convened in February 1964.[56]

As the council meeting approached, the party leadership voiced pessimism about the negotiations. The party's demands were numerous, and Eshkol agreed to only some of them. Most centrally, he refused to consent to budget IL 50 million (a sum equivalent to 1.25 percent of the national budget) to poverty relief, development in the Arab sector, and large families.[57] The party's Political Committee resolved that it could not recommend to the council that it accept the agreement unless Eshkol made further concessions.[58] In mid-February, Ya'ari and Hazan met with Eshkol, who made it clear that he had no intention of giving any more ground.[59] A few days later the council voted overwhelmingly against joining the government.[60] Mapai and Ahdut Ha'avodah were furious. Eshkol accused Mapam of sabotaging the labor camp and of thinking only of its own narrow interests.[61] The following month Mapai and Ahdut Ha'avodah resumed negotiations over an alliance without Mapam. In mid-April, the Tenth Council of Hakibbutz Ha'artzi convened and reasserted the movement's independent line, which sharply rejected such an alliance.[62]

As with Mapam's decision not to join the government in 1961, it is not easy to get past the ideological veneer of the party's internal deliberations to discern the political and social reasons for the decision it made in 1964. Even if we accept that the specific policy issues, in particular the IL 50 million demand, was a consideration, the fact that the discussions to join the government and over the establishment of the Alignment were being conducted in parallel would seem to indicate that many in Mapam were concerned that joining the government would be the first step toward an electoral alliance. And, in fact, when Mapam refused to join the government, it removed itself from the negotiations over the Alignment. At the same time, the party leadership was nevertheless able to avoid being seen by the Israeli public as a party that refused all ties with other forces, while also giving some hope to those of its members who supported an electoral alliance by proposing a "pioneering compact" with Ahdut Ha'avodah and Min Hayesod. The Mapam leadership encouraged this initiative in order to give some hope to those of its members who sought to promote labor unity. But neither of those other movements was really interested in such an idea, so the probability of its occurring was nil.[63] The principal motivation for Mapam's efforts in this direction was simply to keep things quiet at home.[64]

Elections to the Sixth Knesset were held in November 1965. Mapam won eight seats (with 6.6 percent of the vote), one seat less than previously.[65] It had successfully maneuvered to maintain its independence, but Mapai and Ahdut Ha'avodah ran together as the Alignment. Yet Mapam now changed its tune radically. Right after the election, its Political Committee laid out the party's demands, and they were presented to Eshkol a few days later. But this time the demands were not framed as ultimatums.[66] *Al Hamishmar* reported at the beginning of January 1966 that significant progress had been made on economic and social issues as well as on ending the military government and on religious coercion. Mapam's institutions soon approved the coalition agreement.[67] The new government was presented to the Knesset on January 12. After a little more than four years in opposition, Mapam was back in government, holding the housing and health portfolios.

Mapam's agreement to join the government at this specific juncture seems inexplicable. It did so just as the country was feeling the brunt of the economic and social consequences of the recessionary policy initiated by Finance Minister Pinhas Sapir in 1964, which deliberately aimed to raise the unemployment rate.[68] Hazan acknowledged that the party had chosen to join the government "cognizant of our economic situation and what awaited the country." Furthermore, in contrast with the "partnership while in conflict" stance Mapam had taken during its previous stint in government, it supported Sapir's policies in the Knesset.[69] It may well be that when the new economic policy became official and Mapam took stock of all its implications, the party sensed that it urgently needed to join the government so as to protect Hakibbutz Ha'artzi's interests. Whatever the case, clearly the harsh recession did not prevent Mapam from entering the government or from doing so without insisting on recession relief as a sine qua non of its entrance.[70] Mapam carried on its established practice of doing one thing and saying another. It joined the government and thereafter gave no serious consideration to leaving it, while at the same time infuriating Eshkol and Sapir with its public condemnations of the government's recessionary policies. Clearly, protecting Hakibbutz Ha'artzi took precedence over opposing an economic policy that was hugely damaging to Israel's working class. In government, Mapam could no longer mobilize urban workers against the government as it had done in opposition and for which it had been handsomely rewarded in the elections to the Histadrut.[71]

This attempt to have its cake and eat it, too, led to unrest within the party. It reinforced the party's democratic current, which now raised the economic banner in its continued critique of the movement and party hierarchy. It also decried Eshkol's security policy, condemning his use of military force in skirmishes on Israel's northern border in 1965–66, in which Israel sought to assert its control over the sources of the Jordan River.[72] Some of the democratic critics decried what they considered military adventurism and declared their opposition to the Alignment not just on economic and political grounds but also on the grounds of security policies. Although these critics were a small minority compared to the alliance of Mapam's right wing and its historical leadership, the combination of security and economic problems strengthened them. In January 1967, in the face of the economic crisis, the Mapam Council convened to reconsider the party's membership in the government. It decided that Mapam should remain where it was for the time being and that the issue would come up for discussion again in a year's time.[73] This put pressure on the party leaders, who now had to prove that they were achieving something in the coalition. During the initial months of 1967, Mapam continued to voice its opposition, often militantly, to many of the government's decisions and to make a series of demands, in particular for cost-of-living wage increases. In the end, however, the Mapam Council resolved that the party's participation in the coalition should not be challenged and that internal debates over the issue should cease.[74]

During the tense waiting period prior to the outbreak of war in June 1967, security issues again came to the forefront of the internal debate within Mapam and Hakibbutz Ha'artzi. Many on the left believed that the government had deliberately escalated tensions with the Arab world so as to enable it to order the IDF's preemptive attack on Egypt and Syria.[75] Hazan and Ya'ari remained, however, loyal to the government. Although they differed about whether the government had exhausted all avenues for avoiding war, they supported its decisions as a matter of national responsibility.[76] They backed Eshkol even when members of the coalition and opposition claimed that the prime minister was indecisive and called for his ouster in favor of Ben-Gurion. They continued to support him even when, under pressure, Eshkol handed the defense portfolio, which he had held, to Moshe Dayan and brought Rafi and Gahal into the coalition, forming a national-unity government.[77] When, however, the government held a vote on going to war on June 4, the Mapam ministers, Mordechai Bentov and Israel Barzilai, did not participate. Their reason was prosaic— they wanted to consult with Hazan and Ya'ari before having their votes entered into the record, but in any case there was a majority without them. Mapam again sat on the fence, even if on this occasion it did not mean to.[78]

Israel's victory in the Six-Day War raised a host of new questions regarding the territories the country had captured—the West Bank, Gaza Strip, Golan Heights, and Sinai Peninsula. The kibbutz movements also had some reservations about the euphoria that overcame the country in the wake of the war. Together, these reservations spurred a sense of partnership among the kibbutz movements. It quickly became apparent, to the chagrin of the Mapam and Hakibbutz Ha'artzi leadership, that young members of the party's right wing were involved in political initiatives to establish closer relations and even to unify the labor parties and kibbutz movements.[79] Mapai and Ahdut Ha'avodah also saw unity as a way of blocking the advance of Moshe Dayan, who had become a hugely popular public figure following the victory. Dayan's hawkishness, his right-wing economic views, his arrogant personality, and his political scheming all made him anathema to many. Mapai and Ahdut Ha'avodah needed Mapam to join them in a front that would unite Mapai's doves and Ahdut Ha'avodah in opposition to Dayan, Rafi, and their sympathizers in Mapai.[80] The coalition party they envisioned would be a theater for contention between opposing forces; they thus saw Mapam's membership in the government, which they hoped would be the first step toward a united labor party, as critical. Mapam's right wing wanted to help stop Dayan and

Rafi, which exacerbated the internal debate over the party's independence. The rival camps grew increasingly more polarized as the plans over founding a unified party advanced.

But the Mapam leadership's position was clear from the start.[81] It ruled not only that cooperation with Rafi was out of the question but also that Mapam would not exclude itself from an effort to unify the labor camp.[82] Hazan and Ya'ari reconciled partnership while in conflict with the internal and external political playing field on which Mapam found itself. If Rafi were to be part of a unified party, Mapam would agree only to an alignment in which it would retain its independence.[83] Ya'ari declared, "We will not give up ideological and organizational autonomy."[84]

During August 1967, it became apparent that Mapai and Ahdut Ha'avodah intended to unite with Rafi and to leave Mapam on the outside. The threat to Mapam's independence had passed, allowing it to carry on talks about a looser alliance in the form of a joint Knesset slate, a new incarnation of the Alignment.[85] At the end of September, the Mapam Central Committee decided that a vote on the Alignment would be held at Mapam's Fifth Congress, scheduled for the winter of 1968, following the unification of the other three parties. The founding congress of the Israeli Labor Party, uniting Mapai, Ahdut Ha'avodah, and Rafi, was held in January 1968. The event intensified the debate within Mapam over cooperation with the new party. Mapam seemed to be on the verge of rupture.

When the Fifth Mapam Congress convened in March, the atmosphere was tense. At the end of the deliberations, the congress voted in favor of the leadership's resolution on the union of the labor parties, but the majority was much less than overwhelming. In fact, the congress's resolution did not actually sanction the Alignment but merely authorized the party leadership to enter into negotiations over running joint slates in national and local elections. The results of those negotiations were to be brought before a second session of the congress for a final decision.[86] That second session convened in November and approved the Alignment agreement with the Labor Party by a two-thirds vote.[87] Although a small contingent left Mapam as a result of this vote, the party remained whole, if not united, and the Alignment became its political home for the next fifteen years. Neither wing of Mapam saw this change as a victory over the other. It simply meant a continuation of the party's established "partnership while in conflict" strategy within the framework of the joint list. Mapam ran with the Labor Party but acted as an opposition group within the alliance, which enabled it to strike a balance between the opposing forces in the party and Hakibbutz Ha'artzi. This antithetical behavior simply added another dimension of disorder to the Alignment, given that the components of the new Labor Party were riven by the rivalries of their own warring factions. The sum total of all this dissension was a large measure of political paralysis. By the 1970s, factional infighting had become the most salient definitive trait of the labor movement and one of the major causes of its impotence.

The infighting in Mapam placed the historic leadership in the role of mediators. Dissension made Hazan, Ya'ari, and their circle indispensable; they thus had good reason to foster dissension so as to ensure their own survival. The rivalry between the sectoral and democratic wings of the party, what party members at the time termed its right and left wings, intensified throughout the 1960s. By the end of the decade, it had reached the state of dividing Hakibbutz Ha'artzi and Mapam socially. The leaders fostered these divisions while condescending to both groups. Ya'ari positioned himself as the leader of the camp advocating Mapam's independence, and Hazan ostensibly led those who favored labor-movement unity. The two of them fostered this public image because it served their interests to have each of them identified with a different social group in the internal struggle. First, this image strengthened each of them individually by making each the patron of one of the two camps. Second, by dividing the forces that sought to restructure the party hierarchy, it enabled the two traditional leaders to maintain their leadership. Third, the rival camps turned their fire against each other, diverting it away from the leaders and the party's oligarchical leadership structure. Fourth, most importantly, Hazan and Ya'ari, standing at the weak point between the party's right and left wings, served as the glue that kept the two sides of Hakibbutz Ha'artzi and Mapam together.

In the 1960s, it became evident that Hazan and Ya'ari indeed differed on central issues; each was invoked by a different side.[88] Their dispute ostensibly marked a break in the unified front that had been the wellspring of the historic leadership's authority in the past. In fact, the public differences between them ironically bolstered their leadership as the two men reinvented themselves as the party's arbiters. Despite the show of conflict, in part a product of their disparate personalities, they complemented each other. Hazan was the more open one and made himself out as a booster of the younger generation. Ya'ari, for his part, was apprehensive of the young and tended to cast a dim eye on grassroots initiatives. But this show of conflict does not mean that they did not share a larger view. The division between them was like that between the good cop and the bad cop; they simply took different approaches to achieve a common goal. Ya'ari may have been accused of suffocating paternalism, but Hazan was an expert at axing new ideas. When there was a real danger that they would lose control, they aligned to counter the threat. They promoted the image that they were divided as a way of avoiding the need to decide in favor of one camp or the other because such a decision would render their roles as arbiters redundant. They made sure that each faction was checked by the other and by the patron who ostensibly headed it. In fact, Hazan did not want unification with the rest of the labor camp any more than Ya'ari wanted complete independence. Despite their disparate public statements, in practice each leader kept the faction he ostensibly led from carrying out its program. The role of arbitrators and conciliators that the two men were sharp enough to adopt made them indispensable, extending their leadership of Hakibbutz Ha'artzi and Mapam for many years beyond the point when it would otherwise have come to an end. But the price of fostering internal dissension while not allowing a new party leadership to emerge was that the movement's internal social and ideological fissure widened to the point that the common framework became ever more tenuous.

By the beginning of the 1970s, following two decades of fierce internal debate, Hakibbutz Ha'artzi and Mapam, like the rest of the labor movement, were so divided that the so-called arbiters were no longer effective. As the elections of 1977 approached, the rival groups in the labor movement organized themselves into well-defined camps, with the Alignment serving as the common framework for their rivalries. The combination of the political paralysis that this division caused, the fact that the labor movement's economic apparatus could no longer provide any more benefits to its supporters, and the fact that erstwhile supporters who had never enjoyed such benefits had abandoned the party in resentment caused the floor to fall out from under the movement at the polls. Those who abandoned the labor movement formed alternative political frameworks, and new connections were made between cultural activities and economic and political activities.

PART THREE

The Cultural Turn

From Indoctrination to Counterculture

THE ISRAELI LABOR MOVEMENT developed, economically and politically, in interaction with an institutionalized cultural space it created.
This interaction may be divided broadly into two stages. The first began
in the prestate era, when the Histadrut, controlled by Mapai, founded its
cultural front, as did Hakibbutz Ha'artzi and Hakibbutz Hameuhad. This
era extended into the early years of the state as Mapai fashioned a Israeli
national cultural and educational system that largely incorporated the values and goals pursued by the Histadrut and the labor movement as a whole.
In the meantime, Hakibbutz Ha'artzi/Mapam and Hakibbutz Hameuhad/
Ahdut Ha'avodah continued to foster their independent cultural fronts.
Taken together, these cultural fronts helped build up the labor movement's
political power throughout this period. Politically and nationally mobilized culture and the mediating role of the party leaderships were highly
concordant with the austerity of the time and the public's high level of
dependence on labor-movement institutions.

In the mid-1950s, a new stage in the development of the labor-movement cultural front began to take form; this transformation was affected
by the economic and social changes I described earlier. It had two largely
contradictory consequences for the labor movement's hegemony in Israeli
society. On the one hand, economic expansion provided the funds needed
to broaden the cultural front by establishing publishing houses, periodicals, and cultural associations. Furthermore, the rise in the standard of
living meant that more and more Israelis had the money and leisure time
to become consumers of culture. On the other hand, these economic and

social changes meant that the political movements lost much of their ability to control the cultural sphere, which grew considerably more autonomous. Several factors caused the greater consumption and loss of control. First, improvements in communications and transport made a variety of cultural activities much more accessible to the populace; the cultural establishment thus had far less control over the kinds of culture to which people were exposed. Second, as daily life in Israel grew to be more and more like that in the West, it opened itself up to new cultural influences and products. The Israeli public was no longer dependent on local productions, which were more easily controlled. Third, the Israeli public's focus switched; during the first stage, culture was primarily high culture and political debate; now people sought light entertainment rather than the products of the ensconced cultural establishment. Fourth, as the cultural space broadened, it also became more commercialized; it was now a market like any other, subject to the laws of supply and demand. To survive, institutionalized culture had to respond to public tastes, even when doing so ran counter to its own goals. Finally, the Israeli cultural space reacted to the rise of a new generation that entered public life in the 1960s. This cohort became significant both as producers and consumers of culture. The integration of new needs, new capacities, and new audiences as well as the political debates that grew out of the cross-cutting interests that economic development created led to a fundamental change in the role played by institutionalized culture with regard to the labor parties' hegemony. Culture turned from a tool of indoctrination to an autonomous space comprising a variety of manifestations of opposition to the establishment. This happened in two stages: the cultural front became a platform for debate, and then culture became an agent of political change.

II

From Cultural Front to Arena for Debate

THE LABOR-MOVEMENT cultural front expanded in the 1950s as part of larger processes through which the growing affluence left Israelis with leisure time that they sought to fill in part with culture. It also reflected, however, the internal debate within the labor movement and the confrontation between its public and its establishment. As already noted, critiques of the labor parties' machines began to be voiced at the beginning of the 1950s; in the second half of that decade, they became much sharper with the emergence of organized groups of opponents.

The intensification of this criticism received further impetus from the rise of a new generation that entered Israeli public life in the 1950s and 1960s. This "generation of the children" (*dor habanim*), as it was termed in the labor movement, was made up of people who had been born in the 1930s and 1940s. It can clearly be seen in figures for Hakibbutz Ha'artzi. Before 1950, only 53 young people who had grown up in the movement's kibbutzim became kibbutz members. Between 1951 and 1960, the kibbutzim gained 715 new members of this type, and between 1961 and 1970 that number rose to 3,439.[1] A census carried out by the movement in 1968 found that this younger generation constituted a significant proportion of the kibbutz population. The movement's seventy-four kibbutzim had a total population of 29,449, of which 17,441 were members or candidates for membership. The eighteen- to thirty-five-year-old age group was larger than any other.[2] The labor movement's younger generation took on an identity of its own, coming of age as it did during a period of ideological crisis, splits and debates in the movement and its constituent parties, and large-scale sociopolitical processes that put the younger generation in conflict with the older generation.[3] This new generation joined other challengers to the party and movement establishments who, because the political system was not open to them, turned their energies to the freer cultural sphere.[4] The party and movement leadership, for its part, preferred to see such debates conducted in cultural rather than political terms and thus encouraged that tendency. This process fundamentally transformed the cultural front. It ceased to be a tool for mobilizing the public and turned inward, becoming a means of managing internal tensions within the labor movement. The front became an arena, and the more strident the confrontations within the labor movement became, the more this front flourished.

The Ideological Crisis of the Left

The internal labor-movement debate that began in the mid-1950s was the local manifestation of a larger ideological crisis in the worldwide socialist movement. The crisis had two principal sources. The first was brought on by Nikita Khrushchev's revelations about Stalinism and by subsequent disappointment with Khrushchev himself. These factors were most salient for the pro-Communist Left in the West. The second emerged from the internal contradictions that came to light in countries ruled by social democratic parties, Israel among them. Social disparities widened, the bureaucracy mushroomed, and the younger generation did not find socialist ideology inspiring. In Israel, the effect of this disillusionment with Stalinism was felt mostly by Mapam and Ahdut Ha'avodah. Mapai was the major victim of the social democratic crisis. In Israel, as elsewhere, the debates that grew out of the crisis of the Left were carried out to a large extent in the cultural arena.[5]

A large part of the Left's crisis revolved around its relationship with the Soviet Union, which in the 1930s and 1940s was a powerful mobilizing and educational symbol for many socialist movements around the world. Both Hakibbutz Ha'artzi and Hakibbutz Hameuhad had from their inceptions deep roots in Marxist–Leninist thinking and the Soviet revolutionary movement. Furthermore, one of the ways in which the leaderships of these movements grappled with the crisis that their kibbutzim faced after independence was to amplify their ideological fervor, in part by intensifying their admiration of the Soviet Union. Their links to international socialism helped kibbutz members cope with the feeling that they had become marginal elements in the new state. It gave them a sense of mission, a message that they were needed in a much larger cause. The two movements looked to the "world of tomorrow," while Hever Hakevutzot and the pro-Western Mapai looked to Western social democracy.[6]

Whereas Hakibbutz Ha'artzi's leaders had sought to be part of the international revolutionary movement and to be its representative in Israel (contending with Maki, the country's non-Zionist Communist Party, for that position), Hakibbutz Hameuhad's leaders saw themselves as part of the movement but also independent. They were enthused by the revolutionary romanticism exuded by the October Revolution and the Red Army's victories in World War II, and they admired Soviet culture and society.[7] In both movements, sympathy for the Soviet Union led to internal fissures. In 1951, Hakibbutz Hameuhad split between the pro-Western supporters of Mapai and the pro-Soviet supporters of Mapam. Some kibbutzim split into two rival communities, and there was an exodus from others of members who wanted to live in a community with an affiliation they could agree with. Mapai's supporters left Hakibbutz Hameuhad and merged with Hever Hakevutzot to form a new movement, Ihud Hakevutzot Vehakibbutzim. In Mapam, Ya'ari and Hazan contended with a group of stalwart Soviet loyalists who flirted with all-out communism. They expelled the leader of this group, Moshe Sneh, and his supporters from the party (and in some cases from the kibbutzim where they lived). Soviet loyalties were also involved in the debates between Hakibbutz Ha'artzi, where enthusiasm for the Soviet model was zealous and not open to question, and Hakibbutz Hameuhad, where more independence of thought was allowed within the larger space of pro-Soviet sentiment. These differences were one of the reasons why Ahdut Ha'avodah left Mapam in 1954. After the split, support for the Soviet Union in Hakibbutz Hameuhad declined but did not vanish entirely until 1956, when the movement took a sharp turn, recounted later in this chapter, which affected Hakibbutz Ha'artzi as well.

The change in the Zionist Left's attitude toward the Soviet Union was an indirect consequence of moves that this country itself made— its repression of the Soviet bloc states and its support of the Arab states. Soviet repression in eastern Europe first became an issue in the debate over whether the Soviet Union should get preference in postwar rehabilitation and economic development or both it and its client states should get equal priority. When Yugoslavia broke with the Soviets in 1948, the Soviet secret police began to carry out purges in eastern Europe with the assistance of local supporters. These purges climaxed with the Prague Trials at the end of 1952 and the Doctor's Plot in early 1953.[8] One of the victims of the former was Mordechai Oren, a member of Hakibbutz Ha'artzi's Kibbutz Mizra and of Mapam, who was arrested on a visit to eastern Europe and sentenced to prison. This crisis continued until Stalin's death on March 5, 1953, and emerged again when protests broke out in Poland and Hungarians staged an armed rebellion at the end of 1956. In parallel, Soviet Middle East policy began to change in 1954. The Soviet Union had supported the establishment of Israel in 1947–48, but in 1954 it began shifting its support to the Arabs. This shift first manifested itself in pro-Arab votes at the United Nations. In 1955, the Soviet Union began supplying arms to the Arab states, beginning with a Czechoslovakian–Egyptian arms agreement through which the Soviets supplied Egypt with advanced weaponry, in particular aircraft, even when it was clear that these arms would be used against Israel in a future confrontation.

The Soviet Communist Party held its Twentieth Party Congress in February 1956. It made a number of innovative ideological decisions that gave the impression that Khrushchev, Stalin's successor, was going to allow more openness of debate and artistic freedom as well as to end the purges. Khrushchev also made what came to be known as his "secret speech," in which he revealed and condemned Stalin's crimes. The congress reopened the debate regarding Hakibbutz Ha'artzi's and Mapam's relation to the Communist cause, especially in the wake of the ejection of the Sneh faction. All sides felt that the congress was an important step forward in the Soviet Union's process of self-criticism regarding the Stalinist regime's deviations.[9] Yet it soon became clear that the new Soviet regime did not live up to the promise of the Twentieth Congress. A few months later, Khrushchev sent armored columns into Hungary to put down the uprising there. He also banned the publication of Boris Pasternak's novel *Dr. Zhivago* (1957) because of its critical portrayal of the Bolshevik Revolution.

Mordechai Oren, the "prisoner of Prague," returned to Israel in May 1956 after four and a half years in a Czechoslovakian prison. He did his best to give the public the impression that he had been treated well so as to explain why his faith in the Soviet Union had not wavered. But given that he had confessed to all the trumped-up crimes his interrogators had accused him of, it was obvious that he had been tortured. Some weeks after his release, Oren began to recount some of his prison experiences, and in April 1957 he published the first in a series of selections from his prison diaries. In 1958, his diaries were published in book form by Sifriyat Poalim, entitled *Notes of the Prisoner of Prague*.[10] His account of his interrogators' brutal behavior served as a further impetus for Hakibbutz Ha'artzi and Mapam to condemn the Soviet Union, especially in light of the fact that Czechoslovakia refused to rehabilitate Oren, not clearing him of all guilt until seven years after he was first imprisoned.

Khrushchev's secret speech became public in June 1956 when a translation was published in the *New York Times*. Although the fact of the speech and its general content were already known, the complete text, in which Khrushchev laid out the crimes of Stalinism in detail, shocked the world and discomfited the Soviet Union's supporters in the West. In Israel, it set off a wave of anti-Soviet sentiment.[11] Mapam and Hakibbutz Ha'artzi members were faced with the problem of either making excuses for their long-standing and almost unreserved support for Stalin or acknowledging that they had been mistaken. The Sinai Campaign of 1956 further deflated support for the Soviet Union. Soldiers fighting in Sinai heard on their field radios the voices of Russian advisers speaking to the Egyptian forces, and in battle and afterward, when collecting the remains of Egyptian forces from the battlefield, they saw the huge quantities of Soviet weaponry that the Egyptians had received just before the war began.[12]

The first-ever official Hakibbutz Ha'artzi delegation to visit the Soviet Union arrived there in the summer of 1957. It was composed of young kibbutz members who were attending the Festival of Democratic Youth. The 150-strong mission also included representatives from Ihud Hakevutzot and Hakibbutz Hameuhad kibbutzim. The entire delegation returned from the visit shocked by what they had seen—and solidly anti-Soviet. Haim Shor, one of Hakibbutz Ha'artzi's delegates, wrote a report in which he described the rottenness and corruption of Soviet society, its discrimination against Jews, and the harsh discipline enforced in the Soviet

Communist youth movement, the Komsomol.[13] Disillusionment swept through a large swathe of the West's Communists and socialists as well as through the intellectuals of Israel's pioneering and kibbutz movements. This crisis of faith was also evident among the members of the younger generation. They demanded change and directed their ire against the labor movement and party establishment.[14]

The Western social democratic Left also experienced ideological bewilderment in the 1950s. It was first brought on by the Suez crisis and the Israeli invasion of the Sinai Peninsula, (the Sinai Campaign, referred to in Israel as Operation Kadesh) on October 30, 1956. France's Socialist government under Prime Minister Guy Mollet persuaded Britain and Israel to embark on a military operation that looked like colonial adventurism of precisely the type that the Left decried. At the same time, the Mollet government was locked in what was perceived as a merciless war against rebels in Algeria who sought independence from French colonial rule. Britain had also disappointed the West's social democrats, especially under Clement Atlee's Labour government of 1945–51, which had continued to pursue capitalist policies.[15]

The crisis of faith among the pro-Communist and social democratic Left occurred alongside another crisis unique to the Israeli labor movement: the labor parties and kibbutz movements lost their capacity to mobilize their followers, especially young ones, on a voluntary basis. In general, young people during the Yishuv and early state period had been obedient, displaying a willingness to take action for the Zionist cause as members of the pioneering youth movements, establishing and bolstering new settlements and serving in the military.[16] But when the Israeli economy entered a stage of strong growth in the early 1950s, the younger generation began to display signs of passive rebellion. They were no longer as willing to put themselves at the service of their movements, seeking instead greater scope for individuality.[17] In the cities, many high school students did not join youth movements; some instead adopted what was called "salon culture," listening and dancing to rock-and-roll and dressing according to the latest fashions. Older ones left the army as soon as they could and enrolled in college with the aim of gaining a high-status and high-earning profession and starting a family. In short, they accepted the lifestyle and standards of the bourgeoisie.[18] In the kibbutzim, the crisis could be seen as (mostly young) members sought to relax after years of sacrifice. They were unmoved by ideology and were interested largely in attaining a higher standard of living.[19] Although this crisis of the pioneering spirit differed in its causes and symptoms from the crisis of the global Left, it also played out almost entirely on the cultural stage.

Hakibbutz Ha'artzi and Mapam's Cultural Front as a Platform for Debate

The turn of Hakibbutz Ha'artzi and Mapam's cultural front to a platform for debate began with the transformation of the oldest Hakibbutz Ha'artzi journal, *Hedim* (Echoes), from a magazine that published articles on culture and works by kibbutz writers and artists into a platform for political debate. *Hedim* had been founded in 1935 as a quarterly that addressed kibbutz life. It played that role for two decades, without ever deviating from the movement's official line, even as it published opinion and ideological articles by the movement's members.[20] At the end of 1956, in the wake of the Twentieth Soviet Party Congress, a debate broke out in the pages of the journal after some members of the movement criticized its long record of support for the Soviet Union. In recent years, one writer wrote, despite the huge demographic and economic growth of the kibbutzim, there had been no parallel progress in social ideology. The superstructure, he argued, lagged far behind the changes in the movement's socioeconomic foundation. Thinking about kibbutz problems had been frozen for more than a decade, and no systematic discussion of the issue had been held. The movement needed to take stock of the past and examine itself in order to learn lessons to apply from here on out, he wrote.[21] Another member demanded that Mapam redefine its connection with the Communist world in a way that would ensure the party's independent status and not require it to identify fully with or accept the Soviets' authority.[22] Other articles made a variety of arguments about the need for a change in ideological orientation.[23] Alongside these calls for change, *Hedim* also saw attempts by the movement leadership to assert its ideological control over the membership.[24] The leadership permitted the journal to play this contradictory role of being platform both for reformers and for the establishment in the hope that allowing critics to sound off would head off actual change. Indeed, that was one of the reasons that Mapam decided in January 1958 to found a new journal, *Basha'ar* (At the Gate), with the express purpose of serving as a place where kibbutz members could engage in extensive theoretical, ideological, and political debate.

Another subject debated in *Hedim* during the late 1950s and early 1960s was the unification of the labor parties.[25] In 1962, the proposal that a number of struggling kibbutzim near the Gaza Strip, including one belonging to Hakibbutz Ha'artzi, merge their agricultural and manufacturing operations so as to benefit from economies of scale (the regional commune) received a great deal of space in the journal.[26] The strident debate set off by the inception of negotiations to establish the Alignment began in 1963, and more and more issues were debated in its pages as time went on. *Hedim*, ostensibly a journal of kibbutz culture, published increasingly more political content. The debates over current issues in its pages were so intense that the journal enjoyed a significant measure of popularity even though at that time Hakibbutz Ha'artzi also published four other periodicals. Just before the Six-Day War, *Hedim* had a circulation of 4,500, of which 3,500 copies went to members of Hakibbutz Ha'artzi. It was read by about a third of the kibbutzim's members.[27]

Another such platform was *Bahativah* (In the Division), which began to come out just as the number of young adults at the kibbutzim began to increase and were organized into Hakibbutz Ha'artzi's Youth Division. Its first issue, published in June 1956, proclaimed that it was meant to provide "information, instruction in the movement's doctrines, and self-expression" for the members of the Youth Division and that Mapam's urban membership had no part in it.[28] Like *Hedim*, *Bahativah* put on display the ideological ferment that expanded after the Sinai Campaign. It, too, staked out an independent position and criticized the movement's leadership from the right. Its December 1956 issue was devoted to a debate over the war. But the establishment's imprint was also notable.[29] In the February 1957 issue, the periodical's editors grappled with the "manifestations of doubt" regarding the Soviet Union that some members of the Youth Division had expressed. It adduced a famous essay by Berl Katznelson, a founder of the Histadrut and Mapai, "In Praise of Confusion and

Condemnation of Cover-Ups," which criticized educators who engaged in indoctrination rather than dialogue. The editors stated that they rejected confusion that involved asking questions and casting doubt. Criticism was important, they stressed, but confusion was an enemy. They focused in particular on "those who cease to believe."[30] The editors' attempt to defend the movement leadership did not go unanswered. The young people charged with "manifestations of skepticism" responded by attacking ideological collectivism and ties with the Soviet Union. The willingness to broaden the cultural arena to include criticism was also visible in the case of an article that reviled the Soviet Union and Leninism. The editors appended a note to it stating that they had deliberated over whether to publish the piece, but in the end deciding that "it is better to debate and clarify the issues in public on the pages of our press and in carrying out these inquiries and debates to reach common conclusions."[31] Young people, however, condemned this positon, which they saw as overly permissive, and contended that the journal should "guide" the membership.[32] An editorial statement responding to this view supported the tactic of inclusion and declared that the editors' rule of thumb was that "it is the right of the younger generation to make its own mistakes."[33]

At the end of 1961, in the wake of the Lavon Affair, *Bahativah* entered a new period. Its pages became the arena in which the supporters of a partnership between Mapam and Min Hayesod wrestled with those who advocated Mapam's independence. Especially prominent in this debate were a group of young kibbutz intellectuals who supported an alliance and advocated joining the government.[34] The supporters of independence also pushed their position in the journal. They demanded that the movement's young people adopt a more revolutionary approach and explained that they opposed a union of the labor parties because it would compel Mapam to make ideological compromises.[35] In the main, however, *Bahativah* was an organ of those who sought ideological renewal in the direction of a union of labor parties. As a result, many readers claimed that the journal was biased.[36] In 1964, it folded following a decision to turn it into a more attractive and professionally produced biweekly renamed *Hotam* (Seal or Impression).

The gradual intensification of Mapam's internal debate led in 1958 to the founding of *Basha'ar*, a periodical designated as an official platform for fleshing out issues within the party. Its first issue came out in January of that year in parallel with Mapam's Third Congress, at which the dispute between the party's and the movement's right and left wings first came to the fore.[37] Until 1963, the debate in this journal focused primarily on attitudes toward the Soviet Union. After that, the main question was the union of the labor parties. Two largely different sets of writers appeared in the journal during these two periods. During the first period, most of them came from the movement's founding generation and some urban party members, but during the second period many young writers of Hakibbutz Ha'artzi's second generation contributed. A single line ran through both periods, however—the struggle between advocates of preservation and advocates of change. Alongside arguments that Mapam should maintain its historical alignment with the Soviet Union,[38] there were articles highly critical of that country.[39] Many articles called for a democratization of socialist society and an understanding that the struggle between capitalism and socialism in industrialized countries would need to be conducted through democratic and not revolutionary means.[40]

In contrast with *Hedim* and *Bahativah*, which were established to allow members of Hakibbutz Ha'artzi to express themselves but gradually turned into forums for airing issues and questions, *Basha'ar* was designated for such debate from the start. As such, it functioned as a place for its writers to let off steam. With its long, boring, and theoretical articles, it was not very popular among kibbutz members.[41] The publication of a journal specifically devoted to political and social discussion reflected part of a shifting attitude toward culture. Channeling disagreements into a cultural instrument relieved the pressure on political institutions, which could continue to pursue conservative policies, avoid change, and avert tremors along the labor movement's ideological faults. Writers for *Basha'ar* could vent their anger, but the leadership could remain on solid ground. Nevertheless, although the leadership had founded *Basha'ar* to serve as a pressure valve, the journal grew ever more strident and blunt in its calls for reform.[42]

The debate also made the pages of Hakibbutz Ha'artzi's periodical *Hashavu'a Bakibbutz Ha'artzi* (This Week in Hakibbutz Ha'artzi), which had been founded in 1950. At first, the movement leadership exercised full control over the weekly newspaper. The paper continued to appear regularly in 1952–53, years in which Hakibbutz Ha'artzi veered leftward, in contrast with *Hedim*, which the leaders shut down at this time because they could not control it. *Hashavu'a Bakibbutz Ha'artzi* served, however, as the establishment's official house organ, with the result that by the mid-1950s hardly anyone read it. Faced with this plunge in its readership and understanding that a newspaper without readers could not serve as a means of controlling the movement, the leaders agreed to grant its editors and writers greater freedom.[43] The newspaper remained loyal to the establishment but also gave voice to the public's needs. As part of this process, it, like other Hakibbutz Ha'artzi/Mapam cultural institutions, became a home for addressing controversies within the movement.

All the central issues that the movement faced from 1956 were thus argued in *Hashavu'a Bakibbutz Ha'artzi*. At the beginning of that year, Meir Ya'ari confronted the meshekists on its pages;[44] following the Twentieth Soviet Party Congress, writers grappled with its revelations and implications;[45] and at the same time members demanded cooperation with the other kibbutz movements.[46] In all these cases, the leadership sought to assert itself against these grassroots voices.[47] Pieces by leaders advocating adherence to the movement's pro-Soviet orientation appeared side by side with articles by kibbutz members who stridently critiqued the movement's official ideology. The journal also displayed the rise of the younger generation, who authored much of its content.[48] At the beginning of the 1960s, writers for the weekly began to demand unification of the labor camp.[49] The paper also covered the battle against outside labor, the debate over the establishment of the "regional commune,"[50] and the campaign to maintain ideological collectivism.[51] In the mid-1960s, it devoted considerable space to the pros and cons of entering the Alignment.[52] In 1964, *Hashavu'a Bakibbutz Ha'artzi* inaugurated a new feature, "Bamat ha-beirur" (Platform for Inquiry), where writers on the right and left contended and Hazan and Ya'ari occasionally interjected with remarks intended to bridge over and reconcile the sparring factions.

Aside from publishing opinion articles written by supporters of different positions, the weekly's staff writers provided extensive coverage of the opponents of the official line that the leadership sought to enforce on controversial issues. The editors presented the debate over the principle of ideological collectivism as proof that the movement was open and democratic. The free manner in which *Hashavu'a Bakibbutz Ha'artzi* covered debates was, however, balanced by its full and detailed presentation of the leadership's position. In fact, the newspaper devoted far more space to the official line than to the opposition's positions. The weekly thus served the leadership's ends at least until the mid-1960s, providing a cultural forum in which movement members could speak their minds without posing any serious threat to the leadership.

Ha-Merkaz le-Tarbut Mitkatemet (Center for Progressive Culture) also changed as a result of economic, social, and political developments in Hakibbutz Ha'artzi and Mapam. In the summer of 1955, it moved to a new and somewhat larger hall on Dizengoff Street in Tel Aviv, taking the name "Tzavta" (Circle of Friends). This upgrade of what had previously been a small club for the arts was enabled by funding from Mapam. As part of the process, an official manifesto for the organization was drafted in 1957, declaring that Tzavta was to serve as a home for artists and would seek to disseminate the values of Hashomer Hatza'ir throughout the Israeli public.[53] In other words, whereas *Basha'ar* looked inward, Tzavta looked outward. The expansion of Tzavta was an initiative by the leadership and as such was just a start. It did not immediately mark any major change in the extent and nature of the institution's activity. During its first years in its new home, Tzavta operated without any central organizing principle and held cultural evenings, each devoted to a particular work of art, usually a book. The lecturers were members of Mapam or Hakibbutz Ha'artzi, with Avraham Shlonsky the most prominent figure featured. Tzavta cultural clubs also operated in other cities, usually without a fixed home or program.

The irregular programming, small turnouts, and crowded quarters changed at the beginning of the 1960s. The immediate cause was that meetings were held at Tzavta during the election campaign of 1961. The party's slogan that year was "Speak the Truth," a call aimed at some of the public figures involved in the Lavon Affair. Young but well-known actors such as Gila Almagor, Eli Gorlitsky, and Uri Zohar appeared at these events, not simply to cap the evening after a series of speeches by party activists but rather as full participants in the campaign.[54] Their involvement signaled a cultural approach that united political and popular messages. In a rare moment of daring, the party leadership decided that Tzavta should move in a more popular direction. Shmuel "Fiska" Firstenberg, a graduate of Hashomer Hatza'ir's Tel Aviv chapter, a member of Kibbutz Yakum, and a former coordinator of Mapam's young guard, was appointed as Tzavta's new director. He led Mapam's election campaign in 1961 and brought artists into it. Firstenberg represented the party's new popular-cultural policy and was the obvious choice to lead the club into its new era. Shlonsky supported the appointment, realizing that under his own leadership Tzavta had not had any influence. His one condition was that the weekly Friday night poetry readings continue. Firstenberg's condition was that the club be open seven days a week and that it move immediately into larger quarters. The move was also necessary because neighbors in the building on Dizengoff Street had filed suit against the club, complaining of the disturbance it caused. In 1963, Tzavta entered a new home in the basement of a building at 11 Mapu Street, and, in accordance with Firstenberg's plan, it was open every evening.[55]

Tzavta became a great success. It stood out as an innovative and unique cultural venue in the city, and nearly every major entertainer, writer, and poet appeared there. Firstenberg also organized a group of young performers into a repertory group that staged shows on a regular basis. The programs included musical performances (from classical to rock), original theater, singalongs, evenings of satire, and also a new feature, the Political Cabaret. The latter, held each Wednesday night, was Firstenberg's innovation and his favorite. In essence, it was a talk show that featured political guests. Unlike in the past, when speakers had to be party members and present its ideas, the Political Cabaret invited speakers as far from Mapam's ideology as the right-wing party Herut. The only criterion was that they had to be people who made headlines—the prime minister, cabinet members, Knesset members, journalists, professors, army commanders, artists, guests from abroad, and intellectuals.

The new cultural stance grew out of the realization that young people would find their way to Tzavta only if it offered them attractive and high-quality entertainment.[56] But the party leadership did not like it. The orientation toward popular amusement turned out to be Frankenstein's monster. One member of the Mapam Secretariat called the Political Cabaret a "bordello," and the leadership as a whole took Firstenberg to task.[57] "There are some not very cheery innovations in Tzavta's activities," said Yitzhak Patish, Mapam's political secretary, when the secretariat took up the issue. "In the symposium programs, Mapam is represented by people who probably don't hold a membership card." Firstenberg, for his part, complained that "the atmosphere outside is favorable, but from inside we are being slandered and criticized." Mapam Knesset member Reuven Arazi claimed that "Our activity is by necessity biased. . . . If we have reason to fear that we will have the lower hand in a specific activity, that activity should be canceled." Hazan was quite specific—all activity at Tzavta should require the leadership's approval.[58] This is in fact what happened. The lively and groundbreaking programming at Tzavta was placed under the purview of a committee that was to oversee its political activity and make the decisions about what issues were to be addressed and what activities were to be held. Yet at the same time that the party reined in Tzavta, it also topped up the club's coffers to enable its continued operation and formed a fund-raising committee for it.[59]

But the party's financial assistance was not sufficient. The decision to offer popular programming rather than purely party content was motivated in part by financial considerations. The party subsidized the club at a fixed annual rate, the same support that had been provided since the beginning of the 1950s, when Tzavta offered only two or three programs a week. But this subsidy was not sufficient to cover costs, and the club needed to ask for special grants from the party when it went into the red. It was this need for additional funds that prompted the club to start charging an admission fee for programs, with the popular entertainment paying for the club's ideological and political events. Firstenberg's talent was convincing performers to appear on a one-time basis for free; he offered payment only to those who appeared regularly. Tzavta put on an average of ten shows a week, and the club was open for much of the day and night.[60]

Despite the party's efforts to control Tzavta, Firstenberg continued to innovate. He was simply responding to the public rather than to the movement, which was less than supportive. He kept pushing boundaries. Two years after the young people of Mishmar Ha'emek scandalized Hakibbutz Ha'artzi's stalwarts by inviting a lecturer from Mapai to speak to them, Firstenberg inaugurated Tzavta's Political Cabaret and began inviting figures from outside Mapam as guest speakers. The program attracted young kibbutz members who came into the big city looking for fun and stimulation as well as Mapam sympathizers and the public at large. The party establishment was appalled—in their view the Political Cabaret legitimized ideological deviation and alliance with the party's rivals in the labor movement. Although Firstenberg still had to submit all his programming to a party committee, the socioeconomic changes in Hakibbutz Ha'artzi and Mapam encouraged him to be daring. He was on the road to a head-on collision with the party leadership.

Sifriyat Poalim, Hakibbutz Ha'artzi's publishing house, also entered a new phase in the mid-1950s. Following the revelations about Stalin's regime, the press almost completely ceased issuing the Soviet literature that had hitherto been its trademark. The word *Leninism* also disappeared from its catalogs; the term *Marxism* continued to appear, but on its own.[61] The ideological earthquake also led to an economic crisis because demand for the house's backlist books plunged.[62] But when Sifriyat Poalim shook free of its pro-Soviet line, it was able to take a more popular approach. It published fewer books that were meant to serve the movement's ideology—many of them were no longer relevant—and began to publish an eclectic selection of popular titles that expressed a humanistic and progressive worldview.[63] In 1964, it issued a collection of essays by the Polish critical Marxist philosopher Leszek Kołakowski, thus breaking with Mapam's official pro-Soviet line.[64] From the beginning of the 1960s on, the press's fiction offerings no longer followed any ideological guidelines. They included works that had been banned behind the Iron Curtain and had criticized what was going on there.[65] The press's offices moved from Merhaviah to Tel Aviv in 1964, marking its metamorphosis from a party press to one seeking a broad swathe of readers with different tastes.

This shift from indoctrination to deliberation was also evident in the daily *Al Hamishmar*, the movement's flagship newspaper and most widely read publication. From its inception, it had filled the dual role of a daily newspaper with a relatively large circulation outside Hakibbutz Ha'artzi and an ideological megaphone for Mapam's leaders. The friction between the two roles frequently caused problems, as was evident, for example, in the crisis over the party's Soviet orientation. When *Al Hamishmar* printed letters and columns by members of Mapam calling for a clean break with the Soviet regime, Ya'ari reprimanded the editor, Ya'akov Amit. The items, Ya'ari claimed, had aggravated the already tense atmosphere in the movement and had even led to demands that Mapam leave the World Peace Council and the Israel–Soviet Friendship Society.[66] Like Sifriyat Poalim and Tzavta, *Al Hamishmar* had to juggle ideological and commercial considerations. Amit explained to members of the Mapam Secretariat that it was difficult to put out a daily newspaper that appealed to the larger public while maintaining it as a platform for the party's ideas and positions. The editors faced a constant battle between interest and partisanship, he said. If the leaders wanted the public to seek out the newspaper, it was necessary to lower its level of partisanship. Printing speeches by Mapam's leaders, Amit insisted, had never brought the party a single new member. *Al Hamishmar* also had an objectivity problem, he admitted: "In practice, there is no freedom in our newspaper—there is a kind of consensual lie [that we allow freedom of speech] . . . [but] we allow no possibility of debate."[67]

Contrary to Amit's account, the fact that the newspaper maintained the party line (as evidenced by its editorials, which entirely accorded with the leadership's positions) did not mean that it was not open to differing opinions. Although its editorial positions closely followed the party line and every word it published was vetted by the leadership, in practice from 1957 on *Al Hamishmar* was no less an arena for internal debate than were *Hedim, Bahativah, Hashavu'a Bakibbutz Ha'artzi*, and *Basha'ar*. The daily did this in the framework of its feature "Bamat ha-beirur," which appeared in the newspaper prior to meetings of the party council (which met every few months) and the annual party congress. In this feature, party members voiced their differing opinions on the issues of the day. Nevertheless, the articles were closely supervised, and not everything submitted was published. "Bamat ha-beirur" first appeared in October 1957, in advance of the Mapam's Third Congress, as a place where attitudes toward the Soviet Union and the October Revolution were argued.[68] Under the party's doctrine of democratic centralism, Ya'ari or Hazan would, prior to each congress, circulate a document outlining the decisions they wanted the congress to make. Kibbutz members were expected to read and comment on this document, and the leaders would revise it in response. When they sent out this outline in 1957 in advance of the congress scheduled for the following year, its readers discovered that despite the shock of Khrushchev's revelations Ya'ari and Hazan did not intend to engage in any serious revision of Mapam's ideology.[69] Ya'ari pointed to this ideological debate as an example of attempts to challenge the principle of ideological collectivism. He was not opposed to disputation but nevertheless argued that it was a sign of "ideological latitude."[70]

For Mapam's Fourth Congress, held in 1963, *Al Hamishmar* turned into a boxing ring for the factions that favored and opposed the party's entry into the Alignment. Ya'ari played a prominent role, using the newspaper as a pulpit from which to pontificate and to rebuke his opponents. Never before had a debate over such a major issue taken place in such a public forum, and never before had the leaders been so unable to impose their will.[71] The disputations in *Al Hamishmar* were supposedly supervised by the leadership, but they revealed the fault lines that ran through Mapam. The newspaper's staff was made up of loyalists to the historic leadership, but they nevertheless displayed an increasing predilection for commercial journalism, responding to the public's interest in free debate. The newspaper's political orientation became less palpable, and so it gained a wide readership.[72] Like Tzavta, *Al Hamishmar* transformed from a partisan tool to an independent entity. As the newspaper grew, the leadership had a harder time controlling it, just as it saw its hold loosen on other components of Hakibbutz Ha'artzi and Mapam's cultural front.

The subversive nature of Hakibbutz Ha'artzi and Mapam cultural activity was clearly evident in another phenomenon, one influenced by economic developments, the search for new content, improvements in access to information, and the attempt to grapple with the Left's ideological crisis as confronted by the leadership's ossification and conservatism. At the beginning of the 1960s, two young faculty members at the Oranim Teachers College, an institution run jointly by the three kibbutz movements, inaugurated a project addressing international relations and political philosophy. Yigal Wagner, a historian, and Michael Strauss, a philosopher, proposed a new reading of Marxist theory, arguing that the traditional understanding of international relations and politics as taking place between the Eastern and Western blocs, between developed and developing countries, and between socialism and capitalism was anachronistic and incorrect. Actual politics, they maintained, crosses ideological boundaries, and blocs that at first glance seem to be ideologically cohesive are in fact divided into rival camps. Against the background of the Right–Left controversy in Hakibbutz Ha'artzi and Mapam, this "theory of camps" garnered exceptional attention in the movement. It was a major influence on students in Hakibbutz Ha'artzi and for a time had a huge and controversial impact on the leadership's agenda.

The theory of camps first reached the public in the summer of 1963 in a series of articles published in the Min Hayesod movement's journal under the collective title "A New World Order." Wagner, Strauss, and another collaborator, Ze'ev Goldschmit, signed the articles with the pen name "A. Gesher," whose tagline was "close to Mapam." This was the time of the battle between Lavon and Ben-Gurion, and the three authors wanted to enable Lavon to say that they were not his supporters but were nevertheless expressing ideas that accorded with his worldview.[73] Lavon himself wrote an unsigned editor's introduction to the articles.[74] The tagline and the content of the articles, which illustrated the authors' theories by means of several international political case studies, aroused fury among Hakibbutz Ha'artzi's leaders. The clear dichotomy that Mapam made between the world of the revolution (or world of tomorrow) and the capitalist-imperialist world was an important part of its political identity and a fundamental element of its theory of stages, which justified the party's constructive participation in the Zionist enterprise prior to the arrival of a future revolutionary era. The theory of camps challenged this view in that it replaced the capitalist–socialist, East–West divide with a view of rival camps within each of the blocs. The conclusion the authors drew from this analysis was that Mapam should support those elements in each bloc with which it shared common interests and goals. This argument contradicted the ideological formulations of the theory of stages, which had helped the Mapam leadership maintain a balance within the party between advocates of revolutionary socialism and supporters of reformist socialism. In other words, the theory of camps menaced the ideological foundation of the traditional power structure in Hakibbutz Ha'artzi and Mapam.

Wagner and Strauss's insight that ideology could not offer a real means of distinguishing between political rivals and allies led them to read Marx in a new way. Marx, they argued, did not always see an extreme revolutionary stance as being the best way to advance the cause of socialism. He did not necessarily define the difference between himself and his opponents according to their ideological affiliation to one or another political camp, but rather according to their concrete positions on the political questions of the day. In their case studies, Wagner and Strauss showed that the differences between political rivals are most salient within rather than between ideological groupings. Political camps will thus be able to find allies in the opposing camp rather than in their own.

In 1963, this was not just a theoretical matter. It had important implications for Mapam's internal debate. The Lavon Affair had led Mapam's right wing to work closely with the Min Hayesod faction in Mapai, cooperation that made unification of the labor parties seem possible and desirable. The concept of a search for political allies within a rival ideological group was thus expressly directed at the emerging idea of the Alignment. The theory of camps gave a stamp of Marxist legitimacy to those who favored cooperation of the various parties within the labor camp and shook the foundations of the claims made by the opponents of cooperation, who swore their loyalty to Marxist theory. They claimed that the advocates of cooperation with Mapai and Ahdut Ha'avodah were ideological unbelievers and heretics. Another relevant element of the theory of camps was that it made a distinction between productive capital and circulating capital. Basing themselves on Marx, the authors argued that productive capital, meaning the capital contained in different industries and embodied in physical development that contributes to general economic progress, is legitimate, despite the fact that it exploits the labor of others. Circulating capital, in contrast, is a function of financial systems and makes no economic contribution because it involves speculative commerce in money rather than investment in production.

This aspect of the theory of camps applied directly to the rapid industrialization then being undergone by the kibbutzim and the larger Israeli society and to the rise of the capitalist welfare state in both Israel and the West in the 1950s. This process raised ideological dilemmas and reservations, given that the kibbutz factories were part and parcel of the capitalist market, employed wage laborers, and exploited their labor to accumulate surplus value. The theory of camps provided an ideological imprimatur to these practices and explained away the ideological issues. In this view, the kibbutzim were still part of the camp of progress and development and had not crossed the line to join the world's reactionary forces. The pro-industrial aspect of the theory of camps fit in perfectly with the economic and social developments the West had undergone during the postwar development era. It was an attempt to grapple, on the theoretical plane, with the challenges that these processes presented to the socialist Left. Kibbutz members who were benefitting from industrialization and wage labor and whose societies were accumulating profit as a result could justify their position ideologically by means of the theory of camps. It was thus especially attractive to Hakibbutz Ha'artzi's right wing, which was identified with the meshekists. The theory constructed a consciousness that corresponded to kibbutz members' economic experience.

Starting in 1959, the theory of camps was taught in classes at Oranim College, where many of the students were kibbutz members in their twenties. These young people were taught to divide the world politically in a different way than they had learned in school, in kibbutz activities, and at home, and they were thus torn between the two conceptions. A number of students from Hakibbutz Ha'artzi were profoundly influenced by the theory of camps, among them Yoram Nimrod of Ein Hahoresh, Allon Gal of Sha'ar Ha'amakim, and Banko Adar of Ein Shemer, and these students became advocates for the theory within the kibbutz movement. Acolytes of the new theory were prominent among those who in the late 1950s began to call for disassociation from the Soviet Union and alliance with the other labor parties in Israel. During and after their studies at Oranim, the supporters of the theory of camps wrote long articles in the movement and party press in which they analyzed world policy and politics in the spirit of "A. Gesher's" analysis. They also authored opinion pieces in which they called for cooperation with Mapai.[75] Wagner and Strauss's students backed up their prodigious output with archival material, press clippings, and readings of international literature and periodicals, which lent their writings an innovative and original cast as well as a level of validity and persuasive power that made it difficult to argue against them. This trend infuriated the movement establishment, which looked on in frustration as one of its most precious ideals, the political education of promising young people, blew up in their faces. When *Bahativah* was replaced by *Hotam* as the mouthpiece of the movement's younger generation, Adar, Gal, and Nimrod became frequent writers for the new publication. The first issue of *Hotam* appeared in March 1964, and the three of them appeared in its pages on an almost weekly basis, writing on a wide variety of subjects. Their strategy was always to deconstruct the ideological dichotomies that lay at the foundation of Mapam's thinking. They wrote in particular about the development of Africa, the Sino–Soviet controversy, and the arguments for and against nuclear armament,[76] in the process roiling Mapam's membership and leadership. The reactions were harsh.[77]

Wagner and Strauss composed a summary of their views for the Mapam periodical *Basha'ar* at the end of 1963. The first part appeared in the issue published that November under the headline "On the Program in the *Communist Manifesto* and Its Theoretical Foundations."[78] The second installment appeared in March 1964. In the next issue, which came out in May, Yosef Shatil, a prominent intellectual who was a member of Kibbutz Ruhama, published a lengthy response. Ironically, Shatil was identified with the party's right wing, but he attacked the assumptions on which Wagner and Strauss built their exposition.[79] Focusing on the installment authors' challenge to the centrality of class struggle between the proletariat and the capitalists, which stood at the center of Mapam's socialist doctrine, Shatil argued that they had disregarded the fact that the proposals put forth in the *Communist Manifesto* were the right ones for their time only. The *Manifesto* should not be read, he maintained, as an analysis that applies to contemporary capitalism. Even if there had been a political distinction between productive and circulating capital when Marx and Engels authored the *Manifesto*, these two types of capital were now aligned against the labor parties. Shatil argued that Wagner and Strauss's claims had serious present-day consequences that should be taken with the utmost gravity. "There is a danger that these ideas will be taken up by the younger generation that grew up on the kibbutzim and that does not have a concrete affiliation with the working class," he warned. He declared that his greatest concern was that the new theory would promote the meshekist interest in ending the movement's partnership with urban workers in favor of cooperation with industrialists.[80] His fears were not unfounded, given that, according to the theory of camps, productive capitalists, who were employers, were a legitimate and positive force of which the kibbutzim were a part. The theory thus threatened the kibbutzim's self-image as allies of the working class and of Mapam as the representative of that class, an image that was already difficult to maintain because of the conflicting interests of the actual kibbutz economy and the urban worker.

The theory of camps fit the changing experience of the kibbutzim in another way as well. Contrary to its name, the theory actually divided political space into more than two legitimate forces. To the opposition between capital and labor it added another dichotomy between types of capital. For the Old Left, the world had been clearly divided between the forces of revolution and the forces of reaction. The theory of camps offered a more complex view. Kibbutz members, who lived in cooperative settlements that were based on the concept that all labor was to be performed by members of the commune yet who had experienced the transformation of the kibbutzim into industrial societies based on outside labor and capitalist mores, needed a view of the world that offered more than a simple binary opposition between revolution and reaction.

It is not surprising, then, that the compatibility of the theory of camps and the meshekist position, which challenged Hakibbutz Ha'artzi's leadership, aroused fear among those leaders. Meir Ya'ari, the movement's "guardian," was especially incensed. As a result, in June 1964 Wagner and Strauss were summoned for ideological interrogation at Hakibbutz Ha'artzi's Central Circle for Socialist Issues, a body that functioned as a sort of official movement think tank. The inquiry took place at Givat Haviva and was attended by the movement's experts in Marxism and a large public. Among the responders to the lecture given by Wagner and Strauss was Eliezer Hacohen, an economist, meshekist, opponent of Ya'ari and Hazan, and member of the movement's and party's right wing. One would have expected him to support the theory of camps, but he attacked its underlying assumptions, declaring that the support of the productive bourgeoisie was not a substitute for the struggle for socialism. He also cast doubt on the scholarly validity of the interpretation offered by those advocates of the new theory who wrote about it in the movement press.[81] The fact that yet another meshekist had attacked the theory of camps demonstrates how broad were the attempts to provide a theoretical foundation for the challenges confronted by the socialist Left in a welfare state. People such as Shatil and Hacohen could be advocates of economic development and rapid industrialization of the kibbutzim but also be loyal to traditional kibbutz values, which could not be reconciled with new theoretical claims like those made by the theory of camps.

Despite its marginality in terms of the number of its sympathizers, the theory of camps found its way into the consciousness of Hakibbutz Ha'artzi and Mapam thanks to the writings of its acolytes in movement journals. But it never got beyond the realm of ideas because its supporters were not allowed to pursue its practical political implications in Hakibbutz Ha'artzi and Mapam. They were able to write about it freely in the movement press thanks to the leadership's loosening hold over these cultural instruments, but part of that loosening was a deliberate act by leaders seeking to contain and control the opposition. The articles that the theory's supporters wrote demonstrated the growing strength of the movement's right wing, but, no less so, they also demonstrated that the leadership was successful in isolating the supporters politically by making sure that their demands remained in the "harmless" cultural sphere and did not leak into the political arena.

Hotam, the principal platform in which Wagner, Strauss, and their followers presented their views, grew out of the political awakening of Hakibbutz Ha'artzi's younger generation in reaction to the Lavon Affair and as manifested in the Group of Eleven. The journal was founded in reaction to the inadequacy of *Bahativah*, the voice of the movement's younger generation, which had been too limited in size and scope to meet the needs of a generation that wanted to put forth new ideas and disseminate them in an attractive and readable format. Although *Hotam* was officially designated as the organ of the Mapam and Hakibbutz Ha'artzi young guard, like all other Mapam publications and activity it remained firmly under the kibbutz members' control.[82]

Hotam began to appear just as Mapam debated whether to join the Eshkol government and enter into the Alignment. Many young people felt that writing in *Hotam* was the only available avenue to express their opinions and assert their influence; the ideas they expressed were not always to the liking of the party and movement leadership. Ya'ari had insisted, before the first issue even appeared, that the journal obey the party,[83] but its editors responded that they needed a totally free rein. According to its editor in chief, Betzalel Lev, the journal's responsibility was precisely to provide a platform for writers who wanted to challenge the movement's congresses and official positions.[84] In this view, he continued the independent line he had taken as editor of *Bahativah*.

As the Alignment between Mapai and Ahdut Ha'avodah took form, and it became clear that Mapam would not join it, the advocates of the theory of camps ratcheted up their participation in *Hotam*. Although their articles focused largely on theoretical analysis of foreign policy, both Israel's and other countries', their subtext was the concrete question of Mapam's position on the unification of the labor movement. When Yoram Nimrod wrote of the "purpose of French nuclear weapons," his aim was to demonstrate that when it came down to it, the question of France's orientation was a fundamental one for Israeli politics and that there were different positions about it within Mapai. In other words, Mapai had members with positions close to Mapam's, and these members should be harnessed as allies in the fight against Ben-Gurion's school of thought. When Banko Adar wrote about the thirtieth anniversary of the Chinese Communists' Long March, his purpose was to show that the Chinese bourgeoisie was divided, just as Mapai was. The implication was that Mapam, too, should align itself with the progressive element in the Israeli bourgeoisie rather than sequester itself behind the barricades of revolutionary socialism.[85] Of course, the opponents of the Alignment did not remain silent. Nahum Shor called for unification, but only of the "pioneering Left."[86] Yet that proposal was essentially meaningless, given that Ahdut Ha'avodah and Min Hayesod had no interest in uniting with Mapam to oppose Mapai.

Not all young members of Mapam and Hakibbutz Ha'artzi accepted the theory of camps and the political positions its advocates took. On the contrary, when the party's Youth Division convened in February 1965, many of those present complained about the dominance in *Hotam* of a handful of followers of Wagner and Strauss who were seeking to use the journal to compel Mapam to change its policies. They charged that the editors had not found and indeed had not made any effort to find enough writers who could present the opposing position.[87] They also protested the fact that these articles opposing the party line were appearing in a Mapam publication.[88] As the elections set for the end of 1965 approached, and when Ben-Gurion left Mapai and founded Rafi, the debate in *Hotam*'s pages intensified. Positions that had previously only been implied were now made concrete. The debate continued after the election as Mapam pondered whether to join the coalition, and it remained intense into 1967. After the Six-Day War, it was supplanted by new issues growing out of Israel's postwar position.

Throughout this period, from *Hotam*'s first appearance in 1964 until the war of 1967, the periodical was home to a level and ferocity of debate that had no precedent in Mapam and Hakibbutz Ha'artzi. The journal became a counterweight to *Al Hamishmar*, which ostensibly remained the stronghold of the historic leadership, although there, too, the leadership's power was waning. So, for example, the Mapam Rikuz resolved to forbid *Hotam* to publish a problematic article attacking Ya'ari and to have it published instead in *Al Hamishmar*, where Ya'ari would have the privilege of publishing a response.[89] The freedom of debate in *Hotam* resulted from the public atmosphere in Hakibbutz Ha'artzi and Mapam, one element of which was the younger generation's sense of its own power and its frustration with the leadership. The internal disagreements about the great questions that Mapam faced did not, however, obscure the fact that all the party's young people shared one thing—a sense that Mapam had to change, despite or because of the conduct of its conservative political leadership and its attempts to balance the two positions in the debate by avoiding coming down on either side.

Hakibbutz Ha'artzi's college, Givat Haviva, also underwent a major metamorphosis in the early 1960s along the lines of what was taking place on the rest of Hakibbutz Ha'artzi and Mapam's cultural front. The socio-economic, political, and ideological developments in the movement and party during the mid-1950s made it ever more difficult to run the kind of ideological adult-education program that the college had been set up to provide. The crisis first became evident at the beginning of 1956. In a letter to Meir Ya'ari, Yehuda Bauer, a member of Kibbutz Shuval and a teacher at the college, faulted the college for not performing its mission. Bauer, who later became one of Israel's leading historians, blamed the failure on a shortage of resources but also noted that "a very dangerous atmosphere of cynicism and indifference to the movement is spreading within it, of concealing hired labor, opposition to mobilizing members." He added that kibbutzim scorned Givat Haviva's work and sent inappropriate people to its cadres course, which was meant to be the flagship of the movement's ideological training programs.[90] The difficulties Bauer cited were brought on by the rise of meshekism as an outgrowth of advances in kibbutz agriculture (even before massive industrialization began), the younger generation's entry into kibbutz life, the general desire for respite after years of self-sacrifice and war, and the relative comfort resulting from the postwar rehabilitation of the kibbutzim. People were less interested in ideology, even before the major ideological crisis that followed Khrushchev's secret speech in 1956. These circumstances eroded Givat Haviva's standing, a process that became even more pronounced when the ideological crisis arrived.

Following Khrushchev's speech and the Sinai Campaign, the college, too, was caught up in the resulting ideological ferment. Hakibbutz Ha'artzi's ideological authority was undermined.[91] Students were not afraid to fire incisive questions at its leaders—for example, about their continuing support for the Soviet Union despite the revelations about Stalin. They soon began to rebel against the one-sidedness of the curriculum and teaching at Givat Haviva and to demand to be allowed to hear other views.[92] The leadership responded by setting up ideological discussion groups at the college, operating under the approval, supervision, and guidance of the movement. In these discussion groups, prominent movement intellectuals formulated theoretical responses to current issues, keeping the debate within the movement so as to avoid presenting a public face of ideological confusion. The most important of these discussion groups, devoted to issues in socialism, grappled with the crisis of loyalty to the Soviet Union. At its first meeting in 1957, the group deliberated on "the dictatorship of the proletariat and the roads to socialism." Two members offered opening lectures, and then discussion commenced. The urgent issues were divided into more specific aspects to be addressed at future meetings, which were to take place on a monthly basis. The strategy of providing movement intellectuals with a forum where they could sound off ensured that they would not exacerbate the crisis of the Left by speaking out publicly.[93]

Alongside the establishment-sponsored discussion groups at Givat Haviva, Hakibbutz Ha'artzi and Mapam sanctioned a number of informal discussion groups for the airing of current political issues against the background of the Left's ideological crisis. The groups were spontaneous local initiatives that arose in advance of Mapam's Fourth Congress of 1963. The participants wanted to engage with pressing issues in a way not possible in the framework of discussions that took place under the rubric of ideological collectivism, which were structured presentations of written manifestos by Ya'ari, Hazan, and their acolytes. Again, the motivation for tolerating these discussion groups was the hope that they would allow dissenters to vent their frustrations within a controlled setting.[94] But the leadership remained conflicted about this activity. In 1965, Ya'ari and Hazan clashed over one such group led by a Hazan loyalist, Moshe Chizik (Khalif) of Kibbutz Eilon. It emerged that Hazan had known about the group and had given his unofficial blessing. Although the discussion took place within very clear boundaries and with a commitment to party discipline,[95] Ya'ari was incensed because, unlike other such groups, all of the members of this one came from the party's right rather than representing a range of opinions. For Ya'ari, this group raised the specter of factionalism in the party, and so he brought the issue before the leadership. Hazan was caught off guard. In an effort to defend himself, he attacked the discussion group, demanding that they operate "by the rules" or desist.[96] At a particularly stormy meeting of Hakibbutz Ha'artzi's Executive Committee in October 1966 that took up the issue of discussion groups supporting labor-movement unification, Hazan declared: "It's poison, destruction, cannibalism, not how a movement operates." Together with Ya'ari, he forced a decision to forbid any discussion group to organize on the basis of a particular political idea, with the exception of groups under movement supervision. The decision also mandated the Mapam Secretariat's establishment of officially sanctioned discussion groups.[97]

Despite this turmoil, no changes were made in Givat Haviva's course offerings. Marxism–Leninism continued to be taught in two of the most important programs, the cadres course and the seminar for movement activists, despite the fact that in other cultural institutions, such as the publisher Sifriyat Poalim, Lenin's thought was no longer packaged together with Marx's.[98] Nor was the college's curriculum revised—in fact, it was reinforced. The cadres course remained at a full three months, and in 1958 a new six-month-long seminar for activists was instituted, aimed at training kibbutz members for work in the movement and party; the syllabus for both remained focused on indoctrination and mobilization. In response, kibbutz members began to vote with their feet simply by not signing up for these courses. An evaluation in 1958 of the fifth cadres course found that many kibbutz members did their best not to stand out at work and in kibbutz activities, fearing that if they took too much initiative, they would be sent to these courses and then assigned to movement and party tasks. That same year, seventeen kibbutzim could not come up with a single candidate for the cadres course, a large jump from nine kibbutzim who could not do so the previous year.[99] This happened at the same time that Ya'ari was castigating kibbutz economic leaders who wanted to truncate the seminar for twelfth graders held at Givat Haviva. The situation only got worse. The ideological crisis as well as the social and economic changes the kibbutzim were undergoing made the movement's ideological activity seem like a burden that kibbutz members wanted to avoid.

One outcome of the ideological crisis and the difficulties at Givat Haviva was that Moshe Chizik was appointed to head Hakibbutz Ha'artzi's Cultural Department, which oversaw the college. Chizik put his full energies into his new post, issuing new guidelines and revamping much of the department's work. He announced that he intended to institute a new year-long course for activists at Givat Haviva and to reinstate the cadre-training course, which had been suspended.[100] But the kibbutzim continued to sidestep compulsory ideological education. A letter that the Cultural Department sent out to the kibbutzim in 1961 serves as evidence of such sidestepping: "We regret to inform you that your kibbutz has not demonstrated any understanding of the vital need that the movement, the kibbutz, and each individual in the kibbutz has for the ideological courses held at Givat Haviva," it said.[101] Repeated attempts to reinstate the ideological training programs at the college remained restricted to paper.

Kibbutz members evaded ideological education for many reasons, economic, social, and political. Among these reasons were burgeoning meshekism, the fact that kibbutz members now had leisure time (meaning that they did not have to sign up for a course at Givat Haviva in order to get a respite from their daily grind), the availability of outside information (radios were now more accessible), and diminishing support for the concept of ideological collectivism. Furthermore, more and more kibbutz members sought professional studies, and the lack of ideological fervor typical of any population moving into the middle class was evidenced at the kibbutzim as well. It took a while for the college to grasp what was going on, but when it did, it gradually began to replace its indoctrination programs with scholarly and cultural activities offered for enrichment and enjoyment.[102] In 1966, for example, half of the activity at Givat Haviva took place in departments relating to general culture rather than in courses devoted to reinforcing ideological collectivism. Study days devoted to a variety of subjects constituted another 22 percent of the college's programming. Educational activity for Hashomer Hatza'ir youth movement constituted 15 percent of the college's curriculum, and the ideological courses and program accounted for only 13 percent. Recall that it was for this latter purpose exclusively that the college was founded in the first place.[103] The nature of the ideological activities also changed. In the absence of interest in ideological education among adults, these programs were aimed at young people who had completed their military service. This group made up 40 percent of those who attended ideological programs. But members of this group, too, often attended such a program but never returned for any other studies. "The younger generation wants education of a different type," said Menahem Rosner, a young teacher at the college.[104] A few years later Givat Haviva's status as an ideological institution was officially pronounced dead. In discussions of its future, members of the movement eulogized its great original mission.[105]

Givat Haviva's failure to realize its vocation as an educational institution aimed at reinforcing Hakibbutz Ha'artzi's ideological identity was belied by the physical development of its campus. The movement invested huge resources in the college—its budget tripled between 1955 and 1965.[106] New buildings were built, and the grounds were tended and beautified until classrooms looked out on expanses of green lawns. Ironically, as the movement's ideological crisis intensified, the economic prosperity of the kibbutzim, which was itself one of the causes of the crisis, benefitted Givat Haviva. Nothing better demonstrated the dialectic interrelationship between economic success, social entrenchment, and the impotence of ideological indoctrination in the cultural sphere.

From Sports for the People to Sports for the Champions

Sports was another area in which the labor movement's institutional culture changed profoundly. The original goal of fostering physical activity as part of labor culture was to hone class consciousness and to foster norms such as cooperation, physical health, and communal leisure enjoyment. But beginning in the mid-1950s the sports organization Hapoel began to adopt practices that went beyond and even contradicted these ideological principles.[107] Volleyball in Hakibbutz Ha'artzi serves as a perfect illustration.

In Israel of the 1950s, volleyball metamorphosed from a popular sport into a professional sport with regard to training standards and competition. In 1956, Hapoel handed over organization of games to the National Sports Association. That same year the National Volleyball League was organized, which quickly came to be dominated by Hakibbutz Ha'artzi kibbutzim. The kibbutz teams' achievements lay at the center of what some people at the time termed a "social psychosis" surrounding volleyball in these communities.[108] As kibbutz teams won resounding victories over other Israeli teams and competed against great eastern European teams, kibbutz volleyball became an antidote to the relative drabness and isolation of kibbutz life. The young players were lionized by the older generation, an exceptional phenomenon given the intergenerational tension at that time. Kibbutz members also constituted the vast majority of Israel's national teams, both men's and women's. Nevertheless, players remained amateurs. They did not receive the kind of professional training common in other countries, nor could they devote themselves full-time to honing their game. Yet their lack of success on the world stage did not in any way diminish the social and athletic experience of the game, neither for the players nor for the larger kibbutz public. Life at many kibbutzim revolved around the volleyball court: talented boys and girls were taken out of school; young men were excused from work in the fields and women from their jobs in order to participate in games. They even received days off, a rare privilege at the time, for team practices before important contests. The huge status enjoyed by volleyball led to friction between, on the one hand, Hapoel, the teams, and the players and, on the other, the kibbutz and movement establishment, which were not at all pleased with the huge prestige the game enjoyed.[109]

Volleyball gradually became an exterritorial enclave in a movement in which, at least in theory, a central authority controlled and structured members' social, economic, cultural, and political lives. The game, like other areas of kibbutz culture, turned into an unsupervised space in which members could exercise independence and self-expression and follow their own preferences and values. Dramatic ideological and political metamorphoses could take place on either side of the net.

Volleyball had ostensibly been chosen as Hakibbutz Ha'artzi's game because of its socialist characteristics. It is tempting to view it as a cultural instrument that reinforced the movement's political establishment and social structure, as it indeed did during the days of barefoot austerity (and volleyball practice) in the 1930s, 1940s, and 1950s, when it remained an amateur pastime. But when the game grew more competitive and professionalized, it served as an engine of social change. At its peak in the 1960s and 1970s, it changed the lives of not just its players but also its kibbutz fans and managers. True, the players lived in kibbutzim and were members of their teams, but their real formative experience was the game, which fostered drive and competitiveness in opposition to the socialist values of cooperating and of placing the community's needs before personal achievement. It removed the players from routine life at their kibbutzim, exposed them to city life and the world, and turned some of them into stars. For kibbutz fans of the game, the volleyball court stood outside the realm of ideological oversight; it was a place the movement did not enter or direct. The figure of the competitive athlete shunted aside that of the pioneer farmer and soldier, the founding generation's ideal.[110] The pioneer was an outsider who served as a beacon to Israeli society; because the pioneer was first and foremost devoted to his kibbutz, the image had helped the movement leadership discipline its members. The athlete, in contrast, was a popular hero who was part and parcel of Israel's larger society and values, including its bourgeois ethos.

The officials and managers who promoted and ran the teams were instrumental in lending the game broader social significance at Hakibbutz Ha'artzi kibbutzim.[111] Consciously or unconsciously, these people, as they recast the amateur game into a professional one, grasped the changes that were taking place in the way the game was understood and the values it expressed. No longer was volleyball a pickup game to be enjoyed by all kibbutz members, a pastime in which the game itself and good sportsmanship were more important than who won. Instead, promising and talented players were selected and trained and to that end needed to be excused from work and study to achieve their highest potential. The leaders of individual kibbutzim and of the movement as a whole were not pleased, but in the end they could not impose their will on the game's impresarios. The latter had a public mandate that grew out of the changing nature of kibbutz life, and one of the changes was that kibbutz members wanted their community to field a winning team. Volleyball was thus not just evidence of the change in kibbutz life—it was one of the instigators of that change.

Socially, the impresarios were much like the meshekists. The movement leadership understood early on that the meshekists were a menace to its control of kibbutz life and thus sought to hold them back. But it never clashed with the boosters of volleyball, despite the fact that the ethos these boosters promoted was in many ways much more radically individualist than the ethos promoted by the meshekists. Competitive sport was openly bourgeois and capitalist in nature and had the power to bring about major social changes precisely because the leadership had much less capacity for exerting control over sport than it did over the economic realm. The movement's leaders could forbid kibbutzim to enter into partnerships with private investors in establishing factories or with other kibbutzim in regional concerns or to hire outside labor (all with limited success). But it could not change volleyball's rules or the nature of the training necessary to produce good players and teams or the way the National Volleyball League and international matches were run, and it could not keep fans away from games. The volleyball court was, of course, always located at the kibbutz's geographic center (as opposed to the fields, factories, and regional concerns the meshekists ran, which were located on the kibbutz perimeter or outside it and thus less of a presence in communal life). This location made volleyball into an agent of radical change, but despite its physical visibility, its huge potency was not immediately evident, and it was thus more effective than meshekism. True, the meshekists were important agents of change in kibbutz society, but the volleyball players, teams, and managers were a social element with practices diametrically opposed to the values promoted by Hakibbutz Ha'artzi's ideology. They thus fractured the leadership's control over kibbutz life. The competitive ethos of volleyball was used to justify an important part of the metamorphosis of kibbutz values between the 1950s and 1970s. Because changes in the areas of politics, economics, and official culture were evident, the leadership could take action to counter them. But volleyball ironically established an antisocialist mode of behavior that undermined the power of the leadership and the movement even while it gave the impression that it was a communal game that brought prestige to Hakibbutz Ha'artzi.

In other words, the volleyball ethos was a major force in turning Hakibbutz Ha'artzi kibbutzim from one-generational, ascetic farming societies imbued with a total ideology into affluent, industrial, multigenerational, and ideologically pluralist communities. The volleyball experience was a microcosm of the historical development the kibbutzim experienced as they grew more competitive, achievement oriented, open to the world, integrated into their surroundings, and no longer at the vanguard of Israeli society. In short, volleyball was a ritual, and, like other cultural practices, it attracted fans who changed society from below.

12

From Broken Boundaries to Autonomy

The Counterculture

The emergence of sports as an agent of change exemplifies a larger process in the cultural arenas of Hakibbutz Ha'artzi and Mapam and of the other parts of the labor movement as institutional culture gave way to autonomy. This change was enabled by the huge economic, social, and political transformation that Israeli and kibbutz society had undergone by the second half of the 1960s. First, the decline of the mediating mechanism created a new behavioral dispensation for expressing powerful opposition to the establishment in the cultural sphere. Second, living conditions in postmaterial society catalyzed a commercialization of culture that compelled it to encompass a wide variety of uncontrolled content. Third, new instruments of culture came into use, most importantly television, which produced new genres that the traditional cultural arena did not know how to participate in or cope with. Fourth, Israel's younger generation began to absorb influences from the international youth culture.

The 1960s saw the entry of a large cohort of young people into Israeli society. Although the Israeli baby boom began after the War of Independence rather than after World War II and thus lagged a few years behind the booms in Europe and the United States, it had much the same effect. There was a sharp leap in the size of the youth population, and this generation grew up in a period of relative tranquility and rapid economic progress. It developed a unique identity and rebellious attitude toward the aspiration for normalization that typified the older generation. The affluence and comfort in which the generation of the 1960s grew up, compared to the conditions experienced by their parents a generation earlier, focused attention on postmaterial values that grew out of an incisive critique of contemporary society. But the parties and movements of the Left, which might have been expected to serve as vehicles for the younger generation's desire to change the world, were in crisis and could offer little inspiration. The new generation thus opposed not just the conservative establishment but also the liberal and socialist establishment. In other words, they were opposed to everything—oppressive schools, conservative parents, stultifying bourgeois culture, capitalist consumerism, chauvinist nationalism, wars, and what they saw as Western imperialism and colonialism in the Third World.

The younger generation in both Israel and the West gave voice to all this opposition in the most accessible arena they found—culture. The result was the counterculture. In Israel, it could be seen in the press, literature, poetry, and theater, but music was the central manifestation of rebellion. From 1968, a rhythm-band scene emerged in clubs in the Tel Aviv area. The Beat Generation's loud music, wild fashions, and drugs were the trademarks of rebellion against the existing order. The protest gained momentum when television broadcasts began in 1968, including satirical programs that made fun of the government, society, and their leaders.[1]

The counterculture also produced a wide variety of critical pamphlets and weeklies, written and read by young people. *Na'ashush* (a nonsense word), a semiunderground paper written by a group of high school students, appeared in Tel Aviv in 1969 and was read by teenagers and soldiers. The writers were heavily influenced by the American and European counterculture. One group of these writers soon split away to form *Ga'ashush* (another nonsense word), which addressed the War of Attrition and Palestinian rights and supported sexual freedom. A similar spirit prevailed among college students. The Hebrew University Student Association's newspaper, *Pi Ha'aton* (Mouth of the She-Ass), was founded in 1958; a decade later it took on a stridently nonconformist tone on these same issues. *Post Mortem* was the University of Haifa student newspaper, founded in 1971 and edited by members of the radical Yesh faction, which controlled the student government there for a short time. It took a radical critical line that infuriated the university administration and the Knesset. The Tel Aviv University student newspaper, *Dorban* (Porcupine), published from 1965 to 1968, featured a scatological satirical column by Hanoch Levin, who would later become a major poet, playwright, and member of the Tel Aviv avant-garde.[2]

Another, if milder, manifestation of the counterculture was the book published in English as *The Seventh Day* (a literal translation of the Hebrew title, *Siah lohamim*, is "Soldiers Speak"), which appeared in Hebrew in October 1967.[3] The book, a collection of conversations with and testimonies of kibbutz soldiers who had fought in the Six-Day War, also served as a critique of the labor and kibbutz movements. Although the book was issued as a single volume, it was the first of a series of three—*After the War* came out in 1968, and *Among Young People* in 1969. The books were a project of a broad-based group of young kibbutz members from all movements who at the beginning of the decade had begun to speak out critically and skeptically about the communities where they had grown up. They were the same people who wrote in *Shdemot* and who participated in the regional discussion groups already mentioned. The conversations recorded in these three postwar collections were a continuation of a culture of discussion that was already well established by the time the war broke out. Like other elements of the counterculture, the culture of discussion took an adversarial stance against the establishment, growing out of these young people's lack of identification—to the point of alienation—with their kibbutzim.[4]

Hakibbutz Ha'artzi and Mapam were fertile ground for the counterculture to grow, serving as a good illustration of the larger trend in Israel and the world. The movement's intellectual tradition emboldened its members in the city and the younger generation at the kibbutzim to take up the neo-Marxist thinking that formed the theoretical center of the New Left. Some of the seminal neo-Marxist works were translated into Hebrew and published by Sifriyat Poalim. The new culture was also brought to the kibbutzim by people such as volunteers from other countries and immigrants from the United States, France, and Latin America, who brought with them newspapers, music, and fashions. Given the radicalism that was an integral element of the counterculture movement, their influence on Hakibbutz Ha'artzi's youth was particularly potent. This influence could be seen in underground newspapers produced and circulated in the movement's schools, in critical theater productions, and in Woodstock-style music festivals. One example was Harei Efrayim high school, which served seventh to twelfth graders from Hakibbutz Ha'artzi kibbutzim in the Ramot Menashe region, southeast of Haifa. In July 1970, the graduating class put on a show called *Ballad of 1970* that protested the oppressive atmosphere of bereavement and death in the lives of Israeli eighteen-year-olds. It was inspired by the American musical *Hair*, which was produced in Israel that same year. The high school show caused a public uproar. In April 1971, the same school held a festival called Purkan '71, featuring the Israeli rock band the Churchills, one of the leading forces in the new culture. Thousands participated. There was also a political cast to the event—members of the Black Panther protest movement were invited to meet with students.[5] A year later 1,500 teenagers from twenty-two schools gathered in Kibbutz Evron for the Spring '72 Festival, "organized in the spirit of the times and [with] a pop atmosphere."[6] A gathering of Hashomer Hatza'ir youth movement's kibbutz division in 1972 "looked like Woodstock," to the great consternation of the youth movement's leadership.[7] Hakibbutz Ha'artzi considered canceling the same event the following year because of its radical look, which clearly reflected the worldwide counterculture. Hashomer Hatza'ir youth movement also involved itself in radical causes, its members participating in tempestuous demonstrations.[8] They also displayed an affinity for other aspects of the protest movement, such as the plays of Hanoch Levin.[9] Although Hakibbutz Ha'artzi nominally controlled the youth movement, it could not prevent the zeitgeist from profoundly affecting its members.

The members of Hakibbutz Ha'artzi's Youth Division—most of whom were soldiers, recently discharged soldiers, and students—had emerged from service in the War of Attrition disheartened, cynical, distrustful of the government, and thus susceptible to the culture of protest. At the height of the despondency that the conflict engendered, the Youth Division began to issue its own periodical, *Hatza'it* (Skirt).[10] It served as a platform for unconventional and defiant ideas, reflecting the counterculture that had developed in the kibbutzim and the dominance of the New Left among young adherents of Hashomer Hatza'ir and the Youth Division.[11] Its writers castigated the conservatism of Golda Meir and Moshe Dayan as well as the public euphoria that followed the Six-Day War as they "sought to spotlight the doves in politics and culture in Israel, which seemed to have lost its aspiration for peace."[12] *Hatza'it* offered protest poetry, short stories, and plays about death and injury, spiced with cynicism and black humor. Mapam's membership in the government and the Alignment fed the youth protest against the labor movement's leadership and created a general atmosphere critical of the establishment. The protest intensified significantly prior to the crisis of confidence brought on by the Yom Kippur War.

Cultural Autonomy in Hakibbutz Ha'artzi and Mapam

The move from breaking down boundaries to achieving autonomy in the labor movement's cultural system, which resulted from a combination of the broadening of the cultural field and the entry of countercultural ideas and forms of expression into Israeli society, could be seen in much of Hakibbutz Ha'artzi and Mapam's cultural arena. This process first became evident at Tzavta, Mapam's cultural center in Tel Aviv, which turned into the creative center of Israel's New Left. Although the New Left was a political current, its major avenue of expression was cultural. Tzavta, already in the avant-garde, sought to make itself into an artistic platform for Israel's New Left not just for artistic and political reasons but also for commercial reasons. Its cultural milieu was that of the worldwide counterculture, and writers, poets, actors, and entertainers who frequently appeared at Tzavta—such as Dan Ben-Amotz, Amos Kenan, and Arik Einstein—identified with the New Left and brought its style and messages into the club.

Tzavta did not just offer the New Left a platform. It molded its material, sponsoring a rally in sympathy with the Vietnam War protestors; an appearance by the American protest singer Pete Seeger; an evening on the American New Left that included a reading of English-language protest and peace poetry; an evening at which Mordechai Oren interviewed the Czech New Left novelist Ladislav Mňačko on the Prague Spring; a solidarity evening with student rebels in Poland, emceed by the *Al Hamishmar* correspondent Sever Plotzker; a discussion of the riots in Poland led by the Polish Jewish sociologist Zygmunt Baumann; a memorial evening for Martin Luther King Jr.; and a "War and Peace in Vietnam" evening at which intellectuals and journalists spoke.[13]

After the Six-Day War, Tzavta also became an important podium for the cause of peace and critique of the government's security and foreign policy (at a time when Mapam was a member of the government). During an evening in honor of the conquest of Jerusalem's Old City, held just a few days after the war, Dan Ben-Amotz declared that he was "revolted by the orgy of tears and weeping conducted at the Western Wall." The microphone was grabbed from him before he even finished his sentence, and an uproar ensued.[14] A month after the end of the war, the club staged a new play by Amos Mokadi and Micha Limor. In an interview in *Hotam*, the playwrights related that they wanted to write something different from the victory albums that were then coming out. As an alternative, they collected testimonies from soldiers who had served in the war. Their drama focused on the personal experience of the fighters and their horror of combat. It included a protest song by Meir Ariel warning against the postwar euphoria, "Jerusalem of Iron," a parody of Naomi Shemer's wildly popular song "Jerusalem of Gold."[15]

At the beginning of 1969, a group of Israeli leftists, including members of Hakibbutz Ha'artzi, began to conduct meetings with Arab counterparts in Europe. The results of the meetings were presented at Tzavta, which in December 1969 staged a new production on the lives of both Israelis and Palestinian Arabs in the shadow of the war. That same year the club also staged an original show with the title *Where Have All the Flowers Gone?*, which presented the absurdity of the war. The critical stance of the production is evidenced by a sharp letter written by an angry viewer, who charged the play with being anti-Zionist.[16] During a symposium with Foreign Minister Abba Eban, devoted largely to the captured territories, Avraham Shlonsky spoke harshly about the spirit of the times and the goals of Zionism. "What [does it mean to be] a chosen people?" he asked. "That the IDF is the best? That we can stage the best [military] attack?"[17] New Left and countercultural figures such as Hanoch Levin and Sylvie Keshet were regulars on Tzavta's stage at this time.

Under Shmuel Firstenberg, Tzavta became a platform for opposition voices within Mapam, opinions that deviated from the official party line, and for opponents of the party as well. In other words, it stood fundamentally in contradiction to the concept and consciousness of a centralized party.[18] The party establishment did not like the free and open dialogue that was Tzavta's trademark. It sought to control it and so increased its oversight of all the Tzavta clubs. Following the Six-Day War, when Tzavta clubs opened in many cities and kibbutzim, the party decided to establish an umbrella body under Mapam's Propaganda and Culture Department that would coordinate and originate programming for the clubs.[19] A secretariat of all the kibbutz Tzavta clubs began to operate in March 1968.[20] A personnel shakeup also took place. Firstenberg, the well-liked and longtime director, was dismissed so that he would have to return the club's reins to the party.[21] The Mapam Rikuz made this decision in October 1967 and named his successor, Shimon Menahem of Kibbutz Dalia, a loyal party member who had just completed a term as coordinator of Mapam's Jerusalem branch.[22] In the remaining months of 1968, the two men served alongside each other, with Firstenberg leaving his post at the beginning of 1969.

The attempt to subordinate Tzavta to the party leadership's authority was not successful, however. The club in Tel Aviv already had a character of its own, and it continued to serve as an outlet for New Left ideas. In 1971, it began to address social issues in response to criticism from young members of Mapam who complained that the party was neglecting domestic policy and focusing on foreign affairs and defense. Dan Ben-Amotz translated the American musical *The Me Nobody Knows* (music by Gary William Friedman, lyrics by Will Holt, 1970), which gave voice to the lives of inner-city youth, and Tzavta staged it. *Al Hamishmar* wrote that the play was "a social explosive."[23] The play's characters spoke of their boring school, pickpocketing, the employment office, time spent in institutions for juvenile delinquents, drug use, and other experiences. Ben-Amotz, in his usual outspoken way, inserted monologues on peace as a critique of Israel's stance in its conflict with the Arabs. "They say that the doves should bring peace, but in the meantime they just shit on Mom's laundry," one character says.[24]

In 1971, the Israeli public seems to have increased the amount of criticism it was willing to stomach. That year saw the birth of a new kind of political satire in Israel, with Tzavta playing a special role. It was the artistic home of Hanoch Levin, a playwright and humorist who flouted conventions and limits and who was brazen in his handling of issues. Levin's satirical revue *You and Me and the Next War* was scheduled for production at Tzavta Tel Aviv, forcing the management to address the tension between, on the one hand, audience preferences, artistic freedom, and the zeitgeist and, on the other, movement discipline and loyalty to party ideology. In the end, it decided to cancel the production on the grounds that it would be a bad influence on the audience, especially on the young. Young people, the management argued, were liable to learn from it that all war was bad, which might cause them not to report for military service to participate in the necessary and just defense of the State of Israel. The show went up nevertheless at Tel Aviv's Barbarim club.

After that, Levin did not even offer his cabaret *Queen of a Bathtub*, a landmark of social protest and political satire in Israel, to Tzavta. Perhaps he realized what the club management's boundaries were, given its allegiance to the Mapam leadership. Opening instead at the Cameri Theater in April 1970, the cabaret caused an unprecedented public uproar that ended in further shows being canceled. Levin returned to Tzavta with his drama *Heffetz*, which opened in March 1971 and caused no controversy. With Tzavta Tel Aviv, he then coproduced *Ya'akobi and Leidenthal*, the first of his plays that he also directed. It opened in December 1972.

Levin's views and the way he presented Israel's tribulations did not sit well with Mapam's doctrines and values. The party's cultural establishment was embarrassed by the hitherto untouched subjects Levin addressed, as was Hakibbutz Ha'artzi's political establishment. Furthermore, Levin's public persona was very far from the image Mapam's leaders wanted to foster for their party. Nevertheless, they reached the conclusion that "it is better to support it, if only so that it be under our control," as party Political Secretary Naftali Feder put it at a meeting of the Mapam Secretariat that addressed Tzavta's role as a satirical theater because it seemed to be losing all constraint.[25]

Levin was not the only one to confront the Tzavta management with dilemmas over its duty to Mapam as opposed to freedom of artistic expression and public tastes. In July 1972, the club presented a satiric show written by Amos Kenan very reminiscent of *Queen of a Bathtub*. Kenan's *Friends Talk about Jesus* received a huge amount of press coverage before it even opened.[26] As a pioneer of political satire in the 1950s and a campaigner for social change, Kenan had been a consistent foe of the Israeli establishment. Following the Six-Day War, he was a leading proponent of withdrawing from the Occupied Territories. A man of the Left and the protest movement, Kenan made many appearances at Tzavta.

Friends Talk about Jesus was so provocative that it was banned by the military censor. Kenan appealed the decision to the Supreme Court, and while the appeal was pending, he and the censor reached a compromise according to which the revue would be performed a small number of times to an invited audience. In the end, the court denied the appeal, declaring that "the play was banned because it is insulting to religious sensibilities, bereaved parents of fallen soldiers, and moral values."[27] Tzavta had no choice but to cancel the show. "We did not want any scandals," Shimon Menahem said. But he denied the claim made by the daily newspaper *Yediot Aharonot* (Latest News) that Mapam had instigated the decision. "Mapam's institutions definitely hold to the decision that Tzavta is an autonomous club that makes its own programming decisions," Menahem responded.[28] His statement was not, however, entirely in accord with the facts because the party had held many discussions about Tzavta and had influenced decisions made by the club's management. The club's freedom did not derive from Mapam adhering to a principle that granted autonomy to its artistic institutions, as Menahem claimed, but simply from Mapam having no choice. That can be seen in Mapam's policy of lending a hand to the counterculture, as Feder told a party meeting. In keeping with this policy, members of the Black Panthers, the most prominent protest group in Israel at the time, made an appearance at Tzavta Tel Aviv in April 1971. The Mapam Secretariat was very worried but approved the program so as to avoid causing a ruckus. To everyone's relief, the evening passed without incident.[29]

In 1970, Tzavta began searching for a better venue to house the wealth of activity the Tel Aviv club offered. The basement on Mapu Street was no longer large enough. In the end, it decided to move into a new space in a commercial building then under construction on Even Gvirol Street. After construction commenced, the Mapam Rikuz took up a suggestion by Amos Kenan that the new building serve as home to a political satire troupe managed by the columnist and screenwriter Haim Heffer and two members of Mapam. Reuven Arazi, a Mapam member of the Knesset, did not like the idea. Naftali Feder, the political secretary, told him: "It's reasonable to assume that if we don't do it, others will, and better that it be ours, even in exchange for a promise of only partial control."[30] The proposal was rejected in the end, but it demonstrated how Mapam was losing control of the club. Most of Tzavta Tel Aviv's programming in the 1970s was popular entertainment and activities, and only a minority of it was political. The political activity sometimes did not please the party establishment, but the leaders had to accept such programs because they realized that any attempt to block them would cause a public outcry.

The bottom line was that Tzavta was hugely popular. It averaged an audience of 30,000 a year for about two hundred performances.[31] Israeli rock's superstars—Arik Einstein, Shalom Hanoch, and the Churchills, the local representatives of American and British popular music—appeared regularly, giving the club a young and progressive character. Even had Mapam patrons wanted to, they could hardly have turned Tzavta back to the days when it was a progressive cultural center with programming that accorded with the party line—the original raison d'être for which it was founded. This new situation came before the Mapam Rikuz. What was the nature of the party's ownership of the club? Menachem Bader, one of Hakibbutz Ha'artzi's senior economic authorities, proposed that Mapam hand the facility over to a public board that would run the club on behalf of the Tel Aviv municipality and the country. Ya'ari and Feder insisted, however, that Tzavta remain in the hands of Mapam and Hakibbutz Ha'artzi.[32]

Tzavta's new home at 30 Even Gvirol, fine and spacious for its time, opened its doors on January 10, 1972. The move showed how commercially successful the club had become, despite the dissatisfaction it caused among Mapam's leaders. In light of changes in its programming and its move in a more commercial direction, Feder told the Mapam Rikuz that "the more Tzavta succeeds, the more the public forgets its connection to Mapam, despite [the club's] great contribution to Israeli art and culture. True, Tzavta is a success story. The public does not identify it with Mapam and we need to think about how to make the public aware once again that it belongs to Mapam." Ya'ari worried that "Mapam will lose Tzavta" and demanded that "it be known that it is our place."[33] Referring to an evening at which the club hosted Yeshayahu Leibowitz and Dan Ben-Amotz in a program emceed by a representative of the radical Siah movement, Ya'ari maintained that "it would be better for Tzavta to be closed than to take that form."[34] The party secretary-general, Meir Talmi declared that "right now, Tzavta is an entertainment device and does not serve Mapam."[35]

Tzavta's avant-garde character during the period 1967–77 represented another stage in the development of Hakibbutz Ha'artzi and Mapam's cultural arena. From 1956 to 1967, the cultural arena served as a place in which the different voices in the movement could be heard, a place of debate. Focusing on this role broadened that arena but also created a situation in which some of its means of cultural expression looked inward and were thus relatively free of outside influence. The logic behind addressing a larger public in the kibbutzim and in Israel as a whole became more evident in the mid-1960s, engendered by economic considerations as well as by a desire to be relevant and up-to-date. It thus led to an openness to new directions in content and values. In the case of Tzavta, this turn outward opened the club to the New Left, turning it into an incubator of its ideas. Firstenberg supported this role because he understood that it was necessary to speak to young people in their own language and that Tzavta would quickly become irrelevant if it did not attract large audiences.[36] When Shimon Menahem took over as manager, he faced facts already on the ground. The club's audiences preferred popular programming, and "every [indication of] rigidity, prohibition of the possibility of debate, is met with a storm of criticism."[37] Mapam was not pleased, but it preferred to see political energies channeled into culture, and so to avoid scandal it had to support artistic freedom. Tzavta thus continued to be a stronghold of the New Left during the 1970s.

The character of Hakibbutz Ha'artzi's and Mapam's newspapers also changed in the wake of the Six-Day War. They, too, began to expand beyond the role of being a platform for internal debate. The expansion of the cultural arena led to a multiplication of publications, including *Al Hamishmar*, *Hotam*, *Basha'ar*, *Hashavu'a Bakibbutz Ha'artzi*, and *Hedim*. A Hakibbutz Ha'artzi committee to examine the role and function of the movement press, set up before the war but not completing its work until afterward, found that the central problem the press presented to the party leadership was discipline.[38] The plethora of periodicals made it harder to exert control over them. The committee thus recommended combining *Hotam* and *Hashavu'a Bakibbutz Ha'artzi* into a single weekly supplement to be published together with the daily *Al Hamishmar* and that the editorial staffs of these publications be united. The committee's members hoped that fewer publications could be more closely supervised and that the newspaper's "adults" could supervise the supplement's "children." Similarly, the committee recommended the merger of *Basha'ar* and *Hedim*.[39] The committee also decided to set up a permanent board to oversee the movement press.[40] During further discussions of the issue by the committee, it transpired that only *Hotam* was seen as problematic because it was functioning for all intents and purposes as an independent ideological entity that promoted an alternative to the official party line.[41] As a result, the Mapam Secretariat rejected the proposal to merge *Basha'ar* and *Hedim*. It did, however, accept the recommendation to turn *Hotam* into a supplement of *Al Hamishmar* and to merge the staffs of the two publications. *Hashavu'a Bakibbutz Ha'artzi* remained independent.[42]

The discussion of the movement press took place against the background of attempts by members of the kibbutz movement and party leadership to assert control over the publications, just as they had sought to take back control of Tzavta soon after the Six-Day War. The insubordinate editors of *Hashavu'a Bakibbutz Ha'artzi* and *Hotam*, Niva Lanir and Yossi Amitai, were dismissed. Lanir, then a young member of Kibbutz Ein Hahoresh (who would later join the staff of *Ha'aretz* as a reporter and columnist), had joined the staff of *Hashavu'a Bakibbutz Ha'artzi* after the war and after completing her military service. Hakibbutz Ha'artzi secretary Haim Shor had brought her and several other new writers in as part of his effort to give the weekly a younger face. Eliyahu Daniel of Kibbutz Ma'abarot had been named editor in chief, the role of the staff's "responsible adult." But Daniel had served for only a short time, resigning suddenly for medical reasons. Shor had then appointed Lanir to fill in for Daniel, and soon thereafter she was formally named to head the publication. The publication had changed dramatically under her leadership, with regard both to content that was sent to the weekly by the leadership and to the content that came from the grass roots. Lanir had given priority to publishing oppositional opinions that lay outside the movement's consensus. She had also put an end to the venerable practice of publishing speeches made at meetings of the movement's Executive Committee, council, and congress. Lanir was one of the leaders of a group that left Mapam in 1969, when it joined the Alignment, to found Siah. It was this act of disloyalty that triggered her dismissal as editor of *Hashavu'a Bakibbutz Ha'artzi*.[43]

At the same time that Lanir was appointed editor of *Hashavu'a Bakibbutz Ha'artzi*, Yossi Amitai, a young member of Kibbutz Gevulot, was named editor of *Hotam*. Also a leader of the group that left Mapam to form Siah, he, too, was dismissed as editor in 1969.[44] Amitai remained, however, a member of the publication's staff, to the chagrin of the historic leadership, which a few months later ousted him from that position as well.[45] Ya'ari and Hazan also personally saw to it that *Hotam* stopped publishing the work of other writers who had bolted from Mapam.[46]

It was no coincidence that Lanir and Amitai were dismissed a short time after Firstenberg was removed from the management of Tzavta and at the same time that *Hotam* became a supplement to *Al Hamishmar*. Hakibbutz Ha'artzi's leadership desperately wanted to reassert its control over the cultural arena. But these personnel changes did not alter the adversarial nature of these cultural instruments. Lanir was replaced by Rubik Rosenthal, a young member of Kibbutz Nahshon who the movement leaders hoped would appeal to the younger generation but accept the leaders' directives. He instead carried on his predecessor's provocative line.[47] Tzavta, as we have already seen, continued to serve as a megaphone for the New Left. The same happened at *Hotam* when Amitai was replaced by Betzalel Lev of Kibbutz Gan Shmuel, a courageous and independent-minded man.

Even after *Hotam* merged with *Al Hamishmar*, writers at *Hotam* continued to enjoy free rein, which was not at all to the liking of *Al Hamishmar*'s management, especially its venerable editor Ya'akov Amit. Amit was subject to constant pressure from Hazan and Ya'ari not to publish "damaging" material. One example was a piece by Banko Adar on the World Peace Council, a Communist front organization. Adar argued that the movement was fundamentally anti-Zionist, supporting Soviet policy and championing terror organizations and extremist rulers. He castigated Ya'ari for supporting Mapam's involvement in the council.[48] When Ya'ari asked Amit to publish his own (Ya'ari's) response to Adar's article, Lev refused to allow it in *Hotam* on the grounds that it was an ad hominem attack on Adar.[49] Ya'ari's response appeared in *Al Hamishmar* instead, but Amit was furious with Lev for refusing to include it in *Hotam*. He shouted at Lev that he, the editor of *Al Hamishmar*, would decide what *Hotam* would print and not print.[50] But the precedent had been set—for the first time Ya'ari, one of the movement's two historic leaders, had been barred from placing an article in a movement periodical.

But *Al Hamishmar* also provided space for attacks on the historic leadership. In early 1971, it published a piece by Eliezer Hacohen that offered a rebuttal to Ya'ari's response to Adar's claims about the World Peace Council. Ya'ari retained the right to respond to any criticism of him in the same issue that the critical article appeared—in other words, Hacohen's piece was sent to him prior to publication so that he could prepare a response that would appear alongside it.[51] The fracas between Ya'ari and Hacohen was so prominent that it came up before the Mapam Rikuz. Ya'akov Amit told the meeting that *Al Hamishmar* had received letters critical of Ya'ari's response and that Ya'ari had pressured him not to print them. The forum was fearful that word of this suppression would leak and lead to the kibbutz public's castigation of the party leadership and the newspaper's editors. Hazan brokered a compromise that the Rikuz accepted—the newspaper would not print letters about the disagreement.[52] For reasons that remain unclear, however, some of the letters, including some that were highly critical of Ya'ari, were printed anyway. Rosenthal, editor of *Hashavu'a Bakibbutz Ha'artzi*, also complained about Ya'ari's special privilege of having the opportunity to respond to criticism in the same issue it was given, thus voicing a concern of many young readers of *Al Hamishmar* that the party's mouthpiece was overly directed by the leadership.[53]

The charges that *Al Hamishmar* was an establishment newspaper and needed to open itself up more, combined with the attacks against the leadership of Hakibbutz Ha'artzi and Mapam, were becoming more and more prevalent in the movement press.[54] At a symposium, members of

Hashavu'a Bakibbutz Ha'artzi's staff argued both sides of this issue, but most of them agreed that it was the job of the newspaper to decentralize the movement, to end ideological collectivism, and above all to be independent.[55] The debate was very similar to that regarding Tzavta and the role of the movement's cultural arena. The conservatives said that internal debates should be conducted in a way that would keep them from intensifying, while the radicals maintained that the press should foster internal debate and democratization, which it believed strengthened the movement rather than tearing it apart. It was the second view that was in fact put into practice, leaving the leadership with the sense that it had lost control of the press. It no longer had the means to regulate the intensity of debate or the debate's public manifestations in the press; at best, it could seek to control the damage.[56] This damage control involved censoring occasional pieces and letters, but each attempt to do so simply aroused further ire against the leadership. The establishment was able to exercise a certain amount of control over *Al Hamishmar*, but *Hotam* remained independent and under the control of the young people of the movement's right wing. "What makes *Hotam* unique?" asked Mapam secretary Naftali Ben-Moshe at a meeting of the party Rikuz in 1971. He answered the question: "There they publish whatever the editor wants, and the party has no control. It may well be that we need to give *Al Hamishmar* more pages, instead of *Hotam*, where the editor behaves as if he is the only authority. . . . *Hotam* stands out for expressing opinions opposed to the party line."[57] Hazan noted that "our press, especially *Hashavu'a Bakibbutz Ha'artzi*, has become [a set of] newspapers that criticize Mapam and destroy it from within."[58]

In casting off the yoke of the leadership, Sifriyat Poalim had long preceded *Hotam*, *Hashavu'a Bakibbutz Ha'artzi*, and Tzavta when it replaced its formerly Marxist catalog with a list of existentialist books. Givat Haviva had ceased to be an instrument of instilling ideological collectivism and had become a center of research and study. The ideological circles had turned into a culture of discussion; although this culture was not political, it bolstered the independence of the kibbutz younger generation. The cultural front thus went through a developmental process that completely reversed its original purpose. It had been established in the

1940s as a means of political indoctrination and education for members of Hakibbutz Ha'artzi and Mapam. At the end of the 1950s, as internal debate emerged, it became a place in which internal politics could be contained and sequestered from the energy of change. At the end of the 1960s, however, the leadership's control of the cultural front was shaken, and the front now served as a platform for catalyzing a challenge to the old power structure. During the 1970s, it was actively acting against the leadership and forcing the leadership's dismemberment.

Something much like this happened along the other parts of the labor movement's cultural front. In the large picture, the counterculture and the social and political protest movement emerged from within the labor movement's social space and looked like an internal rebellion. Although it was a local phenomenon, it was also part of a larger trend in the West. The counterculture was led by young members of the middle class who were in fact products of the establishment they protested against. Much of the zeitgeist took form in the instruments that had traditionally belonged to the mobilized culture of the Left but that declared their independence to voice values and messages opposed to the establishment that had created them. Party and movement newspapers and journals grew more and more autonomous, voicing criticism of the apparatuses that they had been intended to serve. Recall the case of *Shdemot*, the journal sponsored by the Ihud Hakevutzot Vehakibbutzim kibbutz movement that became a mouthpiece for criticism of the kibbutzim and the labor movement as a whole. A similar thing happened at *Davar*, the daily newspaper published by the Histadrut and for all intents and purposes Mapai's organ for a long time. Ohad Zamora was appointed editor of the newspaper's weekend magazine, *Davar Hashavua* (Item of the Week), in 1964. He recruited a group of young, independent writers who wanted to write what was on their minds (among them Nahum Barnea, Doron Rosenblum, Michael Handelsaltz, Eli Mohar, Dani Kerman, Yair Garboz, and Yonatan Gefen). They produced a critical and trailblazing publication that was a leading force in the transition from a mobilized to an independent press. The same thing could be seen in Israel's radio stations. Broadcasting was a state-owned cultural institution, and although that meant it technically was not partisan, in practice, like the school system, it was controlled by elements of the labor movement.

Until 1960, there had been just two stations, Reshet Alef (Station A) and Galei Tzahal (the IDF station), but in 1960 another station, Reshet Bet (Station B), was launched with an "easy-listening" program. It offered popular music and broadcast commercials, unlike the more serious stations, which were more establishment oriented. Reshet Bet was more innovative and controversial.[59] Galei Tzahal, the IDF radio station, also offered popular entertainment, especially after 1967. This decision led to tension between the station's director, Yitzhak Livni, and his superiors in the Defense Ministry, who wanted the station to be more official.[60] Television broadcasts, which commenced in Israel in 1968 (also as part of the state broadcasting authority), symbolized more than anything else the breaking of conventions of the establishment's cultural front. In the years 1970–73, the satiric program *Lul* made fun of the country's founding myths. A situation comedy, *Hedva and Shlomik*, which debuted in 1971, was a social satire centered on a young couple who had left their kibbutz and were trying to adjust to city life. Another sharply satirical program, *Nikui Rosh* (Head Cleaning), came onto the screen in 1974. It offered skits making fun of things that had hitherto been taboo in the media, such as ethnic protest, drug use, and political developments. The program was highly controversial, and Arnon Zuckerman, the director of the state television station, had to stand up to pressure from leaders who demanded that the program be canceled. *Nikui Rosh* continued until 1978 and was hugely popular.[61] The limits of establishment culture had been broken down, as the test case of Hakibbutz Ha'artzi and Mapam demonstrates. Their experience was a microcosm of a larger process by which cultural institutions founded to serve as purveyors of established ideology turned into agents of change.

From Politics to Culture, from Culture to Politics

The metamorphosis of mobilized culture into the counterculture was directly related to the erosion of the Israeli labor movement's traditional political frameworks and its loss of support. The connection between politics and culture could be seen in a number of major phenomena. One was that the split of the hegemonic Left, which on the political level seemed to result in a number of currents with different orientations, looked from the cultural side like a split between the establishment and a single counterculture that united any number of aspects of opposition to the existing establishment. Demonstrations, processions, discussion groups, rallies, and articles in periodicals—whether by members of Siah, the Black Panthers, or the post–Yom Kippur War protestors—all furthered an agenda centered on the rights of the individual and minorities, pluralism, democracy, and opposition to state control of society.[62] This process brought together advocates of democracy, sectoral interests, and the poor under a single overarching ideology that united the different currents of protest against the establishment.[63] The counterculture looked like a new and revamped left-wing ideology, but it differed fundamentally from classic leftism in several ways. First, most of its supporters did not define themselves as leftists. They preferred the label *democratic* or one of its variants. Second, the counterculture addressed not the distribution of income in society but the rights of the individual. Third, it shed the Left's traditional aspiration to offer a total vision of a new social, economic, political, and cultural order. Rather, it took positions on specific issues without making a real attempt to fashion an ideology that could subsume and explain those positions. Fourth, in political terms it became an ally of the Right, which also sought to take government out of the hands of the old socialist and labor parties.[64]

The second phenomenon that demonstrated the connection between politics and culture was the younger generation's large role in political protests. The conventional scholarly consensus is that the youth protest of the 1960s was a subculture of the contemporary youth culture, which developed in the framework of what educational psychology calls the "psychosocial moratorium period,"[65] the time in which young people create for themselves a space for independent expression, unconnected to the culture of their parents and events around them—that is, in the young people's language, they "dropped out." But a larger perspective shows that the consensus is wrong. Detaching themselves from existing parties, organizations, and social norms was the way members of the younger generation directly involved themselves in political events of the time. The antiestablishment values this generation voiced had an actual political consequence, weakening the establishment. "Dropping out" granted young people a relatively large range of freedom of action, action that actually heralded social and political processes to which the older generation would only later respond. The "quiet revolution" of the Israeli younger generation of the 1950s, expressed in its reluctance to enlist in the labor movement's traditional projects (such as taking on military command and careers and settling the land), cast light on the functional nature of labor-movement mobilization during the state's first two decades. But it took the labor movement's leaders a decade to realize that they lacked any real ideological foothold in the public. Likewise, the counterculture of the younger generation, which came to the fore in the second half of the 1960s, demonstrated that the labor movement had exhausted the potential of its functional mobilization apparatus and had thus lost its legitimacy. In practice, the counterculture heralded the draining away of labor's traditional voters, which would reach its climax a decade later, at the end of the 1970s.

The third phenomenon that illuminated the connection between culture and politics was that initiatives that began by breaking down the boundaries of the cultural framework went on to break down political boundaries as well. Of course, a cultural Left came into being under the rubric of the Left, which began to focus on culture itself (that is, on the way in which people think and communicate as embodied in discourse) as an arena in which to fight for change (especially in academe and among intellectuals).[66] But a large part of this cultural activity was charged with political motivation, addressing more concrete and conventional issues. The hardcore socialist Left has long claimed that those who abandoned party politics in favor of cultural and extraparliamentary activity in the 1960s and 1970s turned apolitical. The opposite is true. The turn in fact demonstrated the creativity of the new politics, which combined political action organized outside the party and movement (for example, in the form of street protests, demonstrations, processions, rallies, festivals, distribution of leaflets) and involvement in public affairs. Culture also served as a space for social and ideological organization and for the creation of a new institutionalized opposition to the movement and party establishment. The organizers of the demonstrations became movement leaders, and extraparliamentary movements turned into political parties that competed with the traditional parties.

The change in the nature of protest and political activity as well as the process through which the protest movement consolidated first on the cultural front and then in alternative frameworks can be seen clearly in the case of members of Hakibbutz Ha'artzi, Mapam, and Hashomer Hatza'ir youth movement. One example was a mass rally to mark the anniversary of the invasion of Czechoslovakia, organized by members of Hakibbutz Ha'artzi and Siah. Arik Einstein sang "A Song I Dreamed about Prague," and Yonatan Gefen read poems he had written. The music festival Pop '70, held in July 1970, ended in rioting and rampaging by many young kibbutz members.[67] In March 1971, a celebrity-studded political festival was held at Kibbutz Shefa'im fields attended by many young kibbutz members.[68] These events not only took place outside Hakibbutz Ha'artzi and Mapam but also linked the participants to outside political and cultural actors who served as the foundation for action outside the movement, which lost power for the reasons described earlier.

The direct form of activity, which included demonstrations, assemblies, and rallies, attracted for the most part the younger generation of the kibbutzim and members of Hashomer Hatza'ir youth movement. It reinforced the connection between the cultural and political arenas, to the point that the differences between the two blurred. The connection was buttressed by the interrelation of the two fields, as a result of which politics became more and more a matter of cultural activity and culture took on more political content. Hakibbutz Ha'artzi and Mapam culture, by nature avant-garde, could innovate more easily than the political establishment, which was by nature more conservative. Culture thus served as a channel through which new ideas could make their way into the movement despite the resistance from the traditional leadership. The unrest caused, for the most part, by the issue of the Occupied Territories led people to seek cultural avenues of expression because the political establishment had long constrained discussion of this issue and related issues. It might have seemed that this process would shore up Hashomer Hatza'ir's control structure, given that the process diverted those who sought change away from decision-making bodies. Yet as the control structure of Hakibbutz Ha'artzi and Mapam fell apart, the movement and party establishment also lost control of the cultural arena, which then became a place in which political change could be pursued.

The movement and party leadership was fully aware that its power was being sapped by political and cultural activity outside their bounds. Mapam secretary-general Meir Talmi called this process "dissolution from within."[69] He was right, inasmuch as the cultural arena served as a corridor through which people left Mapam, an intermediate stage in which young people developed political awareness and then came to realize that the party's control structure and ossification constrained the expression of their ideas because it was guided by contradictory political and economic interests that canceled each other out. In the spring of 1974, young people of Hakibbutz Ha'artzi sought to address the migration of Mapam members into extraparliamentary activity by proposing the establishment of a body, Dor Hahemshekh (Continuing Generation), as a home for young people who wanted to be politically involved but saw no way to do so within the party. The established leadership aborted the initiative.[70] At a discussion of the proposal in the Mapam Rikuz, Hazan voiced concern that these young people, whom he said had been affected by the post–Yom Kippur War turmoil, would seek to capture key party positions.[71] He, Ya'ari, Naftali Feder, and others feared that the shift into extraparliamentary political activity taking place outside Mapam would impair their control of the party, which in any case was weaker than ever. In other words, they deliberately pushed young people out of the party in the attempt to retain control over both the party and the young people.

The cultural arena in which opponents of the labor-party establishment operated began in the 1970s to provide fertile ground for the establishment of new political forces fueled by opposition to the existing parties and offering themselves as alternatives to the labor hegemony. The consolidation of cultural protest into political power seeking an end to labor-movement rule commenced immediately following the Yom Kippur War. As already noted, people exited the labor movement in three directions. First, working-class Mizrahim shifted their allegiance to other parties, mostly the Likud. A second group sought to pursue its sectoral interests, while a third took up a democratic agenda focused on individual and human rights. The first group simply moved to another existing party, but the other two used the cultural arena as a space in which they could found new parties. Despite their differences, however, the members of the three groups made the same arguments, which united them into a single front. In the elections of 1977, they cast protest votes, either for the Likud or for dovish liberal parties. The political weakness of the Rabin government further motivated them, as did the prime minister's public image as a political novice and a series of corruption scandals that erupted during his term. These factors and events reinforced the sense that the labor movement—that is, the Alignment—was crooked and that it had to be ejected from office in the name of democracy and equality.[72]

The Alignment thus entered the elections of 1977 opposed not just by the Likud but also by a protest front of three parties led by and appealing to former labor voters—Dash, Ratz, and Sheli. These three parties shared an overall ideological agenda, so they held discussions before the election about uniting into a single front.[73] Although that did not happen, they together represented all aspects of the critique of the established labor movement and served as political homes for those who had abandoned it. They frightened the Alignment, which felt closer to losing power than it ever had before.[74]

On Election Day, May 17, 1977, the labor movement's worst fears were realized. Dash, the most moderate of the three alternative parties, running on a vague platform that centered mostly on ousting the Alignment, performed the best. It won fifteen seats, more than any new party ever had. Most of its voters had previously voted for the Alignment.[75] Sheli won two seats, and Ratz, which had won three seats in the previous election, declined to just one. Another seat went to Shmuel Flatto-Sharon, a businessman who had moved from France to Israel two years earlier while under investigation in a massive embezzlement case in France. He also attracted protest votes. In other words, the protest front won a total of nineteen seats, precisely the number the Alignment lost in comparison with its performance in the previous election. The Alignment won thirty-two seats, but the Likud won forty-two, enabling it to form a government. Twenty years earlier, the stage for the upheaval had been set. Now it played out.

Conclusion

The Socialist Paradox

THE HISTORICAL PROCESS described here with regard to Hakibbutz Ha'artzi and Mapam proceeded in five stages. In the first, during the first half of the twentieth century, Hashomer Hatza'ir graduates who immigrated to Palestine built up a conglomerate of economic, political, and cultural bodies that together constituted a *movement*. The internal structure of this movement followed the lines of the mass-party model that had emerged in Europe—a strict hierarchy with the leadership on top, the members of the apparatus in the middle, and voters on the bottom. Political power was divided unequally between these levels, creating a situation in which an ensconced leadership maintained a functional relationship with a party machine; the machine campaigned to get the party votes at election time, in exchange for which the leadership saw to it that party activists received social services and employment from economic organizations associated with the party—the kibbutzim. Voters were enlisted through ideological activity that took place, for the most part, in the campaign period leading up to elections. Up until the mid-1950s, this bifurcated political structure did not have major economic ramifications. During Israel's initial years of widespread scarcity, the benefits that Hakibbutz Ha'artzi and Mapam could provide were limited, and the standard of living enjoyed by party activists was not all that higher than that of the population at large. Those benefits thus did not arouse discontent among most supporters.

In the second stage, Hakibbutz Ha'artzi and Mapam's apparatus became institutionalized and succeeded in achieving its goal of improving the living conditions of its members. The main factor in this success was the fact that Israel's economy, like the economies of western Europe countries and elsewhere, grew rapidly. This post–World War II era of prosperity was led by the United States and was based on the expansion of manufacturing, growth of consumption, a rising standard of living across the board, and the emergence of a state-produced middle class, of which in Israel kibbutz members were a part. In large measure, the success of this process, which created an affluent society of a sort that no one had previously experienced, was unexpected. One of the main consequences was that the bifurcated political structure of the mass parties now took on economic significance. Apparatus activists (kibbutz members in the case of Hakibbutz Ha'artzi and Mapam), the cogs in the party machines, enjoyed high economic and social mobility. Their move into the new middle class left the larger pool of voters behind, creating a state of glaring inequality.

The third stage was one of confrontation and contradiction. Unequal economic development prompted a variety of responses within Hakibbutz Ha'artzi and Mapam. One group adopted neoliberal principles, seeking to bolster its own economic success even at the price of exacerbating inequality. A second group, critical of the growing inequality, pressed for democratic reforms in the labor parties and movement. This group first worked within existing structures to promote more equitable economic and social policies and after the Six-Day War also voiced sharp criticism of the labor-led government's foreign and security policies. Part of this group was strongly influenced by the New Left movements of western Europe and North America. A third group consisted of people who had not enjoyed the economic benefits supplied by the movement machine and who grew disillusioned with and felt discriminated against by it. This group formed a number of new parties and movements. Although these three groups disagreed with and contended with each other, they formed a common front of resistance to Hakibbutz Ha'artzi and Mapam's establishment, the major target of their criticism.

The fourth stage was one of repression and control. Hakibbutz Ha'artzi and Mapam leaders found themselves facing internal unrest and challenged by new political ideas and initiatives. They could not halt the economic and social development that had brought on these phenomena, but they attempted to bring it under control and mitigate its effects and in doing so to ensure their own survival. As a result of this conservative response, the establishment became preoccupied with managing internal tensions rather than seeking to offer a comprehensive response to the structural challenges that were bringing about the decline of the movement. Hakibbutz Ha'artzi and Mapam's leadership took on the role of mediators between rival tendencies in the movement. One product of these mediating efforts was the Alignment, a political framework that united the different parts of the labor movement. This top-down solution, however, did not prevent the loss of support from the grass roots. In the 1970s, a new strategy was tried. The Alignment government pursued a new economic and social policy involving the creation of a social safety net and the pursuit of egalitarian economic policies, which it hoped would provide a new basis for mobilizing support for the movement and regain it the support of the lower classes. But by this time the labor movement's internal ruptures and its estrangement from many parts of the public were too profound to bridge. Furthermore, the new policies fired up opposition from the sectoralist neoliberals.

In the fifth stage, Hakibbutz Ha'artzi and Mapam, as part of the political framework of the Alignment, lost huge numbers of erstwhile supporters. Some of these former supporters, especially Mizrahim and the economically weakest voters, switched to Likud. Another group of mostly better-off voters favored three new protest parties. These voters no longer stood to gain any economic or social benefit from supporting the labor movement and its machine. Some had enjoyed such benefits in the past but no longer needed them, whereas others had not enjoyed them and saw no hope of doing so in the future. Whereas working-class and Mizrahi voters shifted their support to other already-existing parties, the protest voters created new parties that ironically had their genesis in the cultural space created by the labor movement.

The political developments of the period in which all this happened transformed Hakibbutz Ha'artzi and Mapam's cultural front. The front had been formed originally to appeal to and enlist the movement's third, outer circle—that is, the public at large. It then turned into a means by which the movement's establishment tried to regulate the internal tensions that had emerged in the second circle, the members of the apparatus, in particular the tension between the sectoralist and democratic trends, which in the parlance of the time were referred to as the movement's right and left wings. The cultural front became an arena for debate, but because all opposition to the establishment was channeled into the cultural sphere, that sphere expanded as the political clashes became more severe. Prosperity brought with it the capacity for creating more culture and an audience that consumed it. The result was an autonomous space that in the 1970s served as fertile ground for the growth of alternative political initiatives. Culture protest turned into political protest that brought down Hakibbutz Ha'artzi and Mapam and contributed, together with the flight of voters to the right, to the loss of the labor movement's hegemony in Israel.

The economic, political, and cultural developments that Hakibbutz Ha'artzi and Mapam went through were part of broader processes that took place in Israel and the Western world. Their specific case may thus offer a few insights on the larger crisis of the Israeli labor movement and even of other parts of the global Left.

First, the case of Hakibbutz Ha'artzi and Mapam shows how an interplay of economic, political, and cultural factors and institutions contributed to the rise of socialist movements during the first half of the twentieth century. At that time, there was a strong correlation between the economic needs of working-class society, the mediating function of party apparatuses, and the mobilizing role of culture. The crisis that followed in the second half of the twentieth century ensued when that correlation was lost. In the age of affluence, working-class voters (both those who had moved up the economic scale and those who were left behind) became steadily more alienated from the hierarchical structure of these movements and thus also to the movements' leaderships and party apparatuses. At the same time, the cultural arena provided a space in which that opposition could organize.

Second, the case of Hakibbutz Ha'artzi and Mapam shows that political structures established during the industrial era were incapable of grappling with the economic and social consequences of the postindustrial era. Between the 1950s and 1970s, working-class movements that developed into mass parties throughout the West had trouble adapting structurally to the age of prosperity. Many of them found themselves riven by centrifugally driven factions. In response, Hakibbutz Ha'artzi and Mapam typically dug in their heels, as did many other such movements in the West. Rather than modifying their political structures to address such far-reaching economic, social, and cultural changes, they let those structures ossify, which further fueled the internal crisis, and so the labor movements imploded.

Hakibbutz Ha'artzi and Mapam together formed a socialist movement that lost its strength when new conditions of production encountered traditional political structures. Their story is an ironic one. Their leaders remained steadfastly Marxist on the theoretical level yet put most of their energies into preserving a political-social superstructure that had been fashioned for a different set of circumstances. In this tactic, they disregarded the very dialectic materialism that they preached and became an extreme example of a socialist paradox. I suggest that much the same happened in other workers movements, both in Israel and around the globe.

Notes

Bibliography

Index

Notes

Introduction

1. David Harvey, *A Brief History of Neoliberalism* (Oxford: Oxford Univ. Press, 2007); Christiane Lemke and Gary Marks, "From Decline to Demise: The Fate of Socialism in Europe," in *The Crisis of Socialism in Europe*, ed. Christiane Lemke and Gary Marks (Durham, NC: Duke Univ. Press, 1992), 12–15; Chronis Polychroniou, ed., *Socialism: Crisis and Renewal* (Westport, CN: Praeger, 1993); Irwin Silber, *Socialism: What Went Wrong? An Inquiry into the Theoretical and Historical Sources of the Socialist Crisis* (London: Pluto Press, 1994); Larry J. Ray, *Social Theory and the Crisis of State Socialism* (Cheltenham, UK: Edward Elgar, 1996); Geoff Eley, *Forging Democracy: The History of the Left in Europe, 1850–2000* (Oxford: Oxford Univ. Press, 2002), 384–457; Donald Sassoon, *One Hundred Years of Socialism: The West European Left in the Twentieth Century* (New York: New Press, 1996), 443–646; Claus Offe, *Contradictions of the Welfare State* (Cambridge, MA: MIT Press, 1984).

2. The term *labor movement* in the Israeli context refers to all the political, economic, and cultural institutions operating under the banner of socialist Zionism in Palestine during the prestate period and after the establishment of the State of Israel. During the period discussed in this book, the labor movement included the Mapai, Ahdut Ha'avodah, and Mapam political parties; the Histadrut labor union; the three kibbutz movements, Hakibbutz Hameuhad, Ihud Hakvutzot Vehakibbutzim, and Hakibbutz Ha'artzi; and some affiliated organizations.

3. Shevach Weiss and Yona Yahav, *Anatomya shel nefila* (Haifa: Shahaf, 1977); Shevach Weiss, *Ha-mahapach* (Tel Aviv: Am Oved, 1977).

4. Avi Shilon, *Menachem Begin: A Life* (New Haven, CN: Yale Univ. Press, 2012), 314–34.

5. Esther Alexander, *Koach ha-shivion ba-kalkala* (Tel Aviv: Hakibbutz Hameuhad, 1990).

6. Ricki Shiv, "Tochnit ha-yetzuv 1985: Kalkala Nechonah oh idiologia," *Iyunim Bitkumat Israel* 23 (2013): 315–49.

7. Nissim Cohen, "Yazmaey medeniut ve-itzuv medinyut tziburit: Ha-mikre shel chok bituach briut mamlachti," *Bitahon Socially* 89 (2012): 5–42; Yitzhak Greenberg,

Anatomia shel mashber yadua merosh: Krisat hevrat a-ovdim bishnot ha-80 (Tel Aviv: Am Oved, 1989).

8. Daniel Rozolio, *Ha-shita ve-ha-mashber* (Tel Aviv: Am Oved, 1999); Ran Hakim, *Ha-kibbutzim be-Israel: Mabat history kalkaly* (Givat Haviva, Israel: Yad Yaari, 2009).

9. Henri Rozenfeld and Shulamit Carmi, "Nichus emtzaim tziburiyim ve-ma'amad beynoni totzar hamdina," *Machbarot Lemechkar ve-Lebikoret* 2 (1979): 43–84; Nachum Gross, "Kalkalat Israel 1954–1967," in *Ha-asor ha-sheni*, ed. Zvi Tzameret and Hanna Yablonka (Jerusalem: Yad Itzhak Ben-Zvi, 2001), 30–46; Amir Ben-Porat, *Heichan hem ha-burganim ha-hem: Toldot ha-burganut ha-Israelit* (Jerusalem: Magnes Press, 1999); Uri Cohen, "Michael sheli ve-hama'avar me-elit mahapechanit le-mamad beynoni," *Israel* 3 (2003): 157–83.

10. A harbinger of this dissent was the publication of a book by Anthony Crosland, *The Future of Socialism* (London: Jonathan Cape, 1956).

11. Lemke and Marks, "From Decline to Demise"; Eley, *Forging Democracy*, 335–36.

12. Paula Kabalo, "Pioneering Discourse and the Shaping of an Israeli Citizen in the 1950s," *Jewish Social Studies* 15, no. 2 (Winter 2009): 82–110; Oded Heilbronner, "Resistance through Rituals: Urban Subcultures of Israeli Youth from the Late 1950s to the 1980s," *Israel Studies* 16, no. 3 (Fall 2011): 28–50.

13. The most important component of Hakibbutz Ha'artzi and Mapam was the youth movement of Hashomer Hatza'ir. In this work, I do not address it directly because that would require a focus on education, which is not the subject here. Furthermore, during the period discussed, Hashomer Hatza'ir's youth movement was fully controlled by Hakibbutz Ha'artzi and Mapam and did not constitute an autonomous body. For further discussion of Hashomer Hatza'ir's youth movement in the years this work focuses on, see Shaul Paz, *Paneinu el ha-shemesh ha-ola* (Sde Boker, Israel: Ben-Gurion Research Institute Press and Bialik Institute, 2017); Ronit Carmeli, "Tmurot be-yachasam shel tze'irey Hashomer Hatza'ir el brit ha-moatsot, el ha-socialism, ve-el ha-ma'rav bi-shnot ha-chamishim ve-ha-shishim shel ha-me'a ha-esrim," PhD diss., Haifa Univ., 2013.

14. Shmuel Noah Eisenstadt, *Tmurot ba-hevra ha-Israelit* (Tel Aviv: Misrad Habitachon, 2004), 35–44; Yael Ishai, *Civil Society in Israel* (Jerusalem: Carmel, 2003), 78; Lev Greenberg, "Mapai bein democratizatsia ve-liberalizatzia: Le-she'elat tokpa shel ha-dichotomya medina/hevra ezrachit," in *Israel: Me-hevra meguyest le-hevra ezrachit?* ed. Yoav Peled and Adi Ophir (Jerusalem: Van Leer Institute and Hakibbutz Hameuhad, 2001), 244–61.

15. Tamar Herman, "New Challenges to New Authority: Israeli Grass Roots Activism in the 1950's," in *Israel: The First Decade of Independence*, ed. S. Ilan Troen and Noah Lucas (Albany: State Univ. of New York Press, 1995), 105–24; Heilbronner, "Resistance through Rituals."

16. See Tal Elmaliach and Anat Kidron, "Mecha'a tzeira be-Israel 1967–1977," *Iyunim Bitkumat Israel* 11 (2017): 78–101.

17. Rozenfeld and Carmi, "Nichus emtzaim tziburiyim"; Gross, "Kalkalat Israel"; Ben-Porat, *Heichan hem ha-burganim ha-hem*; Cohen, "Michael sheli."

18. In 1977, Hakibbutz Ha'artzi numbered more than 30,000 people in seventy-eight kibbutzim. Beginning in 1961, the kibbutzim as a whole in general suffered from a negative demographic balance. However, from 1967 until the 1980s it consistently improved. See Ha-Kibbutzim ve-Uchlusiatam, Israel Central Bureau of Statistics, publication no. 1327, n.d., at https://www.cbs.gov.il/he/publications/DocLib/2008/kibo5/pdf/h_print.pdf, last modified July 17, 2019.

19. Alon Gan, "Chasufim ba-tzariach ve-siach lochamim ke-tzirey zehut mitpatzlim," *Israel* 13 (2008): 267–96.

20. See Uri Izhar, *Bein hazon le-shilton: Mifleget Ahdut-Ha'avoda-Poalei-Zion bi-shnot ha-yeshuv ve-hamedina* (Ramat Efal, Israel: Yad Tabenkin, 2005); Yaakov Tzur, *Min ha-yam ad ha-midbar: Tabenkin ve-Hakibbutz Hameuhad ba-emuna u-Bama'avak le-shlemut ha-Aretz* (Jerusalem: Yad Yitzchak Ben tzvi, 2015); Henry Near, *The Kibbutz Movement: A History* (Jerusalem: Magnes Press, 1997); Avi Ahronson, *Hakamat ha-takam* (Efal, Israel: Yad Tabenkin, 2002); Alon Gan, "Ha-siach shegava: Tarbut ha-sichim ke-nisayon le-gibush zehut me-ya-chedet ba-dor ha-sheny ba-kibbutzim," PhD diss., Tel Aviv Univ., 2002. This lack of attention is even more surprising considering the vast literature about kibbutz economy. See, for example, Avraham Brom, *Tamid shanui be-Machloket: Ha-hitpatchut ha-kalkalit ve-hahevratit shel ha-tnua ha-Kibbutzit me-kom ha-medina* (Tel Aviv: Hakibbutz Hameuhad, 1986); Haim Barkai, *Hitpatchut ha-meshek ha-kibbutzi* (Jerusalem: Machon Falk, 1980); Zeev Tzur, *Hakibbutz Hameuhad be-yeshuva shel ha'aretz* vol. 4 (Tel Aviv: Hakibbutz Hameuhad, 1986); Rozolio, *Ha-shita ve-ha-mashber*; Hakim, *Ha-kibbutzim be-Israel*. Biographies of the leaders of Hakibbutz Ha'artzi/Mapam naturally focused on political and ideological activity. See Aviva Halamish, *Kibbutz, Utopia, and Politics: The Life and Times of Meir Yaari, 1897–1987* (Boston: Academic Studies Press, 2017); Zeev Tzahor, *Hazan: Tnu'at hayim* (Jerusalem: Yad Yitzhak Ben-Zvi; Givat Haviva, Israel: Yad Yaari, 1997). Studies of Hakibbutz Ha'artzi and Mapam's cultural arena have not connected the cultural activity to economic developments but have rather focused largely on the relationship of culture and politics. See Tal Elmaliach, "The Israeli Left between Culture and Politics: Tzavta Club and Mapam 1956–1973," *Journal of Israeli History* 33, no. 2 (Sept. 2014): 169–83.

21. See, for example, David Zayit, *Halutzim ba-mavoch ha-politi: Ha-tnua ha-kibutzit 1927–1948* (Jerusalem: Yad Yitzhak Ben-Zvi, 1993); Elkana Margalit, ed., *Ha-smol ha-meuhad* (Givat Haviva, Israel: Yad Yaari, 1991); Eli Tzur, *Nofey ha-ashlaya* (Sde Boker, Israel: Ben-Gurion Research Institute Press, 1998); Eli Tzur, ed., *Lo yuchlu biladeynu: Emdot Mapam bi-she'elot hutz u-vitahon 1948–1956* (Givat Haviva, Israel: Yad Yaari; Ramat Efal, Israel: Yad Tabenkin, 2000).

22. Avi Bareli and Nir Keidar, "Mamlachtiut Israelit," Israeli Institute for Democracy, 2011, https://www.idi.org.il/media/3498/pp_87.pdf; Avi Bareli, "Ha-mamlachtiut

ve-tnuat ha-avodah bereshit shnot ha-chamishim: Hanachot mivniot," in *Etgar haribo-nut: Yetzira ve-hagut ba-asor ha-rishon la-medina*, ed. Mordechai Bar-On (Jerusalem: Yad Itzhak Ben-Zvi, 1999), 23–44; Avi Bareli, "'Mamlakhtiyut': Capitalism and Socialism during the 1950s in Israel," *Journal of Israeli History* 26, no. 2 (2007): 201–27.

23. Yosef Gorni, "He-asor ha-mufla: Hirhurim al he-asor ha-rishon be-shnat hayovel la-medina," in *Ha-asor ha-rishon*, ed. Zvi Tzameret and Hanna Yablonka (Jerusalem: Yad Itzhak Ben-Zvi, 1997), 363–70; Eisenstadt, *Tmurot*, 35–44; Zeev Tzahor, "Hitkarshut ha-laba ha-yokedet," in *Itzuv ha-Israeliyut* (Tel Aviv: Am Oved and Sapir College, 2007), 102–15.

24. Dan Horowitz and Moshe Lissak, *Trouble in Utopia: The Overburdened Polity of Israel* (Albany: State Univ. of New York Press, 1989).

25. For a critical discussion of the development of sociological research of Israeli so-ciety, see Uri Ram, *The Changing Agenda of Israeli Sociology* (Albany: State Univ. of New York Press, 1995), and Yoav Peled and Gershon Shapir, *Mihu Israeli* (Tel Aviv: Tel Aviv Univ. Press, 2005), 44–54.

26. Lev Greenberg, *Ha-histadrut me'al hakol* (Jerusalem: Nevo, 1993); Ben-Porat, *Heichan hem ha-burganim ha-hem*; Shlomo Svirsky and Dvora Bernstein, "Mi avad bema? Avur mi utmurat ma? Hapituah hakalkali shel Israel ve-halukat ha'avoda ha'adatit," in *Ha-hevra ha-Israelit: Hebetim bikortiyim*, ed. Uri Ram (Tel Aviv: Brerot, 1993), 120–47; Michael Shalev, "Ovdim, medina umashber: Hakalkala hamedinit shel Israel," in *Ha-hevra ha-Israelit*, ed. Ram, 148–71; Gershon Shafir, *Land, Labor, and the Origins of the Israeli–Palestinian Conflict* (Cambridge: Cambridge Univ. Press, 1989).

27. Yonatan Shapira, *Elite le-lo mamshichim* (Tel Aviv: Sifriyat Poalim, 1984).

28. See, for example, Sami Shalom Chetrit, *Ha-ma'avak ha-Mizrahi be-Israel* (Tel Aviv: Am Oved, 2004), 119–79; Ben-Porat, *Heichan hem ha-burganim ha-hem*, 168–69; Peled and Shapir, *Mihu Israeli*, 116–17, 260–62.

29. For a critique of the historical value of sociological research, see Avi Bareli, "Ha-dimuy ha-Bolsheviki shel Mapay be-siah ha-zikaron ha-Israeli," in *Tarbut, zikaron ve-historya*, vol. 2, ed. Meir Hazan and Uri Cohen (Jerusalem: Tel Aviv Univ. and Zalman Shazar Center, 2012), 249–562; Israel Kolat, "Ha-histadrut ashema bakol?" (a critique of Lev Greenberg, *Ha-histadrut me'al hakol*), *Iyunim Bitkumat Yisrael* 9 (1999): 578–85; Yaakov Shavit, "Be-hipus ahar ha-burganut ha-Israelit" (a critique of Amir Ben-Porat, *Heichan hem ha-burganim ha-hem*), *Cathedra* 95 (2000): 159–64; Shmuel Hirsh and Uri Cohen, "He'arot al ha-sociologia ha-Israelit bi-rei mi-yeshuv le-medina," *Iyunim Bitku-mat Yisrael* 10 (2000): 317–52. See also Yechiam Weitz, ed., *Bein hazon le-revizia* (Jerusa-lem: Merkaz Zalman Shazar, 1997), and Tuvia Friling, ed., *Tshuva le-amit post Tziony* (Tel Aviv: Yediot Sfarim, 2003).

30. Adi Portugez, "Mi-smol sotzi'alisti li-smol hadash: Zramim ba-tzibur u-va-politikah be-Israel bein ha-shanim 1967–1982," PhD diss., Bar Ilan Univ., 2008); Gan, "Ha-siach shegava"; Danny Gutwein, "Ha-chalutziut ha-burganit: Tarbut popularit ve-haetos shel ma'amad ha-beynaim ha-mimsadi, shirei Naomi Shemer 1956–1967," *Israel*

20 (2012): 20–80; Gadi Taub, "Shnot ha-shishim ha-Amerikaniot be-Israel: Me-mered le-konformiut," *Iyunim Bitkumat Israel* 13 (2003): 1–28; Avner Cohen, "Ha-smol ha-Israeli bein idiologya liberalit le-meoravut hevratit," in *Hevra ve-kalkala be-Israel: Mabat histori ve-achshavi*, ed. Avi Bareli, Danny Gutwein, and Tuvia Friling (Sde Boker, Israel: Ben-Gurion Research Institute Press, 2005), 855–74.

31. David Harvey, *The Condition of Postmodernity: An Enquiry into the Origins of Cultural Change* (Cambridge, MA: Blackwell, 1990); Richard Rorty, *Achieving Our Country: Leftist Thought in Twentieth-Century America* (Cambridge, MA: Harvard Univ. Press, 1997).

32. Moshe Lissak and Dan Horowitz, "Gius polity ve-binui mosdot ba-yeshuv ha-yehudi bi-tkufat ha-mandat," and Emanuel Gutman, "Miflagut u-machanot: Yetzivut ve-shinui," both in Ha-ma'arechet ha-politit be-Israel, ed. Moshe Lissak and Emanuel Gutman (Tel Aviv: Am Oved, 1979), 51–81, 122–70; Benyamin Neuberger, Mimshal ve-politica (Ra'anana, Israel: Open Univ., 1997), 31–32. See also Yonatan Shapira, Achdut ha-avoda ha-historit: Otzmato shel irgun polity (Tel Aviv: Am Oved, 1975).

33. Anita Shapira, *Ha-halicha al kav ha-ofek* (Tel Aviv: Am Oved, 1988), 374.

1. The Emergence of the Kibbutz Movement
and the Rise of the Mediating Mechanism

1. Tzvi Lam, *Tnuot ha-noar ha-Tzioniot be-mabat le-achor* (Tel Aviv: Sifriyat Poalim, 1991).

2. The decision according to which the kibbutzim of graduates of Hashomer Hatza'ir youth movement should be affiliated solely with Hakibbutz Ha'artzi was accepted by a conference of Hashomer Hatza'ir world youth in 1930 in Czechoslovakia.

3. Yehuda Slutsky, "Mekoma shel ha-idea ha-mechavenet be-hit'havut ha-kvutza be-Israel," in *Heiseg history bi-tmurotav*, ed. Avigil Paz-Yishayahu and Yosef Gorni (Sde Boker, Israel: Ben-Gurion Research Institute Press, 2006), 43–54; Israel Kolat, "Le-mekoma shel ha-idea be-hit-havut ha-kvutza ba-aretz," in *Heiseg history bi-tmurotav*, ed. Paz-Yishayahu and Gorni, 55–58.

4. Haim Dribkin-Darin, *Ha-hevra ha-acheret* (Tel Aviv: Sifriyat Poalim, 1961), 256–70.

5. Tal Elmaliach, *Ha-ta'asia ha-kibutzit 1923–2007* (Givat Haviva, Israel: Yad Yaari, 2009).

6. Muki Tzur and Yuval Danieli, eds., *Livnot ve-lehibanot ba: Sefer Shmuel Mistechkin: Adrichalut ha-kibbutz be-tichnunu* (Tel Aviv: Hakibbutz Hameuhad, 2008), 88, 113–15; Israel Feinmaster, *Hakibbutz be-tichnuno* (Tel Aviv: Sifriyat Poalim, 1984), 89; Eyal Amir, "Dirat ha-megurim ba-kibbutz: Ideoligia ve-tichnun" (PhD diss., Technion, 1997), 131, 139.

7. Shevach Weiss, *Am ve-eda: Kovetz mechkarim be-nosei manhigut ve-peilut politit be-kerev ha-olim u-bnei ha-edot ha-lo Ashkenaziot* (Haifa: Univ. of Haifa, 1974).

8. Bareli and Keidar, "Mamlakchtiut Israelit."

2. The Politicization of Hakibbutz Ha'artzi

1. Tal Elmaliach, "Hashpa'at moreshet tnuat ha-noar Hashomer Hatza'ir ba-Kibbutz Ha'artzi ve-Mapam," *Israel* 23 (2015): 257–84.

2. See Zayit, *Halutzim*, 76–77.

3. Meir Ya'ari (1897–1987) was born in Galicia. He headed Hashomer Hatza'ir in Vienna and served as an officer in the Austrian army during World War I. He immigrated to Palestine in 1921, soon becoming the leader of Hashomer Hatza'ir there and in the Diaspora. He was a member of Kibbutz Merhavia and served in the Knesset from 1949 to 1973. Ya'akov Hazan (1899–1992) was born in Brest-Litovsk, Poland, and headed Hashomer Hatza'ir in Warsaw. He immigrated to Palestine in 1923 and joined Ya'ari in leading the movement. He was a member of Kibbutz Mishmar Haemek and served in the Knesset from 1949 to 1973. For further discussion of the "historic leadership," see Tzahor, *Hazan*; Aviva Halamish, *Meir Ya'ari: Biografiyah kibutzit 1897–1947, hamishim ha-shanim ha-rishonot* (Tel Aviv: Am Oved, 2009); and Aviva Halamish, *Meir Yaari: Ha-admor mi-Merchavia, shnot hamedina* (Tel Aviv: Am Oved, 2012). Halamish's biography of Ya'ari has also been published in English: *Kibbutz, Utopia, and Politics.*

4. Aviva Halamish, "The Historic Leadership of Hakibbutz Ha'artzi: The Power of Charisma, Organization, and Ideology," *Journal of Israeli History* 23, no. 1 (Mar. 2012): 45–66.

5. Anita Shapira, *Berl* (Tel Aviv: Am Oved, 1981); Baruch Kanari, *Tabenkin be-eretz Israel* (Sde Boker, Israel: Ben-Gurion Research Institute Press, 2003).

6. Zayit, *Halutzim*, 75, 101.

7. Eli Tzur, *Nofey ha'ashlaya* (Sde Boker, Israel: Hamerkaz Le-Moreshet Ben-Gurion, 1998).

8. Tzur, *Nofey ha'ashlaya.*

9. Anita Shapira, "'Black Night–White Snow': Attitudes of the Palestinian Labor Movement to the Russian Revolution, 1917–1929," in *Essential Papers on Jews and the Left*, ed. Ezra Mendelsohn (New York: New York Univ. Press, 1997), 236–71.

10. Yonatan Shapira, "Ha-mekorot ha-historiyim shel ha-demokratya ha-Yisraelit: Mapai kemiflaga dominantit," in *Ha-hevra ha-Israelit*, ed. Ram, 40–53; Danny Gutwein, "Al ha-stira bein ha-etos ha-halutzi la-idiologya ha-sotzyalistit bi-tnuat ha-avoda ha-Yisraelit: David Ben-Gurion ve-Yitzhak Ben-Aharon 1948–1967," *Iyunim Bitkumat Israel* 20 (2010): 208–48.

11. For further reading, see Maurice Duverger, *Political Parties: Their Organization and Activity in the Modern State* (New York: Wiley, 1954; London: Methuen, 1964); Peter Mair, *Party System Change: Approaches and Interpretations* (Oxford: Clarendon Press; New York: Oxford Univ. Press, 1998).

12. Eley, *Forging Democracy*, 83–84, 111, 296.

13. Ray, *Social Theory*, 79, 91–94.

14. Avi Bareli, *Authority and Participation in a New Democracy: Political Struggles in Mapai, Israel's Ruling Party, 1948–1953* (Boston: Academic Studies Press, 2014), 295–97; Rozenfeld and Carmi, "Nichus emtzaim tziburiyim."

15. Michael Denning, *The Cultural Front* (New York: Verso, 1996); Julian Jackson, *The Popular Front in France 1934–38* (Cambridge: Cambridge Univ. Press, 1988); Eley, *Forging Democracy*, 113–15.

16. Zayit, *Halutzim*, 78–81.

17. Ya'ari served as Mapam's general secretary until 1972, and Hazan headed Mapam's Knesset faction for many years, but both were exempted from rotation. The other important figures in the party were the secretary of the party Central Committee and the party's political secretary. The party's prominent institutions were its Central Committee, the Rikuz Mapam (Inner Circle committee), the secretariat, and the Political Committee. These institutions met on a regular basis (the Central Committee, the Rikuz, and the secretariat met weekly). The party also convened a council every two months or so and held a party congress every few years. Mordechai Bentov (Kibbutz Mishmar Haemek, 1900–1985) served as minister of development (1955–61) and as minister of housing (1966–69); Israel Barzilay (Kibbutz Negba, 1913–70) served as health minister (1955–59, 1966–69) and briefly as minister of postal services and minister without portfolio. Victor Shem-Tov (Jerusalem, 1915–2015) served as minister without portfolio (1969–70), as health minister (1970–77), and briefly as minister of social welfare. Natan Peled (Kibbutz Sarid, 1913–92) served as minister of immigrant absorption (1970–74). Shlomo Rozen (Kibbutz Sarid, 1905–85) served as minister of immigrant absorption (1974–77) and briefly as minister of housing.

18. Tal Elmaliach, "Ketz ha-hanhaga ha-historit: Kalkala, chevra ve-politica ba-Kibbutz Ha'artzi ve-Mapam 1956–1973," *Iyunim Bitkumat Israel* 24 (2014): 306–31; Halamish, "The Historic Leadership."

19. Census of Hakibbutz Ha'artzi, published in *Hashavu'a Bakibbutz Ha'artzi*, Dec. 2, 1955; see also *Al Hamishmar*, Sept. 5, 1956.

20. Kibbutz members constituted about two-thirds of Mapam's Knesset faction. The Arab sector was represented on a regular basis by one member in the Knesset. The urban group, which included on average two-thirds of the voters, received the lowest representation relative to its size. In the Third (1955), Fourth (1959), and Fifth (1961) Knessets, only three out of nine Mapam Knesset members were city dwellers; in the Sixth Knesset (1965) only two out of eight; in the Seventh Knesset (1969) only one out of seven; and in the Eighth Knesset (1974) only two out of seven. An urban member of Mapam did not serve in the cabinet until 1969, when Victor Shem-Tov was appointed minister without portfolio; in 1970 he became minister of health.

21. For the number of Mapam members, see Mapam Secretariat meeting, minutes, Aug. 8, 1956, file 811(4)63.90, Hashomer Hatza'ir Archive (HHA). For the number of voters, the number of party members in the kibbutzim, the city, and the Arab sector was subtracted from the average number of voters in the 1950s and 1960s.

22. Only a very small number of the urban or Arab members managed to get a share of the political power reserved for kibbutz members. Also, Mapam's party apparatus included very few salaried positions. Mapam's "twin," Ahdut Ha'avodah, had around 2,000 jobs on offer in the party, the government, and Histadrut institutions. That number seems large in contrast to the number of salaried positions in Mapam, where, in any case, they were low-level positions. See Izhar, *Bein hazon le-shilton.*

23. Hakibbutz Ha'artzi and Mapam's relations with Arabs were under the purview of special departments founded for that purpose in both bodies (the Arab Department of Hakibbutz Ha'artzi and the Arab Department of Mapam).

24. Zayit, *Halutzim*, 25–28, 102–19, 148–244.

25. See Aviva Halamish, "Loyalties in Conflict: Mapam's Vacillating Stance on the Military Government, 1955–1966, Historical and Political Analysis," *Israel Studies Review* 33, no. 3 (2018): 26–53. For further discussion, see Tzur, *Lo yuchlu biladeynu.*

26. The idea of stages as a theoretical solution emphasizes the tension between nationality and socialist revolution and was developed in Hakibbutz Ha'artzi under the influence of the teachings of Dov (Ber) Borochov (1881–1917), an inspirational Marxist-Zionist thinker and the leader of socialist Zionism in its early period.

27. Elmaliach, "Hashpa'at moreshet tnuat ha-noar."

28. Elmaliach, "Hashpa'at moreshet tnuat ha-noar."

29. Naftali Feder, *Pagashti anashim* (Tel Aviv: Israel Buch, 1998), 94. For further background, see Alon Pauker, "Hakibbutz Ha'artzi u-vrit ha-mo'atzot be-asor ha-atzma'ut ha-rishon," *Iyunim Bitkumat Israel* 22 (2012):64–90.

3. Founding Hakibbutz Ha'artzi and Mapam's Cultural Front

1. Denning, *The Cultural Front*; Jackson, *The Popular Front*; Pat Francis, "The Labor Publishing Company," *History Workshop Journal* 18, no. 1 (1984): 115–23; Jonathan Ree, *Proletarian Philosophers: Problems in Popular Culture in Britain 1900–1940* (Oxford: Clarendon Press, 1984), 1–6; Richard Bodoek, *Proletarian Performance in Weimar Berlin: Agitprop, Chorus, and Brecht* (Columbia, SC: Camden House, 1997), 40–44; Edward Mortimer, *The Rise of the French Communist Party* (London: Faber, 1984), 21.

2. Yehuda Slutsky, *Mavo le-toldot tnu'at ha-avodah ha-yisre'elit* (Tel Aviv: Am Oved, 1973); Ben-Ami Feingold, "Tarbut u-ma'amad: Ohel—aliyato u-nefilato shel te'atron po'alim," *Iyunim Bitkumat Israel* 15 (2005): 72–349; Emanuel Gil, *Sipuro shel ha-poel* (Tel Aviv: Hakibbutz Hameuhad, 1976).

3. Tzvi Tzameret, "Ben Tzion Dinur: Intelektual boneh medina," *Htziyonut*, Kaf-Alef 1998, 321–32, and "Zalman Aran ve-ma'arechet ha-chinuch," in *Ha-asor ha-sheni*, ed. Tzameret and Yablonka, 61–79.

4. Tzvi Tzameret, *Hitpatchut ma'arechet ha-chinuch*, unit 7 in the series Israel in the First Decade (Ra'anana, Israel: Open Univ., 2003), 47–48.

5. Izhar, *Bein hazon le-shilton*, 151–52.

6. Avraham Shlonsky (1900–1973) was born in Ukraine, immigrated to Palestine in 1921, and spent his first years as a pioneer. He later moved to Tel Aviv and became a leading figure in the cultural life of the prestate era and the first decades after the establishment of Israel.

7. Hagit Halperin, *Ha-maestro: Hayav vi-yetzirato shel Avraham Shlonsky* (Tel Aviv: Sifriyat Poalim, Hakibbutz Hameuhad, 2011), 481–99.

8. The first evidence of a clear demand to gather a cultural conference is in Hakibbutz Ha'artzi Executive Committee meeting, minutes, July 4, 1930, file 3543(3)5-1.10, HHA.

9. Report in preparation for the Hakibbutz Ha'artzi Fifth Council, June 1935, file (1)2.20.5, HHA.

10. Eli Tzur, "Hakibutz Ha'artzi, ha-omanut ha-mesharetet ve-hareka ha-history," in *Aomanut be-sheirut ra'aion*, ed. Shlomo Shealtiel (Givat Haviva, Israel: Yad Yaari; Sde Boker, Israel: Ben-Gurion Research Institute Press, 1999), 13–25.

11. A report about Sifriyat Poalim for 1973–75, submitted to Hakibbutz Ha'artzi Executive Committee, Mar. 1977, file 2411(2)16.24, HHA.

12. Giora Manor, "Holchim le-Tzavta," *Hotam*, Jan. 7, 1972.

13. Regulations of Tzavta, n.d., 1957, files (7)22.23, HHA.

14. "Valleyball," in *Entziklopedia le-tarbut ve-le-sport*, ed. Y. Aviram and others (Tel Aviv: Am Oved, 1959).

15. Haim Kaufman, "Sport le-alufim ao le-alafim," *Etmol* 199 (2008): 55–57, and "Hazika ha-ra'ayonit bein sport ha-Poalim le-bein hit'agdut Hapoel be-tkufat ha-mandat," *Betnnua*, Gimel 1995, 56–77.

16. This explanation is based on the "conflict approach," which sees sports as a means for a social group to increase its status. See Amir Ben-Porat, "Opium la-hamonim, kaduregel ve-leumiyut aim hakamat ha-medina," in *Sport, arachim ve-politica*, ed. Ilan Gur Zeev and Roni Lidor (Hulon, Israel: David Rochgold, 2007), 137–39.

17. Michah Shamban, interview, *Hashavu'a Bakibbutz Ha'artzi*, July 1, 1964; Yuval Danieli, "Ha-shanim ha-muflaot shel Hapoel ha-Ma'apil," Sept. 2011, file 133.150(2)5202, HHA; Yeval Barkai, "Be-zchut ha-bulgarin ve-hagalitzaim," *Hadaf Ha-Yarok*, Apr. 4, 1997.

18. Tzur, "Hakibutz Ha'artzi, ha-omanut ha-mesharetet."

19. Regulation of Givat Haviva, n.d., file 2507(2)1.16, HHA.

20. Committee for Lectures meeting, Aug. 15, 1952, file 2107(2)5.22, HHA; summary of the third session of the course for the movement's activists, Nov. 7, 1954–Jan. 27, 1955, file 62.3(4)476 ה, HHA; proposal of a plan for a cadres course, session 2, Jan. 1, 1954–Feb. 27, 1954, file 476(4)62.3, HHA.

21. Leaflet from seminars in Givat Haviva, 1949–52, file 3917(2)2.1.40, HHA; Hakibbutz Ha'artzi Executive Committee meeting, Oct. 17–18, 1954, file 3553(11)5-6.10, HHA; summary of Tav-Shin-Yod-Gimal, Nov. 5, 1953, file (5)95-13.7, HHA.

4. From a Developing to a Developed Society

1. On the steady trend, see data on gross domestic product per capita in Israel during the years 1950–2005 in *Shishim shana be-rei ha-statistica* (Jerusalem: Israel Main Institute for Statistics, May 1998), at http://www.cbs.gov.il/statistical/statistical60_heb.pdf. A postindustrial society is characterized by new manufacturing technologies, which reduce the working labor, a decreased manufacturing sector compared to the service sector, and the emergence of knowledge and research as the main sources for growth. See Daniel Bell, *The Coming of Post-industrial Society: A Venture in Social Forecasting* (New York: Basic Books, 1973).

2. Gross, "Kalkalat Israel."

3. See Alan Dowty, *Israel/Palestine* (Cambridge: Polity Press, 2008), 69–96; Benny Morris, *Righteous Victims: A History of the Zionist–Arab Conflict 1881–1999* (New York: Knopf, 1999), 121–258. For further reading, see Itamar Rabinovich, *The Lingering Conflict: Israel, the Arabs, and the Middle East 1948–2012* (Washington, DC: Saban Center for Middle East Policy, Brookings Institution Press, 2011).

4. Benn Steil, *The Battle of Bretton Woods: John Maynard Keynes, Harry Dexter White, and the Making of a New World Order* (Princeton, NJ: Princeton Univ. Press, 2013); Robert Lekachman, *The Age of Keynes* (New York: Random House, 1966), 179.

5. Avner Molcho, "Kapitalism ve-haderech ha-Americanit be-Israel: Perion, nihul ve-ha-etos ha-kapitalisty ba-siua ha-techny shel artzot habrit be-shnot ha-chamishim," in *Hevra ve-kalkala be-Israel*, ed. Bareli, Gutwein, and Friling, 263–94; Tony Judt, *Postwar: A History of Europe since 1945* (New York: Penguin Press, 2005), 63–129.

6. Molcho, "Kapitalism ve-haderech ha-Americanit be-Israel"; Judt, *Postwar*.

7. David Levi-Faur, "The Developmental State: Israel, South Korea, and Taiwan Compared," *Studies in Comparative International Development* 33, no. 1 (1988): 65–93.

8. Haim Barkai, *Yemei Bereshit shel ha-meshek ha-Israeli* (Jerusalem: Mosad Biyalik, 1990), 59.

9. Molcho, "Kapitalism."

10. Between 1952 and 1964, Israel received $833 million in reparation payments from West Germany. See *Ha-shilumim ve-hashpa'attam* (Jerusalem: Bank of Israel, Dec. 1965).

11. Between 1951 and 1959, the Israeli government received $284 million (after deduction of expenses such as redemption and interest) from the sale of Israel Bonds. Between 1960 and 1969, it received another $307 million. See Yechiel Rechavi and Asher Veingerten, *Yovel shanim le-gius hon hitzoni be-emtzaut irgun ha-bonds* (Jerusalem: Bank of Israel, Sept. 6, 2004), at http://www.boi.org.il/deptdata/neumim/neum163h.pdf.

12. David Levi-Faur, *Ha-yad ha-lo ne'elama: Ha-politica shel ha-tius be-Israel* (Jerusalem: Yad Itzchak Ben Tzvi; Haifa: Univ. of Haifa, 2001), 36–37.

13. Michal Sapir, *Ha-yesh ha-gadol: Biografya shel Pinchas Sapir* (Tel Aviv: Miskal, 2011), 455.

14. In 1956–57, ninety-six kibbutzim and moshavim (twenty of them in Hakibbutz Ha'artzi) entered into debt arrangements sponsored by the Israeli government (see Rozolio, *Ha-shita ve-ha-mashber*, 115–19; kibbutzim correspondence in the matter of the debt arrangements, file 2595(7)15.8, HHA). In January 1957, the minister of agriculture, Kadish Luz (a member of Kibbutz Degania Bet), founded a special committee to study the difficulties faced by agricultural settlements. It was chaired by David Horowitz, the governor of the Bank of Israel. In 1960, the committee submitted its final report, which led to a reform that improved the situation for the agricultural sector. The kibbutzim's financial situation also improved thanks to the establishment of a new collective-credit (*ashrai merukaz*) department in the Ministry of Agriculture in 1957, which focused on helping kibbutzim and moshavim achieve financial sustainability (see L. Sha'ashua, Y. Goldsmit, and B. Trabelsy, *Ha-shpa'at ha-misgeret shel ha-ashray ha-merukaz al ha-hashka'ot ba-kibutzim* [N.p.: Ha-Yechida Ha-Bein Kibbutzit Le-Hadracha Kalkalit, June 1977], and Rozolio, *Ha-shita ve-ha-mashber*, 118–19).

15. Yonina Talmon-Gerber, *Yachid ve-hevra ba-kibbutz* (Jerusalem: Magnes Press and Hebrew Univ., 1970), 288–99; Shlomo Ekshtein, *Shituf bein kafri be-michun haklai* (Rehovot, Israel: Hamacon le-Cheker ha-Hityashvut, 1969), 1–11; Yehuda Don, *Industrialization of a Rural Collective* (Aldershot, UK: Avebury, 1988), 37–40.

16. *Symposium on Regional Cooperation* (N.p.: Ihud ha-Kvutzot ve-Hakibbutzim, Apr. 1962).

17. Hakibbutz Ha'artzi Lamed-Bet Council meeting, minutes, Mar. 29–31, 1956, file (1)5-8.20, HHA.

18. Tzur, *Hakibbutz Hameuhad*, 4:40.

19. "Megama u-maas," Feb. 1969, file 2834(3)254.8, HHA.

20. Don, *Industrialization*, 10.

21. Data refer to all kibbutz movements. See Barkai, *Hitpatchut ha-meshek*, 193; Reuven Cohen, *Ha-Yeshuv ve-ha-kvutza: Yesodot ve-tahalichim* (Tel Aviv: Hakibbutz Hameuhad, 1969), 15.

22. This trend could be seen, for example, in the decrease of 47,000 working days in agriculture in the kibbutz economy between 1959 and 1961 (from 1.134 million to 1.087 million), while at the same time the number of working days in industry rose by 67,000 (from 235,000 to 302,000). See Shlomo Rosen, interview, *Al Hamishmar*, Dec. 21, 1963, and Yaakov Kondor, *Kalkalat Israel* (Tel Aviv: Shoken, 1984), 32.

23. Elmaliach, *Ha-ta'asia ha-kibutzit*, 58–60.

24. Yaakov Arnon, *Meshek be-sichrur* (Tel Aviv: Hakibbutz Hameuhad, 1981), 48; Yitzchak Greenberg, *Pinchas Sapir: Biografia kalkalit ve-politit* (Tel Aviv: Resling, 2011).

25. Elmaliach, *Ha-ta'asia ha-kibutzit*, 23–41.

26. Brom, *Tamid shanui*, 43.

27. Elmaliach, *Ha-ta'asia ha-kibutzit*, 47–50.

28. Brom, *Tamid shanui*, 48.

29. Don, *Industrialization*, 48; reports for 1967–68 come from file (10)8-71.1, HHA.

30. Data from *Al Hamishmar*, Dec. 29, 1967,

31. Data from *Al Hamishmar*, Dec. 30, 1971.

32. For further reading, see Hakim, *Ha-kibbutzim be-Israel*.

33. See, for example, Mapam Central Committee, minutes, June 13, 1960, file 790(6)64.90, HHA; Mapam Central Committee meeting, minutes, June 22, 1960, file (4)68.90, HHA.

34. Ofer Bord, *Kesef ha-shod mi-yad ha-horeg: Ha-tnua ha-kibutzit ve-heskem ha-shilumim, ha-pitzuyim, ve-hashavat ha-rechush mi-germanya* (Sde Boker, Israel: Ben-Gurion Research Institute Press, Yad Tabenkin, Yad Yaari, and the Institute for Research of the Jewish National Fund, 2015).

35. Bord, *Kesef ha-shod mi-yad ha-horeg*.

36. Allon Gal, "Envisioning Israel: The American-Jewish Tradition," in *Envisioning Israel: The Changing Ideals and Images of North American Jews*, ed. Allon Gal (Detroit: Wayne State Univ. Press; Jerusalem: Magnes Press, 1996), 13–40; Jonathan Sarna, "A Projection of America as It Ought to Be: Zion in the Mind's Eye of American Jews," in *Envisioning Israel*, ed. Gal, 41–59.

37. Shulamit Reinharz, "Irma 'Rama' Lindheim: An Independent American Zionist Woman," *Nashim: A Journal of Jewish Women's Studies and Gender Issues* 1 (Winter 1998): 106–35; Allon Gal, "Brandeis and Hashomer Hatza'ir," *Yaad* 8, no. 26 (Nov. 1991): 66–70.

38. Avraham Schenker, "Progressive Zionism in America," in *Against the Stream: Seven Decades of Hashomer Hatza'ir in North America*, ed. Ariel Hurwitz (Givat Haviva, Israel: Yad Yaari, 1994), 273–95.

39. Folders (1)5-1-4, (2)5-1-4, (5)5-1-4, (10)8.10/8-8-1, Kibbutz Ein Hashofet Archive.

40. For further dissection of the contradiction between ideology and ethos in the Israeli labor movement and the rise of the "bourgeois pioneering," see Gutwein, "Al ha-stira" and "Ha-chalutziut ha-burganit."

41. Hakibbutz Ha'artzi Lamed-Bet Council meeting, minutes, Mar. 1956, file (1)5-8.20, vol. Bet, HHA; Hakibbutz Ha'artzi Ninth Council, May 29–June 1 1958, file (2)5-9.20, HHA.

42. One-third of the kibbutzim needed some financial help to handle previous debts, but they could now rely on their profitability and assistance from the state, the Jewish Agency, and Histadrut, obtained when Mapam was part of the coalition, to pay off those debts. See Yaakov Amit, speech at Hakibbutz Ha'artzi Tenth Council, Apr. 10–13, 1963, file 3588(1)5-13.20, HHA. Regarding the annual income for a kibbutz member, see *Doch ha-va'ada le-bdikat halukat ha-hachnasa ha-le'umit be-Israel* (Jerusalem: Bank of Israel, Dec. 1966), 182.

43. Report in preparation for Hakibbutz Ha'artzi Lamed-Vav Council, May 1966, file (2)5-14.20, HHA.

44. Barkai, *Hitpatchut ha-meshek*, 2, 110, 141, 144, 149, 153.

45. Alon Gan, "Shinuyim hevrati'im ba-tnua ha-kibbutzit be-shnot ha-shishim," *Iyunim Bitkumat Israel* 16 (2006): 343–72; see also the discussion about cooperation, consumerism, and equality in Hakibbutz Ha'artzi Ninth Council, May 1958, file 3586(2)25-9.20, HHA.

46. *Doch ha-va'ada*, 30–33, 182; Ch. Nun, "Ramat ha-chaim shel ha-mishpacha ha-ovedet," *Ha-Meshek ha-Shitufi: Beteon le-Sheelot Kalkala, Cooperatzia ve-Meshek Poalim* 16–17, nos. 592–93 (Aug. 16, 1964): 11–12.

47. *Netunim statistim* (N.p.: Ha-Machon le-Mechkar Kalkali ve-Hevrati ha-Histadrut ha-Klalit, Apr. 1969), 39.

48. *Ha-doch ha-klali* (Jerusalem: Bank of Israel, 1970), 79.

49. Heilbronner, "Resistance through Rituals"; Anat Helman, *Bigdei ha-eretz ha-chadasha: Medinat Israel be-rei ha-ofna* (Jerusalem: Merkaz Zalman Shazar, 2012).

50. Levi-Faur, *Ha-yad ha-lo ne'elama*, 36–37.

51. Ch. D. Moshayov, "Shloshet ha-sektorim ba-meshek ha-Israeli," *Ha-Meshek ha-Shitufi: Beteon le-Sheelot Kalkala, Cooperatzia ve-Meshek Poalim* 16–17, nos. 592–93 (Aug. 16, 1964): 10–11.

52. Shlomo Morgenshtern, "Ha-zchuyot ha-socialiot shel ovdei ha-Histadrut: Hitpatchuiot ve-nesigot," *Ha-Meshek ha-Shitufi: Beteon le-Sheelot Kalkala, Cooperatzia ve-Meshek Poalim* 16–17, nos. 592–93 (Aug. 16, 1964): 14–15.

53. Rozenfeld and Carmi, "Nichus emtzaim tziburiyim."

54. Gutwein, "Ha-chalutziut ha-burganit."

55. See "State Socialism," Lexico, n.d., at http://www.oxforddictionaries.com/definition/english/state-socialism.

56. See Raymond Williams, "Capitalism," in *Keywords: A Vocabulary of Culture and Society*, rev. ed. (New York: Oxford Univ. Press, 1983), 52; Levi-Faur, *Ha-yad ha-lo ne'elama*, 262.

57. Uri Cohen and Eitan Orkibi, "Universita ve-shilton—me-shutfut le-imut: Ha-elita ha-academit ve-nisuach ha-bikoret le-mahapach 1977," *Alpaim* 33 (2008): 149–86.

58. For further discussion of the political system and higher education in Israel in this period, see Uri Cohen, "Ha-intelectual ha-ta'hor ba-politica ao elita academit be-mashber: Meoravut ha-universita ha-ivrit be-parashat Lavon," *Iyunim Bitkumat Israel* 14 (2004): 191–229; Michael Keren, *Ha-et ve-hacherev: Levateia shel ha-intiligentzia ha-Israelit* (Tel Aviv: Ramot, 1991), 7; Pitter Y. Medding, *Mapai in Israel: Political Organization and Government in a New Society* (Cambridge: Cambridge Univ. Press, 1972), 62.

59. Doron Timor and Uri Cohen, "Yachas ha-kibbutzim le-mosdot ha-haskalah ha-gvo'ha: Me-dchi'ya ve-histaygut le-hishtalvut," *Iyunim Bitkumat Israel* 23 (2014): 378–410.

60. Tal Elmaliach, "Sport, hevra, politica ve-ideologia: Hakibbutz Ha'artzi–Hashomer Hatza'ir ve-hakaduraf," *Cathedra* 157 (2015): 155–74.

61. The critical sociologists have discussed Mapai's mechanism for distributing privileges in detail. See, for example, Peled and Shapir, *Mihu Israeli*, 59–99, and Rozenfeld and Carmi, "Nichus emtzaim tziburiyim."

62. Gan, "Shinuyim hevrati'im."

63. Bareli, *Authority and Participation*, 81–83.

64. Brom, *Tamid shanui be-Machloket*, 22.

65. "Hakibbutz Ha'artzi pote'ach ha-yom et ve'idato ha-11," *Al Hamishmar*, Feb. 21, 1969; *Ha-kibbutzim ve-uchlusiyatam: Tmurot demografiot ba-shanim 1961–2005* (Jerusalem: Israeli Central Bureau of Statistics, June 2008), 10; report submitted on a discussion regarding the inequality in Hakibbutz Ha'artzi, 1972, file 253.8(5)2833, HHA.

66. Data based on David Spektor, "Ma hidshah shnat tav-shin-yod-daelt be-chaye'i Hakibbutz Ha'artzi," *Hashavu'a Bakibbutz Ha'artzi*, Sept. 26, 1954; "Hakibbutz Ha'artzi pote'ach ha-yom et ve'idato ha-11."

67. Moshe Lissak, *Ha-aliya ha-gdola be-shnot ha-chamishim: Kishlono shel kur ha-hituch* (Jerusalem: Mosad Bialik, 1999), 78–132.

68. Izhar, *Bein hazon le-shilton*, 212.

69. *Doch ha-va'ada le-bdikat*, 4, 7, 12, 58; Nun, "Ramat ha-chaim"; Avi Bareli and Uri Cohen, "Ha-siach ha-tziburi be-Mapai likrat shvitat ha-academaim be-shenat 1956," *Cathedra* 143 (2012): 153–84.

70. Mapam Central Committee meeting, minutes, Aug. 8, 1956, file 811(4)63.90, HHA; Y. Yechezkel to Itzchak Patish, May 29, 1959, file 789(2)111.90, HHA.

71. Yechiam Weitz, "Miflaga mitmodedet aim kishlona: Mapai nochach ha-totzaot ba-bchirot la-Knesset ha-shlishit," *Cathedra* 77 (1996): 124–34.

72. Izhar, *Bein hazon le-shilton*, 203.

73. Bareli, *Authority and Participation*, 236; Avi Bareli, "Mapai and the Oriental Jewish Question in the Early Years of the State," *Jewish Social Studies* 16, no. 1 (Fall 2009): 54–84; Dov Hanin, "Me-Eretz Israel ha-ovedet le-Eretz Israel ha-shniya: Siach umedini-yut hevratit be-Mapai shel shnot ha-chmishim," in *Shilton ha-hon be-Israel*, ed. Danny Filc and Uri Ram (Jerusalem: Van Leer institute; Tel Aviv: Hakibbutz Hameuhad, 2004), 131–63; Izhar, *Bein hazon le-shilton*, 218.

74. *Doch ha-va'ada le-bdikat*, 160–66.

75. Nun, "Ramat ha-chaim."

76. Ben-Porat, *Heichan hem ha-burganim ha-hem.*

77. *Doch ha-va'ada le-bdikat*, 144.

78. Avi Pikar, "Reshita shel ha-aliya ha-selektivit be-shnot ha-chamishin," *Iyunim Bitkumat Israel* 9 (1999): 338–94; Bareli, "Mapai and the Oriental Jewish Question."

79. Edna Bonacich, "A Theory of Ethnic Antagonism: The Split Labor Market," *American Sociological Review* 37, no. 5 (Oct. 1972): 547–59; Harald Bauder, *Labor Movement: How Migration Regulates Labor Markets* (New York: Oxford Univ. Press, 2006).

80. Danny Gutwein, "He'arot al ha-yesodot ha-ma'amadi'im shel ha-kibush," *Theoria ve-Bikoret* 24, no. 203 (2004): 203–11, and "Al kalkala ve-de'a kduma," *Theoria ve-Bikoret* 26, no. 286 (2005): 286–96.

81. Tom Navon, "Ha-mitun: Tziun derech ba-historia ha-politit-kalkalit shel Israel, 1964–1967," *Iyunim Bitkumat Israel* 26 (2016): 386–429. I am grateful to Tom Navon for giving me access to his materials and for sharing with me his great knowledge about this subject.

82. Navon, "Ha-mitun."

83. Izhar, *Bein hazon le-shilton*, 396.

84. Momi Dahan, "Aliyat ai-hashivyon ha-kalkali," in *Me-meoravut memshaltit le-kalkalat shuk, ha-meshek ha-Israeli 1985–1998*, ed. Avi Ben-Basat (Tel Aviv: Am Oved, 2001), 610–56.

85. Tamar Guzansky, *Atzma'ut kalkalit—keitzad? Sikumim be-hitpatchuta ha-kalkalit shel Israel* (Tel Aviv: Iyun, 1969), 125.

86. Guzansky, *Atzma'ut kalkalit—keitzad?*

87. Johnny Gal, *Ha-omnam netel me-ratzon? Sipura shel ha-hitmodedut aim ha-avtala 1920–1995* (Sde Boker, Israel: Ben-Gurion Research Institute Press, 2002), 133–34.

5. A Postmaterial Society

1. Sapir, *Ha-yesh ha-gadol*, 458; Carol Schwartz Greenwald, *Recession as a Policy Instrument: Israel 1965–1969* (Rutherford, NJ: Fairleigh Dickinson Univ. Press, 1973), 106.

2. Eliyahu Kanovsky, *The Economic Impact of the Six-Day War: Israel, the Occupied Territories, Egypt, Jordan* (New York: Praeger, 1970), 74–77, 64–65.

3. Kanovsky, *Economic Impact of the Six-Day War*, 42–55.

4. Kanovsky, *Economic Impact of the Six-Day War*, 92–95.

5. Kanovsky, *Economic Impact of the Six-Day War*, 60.

6. Richard W. T Pomfret, *Trade Policies and Industrialization in a Small Country: The Case of Israel* (Tubingen, Germany: Mohr, 1976), 70.

7. Arieh Bergman, *Ha-ta'asiya ve-mediniyut ha-ti'us be-Israel: Sugiyot ikariot 1965–1985* (Jerusalem: Bank of Israel, 1986), 3–7.

8. Shlomo Shtenger, *Ha-ta'asia ha-kibbutzit* (N.p.: Igud ha-Taasia Hakibbutzit, 1971), 11.

9. "Ha-ta'asia ha-kibbutzit be-shnat tashlav," *Al Hamishmar*, May 3, 1973.

10. Data from *Al Hamishmar*, Dec. 30, 1971.

11. *Hadoch ha-shanati* (Jerusalem: Bank of Israel, 1973), 3–4.

12. Compare *Hadoch ha-shanati* (1973), 79, and *Hadoch ha-shanati* (Jerusalem: Bank of Israel, 1970), 126.

13. *Shishim shana be-rei ha-statistica*, 10.

14. According to Haim Barkai, the standard of living in the kibbutz in the mid-1960s was similar to that of the sixth decile in the city (*Hitpatchut ha-meshek ha-kibbutzi*, 162). In an interview Barkai gave in 1976, he claimed that by that point the kibbutz standard of living had become similar to that of the eighth decile (Haim Barkai, interview,

Al Hamishmar, Jan. 23, 1976). See also Shimon Shor, ed., *Hitpatchuyot be-kalkalat Israel ve-hashpa'atan al ha-kibbutz* (N.p.: Hakibbutz Ha'artzi, Nov. 1975), 2–3, 105.

15. Ronald Inglehart, "The Silent Revolution in Post-industrial Societies," *American Political Science Review* 65 (1971): 991–1017.

16. Data from *Netunim statistim 1968–1971* (N.p.: Ha-Machon le-Mechkar Kalkali ve-Chevrati, ha-Histadrut ha-Klalit, Apr. 1972).

17. Avraham Doron, "Medinyut ha-revacha ve-ha-bitachon ha-socialy ba-asor hashlishi," in *Ha-asor ha-shlishi,* ed. Zvi Tzameret and Hanna Yablonka (Jerusalem: Yad Itzhak Ben-Zvi, 2008), 115–28.

18. Ya'akov Arnon, "Ha-mediniyut ha-kalkalit be-1974," *Rev'on le-Kalkala,* Kaf-Alef, 83 (Dec. 1974): 7–15.

19. Dudi Natan, "Ha-mediniyut ha-kalkalit shel memshelet Rabin, 1974–1977," MA thesis, Univ. of Haifa, 2007, 4.

20. Ya'akov Arnon, "Ha-mediniyut ha-kalkalit be-1976," *Rev'on le-Kalkala,* Kaf-Gimel, 88–89 (Apr. 1976): 3–14.

21. Chaim Bar-lev, minister of industry and commerce, interview, *Al Hamishmar,* Nov. 20, 1973.

22. David Gordon, "Yemei herum ba-ta'asia ha-kibbutzit," *Al Hamishmar,* Dec. 6, 1973; Don, *Industrialization,* 48.

23. For further details of these government actions, see Amos Shifris, *Memshelet Rabin ha-rishona 1974–1977* (Tzur Igaal, Israel: Porat, 2013), 128–66.

24. Natan, "Ha-mediniyut ha-kalkalit shel memshelet Rabin"; Shlomo Svirsky, "1967: Tafnit kalkalit be-Israel," in *Hevra ve-kalkala be-Israel,* ed. Bareli, Gutwein, and Friling, 91–116. See also Hakibbutz Ha'artzi Executive Committee meeting, minutes, Dec. 12, 1975, file (6)5-9.10, HHA.

25. Doron, "Medinyut ha-revacha"; Michal Ofir and Tami Eliav, *Kitzba'ot ha-yeladim be-Israel: Mabat history ve-re'iya bein-leumit* (N.p.: Hamosad Lebituach Leumi, Dec. 2005), 5; Johnny Gal, "Al metutelet bituach ha-avtala be-Israel 1972–2003," *Bitachon Socialy* 67 (2004): 109–43.

26. *Al Hamishmar,* July 2 and 5, 1974.

27. Johnny Gal, *Bitachon socialy be-Israel* (Jerusalem: Magnes Press, 2004), 29–31; Gutwein, "Al ha-stira."

6. The Decline of the Mediating Mechanism

1. Amiram Gonen, "Bchina geografit shel ha-tacharut ha-electoralit bein ha-maarach ve-halikud ba-arim ha-yehudiot be-Israel, 1965–1981," *Medina, Mimshal Veyachasim Bein-leumi-im* 19–20 (1982): 63–87; Cohen and Orkibi, "Universita ve-shilton"; Yonatan Shapira, *Lashilton bachartanu: Darka shel tnuaat ha-Cheirut* (Tel Aviv: Am Oved, 1989).

2. Amir Bar-Or, "Min ha-yesod: Naftuleyah shel tnua politit," *Iyunim Bitkumat Israel* 4 (1994): 478–93.

3. *Al Hamishmar*, Dec. 30, 1965.

4. For further discussion, see Reuven Shapira, *Ha-emet al ha-kibbutz* (Haifa: Pardes, 2013).

5. Hakim, *Ha-kibbutzim be-Israel*, 103, 121.

6. Barkai, *Hitpatchut ha-meshek*, 178; Hakim, *Ha-kibbutzim be-Israel*, 59–60, 94; Elmaliach, *Ha-ta'asia*, 107.

7. Molcho, "Kapitalism."

8. See Hakibbutz Ha'artzi Ninth Council, minutes, May 1958, file (2)5-9.20, HHA.

9. Report on students of Hakibbutz Ha'artzi, Feb. 25, 1973, file 3627(4)9.5, HHA.

10. Kibbutzim students had a significant role in the establishment of the Group of Eleven, Siah, the Movement for Peace and Security, and more. For further discussion, see Portugez, "Mi-smol sotzi'alisti."

7. Internal Divisions in the Labor Movement

1. For further discussion, see Baruch Zisser, *Al yemin ve-al smol* (Jerusalem: Shoken, 1999), 32.

2. Israel was not alone in seeing the traditional labor movement abandoned by neoliberals, leftists of the old and new variety, and the working class. The same thing happened in many European countries. See Eley, *Forging Democracy*, 386–403.

3. Rozenfeld and Carmi, "Nichus emtzaim tziburiyim"; Ben-Porat, *Heichan hem ha-burganim ha-hem.*

4. Rachel Tokatli, "Dfusim politim be-yachasey ha-avoda be-Israel," PhD diss., Tel Aviv Univ., 1979, 112. For further discussion, see Avi Bareli and Uri Cohen, *The Academic Middle-Class Rebellion* (Leiden: Brill, 2017).

5. Ministerial Committee for Economics meeting, minutes, Oct. 13, 1964, folder 8/16700-ג, Israel State Archive, Jerusalem; see also Navon, "Ha-mitun."

6. Avraham Michael and Refael Bar-El, *Shvitot be-Israel: Gisha kamutit* (Ramat Gan, Israel: Ha-Machon Le-Kidum Yachasey Avoda, Bar-Ilan Univ., 1977), 37–38.

7. *Davar*, Jan. 5, 1966.

8. Shalev, "Ovdim."

9. Michael and Bar-El, *Shvitot be-Israel*, 36–38.

10. Michael and Bar-El, *Shvitot be-Israel*, 65.

11. The term *meshekists* (*mishkistim*) originated with a group at Kibbutz Ein Harod that in the second half of the 1920s sought to promote and ground the local kibbutz economy at the expense of support for a nationwide kibbutz movement. Over time, the term came to be used in the other kibbutz movements, mostly with a negative connotation. For further discussion, see Moshe Breslavsky, *Tnua'at ha-poalim ha-Eretz Israelit*, vol. 2 (Tel Aviv: Hakibbutz Hameuhad, 1957), 84; Shapira, *Ha-halicha*, 166; Menachem Rozner, Yitzhak Ben David, Alexander Avnat, Nani Cohen, and Uri Leviatan, *Hador ha-sheny: Ha-kibbutz bein hemshech le-tmura* (Tel Aviv: Sifriyat Poalim, 1978), 297; Menachem

Topel, "Ha-technokratim ke-elita kibutzit," in *Elitot hadashot be-Israel*, ed. Eliezer Ben Refael (Jerusalem: Mosad Bialik, 2007), 255–74.

12. Topel, "Ha-technokratim."

13. Topel, "Ha-technokratim."

14. Meir Ya'ari, "Al gilu'im mad'igim," *Hashavu'a Bakibbutz Ha'artzi*, Jan. 27, 1956.

15. Meir Ya'ari, "Al gilu'im mad'igim," *Hashavu'a Bakibbutz Ha'artzi*, Jan. 27, 1956.

16. Israel Pinchasi, "Beshel ma ha-tocheca?" *Hashavu'a Bakibbutz Ha'artzi*, Feb. 24, 1956.

17. *Hashavu'a Bakibbutz Ha'artzi*, Feb. 24, 1956.

18. Ra'anan Weitz, *Ha-kfar ha-Israeli be-idan ha-technologya* (Tel Aviv: Am Oved, 1967), 283–84.

19. Dov Markovitz, "Me-she'elot ha-shituf ha-ezory," *Hedim* 71 (Sept. 1962); "Pe'iley ha-ezorim be-diyun al ha-shituf ha-ezory," *Hashavu'a Bakibbutz Ha'artzi*, June 1, 1962.

20. Hakibbutz Ha'artzi Executive Committee meeting, minutes, May 1962, file 3555(7)5-7.10, HHA; Shlomo Rozen, "Ha-shituf ha-ezory," *Hedim* 71 (Sept. 1962).

21. For further discussion of "acceptable behavior," see Tamar Herman, *Me-lemala lemata: Tnu'ot hevratiot u-mecha'a politit*, vol. 2 (Ra'anana, Israel: Open Univ., 1995), 145.

22. Harvey, *A Brief History of Neoliberalism*, 110.

23. Portugez, "Mi-smol sotzi'alisti."

24. This merger included two other groups also: Oded, a group of young activists of Mizrahi origin, and a group that split from the Labor Party under the leadership of General (ret.) Meir Amit.

25. Along with its democratic characteristics, the struggle against Ben-Gurion also aimed to maintain the status of certain social groups affiliated with the Histadrut—that is, to maintain the unequal social structure. See Cohen, "Ha-intelectual ha-ta'hor"; Greenberg, "Mapai bein demokratizatzia le-liberalizatzia"; Bar-Or, "Min ha-yesod."

26. For further discussion of the Lavon Affair, see Eyal Kafkafy, *Lavon—anti mashiach* (Tel Aviv: Am Oved, 1998), 379–98.

27. Mapam Central Committee meeting, minutes, Apr. 21, 1958, file 790(6)64.90, HHA.

28. Imri Ron, interview by the author, Mishmar Ha'emek, Dec. 30, 2008; Danny Zamir, interview by the author, Mishmar Ha'emek, Apr. 7, 2009; Reuven Shapira, interview by the author, Gan Shmuel, May 24, 2009.

29. *Hashavu'a Bakibbutz Ha'artzi*, Sept. 14 and 29, Oct. 26, 1962.

30. Hakibbutz Ha'artzi Executive Committee meetings, minutes, Nov. 18–19, Dec. 7–8, 1962, file 3558(14)5-10.10, HHA. See also reports in *Hashavu'a Bakibbutz Ha'artzi*, Nov. 30 and Dec. 21, 1962.

31. Hakibbutz Ha'artzi Executive Committee meeting, minutes, Dec. 7–8, 1962, file 3558(14)5-10.10, HHA.

32. Hakibbutz Ha'artzi Tenth Council, Apr. 10–13, 1964, file 3558(1)5-13.20, HHA.

33. Gan, "Ha-siach shegava," 57.

34. Gan, "Ha-siach shegava," 61.

35. On the protest in Hakibbutz Hameuhad, see Izhar, *Bein hazon le-shilton*, 426, 432, 437, 453.

36. Tamar Herman, "Aliato shel va'ad ha-shalom ha-Israeli u-nefilato," *Ha-tziyonut*, Yud-Zain 1993, 245–60; Eli Tzur, "Le-hi'ot am hofshi be-artzenu: Ha-liga le-meni'at kfia datit be-hekshera ha-history," in *Medina ba-derech: Ha-hevera ha-Israelit ba-asorim ha-rishonim*, ed. Anita Shapira (Jerusalem: Merkaz Zalman Shazar, 2001), 205–38.

37. For further discussion, see Tamar Herman, "Me-brit shalom le-shalom achshav: Ha-patzifism ha-pragmaty shel machaneh ha-shalom be-Israel," PhD diss., Tel Aviv Univ., 1989, 258–80.

38. Adi Portugez, "Tnuat smol Israeli hadash: Smol hadash be-Israel," *Israel* 21 (2013): 225–52.

39. Ehud Shprintzak, *Nitzaney politica shel de-legitimizatzia be-Israel 1967–1972* (Jerusalem: Hebrew Univ., 1983).

40. Between the end of the Six-Day War and the beginning of 1969, a total of 234 Israeli soldiers and 47 civilians were killed in security incidents, and 1,288 were injured. In March 1969, the War of Attrition broke out. In this conflict, which lasted until August 1970, a total of 369 Israeli soldiers were killed, and 999 were injured. From then until 1972, another 214 Israelis were killed in security incidents, and 822 were injured (data from *Al Hamishmar*, June 6, 1972).

41. Meir Chazan, "Yozmat Nachum Goldman le-hipagesh aim Natzer be-shnat 1970," *Iyunom Bitkumat Israel* 14 (2004): 255–84.

42. "Korbanot prag shuv muka'im," *Davar*, May 2, 1970; Yigal Laviv, "Bno shel ha-sar Sem-Tov yazym et ha-michtav le-rosh ha-memshalah," *Ha'aretz*, Apr. 28, 1970.

43. Yigal Alon, minister of education, meeting with the writers of the letter, May 5, 1970, folder 03-8048, ISA.

44. *Hatza'it*, Oct. 1970.

45. Rikuz Mapam meeting, minutes, Mar. 13, 1972, file (3)79.90, HHA.

46. "Mapam tova'at hafsakat nishul ve-hitnachlut ba-retzu'a," *Al Hamishmar*, Mar. 16, 1972.

47. Mapam Secretariat meeting, minutes, Apr. 3, 1972, file 811(2)63.90, HHA.

48. Dalya Shchori, "Dayan: Pinui ha-pitcha ne'esa le-lo hachlatat memshala u-bli hora'at ha-matkal," *Al Hamishmar*, May 17, 1972.

49. Mapam Political Committee meeting, minutes, Aug. 9, 1972, file 90.122(9)847, HHA; "Mapam Tova'at diun hozer ba-memshala be-inyan ha-akurim," *Al Hamishmar*, Aug. 10, 1972.

50. Mordechai Oren, "Ha-demagogya ha-hitnachlutit ha-mishtolelet," *Al Hamishmar*, Mar. 21, 1972; Ytzchak Shor, "Be-mivtza tzva'I punu revavot ha-tzoadim aim ha-hachlata le-vatel et ha-tzeada ha-yod-het," *Al Hamishmar*, Mar. 22, 1972; "Rosh ha-memshala hetila mishkala ha-ishi le-ma'an hasarat hatzaot ha-opozitzia," *Al Hamishmar*, Mar. 28, 1972.

51. "Ha-atzuma: Rak hatzi emet," *Al Hamishmar*, Apr. 9, 1972.

52. Mordechai Oren, "Golda Meir nozefet be-sarei Mapam," *Al Hamishmar*, July 28, 1972.

53. *Al Hamishmar*, Mar. 28, 1972.

54. "Ha-ma'aracha lekiuma ve-atida shel medinat Israel adain be-itzuma," *Al Hamishmar*, Apr. 18, 1972.

55. Ya'akov Hazan, "Ivut ve-siluf shel dvarim," *Hashavu'a Bakibbutz Ha'artzi*, Apr. 28, 1972.

56. Rikuz Mapam meeting, minutes, July 12, 1973, file (4)79.90, HHA.

57. Rikuz Mapam meeting, minutes, Oct. 2, 1973, file (5)79.90, HHA.

58. Rikuz Mapam meeting, minutes, May 25, 1972, file (3)79.90, HHA.

59. Rikuz Mapam meeting, minutes, June 12, 1972, file (3)79.90, HHA.

60. Quoted in "Emdat Mapam be-inyan Biram, Rafiach ve-hok Hausner: Be-diunei ha-ma'arach," *Al Hamishmar*, Aug. 18, 1972.

61. Gavriel Shtern, "Harov ba-memshala hechlit neged hatarat shuvam shel toshvei Ikrit ve-Biram el kfaryehem," *Al Hamishmar*, Apr. 24, 1972.

62. Rikuz Mapam meeting, minutes, July 31, 1972, file (3)79.90, HHA.

63. Rikuz Mapam meeting, minutes, Aug. 21, 1972, file (3)79.90, HHA; Yechiel Limor, "Tzeirei Mapam hitmardu: Ki'imu atzeret lema'an ha-akurim benigud le-hachlatat ha-hanhaga," *Maariv*, Aug. 23, 1972.

64. Rikuz Mapam meeting, minutes, Apr. 2, 1973, file (3)79.90, HHA.

65. Gavriel Shtern, "Golda: Er'u harigot mach'ivot; Dayan: Biglal shikul da'at mut'e shel ktzinim," *Al Hamishmar*, July 10, 1972.

66. "Asrot haveri kibbutzim hefginu leyad Akraba," *Al Hamishmar*, Apr. 3, 1973.

67. Nachum Barne'a, "Ha-shtachim hasgurim ve-hahitnachlut," *Davar*, Feb. 1, 1973.

68. Report about the relationship between the university establishment and the students, 1969, file 310, Hebrew Univ. Archive, Jerusalem.

69. Amos Gal, "Ha-hatzaga ha-gdola be-shfeya holida dmama daka," *Davar*, Apr. 14, 1969; "Ha-studentim Le-re'iyat heshbon hitpar'u emesh be-Haifa," *Maariv*, June 2, 1969; Yechiel Limor, "Ofnat ha-meri hegi'a le-Universitat Yerushalaim," *Maariv*, Dec. 19, 1969; Yechiel Limor, "Nesi'ut hitachdut ha-studentim dana ba-shvita ba-fakulta le-mishpatim," *Maariv*, Feb. 18, 1972; A. Gazit, "Al ha-barikadot, al habchinot," *Maariv*, Mar. 31, 1972; Tel Aviv University Law School Student Council to Yuval Ne'eman, Dec. 27, 1971, no file number, Tel Aviv Univ. Archive; head of the national Student Council to the university presidents, Mar. 10, 1972, no file number, Tel Aviv Univ. Archive.

70. Gidon Sapiro, "Mi hishtalet al ha-studentim be-universitat Hifa," *Davar*, Apr. 3, 1972; *Zo Ha-Derech*, Mar. 15, 1973; Shlomo Svirsky, *Kampus, hevra u-medina* (Jerusalem: Mifras, 1982).

71. Dov Goldshtein, "Reayon ha-shavua aim Moti Ashkenazi," *Maariv*, Feb. 7, 1974; "Moti Ashkenazi machriz al mivtza 101 elef hatimot lehadachat Dayan," *Maariv*, Feb. 17,

1974; Motty Ashkenazy, "Tnuat ha-mecha'a she-le'achar milchemet Yom Kipur: Mabat retrospectivy," in *Ha-asor ha-shlishi*, ed. Tzameret and Yablonka, 165–70.

72. Motti Ashkenazy, "Da me'ain bata u-lean ata holech," in *Trauma leumit: Milchemet Yom Ha-Kipurim achrey shloshim shana ve-od milchama*, ed. Moshe Shemesh and Zeev Drori (Sde Boker, Israel: Ben-Gurion Research Institute Press, 2008), 368–78.

73. Dayan quoted in Meron Medzini, *Golda: Biografya politit* (Tel Aviv: Yediot Sfarim, 2008), 591.

74. Ashkenazy, "Da me'ain bata."

75. "Lema'ala me-aseret alafim aish hatmu al atzumat shalom achshav," *Al Hamishmar*, Dec. 5, 1973.

76. *Al Hamishmar*, Aug. 1, 1974.

77. *Al Hamishmar*, Oct. 28, 1974.

78. *Al Hamishmar*, Feb. 21, 1975.

79. *Al Hamishmar*, Feb. 25, 1975.

80. *Al Hamishmar*, Jan. 11, 1976.

81. *Al Hamishmar*, Jan. 29, 1976.

82. Shalom Chetrit, *Ha-maavak ha-mizrahi be-Israel*; Bryan K. Roby, *The Mizrahi Era of Rebellion: Israel's Forgotten Civil Rights Struggle, 1948–1966* (Syracuse, NY: Syracuse Univ. Press, 2015), 101.

83. The survey, conducted among twenty branches of Mapam (2,030 participants), found that 830 of the participants (40.8 percent) lived in transit camps or immigrant settlements; 750 (36.9 percent) were of North African and Middle Eastern origin; 1,212 (59.7 percent) were blue-collar workers; and 595 (49 percent) of the blue-collar workers did not have a permanent job or a stable income. Although these numbers might seem impressive, we must remember that less than half of Mapam's members were from the city, so the real share of what could be defined as the "proletariat" population among the party members was actually less than 25 percent. The survey's results are given in Mapam Secretariat meeting, minutes, Aug. 8, 1956, file 811(4)63.90, HHA.

84. Mapam Secretariat meetings, minutes, Apr. 3, 1956, file (3)63.90, and Aug. 8, 1956, file 811(4)63.90, HHA; Hulon branch to the Mapam Assembly, Nov. 11, 1959, file 789(2)111.90, HHA; report of activities in December 1966, Tel Aviv branch, Mapam, file 1048(6)318.90, HHA.

85. Izhar, *Bein hazon le-shilton*, 175, 207.

86. Roby, *Mizrahi Era of Rebellion*, 101.

87. Roby, *Mizrahi Era of Rebellion*, 86–136.

88. Bareli and Cohen, "Ha-siach ha-tziburi"; Weitz, "Miflaga mitmodedet am kishlona."

89. Yfaat Weiss, *Vadi Salib: Ha-nochach ve-ha-nifkad* (Jerusalem: Van Leer Institute; Tel Aviv: Hakibbutz Hameuhad, 2007); report by the Public Investigation Committee of Vadi Salib on incidents of July 9, 1959, folder 4/7253, ISA.

90. Izhar, *Bein hazon le-shilton*, 218–23.

91. Gonen, "Bchina geografit."

92. "Mafginim hitnagshu aim ha-mishtara be-hafganot 1 be-may bedimona," *Maariv*, May 2, 1966; Yitzchak Yitzchaki, "Alfei olim hefginu ve-shavtu," *Davar*, May 2, 1966.

93. Izhar, *Bein hazon le-shilton*, 132, 207, 210, 212, 213, 345, 396, 403, 447.

94. *Davar*, Mar. 3 and 13, 1966; *Al Hamishmar*, Mar. 9 and 10, 1966.

95. Zalman Livne to the Mapam Propaganda Department, July 7, 1967, file 789(2)111.90, HHA.

96. Mapam Jerusalem Branch Secretariat meeting, minutes, Jan. 5, 1975, file 842(7)83.90, HHA.

97. Report on demonstration of May 1, 1967, May 25, 1967, file 789(2)111.90, HHA.

98. Izhar, *Bein hazon le-shilton*, 416.

99. Ya'akov Vilan to Hakibbutz Ha'artzi Secretariat, Apr. 4, 1958, file 811(4)63.90, HHA.

100. See a report that Ben-Moshe wrote to the Mapam Assembly, 1963, in Naftali Ben-Moshe, *Asif: Kovetz ma'amarim* (N.p.: Asif, 1994), 62.

101. Tzvi Zakai to Meir Talmi, May 25, 1966, file 858(4)190.90, HHA.

102. Ya'akov Vilan to Mapam Secretariat, Dec. 18, 1959, and Shlomo Atir to the Hakibbutz Ha'artzi Professional Department, Sept. 28, 1967, file 789(2)111.90, HHA.

103. Haifa Branch of Mapam young guard to the kibbutzim, Dec. 30, 1966; Hakibbutz Ha'artzi Secretariat to Mapam Assembly, Jan. 24, 1967; Mapam Secretariat to Kibbutz Nachshonim, Jan. 24, 1967; Mapam Secretariat to Kibbutz Ramat Hashofet, Jan. 23, 1967: all in file 1188(3)458.90, HHA.

104. Henriette Dahan Kalev, *Ha-hachmatza ha-gdola shel ha-demokratya ha-Israelit: Ha-zikaron ha-traumati ke-moreshet shel Meha'ot Vadi Salib* (N.p.: Israeli Institute for Democracy, 2009), 5; Shalom Chetrit, *Ha-maavak ha-Mizrahi*, 136–74.

105. See, for example, *Al Hamishmar*, Jan. 13, 1971; *Maariv*, Mar. 25, 1971; *Davar*, May 18, 1971. See also Dvora Berenstein, "Ha-panterim ha-shchorim ke-tnuat mecha'a: Kri'at tegar la-medina u-lesdarei'a," in *Ha-asor ha-shlishi*, ed. Tzameret and Yablonka, 104–14.

106. Shapira, *Lashilton bachartanu*, 176.

107. Yona Yagol, *Ketz ha-hagmonya: Nefilat ha-ma'arach ve-aliyat ha-Likud* (Hulon, Israel: Yesod, 1978), 91.

8. The Rebellion Within

1. Protocols of Hakibbutz Ha'artzi Ninth Council, May 29–June 1, 1958, file (2)9.20-5, HHA.

2. Protocols of Hakibbutz Ha'artzi Tenth Council, Apr. 10–13, 1963, file 3588(1)5-13.20, HHA.

3. The leadership included Dany Zamir (Mishmar Haemek), Asaf Nahir (Sha'ar Ha'amakim), Reuven Shapira (Gan Shmuel), Banko Adar (Ein Shemer), Ran Cohen (Gan Shmuel), and Yossi Amitai (Gvulot).

4. Newspaper articles related to the congress, file 3590(1)5-15.20, HHA.

5. Mapam Central Committee meeting, minutes, July 15, 1970, file (1)68.90, HHA. See also Benko Adar, "Mapam: Levatim shel tmura—ironim, kibbutznikim ve-dor ha-hemshech," *Hotam*, Aug. 6, 1971.

6. Letters to the editor in *Hashavu'a Bakibbutz Ha'artzi*, Aug. 27, 1971, and *Al Hamishmar*, July 28, 1971; Meir Ya'ari's responses in *Hashavu'a Bakibbutz Ha'artzi*, June 4, 1971, and *Al Hamishmar*, Aug. 6, 1971; Benko Adar, "Mapam: Levatim shel tmura—ha-manhig ve-ha-machaneh," *Hotam*, July 30, 1971.

7. Rikuz Mapam meetings, minutes, Oct. 25 and Nov. 1, 1971, file 79.90(2), HHA, and Nov. 3, 1971, file 811(11)63.90, HHA.

8. Rikuz Mapam meeting, minutes, Sept. 26, 1972, file (3)79.90, HHA.

9. See survey in *Hotam*, Feb. 4, 1977.

10. Hakibbutz Ha'artzi Thirty-Ninth Council, Oct. 1972, file 18.20-5(1)3593, HHA; Reuven Shapira to the editor, *Hashavu'a Bakibbutz Ha'artzi*, Nov. 17, 1972.

11. Rikuz Mapam meeting, minutes, Sept. 10, 1973, file (5)79.90, HHA.

12. For further reading on the end of Ben-Gurion's and Tabenkin's careers, see Avi Shilon, *Ben-Gurion: His Later Years in the Political Wilderness* (Lanham, MD: Rowman and Littlefield, 2016), and Izhar, *Bein hazon le-shilton*.

13. Keith Laybourn, *A Century of Labour: A History of the Labour Party, 1900–2000* (Phoenix Mill, UK: Sutton, 2000), 108.

9. The Leadership's Response

1. Bareli and Cohen, "Ha-siach ha-tziburi."

2. Shalev, "Ovdim."

3. See resolutions of Hakibbutz Ha'artzi Ninth Council, May 1958, file (2)5-9.20, HHA; proposals from Hakibbutz Ha'artzi Economic Department, Feb. 1964, file 2833(5)253.8, HHA.

4. Hakibbutz Ha'artzi Executive Committee meeting, minutes, Feb. 22–23, 1955, file (7)95-4.23, HHA.

5. See guiding materials from 1965–66, files 71.1-8(5), 8-93.1, HHA.

6. Regional factories to Hakibbutz Ha'artzi Economic Department, July 17, 1967, file 72.1-8(1), HHA.

7. Tzur, *Hakibbutz Hameuhad*, 40.

8. Meir Ya'ari, "Nekudot ha-moked asher ba-ma'aracha," *Al Hamishmar*, July 28, 1961.

9. "Ha-mif'alim ha-ezori'im: Al seder yoma shel brit ha-tnua ha-kibbutzit," *Al Hamishmar*, Oct. 20, 1968.

10. Survey by the Association of Kibbutz Industry, Nov. 1969, file 72.1-8(8), HHA.

11. See, for example, a description of such a phenomenon in the Kibbutz Ramat Hashofet factory, ARAD, file (4)8-10.1, HHA.

12. Symposium in *Al Hamishmar*, Dec. 30, 1966; Hananyah Nahor to *Al Hamishmar*, Sept. 28, 1966; Shlomo Rozen, "Orot ve-tazlalim ba-shituf ha-ezory," *Hashavu'a Bakibbutz Ha'artzi*, June 1, 1962.

13. Tzur, *Hakibbutz Hameuhad*, 40.

14. Tzur, *Hakibbutz Hameuhad*, 36.

15. Moshe Chizik, "Aim hakamat brit ha-tnua ha-kibbutzit," *Hedim* 75, Nov. 1963; Meir Ya'ari, "Shutfut melakedet," *Al Hamishmar*, Nov. 1, 1963.

16. The writers of the Letter of the Twelfth Graders, for example, were invited for a meeting with Yigal Allon, the minister of education. Prime Minister Golda Meir spoke of them differently than she did of other groups of protestors, saying that "they are not reckless like members of Matzpen" (Knesset Foreign Affairs and Defense Committee meeting, minutes, May 15, 1970, folder ג' 16707-06, ISA). On varying approaches to different cases of protest after the Yom Kippur War, see Eva Etzioni-Halevy and Moshe Livne, "The Response of the Israeli Establishment to the Yom Kippur War Protest," *Middle East Journal* 31, no. 3 (Summer 1977): 281–96.

17. Elmaliach, "The Israeli Left between Culture and Politics."

18. See interviews with Meir in *Maariv*, Feb. 26, 1969, and *Al Hamishmar*, Apr. 2, 1969.

19. Tzahor, *Hazan*, 254.

20. Mapam Secretariat meeting, minutes, Oct. 26, 1970, file 79.90(1), HHA.

21. See, for example, articles by Meir Ya'ari in *Al Hamishmar*, Oct. 27, 1969; by Peretz Merchav in *Al Hamishmar*, July 20, 1970; and by Dov Bar-Nir in *Al Hamishmar*, Dec. 4, 1970. For further discussion of the tactic of "moral panic," see Tali Lev and Yehuda Shenhav, "Kinunu shel ha-oyev mibifnim: Hapanterim hashchorim kemusa shel panica musarit," *Sociologia Israerlit* 12, no. 1 (2010): 135–58.

22. See, for example, *Al Hamishmar*, Feb. 6, 13, and 27, 1970.

23. See, for example, *Basha'ar*, Feb.–May 1969, Nov.–Dec. 1971; *Al Hamishmar*, Oct. 30 and Nov. 6, 1970.

24. Miryam Bustan, interview by the author, Gan Shmuel, Oct. 5, 2006.

25. Meir Ya'ari, "Ha-poschim al shney ha-se'ifim," *Al Hamishmar*, Aug. 17, 1973.

26. Rikuz Mapam meeting, minutes, June 18, 1973, file (4)79.90, HHA.

27. Lev and Shenhav, "Kinunu shel ha-oyev mibifnim," 13.

28. Timor and Cohen, "Yachas ha-kibbutzim."

29. Yitzchak Ben-David, *Avoda ba-kibbutz: Metziut ve-she'ifot* (N.p.: Center for Research of Rural Settlements and Brit ha-Tnua ha-Kibbutzit, 1975), 10, 54.

30. Yechiel Harari to Hakibbutz Ha'artzi Secretariat, Apr. 25, 1972, file ה-88.3(1), HHA.

31. Report in *Al Hamishmar*, Jan. 19, 1971.

32. Report in *Al Hamishmar*, Dec. 8, 1969.

33. Report in *Al Hamishmar*, June 4, 1970.

34. Yitzhak Ben-Aharon, "Oz li-tmura be-terem por'anut," published simultaneously in *Davar* and *Lamerchav* (the Ahdut Ha'avodah daily) on January 11, 1963, and in a shorter version in *Al Hamishmar* three days later.

35. Izhar, *Bein hazon le-shilton*, 357, 360, 362.

36. Gutwein, "Al ha-stira."

37. See *Al Hamishmar*, Jan. 11 and July 6, 1967.

38. Menachem Hofgong, *Mecha'a ve-chem'a: Hashpa'at hafganot ha-panterim ha-shchorim al haktza'ot le-tzorchei hevra u-revacha* (Jerusalem: Nevo, 2006); Gal, *Bitachon socialy be-Israel*, 28–32; Gutwein, "Ha-chalutziut ha-burganit."

39. Doron, "Medinyut ha-revacha."

40. Natan, "Ha-mediniyut ha-kalkalit," 21.

41. Yossi Tamir, *Shinuyim be-dfusei ha-oni be-auchlusiat ha-schirim be-Israel 1969–1975: Megamot klaliot* (Jerusalem: Hamosad le-Bituach Leumi, Mechkar 18, 1977).

42. *Shnaton ha-memshala* (Jerusalem: Tav-Shin-Lamed-Chet, 1976), 125–28.

10. Political Paralysis

1. Shapira, *Ha-halicha*, 373.

2. Eisenstadt, *Tmurot*, 36.

3. Richard S. Katz and Peter Mair, "Changing Models of Party Organization and Party Democracy: The Emergence of the Cartel Party," *Party Politics* 1, no. 1 (1995): 5–31.

4. Laybourn, *A Century of Labour*, 98.

5. Seymour M. Lipset and Stein Rokkan, *Party Systems and Voter Alignments: Cross-National Perspectives* (New York: Free Press, 1967).

6. In *A Brief History of Neoliberalism*, David Harvey uses the term *embedded liberalism* to define the economic mechanism of the capitalistic welfare state.

7. For further discussion, see Yossi Beilin, *Mechiro shel ihud* (Tel Aviv: Revivim, 1985).

8. For further discussion, see Shifris, *Memshelet Rabin*.

9. Izhar, *Bein hazon le-shilton*, 297.

10. Izhar, *Bein hazon le-shilton*, 289, 374.

11. Izhar, *Bein hazon le-shilton*, 274.

12. Izhar, *Bein hazon le-shilton*, 260, 263, 315, 389. See also Tzur, *Min ha-yam ad ha-midbar*, 312.

13. Tzur, *Min ha-yam ad ha-midbar*, 241.

14. Tzur, *Nofey ha'ashlaya*, 283–310.

15. Meir Ya'ari, speech in Hakibbutz Ha'artzi Lamed-Bet Council, Mar. 29–31, 1956, file (1)5-8.20, vol. 1, HHA; see also Ya'akov Hazan, "Keitzad nitkadem likrat ha-shalom," *Hedim* 52 (Jan. 1957).

16. *Al Hamishmar*, Nov. 8, 1956; Mapam party-center assembly, minutes, Jan. 31, 1957, file 819(1)68.90, HHA.

17. Under the Eisenhower Doctrine, a Middle Eastern country could request American economic assistance or aid from US military forces if it were being threatened by armed aggression from another state. The doctrine's goal clearly was to stand against the Soviet Union in the struggle over the control of the Middle East. For further details, see Nadav Safran, *Medinat Israel ve-yachasei'ha aim artzot ha-brit* (Jerusalem: Shoken, 1979). For Mapam's stand regarding the doctrine, see *Al Hamishmar*, Jan. 31 and Feb. 8, 1957.

18. Mapam Political Committee meeting, minutes, July 23, 1958, file 803(5)121.90, HHA.

19. *Al Hamishmar*, Dec. 29, 1958.

20. *Al Hamishmar*, June 30 and July 3, 1959.

21. *Al Hamishmar*, June 30 and July 3, 1959.

22. *Al Hamishmar*, June 30 and July 3, 1959.

23. Mapam party-center assembly, minutes, Dec. 16, 1959, file (3)68.90, HHA.

24. *Al Hamishmar*, Jan. 21, 1960.

25. See the criticism of the party by Naftali Ben-Moshe (leader of Mapam's urban working-class sector) in his book *Asif*, 62.

26. Mapam Political Committee meeting, minutes, Mar. 8, 1956, file (4)121.90, HHA.

27. *Al Hamishmar*, Dec. 25, 1958.

28. *Al Hamishmar*, May 12, 1959.

29. *Al Hamishmar*, Oct. 18, 1959.

30. *Al Hamishmar*, Jan. 5, 1961.

31. Ben-Moshe, *Asif.*

32. Mapam Central Committee meeting, minutes, Jan. 16, 1961, file (4)68.90, HHA; Mapam Secretariat meeting, minutes, Feb. 8, 1961, file (4)65.90, HHA.

33. *Al Hamishmar*, Feb. 2, 1961.

34. *Al Hamishmar*, Aug. 24, 1961.

35. Mapam Political Committee meeting, minutes, Oct. 12, 1961, file 803(2)121.90, HHA.

36. Mapam Executive Committee meeting, minutes Dec. 10, 1959, file 790(6)64.90, HHA.

37. Mapam Secretariat meetings, minutes, Oct. 18 and 25, 1961, file (5)65.90, HHA.

38. Mapam Central Committee meeting, minutes, Oct. 26, 1961, file (5)68.90, HHA.

39. Yigal Alon to Israel Galili, Apr. 27, 1961, correspondence file, Yigal Alon Archive, Kibbutz Ginosar.

40. See *Al Hamishmar*, Oct. 14, 1960, and Jan. 12, 1961.

41. See Ya'akov Hazan, "Likrat ha-he'archut ha-hadasha," *Hedim* 69 (Jan. 1962). For Mapai's stand regarding the inclusion of Mapam in the government, see Greenberg, *Pinchas Sapir*, 200.

42. *Al Hamishmar*, Jan. 16, 1962.

43. Greenberg, *Pinchas Sapir*, 203–15; Nadav Kalinov-Malul and Rut Kalinov-Malul, *Ha-hitpatcut ha-kalkalit shel Israel* (Jerusalem: Academon, 1968), 8.

44. *Al Hamishmar*, Feb. 16, 1962.

45. *Al Hamishmar*, May 15 and July 17, 1962.

46. *Al Hamishmar*, Dec. 17, 23, 25, 26, 31, 1962.

47. See Richard Weintraub's speech in Hakibbutz Ha'artzi Executive Committee meeting, quoted in *Hashavu'a Bakibbutz Ha'artzi*, Mar. 1, 1963.

48. *Al Hamishmar*, Mar. 7, 1962, and Apr. 21, 1963; *Hashavu'a Bakibbutz Ha'artzi*, Mar. 12, 1963.

49. Halamish, *Meir Ya'ari: Biografiyah*, 154.

50. Zaki Shalom, "Hitpatrut Ben Gurion me-rashut ha-memshala," *Iyunim Bitkumat Israel* 5 (1995): 608–14; Ychiam Weits, "Preida me-ha'av ha-meyased: Prishato shel Ben-Gurion me-rashut ha-memshala be-1963," in *Medina ba-derech*, ed. Shapira, 73–108; Michael Bar-Zohar, *Ben-Gurion*, vol. 3 (Tel Aviv: Zmura Beitan, 1987), 1519–59.

51. *Al Hamishmar*, June 21, Aug. 9, and Aug. 16, 1963.

52. Mapam Political Committee meeting, minutes, Oct. 7, 1963, file 803(6)121.90, HHA.

53. *Al Hamishmar*, Oct. 16, 1963.

54. Mapam Political Committee meeting, minutes, Jan. 1, 1964, file 803(6)121.90, HHA.

55. *Al Hamishmar*, Jan. 3 and 10, 1964.

56. Mapam Central Committee meeting, minutes, Jan. 15, 1964, file '8192(6)68.90, HHA; Mapam Political Committee meetings, minutes, Jan. 22 and 30, 1964, file 803(6)121.90, HHA.

57. *Al Hamishmar*, Feb. 6, 1964.

58. Mapam Political Committee meeting, minutes, Feb. 10, 1964, file 803(6)121.90, HHA.

59. *Al Hamishmar*, Feb. 13, 1964.

60. A total of 301 members voted against joining the government, 16 supported it, and 55 abstained. See *Basha'ar*, Mar. 1964.

61. *Al Hamishmar*, Feb. 23 and Mar. 13, 1964.

62. *Al Hamishmar*, Apr. 12, 1964.

63. Mapam Political Committee meeting, minutes, Feb. 17, 1964, file 803(6)121.90, HHA. See also Izhar, *Bein hazon le-shilton*, 357–62.

64. See Peretz Merchav, *Toldot tnuat ha-poalim be-Eretz Israel* (Tel Aviv: Sifriyat Poalim, 1967), 284.

65. *Al Hamishmar*, Nov. 10, 1965,

66. Mapam Political Committee meeting, minutes, Nov. 11, 1965, and Jan. 7, 1966, file 803(8)121.90, HHA.

67. *Al Hamishmar*, Jan. 3, 1966; Mapam Political Committee meeting, minutes, Jan. 7, 1966, file 803(8)121.90, HHA.

68. The Sapir Plan was published prior to Mapam's joining the government. See *Al Hamishmar*, Jan. 6, 1966.

69. See Hazan's speech in *Al Hamishmar*, Aug. 7, 1966; see also Arieh Krampf, "Kinuno shel musag ha-astzmaut ha-kalkalit ba-siach ha-Israeli," *Iyunim Bitkumat Israel* 19 (2009): 1–34.

70. Mapam Political Committee meeting, minutes, Jan. 7, 1966, file 803(8)121.90, HHA.

71. Mapam Central Committee meeting, minutes, Feb. 17, 1966, file (1)68.90, HHA.

72. Mapam Political Committee meeting, minutes, Jan. 7, 1966, file 803(8)121.90, HHA.

73. *Al Hamishmar*, Jan. 8, 1967.

74. Mapam Central Committee meeting, minutes, Mar. 22, 1967, file '68.90(8)8192, HHA.

75. Mapam Secretariat meeting, minutes, May 26, 1967, file '65.90(14)8182, HHA; Elazar Peri, "Hitgonenut, bitachon ve-shalom Keitzad?" *Al Hamishmar*, Apr. 21, 1967; the Mula Agin Affair is mentioned in Tzahor, *Hazan*, 244.

76. Halamish, *Meir Yaari: Ha-admor mi-Merchavia*, 211.

77. *Al Hamishmar*, May 5, June 2 and 6, 1967; Mapam Secretariat meeting, minutes, June 6, 1967, file '65.90(14)8182, HHA; Halamish, *Meir Yaari: Ha-admor mi-Merchavia*, 212.

78. Halamish, *Meir Yaari: Ha-admor mi-Merchavia*, 215.

79. Mapam Secretariat meeting, minutes, Sept. 9, 1967, file '65.90(14)8182, HHA.

80. Mapam Political Committee meeting, minutes, Sept. 6, 1967, file (4)122.90, HHA.

81. Mapam Political Committee meeting, minutes, June 19, 1967, file (4)122.90, HHA; *Al Hamishmar*, July 18, 1967.

82. Mapam Political Committee meeting, minutes, June 29, 1967, file (4)122.90, HHA.

83. Meir Ya'ari, "Al shlosha dvarim," *Al Hamishmar*, July 7, 1967.

84. Mapam Central Committee meeting, minutes, July 20, 1967, file '68.90(8)8192, HHA.

85. Mapam Political Committee meeting, minutes, Sept. 6, 1967, file (4)122.90, HHA.

86. *Al Hamishmar*, Mar. 24, 1968.

87. The results of the vote were: 433 (64.4 percent) against, 239 (35.6 percent) for, and 5 absent. See *Al Hamishmar*, Nov. 24, 1968.

88. See personal correspondence between Hazan and Ya'ari, 1965, file (6)4.30.95, HHA.

11. From Cultural Front to Arena for Debate

1. Rozner et al., *Hador ha-sheny*, 17.

2. Census carried out by the movement in 1968, file 2834(7)254.8, HHA.

3. Gan, "Ha-siach shegava"; Yossi Beilin, *Banim be-tzel avotam* (Tel Aviv: Revivim, 1984); Rozner et al., *Hador ha-sheny*.

4. Gadi Wolfsfeld, *The Politics of Provocation: Participation and Protest in Israel* (Albany: State Univ. of New York Press, 1988), 163.

5. Gerd-Rainer Horn, *The Spirit of 1968: Rebellion in Western Europe and North America, 1956–1976* (New York: Oxford Univ. Press, 2007), 144–46.

6. Pauker, "Hakibbutz Ha'artzi"; Reuven Shapira, "Ha-aratzat brit ha-moatzot ba-tnu'ot ha-kibbutziot ha-rashiot: Hisradut manhigim be-shlav ai-ye'ilutam ve-oligar-chizatzia be-Israel," *Hamerchav Hatziburi* 5 (2011): 92–121.

7. Izhar, *Bein hazon le-shilton*, 97.

8. In the Prague Trials, Czechoslovakian Communist leaders were accused of being agents of American imperialism. Eleven of the fourteen men so accused were of Jewish origin, and the trial displayed clear antisemitic characteristics. In the Doctor's Plot, nine doctors, six of them Jewish, were charged with attempting to poison the Soviet leadership. After Stalin's death, the country's new leadership acknowledged that the plot was a fabrication and exonerated the defendants.

9. Mapam Political Committee meeting, minutes, Mar. 28, 1956, file 121.90(3), HHA; Moshe Chizik, "Ha-chidushim ha-ra'aioni'im ve-ha-politi'im shel ha-veida ha-esrim," *Hedim* 50 (July 1956).

10. Mordechai Oren, *Reshimot asir Prague* (Tel Aviv: Sifriyat Poalim, 1958).

11. Hazan had already mentioned the speech, with its criticism of Stalinism, in March 1956. See Mapam Political Committee meeting, minutes, Mar. 28, 1956, file 121.90(3), HHA.

12. Imri Ron, interview by the author, Mishmar Ha'emek, Dec. 31, 2008.

13. Beilin, *Banim be-tzel avotam*, 170.

14. See articles by Eliezer Hacohen, Shlomo Ytzchaki, and Loshek Grol in *Hedim* 55 (Oct. 1957); see also articles in the "Bamat ha-beirur" section in *Al Hamishmar*, Oct. 4, 1957.

15. Gerd-Rainer, *The Spirit of 1968*, 131–38.

16. Anita Shapira, *Yehudim ḥadashim, Yehudim yeshanim* (Tel Aviv: Am Oved, 1997), 122–54.

17. See articles in *Davar*, Nov. 13, 1950, and Jan. 28, 1951, and in *Maariv*, June 14, 1962; see also Heilbronner, "Resistance through Rituals."

18. Education and Culture Committee meeting, Seventh Knesset, minutes, Feb. 23, Mar. 9 and 16, 1970, folder ב-3\186, ISA; Education and Culture Committee meeting, Seventh Knesset, Dec. 15, 1976, folder ב-10\1, ISA; Tel Aviv Town Hall Twelfth Council, meeting no. 9, minutes, July 14, 1974, Tel Aviv Municipality Archive. See also Pola Kabalo, "Ezrachim mitbagrim—kinus ha-talmidim be-Sheich Munis: Hitnagshut, dialog, ve-mifgash," *Israel* 4 (2003): 123–54; Kabalo, "Pioneering Discourse"; Eli Tzur, "Bdidut ha-manhig ha-zaken," *Ha-Tziyonut*, Kaf-Bet 2000, 283–310; Cohen, "Michael sheli"; Heilbronner, "Resistance through Rituals."

19. For further reading, see Alon Pauker, "Utopia be-svach ha-stirot: Hashva'a bein ha-dimuim ha-atzmi'im shel ha-tnutot hakibutziot be-asor ha-rishon la-medina," PhD diss., Tel Aviv Univ., 2005.

20. See the summary of *Hedim* activity in the years 1960–70 in *Hedim* 92 (Feb. 1970).

21. Yosef Shamir, "Ktzat heshbon nefesh," *Hedim* 49 (Apr. 1956).

22. Menachem Rozner, "Ha-veida ha-esrim le'or hatmurot she-achareiah," *Hedim* 52 (Jan. 1957).

23. Eliezer Hacohen, "Dreachim la-socialism," *Hedim* 53 (Apr. 1957), and *Hedim* 55 (Oct. 1957); Menachem Rozner, "Ha-veida ha-esrim le'or hatmurot she-achareiah," *Hedim* 52 (Jan. 1957).

24. See, for example, articles by Ya'ari in *Hedim* 50 (July 1956), 51 (Oct. 1956), and 55 (Oct. 1957).

25. Moshe Chizik, "Ha-ma'avak al derecho alternativit ve-ba'ayot ha-hazit ha-me'uchedet," *Hedim* 62 (Aug. 1959); Moshe Chizik, "Shituf peula ve-ihud ba-tnua ha-kibbutzit," *Hedim* 64 (Apr. 1960).

26. Symposium on regional cooperation, *Hedim* 71 (Sept. 1962).

27. Survey of the Hakibbutz Ha'artzi journals, spring 1967, and report Hakibbutz Ha'artzi Committee for the Study of the Movement's Journals, Aug. 1967, file 25.27(4)1868, HHA.

28. The editors in chief of *Bahativah* were right-wing Mapam activists such as Betzalel Lev (Gan Shmuel) and Menachem Shelach (Mishmar Haemek). Haim Shor (Shuval) also played a significant role in editing the journal (Ada Sade [Prich], interview by the author, Maabarot, Mar. 4, 2012).

29. See, for example, an article about Yaari's speech in *Bahativah*, Jan. 1957.

30. *Bahativah*, Feb. 1957.

31. *Bahativah*, Oct. 1958.

32. *Bahativah*, Jan.–Feb. 1959.

33. *Bahativah*, Dec. 1958.

34. See articles by Allon Gal, Yoram Nimrod, and Benko Adar in *Bahativah*, Dec. 1961 and Sept. 1962.

35. *Bahativah*, Apr. 1963.

36. Mula Agin, "He-arot le-tmiha," *Bahativah*, June 1963; "Bamat ha-beirur," *Hashavu'a Bakibbutz Ha'artzi*, Mar. 13, 1964.

37. Mapam Secretariat meeting, minutes, Nov. 13, 1957, file '63.90(7)8112, HHA.

38. See, for example, *Basha'ar*, Aug. 1958 and Mar. 1962.

39. See, for example, *Basha'ar*, Jan., Mar., June, and Aug. 1958.

40. See, for example, *Basha'ar*, Dec. 1959.

41. *Basha'ar* was read by 14.1 percent of Hakibbutz Ha'artzi members. See a report by the Hakibbutz Ha'artzi Committee for the Study of the Movement's journals, Aug. 1967, file 25.27(4)1868, HHA.

42. *Basha'ar*, Jan. 1960, Jan.–Feb. 1966, Mar.–Apr. 1966.

43. An interview with former editors in chief of *Hashavu'a Bakibbutz Ha'artzi* in *Hashavu'a Bakibbutz Ha'artzi*, Mar. 9, 1973.

44. See the articles by Meir Ya'ari and Israel Pinchasi in *Hashavu'a Bakibbutz Ha'artzi*, Jan. 27 and Feb. 24, 1956; see also reports from the Hakibbutz Ha'artzi Lamed-Bet Council, *Hashavu'a Bakibbutz Ha'artzi*, Apr. 6 and 20, 1956.

45. Meir Ya'ari quoted in reports from the Hakibbutz Ha'artzi Lamed-Bet Council, *Hashavu'a Bakibbutz Ha'artzi*, Apr. 6, 1956.

46. Reports from the Hakibbutz Ha'artzi Lamed-Bet Council, *Hashavu'a Bakibbutz Ha'artzi*, Apr. 6 and 20, 1956.

47. Resolution of Hakibbutz Ha'artzi Executive Committee, June 26–27, 1956, *Hashavu'a Bakibbutz Ha'artzi*, July 20, 1956.

48. Resolution of Hakibbutz Ha'artzi Executive Committee, Oct. 24–25, 1956, and other articles in *Hashavu'a Bakibbutz Ha'artzi*, Nov. 11, 1956. See also articles and reports in *Hashavu'a Bakibbutz Ha'artzi*, Dec. 28, 1956; May 3, 1957; and Sept. 4, 1959.

49. See *Hashavu'a Bakibbutz Ha'artzi*, Mar. 17, 1961.

50. See *Hashavu'a Bakibbutz Ha'artzi*, June 1, 1962.

51. See *Hashavu'a Bakibbutz Ha'artzi*, Sept. 14 and 29, Oct. 26, 1962.

52. *Hashavu'a Bakibbutz Ha'artzi*, Feb. 1 and Mar. 29, 1963.

53. Tzavta regulations, file 22.23(7), HHA.

54. Giora Manor, "Holchim le-Tzavta," *Hotam*, Jan. 7, 1972.

55. Manor, "Holchim le-Tzavta."

56. Shmuel Firstenberg, interview in *Hotam*, Jan. 17, 1968.

57. Shmuel Firstenberg, interviews by the author, Tel Aviv, Dec. 29, 2005, and Jan. 15, 2006.

58. Mapam Secretariat meeting, minutes, June 24, 1965, file 65.90(10)818, HHA.

59. Correspondence about Tzavta, 1968, file 22.23(7), HHA.

60. Firstenberg, interviews by the author.

61. David Hanegbi to Yaakov Hazan, n.d., 1956, file 36.24(52')2431, HHA; David Hanegbi to "Simcha," Nov. 15, 1957, file 2.24(1)2395, HHA; Sifriyat Poalim catalogs for 1954 and 1959, file 2.24(1)2395, HHA.

62. David Hanegbi to Hakibbutz Ha'artzi Secretariat, Apr. 21, 1956, file 36.24(52')2431, HHA.

63. Tzvi Zohar to David Hanegbi, June 12, 1960, file 10.24(1)2405, HHA; correspondence, file 12.24(2)2407, HHA.

64. Leszek Kołakowski, *Al ha-reshut netuna* (Tel Aviv: Sifriyat Poalim, 1964).

65. Nathan Shacham, *Sifriyat Poalim—50 shana* (Tel Aviv: Sifriyat Poalim, 1989), 33–37.

66. Mapam Secretariat meeting, minutes, Nov. 14, 1956, file 63.90(4)811, HHA. The World Peace Council was founded in August 1948 as a Soviet initiative, operated local

centers all over the world, and held international conventions. Mapam took part in this movement through the Vaad Hashalom ha'Israeli (Peace Committee of Israel), which the party controlled.

67. Mapam Secretariat meeting, minutes, May 15, 1956, file 62.90(7)778, HHA.

68. "Bamat ha-berur likrat ha-ve'ida ha-shlishit shel Mapam," *Al Hamishmar*, Oct. 4, 1957.

69. See, for example, Dov Yosefi, "Tafkid ha-ve'ida ha-shlishit shel Mapam," *Al Hamishmar*, Nov. 1, 1957.

70. Meir Ya'ari, speech in the Hakibbutz Ha'artzi Lamed-Gimel conference, quoted in *Al Hamishmar*, Mar. 20, 1959.

71. See, for example, Efraim Reiner's articles in *Al Hamishmar*, Apr. 5 and Aug. 30, 1963, and Eliezer Hacohen's articles in *Al Hamishmar*, Oct. 2, 9, and 18, 1963.

72. Report of Hakibbutz Ha'artzi's Committee for the Study of the Movement's Journals, Aug. 1967, file 25.27(4)1868, HHA.

73. Yigal Vagner, interview by the author, Oranim College, Jan. 17, 2010.

74. Kafkafy, *Lavon*, 408.

75. See articles by Yoram Nimrod, Allon Gal, and Benko Adar in *Bahativah*, June, Aug., and Sept. 1962 and Feb. 1963.

76. See articles by Nimrod, Gal, and Adar in *Hotam*, Mar. 17, Apr. 14, and June 9, 1964.

77. See articles by Nachum Shor in *Hotam*, Apr. 28, 1964, and by Mula Agin in *Hotam*, June 9, 1964.

78. Michael Strauss and Yigal Wagner, "Al ha-tochnit *She-ba-manifest ha-comonisty* ve-yesodotei'a ha-iuni'im," *Basha'ar*, Nov. 1963.

79. *Basha'ar*, May 1964.

80. *Basha'ar*, May 1964.

81. Eliezer Hacohen, *Sivchei kalkala u-medina* (Tel Aviv: Sifriyat Poalim, 1977), 274–83.

82. See Hakibbutz Ha'artzi Young Guard resolutions in *Al Hamishmar*, Mar. 18, 1962, and Mapam Secretariat, resolutions, Feb. 7, 1963, file '65.90(8)818ב, HHA. *Hotam*'s editors in chief and most members of its editorial board were Kibbutz members and affiliated with the right wing of Hakibbutz Ha'artzi and Mapam.

83. Mapam Secretariat meeting, minutes, Feb. 7, 1964, file '65.90(8)818ב, HHA.

84. Protocols of Hakibbutz Ha'artzi Committee for the Study of the Movement's journals, n.d., file 25.27(4)1868, HHA.

85. See articles by Adar and Nimrod in *Hotam*, June 9, 1964.

86. See articles by Shor in *Hotam*, June 23 and July 7, 1964.

87. Report regarding a discussion about *Hotam* in the Mapam Young Guard Council, Feb. 16–17, 1965, *Hashavu'a Bakibbutz Ha'artzi*, Feb. 26, 1965.

88. See the discussion about *Hotam* reported in *Hotam*, Mar. 3, 1965.

89. Rikuz Mapam meeting, minutes, July 26, 1966, file 79.90(1), HHA.

90. Yehuda Bower to Meir Yaari, Mar. 5, 1956, file 14.7-95(5), HHA.

91. Interview with Yechiel Harari, *Hashavu'a Bakibbutz Ha'artzi*, July 20, 1973.

92. See, for example, questions for participants in the Hakibbutz Ha'artzi seminar at the end of the 1950s and in the early 1960s, files 14.7-95(5), 17.7-95(2), HHA; summary of short-term ideological seminars, file 2.1.40(1)3917, HHA.

93. Summary of first appointment, Feb. 24, 1957, file ח-62.3(4)476, HHA.

94. This activity was mentioned in a report about the Hakibbutz Ha'artzi Young Guard Fourth Council in *Hotam*, July 21, 1965.

95. Moshe Chizik to Ya'akov Hazan, Aug. 24, 1965, file 4.30.95(6), HHA.

96. Hakibbutz Ha'artzi Secretariat meeting, minutes, Dec. 9, 1965, file 7.5(4)3625, HHA.

97. Hakibbutz Ha'artzi Executive Committee meeting, minutes, Oct. 20, 1966, file 10-10.5(1)3558, and Dec. 14, 1966, file 10.10-5(1)3558, HHA; Meir Talmi to Moshe Chizik, Sept. 19, 1966, file ח-77.3(4), HHA; Mapam Secretariat meeting, minutes, Dec. 29, 1966, file 65.90(13), HHA; plan for a supervised discussion group, n.d., file ח-77.3 (4), HHA.

98. Summary of the fourth cadres course, 1957, file 1.1-40(6)3916, HHA.

99. Nachum Boneh to Hakibbutz Ha'artzi Secretariat, Jan. 14, 1958, file ח-62.3(4)476, HHA.

100. Hakibbutz Ha'artzi Culture Department meeting, minutes, July 31, 1958, file 5.22(2)2107, HHA.

101. Hakibbutz Ha'artzi Culture Department to the kibbutzim, Nov. 22, 1961, file 9.22(4)2110, HHA.

102. Several institutions were founded under the aegis of Givat Haviva in the 1960s and 1970s, such as the Arab-Jewish Institute and the Institute for Research on the Kibbutz Movement.

103. Givat Haviva general report for 1965–66, file 13.16(5)2519, HHA.

104. Givat Haviva general report for 1965–66, file 13.16(5)2519, HHA; plan for Hashomer Hatza'ir youth-movement activity in Givat Haviva, 1960, file 77.1-3(1)589, HHA; discussion about cadres course, 1964, file 3.16(4)2509, HHA.

105. Ychiel Harari to Hakibbutz Ha'artzi Secretariat, Apr. 25, 1972, file ח-88.3(1)503, HHA; summary of the discussion about the future of Givat Haviva, Mar. 1, 1976, file 3.16(4)2509, HHA.

106. Givat Haviva general report for 1965–66, file 13.16(5)2519, HHA.

107. Kaufman, "Sport la-alufim ao la-alafim"; Gil, *Sipuro shel ha-poel.*

108. Yuval Daniely, interview by the author, Givat Haviva, Sept. 30, 2014; Shlomo Shealtiel, interview by the author, Givat Haviva, Sept. 30, 2014.

109. Hapoel Hama'apil file, 133.150(1)5202, HHA.

110. Yuval Danieli, "Ha-shanim ha-mufla'ot shel Hapoel Hama'apil," Sept. 2011, file 133.150(2)5202, HHA.

111. Such as Michah Shamban (1919–2013), Tvi Sinto (1933–69), Amaniahu Levavi (1925–89), and others.

12. From Broken Boundaries to Autonomy

1. For further discussion of the counterculture in Israeli, see Oz Almog, *Pridah mi-Srulik: Arakhim ba-elitah ha-Isre'elit* (Haifa: Univ. of Haifa and Zmora Bitan, 2004), 114, 146; Arie M. Dubnov, "The Missing Beat Generation: Coming of Age and Nostalgism in Arik Einstein's Music," *Jewish Social Studies* 21, no. 1 (Fall 2015): 49–88; Ari Katorzah, "Hamachar eino yodea—rock 'n' roll: Hadat ha-Amerikanit ha-chadasha," *Resling* 6 (1999): 1–13; Moti Regev, "Sof onat ha-tapuzim," *Theoria ve-Bikoret* 12–13 (1999): 251–59.

2. See articles in *Maariv*, June 11, 1970; *Davar*, July 7, 1970; and *Yediot Acharonot*, May 25, 1973. For further discussion, see Almog, *Pridah mi-Srulik*, 129, 139, 898. For Hanoch Levin's writings, see his website at http://www.hanochlevin.com/young-04/p49 (last modified May 23, 2018).

3. Avraham Shapira, ed., *Siach lochamim: Pirkey hakshava ve-hitbonenut* (N.p.: Hotza'at HaIhud, 1967).

4. Gan, "Ha-siach shegava."

5. *Al Hamishmar*, Apr. 25, 1971.

6. *Al Hamishmar*, Apr. 2, 1972.

7. *Al Hamishmar*, Apr. 28, 1972.

8. *Al Hacoma*, July 3, 1968.

9. *Al Hacoma*, Jan. 4, 1969.

10. Gan, "Ha-siach shegava," 263.

11. *Hatza'it*, Apr. 1970.

12. *Hatza'it*, Apr. 1970.

13. Tzavta weekly program, *Al Hamishmar*, May 19, 1967, and Mar. 4, 1968.

14. Quoted in Almog, *Pridah mi-Srulik*, 439.

15. See Moshe Nathan, *Ha-milchama al Yerushalaim* (Tel Aviv: Otpaz, 1968), 345.

16. Reports on Tzavta activities, file 23.1(3), HHA.

17. Reports on Tzavta activities, file (3)23.1, HHA.

18. Michal Snonit, "Metamorfoza: Tzavta al saf tkufa hadasga," *Hotam*, Aug. 14, 1970.

19. *Al Hamishmar*, May 11, 1969.

20. List of Tzavta regional managers, Oct. 23, 1968, file 8.15(3), HHA.

21. Snonit, "Metamorfoza."

22. Snonit, "Metamorfoza."

23. *Al Hamishmar*, Jan. 1, 1971.

24. Quoted in *Al Hamishmar*, July 12, 1972.

25. Mapam Secretariat meeting, minutes, Apr. 21, 1971, file 79.90(2), HHA.

26. *Yediot Acharonot*, July 31, 1972.

27. Quoted in *Al Hamishmar*, Nov. 11, 1972.

28. Quoted in *Yediot Acharonot*, Aug. 31, 1972.

29. Mapam Secretariat meeting, minutes, Apr. 1971, file 79.90(2), HHA.

30. Rikuz Mapam meeting, minutes, Apr. 21, 1971, file (2)79.90, HHA.

31. Tzavta annual report, 1971, file 22.23(4), HHA.

32. Rikuz Mapam meeting, minutes, Mar. 16, 1970, file (1)79.90, HHA.

33. Rikuz Mapam meeting, minutes, Feb. 19, 1970, file (3)79.90, HHA.

34. Rikuz Mapam meeting, minutes, Jan. 13, 1975, file 209.90(9), HHA.

35. Rikuz Mapam meeting, minutes, Jan. 20, 1975, file 209.90(9), HHA.

36. Shoshana Pilus, "Mar Tzavta," *Hotam*, Jan. 1, 1968.

37. Quoted Snonit, "Metamorfoza."

38. Survey of the Hakibbutz Ha'artzi journals, spring 1967, and report by the Hakibbutz Ha'artzi Committee for the Study of the Movement's Journals, Aug. 1967, file 25.27(4)1868, HHA.

39. Mapam Secretariat meeting, minutes, Oct. 3, 1968, file '65.90(16)8182, HHA.

40. Final report by Hakibbutz Ha'artzi's Committee for the Study of the Movement's Journals, Aug. 1967, file 25.27(4)1868, HHA.

41. Report on Hakibbutz Ha'artzi Executive Committee meeting, *Hashavu'a Bakibbutz Ha'artzi*, Apr. 26, 1968.

42. Report on Hakibbutz Ha'artzi Executive Committee meetings, *Hashavu'a Bakibbutz Ha'artzi*, Apr. 26 and June 21, 1968; Mapam Secretariat meetings, minutes, June 4, 1969, May 21, 1969, file '65.90(17)8182, HHA.

43. *Hashavu'a Bakibbutz Ha'artzi*, Mar. 9, 1973; Niva Lanir, telephone interview by the author, Jan. 27, 2013.

44. Mapam Secretariat meetings, minutes, May 5 and June 4, 1969, file '65.90(17)8182, HHA.

45. Rikuz Mapam meeting, minutes, Mar. 3, 1970, file (1)79.90, HHA.

46. Rikuz Mapam meeting, minutes, July 6, 1970, file (1)79.90, HHA.

47. *Hashavu'a Bakibbutz Ha'artzi*, Mar. 9, 1973

48. *Hotam*, Nov. 27, 1970.

49. *Al Hamishmar*, Dec. 4, 1970.

50. Betzalel Lev and Haim Shor to Ya'akov Amit, July 1970, file 1848(4)5.27, HHA.

51. *Al Hamishmar*, Jan. 8, 1971.

52. Rikuz Mapam meeting, minutes, Jan. 11, 1971, file (2)79.90, HHA.

53. *Al Hamishmar*, Jan. 20, 1971.

54. See, for example, articles by Benko Adar in *Hotam*, July 30, Aug. 6, Aug. 13, 1971, and other days.

55. *Hashavu'a Bakibbutz Ha'artzi*, May 21, 1971.

56. Rikuz Mapam meeting, minutes, Jan. 18, 1971, file 79.90(2)862, HHA.

57. Rikuz Mapam meeting, minutes, Aug. 16, 1971, file 79.90(2)862, HHA.

58. Rikuz Mapam meeting, minutes, Aug. 11, 1971, file 79.90(2)862, HHA.

59. Nachum Barnea, "Ha-gal ha-ze ta'im, nifla, hu marveh kol kach," *Davar*, Sept. 19, 1969; Almog, *Prieda me-Srulik*, 98–101.

60. Almog, *Prieda me-Srulik*, 176.

61. Almog, *Prieda me-Srulik*, 192–215.

62. Herman, *Me-lemala lemata*, 214–16; Shprintzak, *Nitzaney politica*; Menachem Moutner, *Yeridat ha-formalism ve-aliyat ha-arachim ba-mishpat ha-Israeli* (Tel Aviv: Maagaley Daat, 1993), 134–36; Dany Koren, ed., *Shkiat ha-miflagot* (Tel Aviv: Hakibbutz Hameuhad, 1998).

63. Herman, *Me-lemala lemata*, 211–13; Herman, "Me-brit shalom le-shalom achshav," 335; Portugez, "Mi-smol sotzi'alisti," 140.

64. Portugez, "Mi-smol sotzi'alisti," 140; Taub, "Shnot ha-shishim ha-amerikaniot be-Israel."

65. Reuven Cahana and Tamar Rapaport, *Neurim ve-hakod ha-bilty formaly* (Jerusalem: Mosad Bialik, 2007), 29, 145–46.

66. Rorty, *Achieving Our Country*.

67. *Al Hamishmar*, July 12, 1970.

68. *Al Hamishmar*, Mar. 7, 1971.

69. Rikuz Mapam meeting, minutes, Mar. 25, 1974, file 70.90(6), HHA.

70. Rikuz Mapam meeting, minutes, Apr. 1, 1974, file 70.90(6), HHA.

71. Rikuz Mapam meeting, minutes, June 10, 1974, file (7)70.90, HHA.

72. For further discussion, see Arieh Avnery, *Hamapolet* (Tel Aviv: Revivim, 1978).

73. Portugez, "Mi-smol sotzi'alisti," 168.

74. Rikuz Mapam meetings, minutes, Jan.–Apr. 1974, file (6)70.90, HHA; see also articles by Benko Adar and Rafel Bankler in *Hotam*, Mar. 29 and Apr. 5, 1974, and by Arieh Avneri in *Davar*, Jan. 31, 1974.

75. For further discussion of the support of the upper middle class in Dash, see Shmuel Noah Eisenstadt, "Hirhurim al shinuy hamapa hapolitit," *Molad* 39–40, no. 8 (1980): 9–14, esp. 6–9; Shevach Weiss, *Hamahapach* (Tel Aviv: Am Oved, 1977); Weiss and Yahav, *Anatomya shell nefila*, 378; Almog, *Preida me-Srulik*, 452; Asher Arian and Michal Shamir, "Shney mahapachim ba-politica ha-Israelit: Madua mahapach 1992 eino ke-mahapach 1977," *Megamot* 4 (1995): 361–87.

Bibliography

Archives

Hashomer Hatza'ir Archive (HHA)
Hebrew Univ. Archive, Jerusalem
Israel State Archive (ISA), Jerusalem
Kibbutz Ein Hashofet Archive

Tel Aviv Municipality Archive
Tel Aviv Univ. Archive
Yigal Alon Archive, Kibbutz Ginosar

Newspapers and Periodicals

Bahativah
Basha'ar
Davar
Ha'aretz
Al Hacoma
Hadaf Ha-Yarok
Al Hamishmar
Hashavu'a Bakibbutz Ha'artzi

Hatza'it
Hedim
Hotam
Lamerchav
Maariv
Yediot Acharonot
Zo Ha-Derech

Interviews by the Author

Bustan, Miryam. Gan Shmuel, Oct. 5, 2006.
Daniely, Yuval. Givat Haviva, Sept. 30, 2014.
Firstenberg, Shmuel. Tel Aviv, Dec. 29, 2005; Jan. 15, 2006.
Lanir, Niva. Telephone interview, Jan. 27, 2013.
Ron, Imri. Mishmar Ha'emek, Dec. 30, 2008.
Sade (Prich), Ada. Maabarot, Mar. 4, 2012.
Shapira, Reuven. Gan Shmuel, May 24, 2009.
Shealtiel, Shlomo. Givat Haviva, Sept. 30, 2014.
Vagner, Yigal. Oranim College, Jan. 17, 2010.
Zamir, Danny. Mishmar Ha'emek, Apr. 7, 2009.

Secondary Sources

Ahronson, Avi. *Hakamat ha-takam*. Efal, Israel: Yad Tabenkin, 2002.

Alexander, Esther. *Koach ha-shivion ba-kalkala*. Tel Aviv: Hakibbutz Hameuhad Press, 1990.

Almog, Oz. *Pridah me-Srulik: Arakhim ba-elitah ha-Isre'elit*. Haifa: Univ. of Haifa and Zmora Bitan, 2004.

Amir, Eyal. "Dirat ha-megurim ba-kibbutz: Ideoligia ve-tichnun." PhD diss., Technion, 1997.

Arian, Asher, and Michal Shamir. "Shney mahapachim ba-politica ha-Israelit: Madua mahapach 1992 eino ke-mahapach 1977." *Megamot* 4 (1995): 361–87.

Arnon, Yaakov. "Ha-mediniyut ha-kalkalit be-1974." *Rev'on le-Kalkala*, Kaf-Alef, 83 (Dec. 1974): 7–15.

———. "Ha-mediniyut ha-kalkalit be-1976." *Rev'on le-Kalkala*, Kaf-Gimel, 88–89 (Apr. 1976): 3–14.

———. *Meshek be-sichrur*. Tel Aviv: Hakibbutz Hameuhad, 1981.

Ashkenazy, Motty. "Da me'ain bata u-lean ata holech." In *Trauma leumit: Milchemet Yom Ha-Kipurim achrey shloshim shana ve-od milchama*, edited by Moshe Shemesh and Zeev Drori, 368–78. Sde Boker, Israel: Ben-Gurion Research Institute Press, 2008.

———. "Tnuat ha-mecha'a she-le'achar milchemet Yom Kipur: Mabat retrospectivy." In *Ha-asor ha-shlishi*, edited by Zvi Tzameret and Hanna Yablonka, 165–70. Jerusalem: Yad Itzhak Ben-Zvi, 2008.

Avnery, Arieh. *Hamapolet*. Tel Aviv: Revivim, 1978.

Bareli, Avi. *Authority and Participation in a New Democracy: Political Struggles in Mapai, Israel's Ruling Party, 1948–1953*. Boston: Academic Studies Press, 2014.

———. "Ha-dimuy ha-Bolsheviki shel Mapay be-siah ha-zikaron ha-Israeli." In *Tarbut, Zikaron vehistorya*, vol. 2, edited by Meir Chazan and Uri Cohen, 249–562. Jerusalem: Tel Aviv Univ. and Zalman Shazar Center, 2012.

———. "Ha-mamlachtiut ve-tnuat ha-avodah bereshit shnot ha-chamishim: Hanachot mivniot." In *Etgar haribonut: Yetzira ve-hagut ba-asor ha-rishon la-medina*, edited by Mordechai Bar-On, 23–44. Jerusalem: Yad Itzhak Ben-Zvi, 1999.

———. "'Mamlakhtiyut': Capitalism and Socialism during the 1950s in Israel." *Journal of Israeli History* 26, no. 2 (2007): 201–27.

———. "Mapai and the Oriental Jewish Question in the Early Years of the State." *Jewish Social Studies* 16, no. 1 (Fall 2009): 54–84.

Bareli, Avi, and Uri Cohen. *The Academic Middle-Class Rebellion*. Leiden: Brill, 2017.

———. "Ha-siach ha-tziburi be-Mapai likrat shvitat ha-academaim be-shenat 1956." *Cathedra* 143(2012): 153–84.

Bareli, Avi, Danny Gutwein, and Tuvia Friling, eds. *Hevra ve-kalkala be-Israel: Mabat histori ve-achshavi*. Sde Boker, Israel: Ben-Gurion Research Institute Press, 2005.

Bareli, Avi, and Nir Keidar. "Mamlakchtiut Israelit." Israeli Institute for Democracy, 2011. At https://www.idi.org.il/media/3498/pp_87.pdf.

Barkai, Haim. *Hitpatchut ha-meshek ha-kibbutzi*. Jerusalem: Machon Falk, 1980.

———. *Yemei bereshit shel ha-meshek ha-Israeli*. Jerusalem: Mosad Biyalik, 1990.

Bar-Or, Amir. "Min ha-yesod: Naftuleyah shel tnua politit." *Iyunim Bitkumat Israel* 4 (1994): 478–93.

Bar-Zohar, Michael. *Ben-Gurion*. Vol. 3. Tel Aviv: Zmura Beitan, 1987.

Bauder, Harald. *Labor Movement: How Migration Regulates Labor Markets*. New York: Oxford Univ. Press, 2006.

Beilin, Yossi. *Banim be-tzel avotam*. Tel Aviv: Revivim, 1984.

———. *Mechiro shel ihud*. Tel Aviv: Revivim, 1985.

Bell, Daniel. *The Coming of Post-industrial Society: A Venture in Social Forecasting*. New York: Basic Books, 1973.

Ben-David, Yitzchak. *Avoda ba-kibbutz: Metziut ve-she'ifot*. N.p.: Center for Research of Rural Settlements and Brit ha-Tnua ha-Kibbutzit, 1975.

Ben-Moshe, Naftali. *Asif: Kovetz ma'amarim*. N.p.: Asif, 1994.

Ben-Porat, Amir. *Heichan hem ha-burganim ha-hem: Toldot ha-burganut ha-Israelit*. Jerusalem: Magnes Press, 1999.

———. "Opium la-hamonim, kaduregel ve-leumiyut aim hakamat ha-medina." In *Sport, arachim ve-politica*, edited by Ilan Gur Zeev and Roni Lidor, 137–39. Hulon, Israel: David Rochgold, 2007.

Berenstein, Dvora. "Ha-panterim ha-shchorim ke-tnuat mecha'a: Kri'at tegar la-medina u-lesdarei'a." In *Ha-asor ha-shlishi*, edited by Zvi Tzameret and Hanna Yablonka, 104–14. Jerusalem: Yad Itzhak Ben-Zvi, 2008.

Bergman, Arieh. *Ha-ta'asiya ve-mediniyut ha-ti'us be-Israel: Sugiyot ikariot 1965–1985*. Jerusalem: Bank of Israel, 1986.

Bodoek, Richard. *Proletarian Performance in Weimar Berlin: Agitprop, Chorus, and Brecht*. Columbia, SC: Camden House, 1997.

Bonacich, Edna. "A Theory of Ethnic Antagonism: The Split Labor Market." *American Sociological Review* 37, no. 5 (Oct. 1972): 547–59.

Bord, Ofer. *Kesef ha-shod mi-yad ha-horeg: Ha-tnua ha-kibutzit ve-heskem ha-shilumim, ha-pitzuyim, ve-hashavat ha-rechush mi-germanya.* Sde Boker, Israel: Ben-Gurion Research Institute Press, Yad Tabenkin, Yad Yaari, and the Institute for Research of the Jewish National Fund, 2015.

Breslavsky, Moshe. *Tnua'at ha-poalim ha-Eretz Israelit.* Vol. 2. Tel Aviv: Hakibutz Hameuhad, 1957.

Brom, Avraham. *Tamid shanui be-Machloket: Ha-hitpatchut ha-kalkalit ve-hahevratit shel ha-tnua ha-kibbutzit me-kom ha-medina.* Tel Aviv: Hakibutz Hameuhad, 1986.

Cahana, Reuven, and Tamar Rapaport. *Neurim ve-hakod ha-bilty formaly.* Jerusalem: Mosad Bialik, 2007.

Carmeli, Ronit. "Tmurot be-yachasam shel tze'irey Hashomer Hatza'ir el brit ha-moatsot, el ha-socialism, ve-el ha-ma'rav bi-shnot ha-chamishim ve-ha-shishim shel ha-me'a ha-esrim." PhD diss., Haifa Univ., 2013.

Chazan, Meir. "Yozmat Nachum Goldman le-hipagesh aim Natzer be-shnat 1970." *Iyunom Bitkumat Israel* 14 (2004): 255–84.

Cohen, Avner. "Ha-smol ha-Israeli bein idiologya liberalit le-meoravut hevratit." In *Hevra ve-kalkala be-Israel: Mabat histori ve-achshavi*, edited by Avi Bareli, Danny Gutwein, and Tuvia Friling, 855–74. Sde Boker, Israel: Ben-Gurion Research Institute Press, 2005.

Cohen, Nissim. "Yazmaey medeniut ve-Itzuv medinyut tziburit: Ha-mikre shel chok bituach briut mamlachti." *Bitachon Socially* 89 (2012): 5–42.

Cohen, Reuven. *Ha-yeshuv ve-ha-kvutza: Yesodot ve-tahalichim.* Tel Aviv: Hakibutz Hameuhad, 1969.

Cohen, Uri. "Ha-intelectual ha-ta'hor ba-politica ao elita academit be-mashber: Meoravut ha-universita ha-ivrit be-parashat Lavon." *Iyunim Bitkumat Israel* 14 (2004): 191–229.

———. "Michael sheli ve-hama'avar me-elit mahapechanit le-mamad beynoni." *Israel* 3 (2003): 157–83.

Cohen, Uri, and Eitan Orkibi. "Universita ve-shilton—me-shutfut le-imut: Ha-elita ha-academit ve-nisuach ha-bikoret le-mahapach 1977." *Alpaim* 33 (2008): 149–86.

Crosland, Anthony. *The Future of Socialism.* London: Jonathan Cape, 1956.

Dahan, Momi. "Aliyat ai-hashivyon ha-kalkali." In *Me-meoravut memshaltit le-kalkalat shuk, ha-meshek ha-Israeli 1985–1998*, edited by Avi Ben-Basat, 610–56. Tel Aviv: Am Oved, 2001.

Dahan Kalev, Henriette. *Ha-hachmatza ha-gdola shel ha-demokratya ha-Israelit: Ha-zikaron ha-traumati ke-moreshet shel Meha'ot Vadi Salib*. N.p.: Israeli Institute for Democracy, 2009.

Denning, Michael. *The Cultural Front*. New York: Verso, 1996.

Ha-doch ha-klali. Jerusalem: Bank of Israel, 1970.

Ha-doch ha-shanati. Jerusalem: Bank of Israel, 1970.

Ha-doch ha-shanati. Jerusalem: Bank of Israel, 1973.

Doch ha-va'ada le-bdikat halukat ha-hachnasa ha-le'umit be-Israel. Jerusalem: Bank of Israel, Dec. 1966.

Don, Yehuda. *Industrialization of a Rural Collective*. Aldershot, UK: Avebury, 1988.

Doron, Avraham. "Medinyut ha-revacha ve-ha-bitachon ha-socialy ba-asor hashlishi." In *Ha-asor ha-shlishi*, edited by Zvi Tzameret and Hanna Yablonka, 115–28. Jerusalem: Yad Itzhak Ben-Zvi, 2008.

Dowty, Alan. *Israel/Palestine*. Cambridge: Polity Press, 2008.

Dribkin-Darin, Haim. *Ha-hevra ha-acheret*. Tel Aviv: Sifriyat Poalim, 1961.

Dubnov, Arie M. "The Missing Beat Generation: Coming of Age and Nostalgism in Arik Einstein's Music." *Jewish Social Studies* 21, no. 1 (Fall 2015): 49–88.

Duverger, Maurice. *Political Parties: Their Organization and Activity in the Modern State*. New York: Wiley, 1954; London: Methuen, 1964.

Eisenstadt, Shmuel Noah. "Hirhurim al shinuy hamapa hapolitit." *Molad* 39–40, no. 8 (1980): 9–14.

———. *Tmurot ba-hevra ha-Israelit*. Tel Aviv: Misrad Habitachon, 2004.

Ekshtein, Shlomo. *Shituf bein kafri be-michun haklai*. Rehovot, Israel: Hamacon le-Cheker ha-Hityashvut, 1969.

Eley, Geoff. *Forging Democracy: The History of the Left in Europe, 1850–2000*. Oxford: Oxford Univ. Press, 2002.

Elmaliach, Tal. "Hashpa'at moreshet tnuat ha-noar Hashomer Hatza'ir ba-Kibbutz Ha'artzi ve-Mapam." *Israel* 23 (2015): 257–84.

———. "The Israeli Left between Culture and Politics: Tzavta Club and Mapam 1956–1973." *Journal of Israeli History* 33, no. 2 (Sept. 2014): 169–83.

———. "Ketz ha-hanhaga ha-historit: Kalkala, chevra ve-politica ba-Kibbutz Ha'artzi ve-Mapam 1956–1973." *Iyunim Bitkumat Israel* 24 (2014): 306–31.

———. "Sport, hevra, politica ve-ideologia: Hakibbutz Ha'artzi–Hashomer Hatza'ir ve-hakaduraf." *Cathedra* 157 (2015): 155–74.

———. *Ha-ta'asia ha-kibbutzit 1923–2007*. Givat Haviva, Israel: Yad Yaari, 2009.

Elmaliach, Tal, and Anat Kidron. "Mecha'a tzeira be-Israel 1967–1977." *Iyunim Bitkumat Israel* 11 (2017): 78–101.

Etzioni-Halevy, Eva, and Moshe Livne. "The Response of the Israeli Establishment to the Yom Kippur War Protest." *Middle East Journal* 31, no. 3 (Summer 1977): 281–96.

Feder, Naftali. *Pagashti anashim*. Tel Aviv: Israel Buch, 1998.

Feingold, Ben-Ami. "Tarbut u-ma'amad: Ohel—aliyato u-nefilato shel te'atron po'alim." *Iyunim Bitkumat Israel* 15 (2005): 72–349.

Feinmaster, Israel. *Hakibbutz be-tichnuno*. Tel Aviv: Sifriyat Poalim, 1984.

Francis, Pat. "The Labor Publishing Company." *History Workshop Journal* 18, no. 1 (1984): 115–23.

Friling, Tuvia, ed. *Tshuva le-amit post Tziony*. Tel Aviv: Yediot Sfarim, 2003.

Gal, Allon. "Brandeis ve-Hashomer Hatza'ir." *Yaad* 8, no. 26 (Nov. 1991): 66–70.

———. "Envisioning Israel: The American-Jewish Tradition." In *Envisioning Israel: The Changing Ideals and Images of North American Jews*, edited by Allon Gal, 13–40. Detroit: Wayne State Univ. Press; Jerusalem: Magnes Press, 1996.

———, ed. *Envisioning Israel: The Changing Ideals and Images of North American Jews*. Detroit: Wayne State Univ. Press; Jerusalem: Magnes Press, 1996.

Gal, Johnny. *Bitachon socialy be-Israel*. Jerusalem: Magnes Press, 2004.

———. "Al metutelet bituach ha-avtala be-Israel 1972–2003." *Bitachon Socialy* 67 (2004): 109–43.

———. *Ha-omnam netel me-ratzon? Sipura shel ha-hitmodedut aim ha-avtala 1920–1995*. Sde Boker, Israel: Ben-Gurion Research Institute Press, 2002.

Gan, Alon. "Chasufim ba-tzariach ve-siach lochamim ke-tzirey zehut mitpatzlim." *Israel* 13 (2008): 267–96.

———. "Shinuyim hevrati'im ba-tnua ha-kibbutzit be-shnot ha-shishim." *Iyunim Bitkumat Israel* 16 (2006): 343–72.

———. "Ha-siach shegava: Tarbut ha-sichim ke-nisayon le-gibush zehut me-yachedet ba-dor ha-sheny ba-kibbutzim." PhD diss., Tel Aviv Univ., 2002.

Gil, Emanuel. *Sipuro shel ha-poel*. Tel Aviv: Hakibbutz Hameuhad, 1976.

Gonen, Amiram. "Bchina geografit shel ha-tacharut ha-electoralit bein ha-maarach ve-halikud ba-arim ha-yehudiot be-Israel, 1965–1981." *Medina, Mimshal Veyachasim Beinleumi-im* 19–20 (1982): 63–87.

Gorni, Yosef. "He-asor ha-mufla: Hirhurim al he-asor ha-rishon be-shnat hayovel la-medina." In *Ha-asor ha-rishon*, edited by Zvi Tzameret and Hanna Yablonka, 363–70. Jerusalem: Yad Itzhak Ben-Zvi, 1997.

Greenberg, Lev. *Ha-histadrut me'al hakol.* Jerusalem: Nevo, 1993.

———. "Mapai bein demokratizatzia le-liberalizatzia: Le-she'elat tokpa shel ha-dichotomya medina/hevra ezrachit." In *Israel: Me-hevra meguyest le-hevra ezrachit?* edited by Yoav Peled and Adi Ofir, 244–61. Jerusalem: Van Leer Institute; Tel Aviv: Hakibbutz Hameuhad, 2001.

Greenberg, Yitzhak. *Anatomia shel mashber yadua merosh: Krisat hevrat a-ovdim bishnot ha-80.* Tel Aviv: Am Oved, 1989.

———. *Pinchas Sapir: Biografia kalkalit ve-politit.* Tel Aviv: Resling, 2011.

Gross, Nachum. "Kalkalat Israel 1954–1967." In *Ha-asor ha-sheni*, edited by Zvi Tzameret and Hanna Yablonka, 30–46. Jerusalem: Yad Itzhak Ben-Zvi, 2001.

Gutman, Emanuel. "Miflagut u-machanot: Yetzivut ve-shinui." In *Ha-ma'arechet ha-politit be-Israel*, edited by Moshe Lissak and Emanuel Gutman, 122–70. Tel Aviv: Am Oved, 1979.

Gutwein, Danny. "Ha-chalutziut ha-burganit: Tarbut popularit ve-haetos shel ma'amad ha-beynaim ha-mimsadi, shirei Naomi Shemer 1956–1967." *Israel* 20 (2012): 20–80.

———. "He'arot al ha-yesodot ha-ma'amadi'im shel ha-kibush." *Theoria ve-Bikoret* 24, no. 203 (2004): 203–11.

———. "Al kalkala ve-de'a kduma." *Theoria ve-Bikoret* 26, no. 286 (2005): 286–96.

———. "Al ha-stira bein ha-etos ha-halutzi la-idiologya ha-sotzyalistit bi-tnuat ha-avoda ha-Yisraelit: David Ben-Gurion ve-Yitzhak Ben-Aharon 1948–1967." *Iyunim Bitkumat Israel* 20 (2010): 208–48.

Guzansky, Tamar. *Atzma'ut kalkalit—keitzad? Sikumim be-hitpatchuta ha-kalkalit shel Israel.* Tel Aviv: Iyun, 1969.

Hacohen, Eliezer. *Sivchei kalkala u-medina.* Tel Aviv: Sifriyat Poalim, 1977.

Hakim, Ran. *Ha-kibbutzim be-Israel: Mabat history kalkaly.* Givat Haviva, Israel: Yad Yaari, 2009.

Halamish, Aviva. "The Historic Leadership of Hakibbutz Ha'artzi: The Power of Charisma, Organization, and Ideology." *Journal of Israeli History* 23, no. 1 (Mar. 2012): 45–66.

———. *Kibbutz, Utopia, and Politics: The Life and Times of Meir Yaari, 1897–1987.* Boston: Academic Studies Press, 2017.

———. "Loyalties in Conflict: Mapam's Vacillating Stance on the Military Government, 1955–1966, Historical and Political Analysis." *Israel Studies Review* 33, no. 3 (2018): 26–53.

———. *Meir Yaari: Ha-admor mi-Merchavia, shnot hamedina.* Tel Aviv: Am Oved, 2012.

———. *Meir Ya'ari: Biografiyah kibutzit 1897–1947, hamishim ha-shanim ha-rishonot*. Tel Aviv: Am Oved, 2009.

Halevi, Nadav, and Rut Kalinov-Malul. *Ha-hitpatcut ha-kalkalit shel Israel*. Jerusalem: Academon, 1968.

Halperin, Hagit. *Ha-maestro: Hayav vi-yetzirato shel Avraham Shlonsky*. Tel Aviv: Sifriyat Poalim, Hakibbutz Hameuhad, 2011.

Hanin, Dov. "Me-Eretz Israel ha-ovedet le-Eretz Israel ha-shniya: Siach umediniyut hevratit be-Mapai shel shnot ha-chmishim." In *Shilton ha-hon be-Israel*, edited by Danny Filc and Uri Ram, 131–63. Jerusalem: Van Leer institute; Tel Aviv: Hakibbutz Hameuhad, 2004.

Harvey, David. *A Brief History of Neoliberalism*. Oxford: Oxford Univ. Press, 2007.

———. *The Condition of Postmodernity: An Enquiry into the Origins of Cultural Change*. Cambridge, MA: Blackwell, 1990.

Heilbronner, Oded. "Resistance through Rituals: Urban Subcultures of Israeli Youth from the Late 1950s to the 1980s." *Israel Studies* 16, no. 3 (Fall 2011): 28–50.

Helman, Anat. *Bigdei ha-eretz ha-chadasha: Medinat Israel be-rei ha-ofna*. Jerusalem: Merkaz Zalman Shazar, 2012.

Herman, Tamar. "Aliato shel va'ad ha-shalom ha-Israeli u-nefilato." *Ha-Tziyonut*, Yud-Zain 1993, 245–60.

———. "Me-brit shalom le-shalom achshav: Ha-patzifism ha-pragmaty shel machaneh ha-shalom be-Israel." PhD diss., Tel Aviv Univ., 1989.

———. *Me-lemala lemata: Tnu'ot hevratiot u-mecha'a politit*. Vol. 2. Ra'anana, Israel: Open Univ., 1995.

———. "New Challenges to New Authority: Israeli Grass Roots Activism in the 1950's." In *Israel: The First Decade of Independence*, edited by S. Ilan Troen and Noah Lucas, 105–24. Albany: State Univ. of New York Press, 1995.

Hirsh, Shmuel, and Uri Cohen. "He'arot al ha-sociologia ha-Israelit bi-rei miyeshuv le-medina." *Iyunim Bitkumat Israel* 10 (2000): 317–52.

Hofgong, Menachem. *Mecha'a ve-chem'a: Hashpa'at hafganot ha-panterim ha-shchorim al haktza'ot le-tzorchei hevra u-revacha*. Jerusalem: Nevo, 2006.

Horn, Gerd-Rainer. *The Spirit of 1968: Rebellion in Western Europe and North America, 1956–1976*. New York: Oxford Univ. Press, 2007.

Horowitz, Dan, and Moshe Lissak. *Trouble in Utopia: The Overburdened Polity of Israel*. Albany: State Univ. of New York Press, 1989.

Inglehart, Ronald. "The Silent Revolution in Post-industrial Societies." *American Political Science Review* 65 (1971): 991–1017.

Ishai, Yael. *Civil Society in Israel.* Jerusalem: Carmel, 2003.

Izhar, Uri. *Bein hazon le-shilton: Mifleget Ahdut-Ha'avoda-Poalei-Zion bi-shnot ha-yeshuv ve-hamedina.* Ramat Efal, Israel: Yad Tabenkin, 2005.

Jackson, Julian. *The Popular Front in France 1934–38.* Cambridge: Cambridge Univ. Press, 1988.

Judt, Tony. *Postwar: A History of Europe since 1945.* New York: Penguin Press, 2005.

Kabalo, Pola. "Ezrachim mitbagrim—kinus ha-talmidim be-Sheich Munis: Hit-nagshut, dialog, ve-mifgash." *Israel* 4 (2003): 123–54.

———. "Pioneering Discourse and the Shaping of an Israeli Citizen in the 1950s." *Jewish Social Studies* 15, no. 2 (Winter 2009): 82–110.

Kafkafy, Eyal. *Lavon—anti mashiach.* Tel Aviv: Am Oved, 1998.

Kanari, Baruch. *Tabenkin be-Eretz Israel.* Sde Boker, Israel: Ben-Gurion Research Institute Press, 2003.

Kanovsky, Eliyahu. *The Economic Impact of the Six-Day War: Israel, the Occupied Territories, Egypt, Jordan.* New York: Praeger, 1970.

Katorzah, Ari. "Hamachar eino yodea—rock 'n' roll: Hadat ha-Amerikanit ha-chadasha." *Resling* 6 (1999): 1–13.

Katz, Richard S., and Peter Mair. "Changing Models of Party Organization and Party Democracy: The Emergence of the Cartel Party." *Party Politics* 1, no. 1 (1995): 5–31.

Kaufman, Haim. "Sport le-alufim ao le-alafim." *Etmol* 199 (2008): 55–57.

———. "Ha-zika ha-ra'ayonit bein sport ha-Poalim le-bein hit'agdut Hapoel be-tkufat ha-mandat." *Betnnua,* Gimel 1995, 56–77.

Keren, Michael. *Ha-et ve-hacherev: Levateia shel ha-intiligentzia ha-Israelit.* Tel Aviv: Ramot, 1991.

Ha-kibbutzim ve-uchlusiyatam: Tmurot demografiot ba-shanim 1961–2005. Jerusalem: Israeli Central Bureau of Statistics, June 2008.

Kołakowski, Leszek. *Al ha-reshut netuna.* Tel Aviv: Sifriyat Poalim, 1964.

Kolat, Israel. "Ha-histadrut ashema bakol?" (a critique of Lev Greenberg, *Ha-histadrut me'al hakol*). *Iyunim Bitkumat Israel* 9 (1999): 578–85.

———. "Le-mekoma shel ha-idea be-hit-havut ha-kvutza ba-aretz." In *Heiseg history bi-tmurotav,* edited by Avigil Paz-Yishayahu and Yosef Gorni, 55–58. Sde Boker, Israel: Ben-Gurion Research Institute Press, 2006.

Kondor, Yaakov. *Kalkalat Israel*. Tel Aviv: Shoken, 1984.

Koren, Dany, ed. *Shkiat ha-miflagot*. Tel Aviv: Hakibbutz Hameuhad, 1998.

Krampf, Arieh. "Kinuno shel musag ha-astzmaut ha-kalkalit ba-siach ha-Israeli." *Iyunim Bitkumat Israel* 19 (2009): 1–34.

Lam, Tzvi. *Tnuot ha-noar ha-Tzioniot be-mabat le-Achor*. Tel Aviv: Sifriyat Poalim, 1991.

Laybourn, Keith. *A Century of Labour: A History of the Labour Party, 1900–2000*. Phoenix Mill, UK: Sutton, 2000.

Lekachman, Robert. *The Age of Keynes*. New York: Random House, 1966.

Lemke, Christiane, and Gary Marks, eds. *The Crisis of Socialism in Europe*. Durham, NC: Duke Univ. Press, 1992.

———. "From Decline to Demise: The Fate of Socialism in Europe." In *The Crisis of Socialism in Europe*, edited by Christiane Lemke and Gary Marks, 1–20. Durham, NC: Duke Univ. Press, 1992.

Lev, Tali, and Yehuda Shenhav. "Kinunu shel ha-oyev mibifnim: Hapanterim hashchorim kemusa shel panica musarit." *Sociologia Israelit* 12, no. 1 (2010): 135–58.

Levi-Faur, David. "The Developmental State: Israel, South Korea, and Taiwan Compared." *Studies in Comparative International Development* 33, no. 1 (1988): 65–93.

———. *Ha-yad ha-lo ne'elama: Ha-politica shel ha-tius be-Israel*. Jerusalem: Yad Itzchak Ben Tzvi; Haifa: Univ. of Haifa, 2001.

Lipset, Seymour M., and Stein Rokkan. *Party Systems and Voter Alignments: Cross-National Perspectives*. New York: Free Press, 1967.

Lissak, Moshe. *Ha-aliya ha-gdola be-shnot ha-chamishim: Kishlono shel kur ha-hituch*. Jerusalem: Mosad Bialik, 1999.

Lissak, Moshe, and Dan Horowitz. "Gius polity ve-binui mosdot ba-yeshuv h-yehudi bi-tkufat ha-mandat." In *Ha-ma'arechet ha-politit be-Israel*, edited by Moshe Lissak and Emanuel Gutman, 51–81. Tel Aviv: Am Oved, 1979.

Mair, Peter. *Party System Change: Approaches and Interpretations*. Oxford: Clarendon Press; New York: Oxford Univ. Press, 1998.

Margalit, Elkana, ed. *Ha-smol ha-meuhad*. Givat Haviva, Israel: Yad Yaari, 1991.

Medding, Pitter Y. *Mapai in Israel: Political Organization and Government in a New Society*. Cambridge: Cambridge Univ. Press, 1972.

Medzini, Meron. *Golda: Biografya politit*. Tel Aviv: Yediot Sfarim, 2008.

Merchav, Peretz. *Toldot tnuat ha-poalim be-Eretz Israel*. Tel Aviv: Sifriyat Poalim, 1967.

Michael, Avraham, and Refael Bar-El. *Shvitot be-Israel: Gisha kamutit.* Ramat Gan, Israel: Ha-Machon le-Kidum Yachasey Avoda, Bar-Ilan Univ., 1977.

Molcho, Avner. "Kapitalism ve-haderech ha-Americanit be-Israel: Perion, nihul ve-Ha'etos ha-kapitalisty ba-siua ha-techny shel artzot habrit be-shnot ha-chamishim." In *Hevra ve-kalkala be-Israel: Mabat histori ve-achshavi,* edited by Avi Bareli, Danny Gutwein, and Tuvia Friling, 263–94. Sde Boker, Israel: Ben-Gurion Research Institute Press, 2005.

Morgenshtern, Shlomo. "Ha-zchuyot ha-socialiot shel ovdei ha-Histadrut: Hit-patchuiot ve-nesigot." *Ha-Meshek ha-Shitufi: Beteon le-Sheelot Kalkala, Co-operatzia ve-Meshsek Poalim* 16–17, nos. 592–93 (Aug. 16, 1964): 14–15.

Morris, Benny. *Righteous Victims: A History of the Zionist–Arab Conflict 1881–1999.* New York: Knopf, 1999.

Mortimer, Edward. *The Rise of the French Communist Party.* London: Faber, 1984.

Moshayov, Ch. D. "Shloshet ha-sektorim ba-meshek ha-Israeli." *Ha-Meshek ha-Shitufi: Beteon le-Sheelot Kalkala, Cooperatzia ve-Meshsek Poalim* 16–17, nos. 592–93 (Aug. 16, 1964): 10–11.

Moutner, Menachem. *Yeridat ha-formalism ve-aliyat ha-arachim ba-mishpat ha-Israeli.* Tel Aviv: Maagaley Daat, 1993.

Natan, Dudi. "Ha-mediniyut ha-kalkalit shel memshelet Rabin, 1974–1977." MA thesis, Univ. of Haifa, 2007.

Nathan, Moshe. *Ha-milchama al Yerushalaim.* Tel Aviv: Otpaz, 1968.

Navon, Tom. "Ha-mitun: Tziun derech ba-historia ha-politit-kalkalit shel Israel, 1964–1967." *Iyunim Bitkumat Israel* 26 (2016): 386–429.

Near, Henry. *The Kibbutz Movement: A History.* Jerusalem: Magnes Press, 1997.

Netunim statistim. N.p.: Ha-Machon le-Mechkar Kalkali ve-Hevrati, ha-Histadrut ha-Klalit, Apr. 1969.

Netunim statistim 1968–1971. N.p.: Ha-Machon le-Mechkar Kalkali ve-Chevrati, ha-Histadrut ha-Klalit, Apr. 1972.

Neuberger, Benyamin. *Mimshal ve-politica.* Ra'anana, Israel: Open Univ., 1997.

Nun, Ch. "Ramat ha-chaim shel ha-mishpacha ha-ovedet." *Ha-Meshek ha-Shitufi: Beteon le-Sheelot Kalkala, Cooperatzia ve-Meshsek Poalim* 16–17, nos. 592–93 (Aug. 16, 1964): 11–12.

Offe, Claus. *Contradictions of the Welfare State.* Cambridge, MA: MIT Press, 1984.

Ofir, Michal, and Tami Eliav. *Kitzba'ot ha-yeladim be-Israel: Mabat history ve-re'iya bein-leumit.* N.p.: Hamosad Lebituach Leumi, Dec. 2005.

Oren, Mordechai. *Reshimot asir Prague.* Tel Aviv: Sifriyat Poalim, 1958.

Pauker, Alon. "Hakibbutz Ha'artzi u-vrit ha-mo'atzot be-asor ha-atzma'ut ha-rishon." *Iyunim Bitkumat Israel* 22 (2012): 64–90.

———. "Utopia be-svach ha-stirot: Hashva'a bein ha-dimuim ha-atzmi'im shel ha-tnutot hakibutziot be-asor ha-rishon la-medina." PhD diss., Tel Aviv Univ., 2005.

Paz, Shaul. *Paneinu el ha-shemesh ha-ola.* Sde Boker, Israel: Ben-Gurion Research Institute Press and Bialik Institute, 2017.

Paz-Yishayahu, Avigil, and Yosef Gorni, eds. *Heiseg history bi-tmurotav.* Sde Boker, Israel: Ben-Gurion Research Institute Press, 2006.

Peled, Yoav, and Gershon Shapir. *Mihu Israeli.* Tel Aviv: Tel Aviv Univ. Press, 2005.

Pikar, Avi. "Reshita shel ha-aliya ha-selektivit be-shnot ha-chamishin." *Iyunim Bitkumat Israel* 9 (1999): 338–94.

Polychroniou, Chronis, ed. *Socialism: Crisis and Renewal.* Westport, CN: Praeger, 1993.

Pomfret, Richard W. T. *Trade Policies and Industrialization in a Small Country: The Case of Israel.* Tubingen, Germany: Mohr, 1976.

Portugez, Adi. "Mi-smol sotzi'alisti li-smol hadash: Zramim ba-tzibur u-va-politikah be-Yisrael bein ha-shanim 1967–1982." PhD diss., Bar Ilan Univ., 2008.

———. "Tnuat smol Israeli hadash: Smol hadash be-Israel." *Israel* 21 (2013): 225–52.

Rabinovich, Itamar. *The Lingering Conflict: Israel, the Arabs, and the Middle East 1948–2012.* Washington, DC: Saban Center for Middle East Policy, Brookings Institution Press, 2011.

Ram, Uri. *The Changing Agenda of Israeli Sociology.* Albany: State Univ. of New York Press, 1995.

———, ed. *Ha-hevra ha-Israelit: Hebetim bikortiyim.* Tel Aviv: Brerot, 1993.

Ray, Larry J. *Social Theory and the Crisis of State Socialism.* Cheltenham, UK: Edward Elgar, 1996.

Rechavi, Yechiel, and Asher Veingerten. *Yovel shanim le-gius hon hitzoni be-emtzaut irgun ha-bonds.* Jerusalem: Bank of Israel, Sept. 6, 2004. At http://www.boi.org.il/deptdata/neumim/neum163h.pdf.

Ree, Jonathan. *Proletarian Philosophers: Problems in Popular Culture in Britain 1900–1940.* Oxford: Clarendon Press, 1984.

Regev, Moti. "Sof onat ha-tapuzim." *Theoria ve-Bikoret* 12–13 (1999): 251–59.

Reinharz, Shulamit. "Irma 'Rama' Lindheim: An Independent American Zionist Woman." *Nashim: A Journal of Jewish Women's Studies and Gender Issues* 1 (Winter 1998): 106–35.

Roby, Bryan K. *The Mizrahi Era of Rebellion: Israel's Forgotten Civil Rights Struggle, 1948–1966.* Syracuse, NY: Syracuse Univ. Press, 2015.

Rorty, Richard. *Achieving Our Country: Leftist Thought in Twentieth-Century America.* Cambridge, MA: Harvard Univ. Press, 1997.

Rozenfeld, Henri, and Shulamit Carmi. "Nichus emtzaim tziburiyim ve-ma'amad beynoni totzar hamdina." *Machbarot Lemechkar ve-Lebikoret* 2 (1979): 43–84.

Rozner, Menachem, Yitzhak Ben David, Alexander Avnat, Nani Cohen and Uri Leviatan. *Hador ha-sheny: Ha-kibbutz bein hemshech le-tmura.* Tel Aviv: Sifriyat Poalim, 1978.

Rozolio, Daniel. *Ha-shita ve-ha-mashber.* Tel Aviv: Am Oved, 1999.

Safran, Nadav. *Medinat Israel ve-yachasei'ha aim artzot ha-brit.* Jerusalem: Shoken, 1979.

Sapir, Michal. *Ha-yesh ha-gadol: Biografya shel Pinchas Sapir.* Tel Aviv: Miskal, 2011.

Sarna, Jonathan. "A Projection of America as It Ought to Be: Zion in the Mind's Eye of American Jews." In *Envisioning Israel: The Changing Ideals and Images of North American Jews,* edited by Allon Gal, 41–59. Detroit: Wayne State Univ. Press; Jerusalem: Magnes Press, 1996.

Sassoon, Donald. *One Hundred Years of Socialism: The West European Left in the Twentieth Century.* New York: New Press, 1996.

Schenker, Avraham. "Progressive Zionism in America." In *Against the Stream: Seven Decades of Hashomer Hatza'ir in North America,* edited by Ariel Hurwitz, 273–95. Givat Haviva, Israel: Yad Yaari, 1994.

Schwartz Greenwald, Carol. *Recession as a Policy Instrument: Israel 1965–1969.* Rutherford, NJ: Fairleigh Dickinson Univ. Press, 1973.

Sha'ashua, L., Y. Goldsmit, and B. Trabelsy. *Ha-shpa'at ha-misgeret shel ha-ashray ha-merukaz al ha-hashka'ot ba-kibutzim.* N.p.: Ha-Yechida ha-Bein Kibbutzit le-Hadracha Kalkalit, June 1977.

Shacham, Nathan. *Sifriyat Poalim—50 shana.* Tel Aviv: Sifriyat Poalim, 1989.

Shafir, Gershon. *Land, Labor, and the Origins of the Israeli–Palestinian Conflict.* Cambridge: Cambridge Univ. Press, 1989.

Shalev, Michael. "Ovdim, medina umashber: Hakalkala hamedinit shel Israel." In *Ha-hevra ha-Israelit: Hebetim bikortiyim,* edited by Uri Ram, 148–71. Tel Aviv: Brerot, 1993.

Shalom, Zaki. "Hitpatrut Ben Gurion me-rashut ha-memshala." *Iyunim Bitkumat Israel* 5 (1995): 608–14.

Shalom Chetrit, Sami. *Ha-ma'avak ha-Mizrahi be-Israel*. Tel Aviv: Am Oved, 2004.

Shapira, Anita. *Berl*. Tel Aviv: Am Oved, 1981.

———. "'Black Night–White Snow': Attitudes of the Palestinian Labor Movement to the Russian Revolution, 1917–1929." In *Essential Papers on Jews and the Left*, edited by Ezra Mendelsohn, 236–71. New York: New York Univ. Press, 1997.

———. *Ha-halicha al kav ha-ofek*. Tel Aviv: Am Oved, 1988.

———, ed. *Medina ba-derech: Ha-hevera ha-Israelit ba-asorim ha-rishonim*. Jerusalem: Merkaz Zalman Shazar, 2001.

———. *Yehudim ḥadashim, Yehudim yeshanim*. Tel Aviv: Am Oved, 1997.

Shapira, Avraham, ed. *Siach lochamim: Pirkey hakshava ve-hitbonenut*. N.p.: Hotza'at HaIhud, 1967.

Shapira, Reuven. "Ha-aratzat brit ha-moatzot ba-tnu'ot ha-kibbutziot ha-rashiot: Hisradut manhigim be-shlav ai-ye'ilutam ve-oligarchizatzia be-Israel." *Hamerchav Hatziburi* 5 (2011): 92–121.

———. *Ha-emet al ha-kibbutz*. Haifa: Pardes, 2013.

Shapira, Yonatan. *Achdut ha-avoda ha-historit: Otzmato shel irgun polity*. Tel Aviv: Am Oved, 1975.

———. *Elite le-lo mamshichim*. Tel Aviv: Sifriyat Poalim, 1984.

———. "Ha-mekorot ha-historiyim shel ha-demokratya ha-Yisraelit: Mapai kemiflaga dominantit." In *Ha-hevra ha-Israelit: Hebetim bikortiyim*, edited by Uri Ram, 40–53. Tel Aviv: Brerot, 1993.

———. *Lashilton bachartanu: Darka shel tnuaat ha-Cheirut*. Tel Aviv: Am Oved, 1989.

Shavit, Yaakov. "Be-hipus ahar ha-burganut ha-Israelit" (a critique of Amir Ben-Porat, *Heichan hem ha-burganim ha-hem*). *Cathedra* 95 (2000): 159–64.

Shifris, Amos. *Memshelet Rabin ha-rishona 1974–1977*. Tzur Igaal, Israel: Porat, 2013.

Shilon, Avi. *Ben-Gurion: His Later Years in the Political Wilderness*. Lanham, MD: Rowman and Littlefield, 2016.

———. *Menachem Begin: A Life*. New Haven, CN: Yale Univ. Press, 2012.

Ha-shilumim ve-hashpa'attam. Jerusalem: Bank of Israel, Dec. 1965.

Shishim shana be-rei ha-statistica. Jerusalem: Israel Main Institute for Statistics, May 1998. At http://www.cbs.gov.il/statistical/statistical60_heb.pdf.

Shiv, Ricki. "Tochnit ha-yetzuv 1985: Kalkala Nechonah oh idiologia." *Iyunim Bitkumat Israel* 23 (2013): 315–49.

Shnaton ha-memshala. Jerusalem: Tav-Shin-Lamed-Chet, 1976.

Shor, Shimon ed., *Hitpatchuyot be-kalkalat Israel ve-hashpa'atan al ha-kibbutz.* N.p.: Hakibbutz Ha'artzi, Nov. 1975.

Shprintzak, Ehud. *Nitzaney politica shel de-legitimizatzia be-Israel 1967–1972,* Jerusalem: Hebrew Univ., 1983.

Shtenger, Shlomo. *Ha-ta'asia ha-kibbutzit.* N.p.: Igud ha-Taasia Hakibbutzit, 1971.

Silber, Irwin. *Socialism: What Went Wrong? An Inquiry into the Theoretical and Historical Sources of the Socialist Crisis.* London: Pluto Press, 1994.

Slutsky, Yehuda. *Mavo le-toldot tnu'at ha-avodah ha-Yisre'elit.* Tel Aviv: Am Oved, 1973.

———. "Mekoma shel ha-idea ha-mechavenet be-hit'havut ha-kvutza be-Israel." In *Heiseg history bi-tmurotav,* edited by Avigil Paz-Yishayahu and Yosef Gorni, 43–54. Sde Boker, Israel: Ben-Gurion Research Institute Press, 2006.

"State Socialism." Lexico, n.d. At http://www.oxforddictionaries.com/definition/english/state-socialism.

Steil, Benn. *The Battle of Bretton Woods: John Maynard Keynes, Harry Dexter White, and the Making of a New World Order.* Princeton, NJ: Princeton Univ. Press, 2013.

Svirsky, Shlomo. "1967: Tafnit kalkalit be-Israel." In *Hevra ve-kalkala be-Israel: Mabat histori ve-achshavi,* edited by Avi Bareli, Danny Gutwein, and Tuvia Friling, 91–116. Sde Boker, Israel: Ben-Gurion Research Institute Press, 2005.

———. *Kampus, hevra u-medina.* Jerusalem: Mifras, 1982.

Svirsky, Shlomo, and Dvora Bernstein. "Mi avad bema? Avur mi utmurat ma? Hapituah hakalkali shel Israel ve-halukat ha'avoda ha'adatit." In *Ha-hevra ha-Israelit: Hebetim bikortiyim,* edited by Uri Ram, 120–47. Tel Aviv: Brerot, 1993.

Symposium on Regional Cooperation. N.p.: Ihud ha-Kvutzot ve-Hakibbutzim, Apr. 1962.

Talmon-Gerber, Yonina. *Yachid ve-hevra ba-kibbutz.* Jerusalem: Magnes Press and Hebrew Univ., 1970.

Tamir, Yossi. *Shinuyim be-dfusei ha-oni be-auchlusiat ha-schirim be-Israel 1969–1975: Megamot klaliot.* Jerusalem: Hamosad le-Bituach Leumi, Mechkar 18, 1977.

Taub, Gadi. "Shnot ha-shishim ha-Amerikaniot be-Israel: Me-mered le-konformiut." *Iyunim Bitkumat Israel* 13 (2003): 1–28.

Timor, Doron, and Uri Cohen. "Yachas ha-kibbutzim le-mosdot ha-haskalah ha-gvo'ha: Me-dchi'ya ve-histaygut le-hishtalvut." *Iyunim Bitkumat Israel* 23 (2014): 378–410.

Tokatli, Rachel. "Dfusim politim be-yachasey ha-avoda be-Israel." PhD diss., Tel Aviv Univ., 1979.

Topel, Menachem. "Ha-technokratim ke-elita kibutzit." In *Elitot hadashot be-Israel*, edited by Eliezer Ben Refael, 255–74. Jerusalem: Mosad Bialik, 2007.

Tzahor, Zeev. *Hazan: Tnu'at hayim*. Jerusalem: Yad Itzhak Ben-Zvi; Givat Haviva, Israel: Yad Yaari, 1997.

———. "Hitkarshut ha-laba ha-yokedet." In *Itzuv ha-Israeliyut*, 102–15. Tel Aviv: Am Oved and Sapir College, 2007.

Tzameret, Tzvi. "Ben Tzion Dinur: Intelektual boneh medina." *Htziyonut*, Kaf-Alef 1998, 321–32.

———. *Hitpatchut ma'arechet ha-chinuch*. Unit 7 in the series Israel in the First Decade. Ra'anana, Israel: Open Univ., 2003.

———. "Zalman Aran ve-ma'arechet ha-chinuch." In *Ha-asor ha-sheni*, edited by Zvi Tzameret and Hanna Yablonka, 61–79. Jerusalem: Yad Itzhak Ben-Zvi, 2001.

Tzameret, Zvi, and Hanna Yablonka, eds. *Ha-asor ha-sheni*. Jerusalem: Yad Itzhak Ben-Zvi, 2001.

———, eds. *Ha-asor ha-shlishi*. Jerusalem: Yad Itzhak Ben-Zvi, 2008.

Tzur, Eli. "Bdidut ha-manhig ha-zaken." *Ha-Tziyonut*, Kaf-Bet 2000, 283–310.

———. "Hakibutz Ha'artzi, ha-omanut-ha-mesharetet ve-hareka ha-history." In *Aomanut be-sheirut ra'aion*, edited by Shlomo Shealtiel, 13–25. Givat Haviva, Israel: Yad Yaari; Sde Boker, Israel: Ben-Gurion Research Institute Press, 1999.

———. "Le-hi'ot am hofshi be-artzenu: Ha-liga le-meni'at kfia datit be-hekshera ha-history." In *Medina ba-derech: Ha-hevera ha-Israelit ba-asorim ha-rishonim*, edited by Anita Shapira, 205–38. Jerusalem: Merkaz Zalman Shazar, 2001.

———, ed. *Lo yuchlu biladeynu: Emdot Mapam bi-she'elot hutz u-vitahon 1948–1956*. Givat Haviva, Israel: Yad Yaari; Ramat Efal, Israel: Yad Tabenkin, 2000.

———. *Nofey ha'ashlaya*. Sde Boker, Israel: Ben-Gurion Research Institute Press, 1998.

Tzur, Muki, and Yuval Danieli, eds. *Livnot ve-lehibanot ba: Sefer Shmuel Mistechkin: Adrichalut ha-Kibbutz be-tichnunu*. Tel Aviv: Hakibbutz Hameuhad, 2008.

Tzur, Yaakov. *Min ha-yam ad ha-midbar: Tabenkin ve-Hakibbutz Hameuhad ba-emuna u-Bama'avak le-shlemut ha-Aretz*. Jerusalem: Yad Itzchak Ben-Tzvi, 2015.

Tzur, Zeev. *Hakibbutz Hameuhad be-yeshuva shel ha'aretz.* Vol. 4. Tel Aviv: Hakibbutz Hameuhad, 1986.

"Valleyball." In *Entziklopedia le-tarbut ve-le-sport,* edited by Y. Aviram and others. Tel Aviv: Am Oved, 1959.

Weiss, Shevach. *Am ve-eda: Kovetz mechkarim be-nosei manhigut ve-peilut politit be-kerev ha-olim u-bnei ha-edot ha-lo Ashkenaziot.* Haifa: Univ. of Haifa, 1974.

———. *Ha-mahapach.* Tel Aviv: Am Oved, 1977.

Weiss, Shevach, and Yona Yahav. *Anatomya shell nefila.* Haifa: Shachaf, 1977.

Weiss, Yfaat. *Vadi Salib: Ha-nochach ve-ha-nifkad.* Jerusalem: Van Leer Institute; Tel Aviv: Hakibbutz Hameuhad, 2007.

Weits, Ychiam. "Preida me-ha'av ha-meyased: Prishato shel Ben-Gurion me-rashut ha-memshala be-1963." In *Medina ba-derech: Ha-hevera ha-Israelit ba-asorim ha-rishonim,* edited by Anita Shapira, 73–108. Jerusalem: Merkaz Zalman Shazar, 2001.

Weitz, Ra'anan. *Ha-kfar ha-Israeli be-idan ha-technologya.* Tel Aviv: Am Oved, 1967.

Weitz, Yechiam, ed. *Bein hazon le-revizia.* Jerusalem: Merkaz Zalman Shazar, 1997.

———. "Miflaga mitmodedet aim kishlona: Mapai nochach ha-totzaot ba-bchirot la-Knesset ha-shlishit." *Cathedra* 77 (1996): 124–34.

Williams, Raymond. "Capitalism." In *Keywords: A Vocabulary of Culture and Society,* rev. ed., 52. New York: Oxford Univ. Press, 1983.

Wolfsfeld, Gadi. *The Politics of Provocation: Participation and Protest in Israel.* Albany: State Univ. of New York Press, 1988.

Yagol, Yona. *Ketz ha-hagmonya: Nefilat ha-ma'arach ve-aliyat ha-Likud.* Hulon, Israel: Yesod, 1978.

Zayit, David. *Halutzim ba-mavoch ha-politi: Ha-tnua ha-kibutzit 1927–1948.* Jerusalem: Yad Itzhak Ben-Zvi, 1993.

Zisser, Baruch. *Al yemin ve-al smol.* Jerusalem: Shoken, 1999.

Index

Adar, Benko, 186–87, 190, 212–13, 251n3
After the War (no author mentioned), 202
Agranat Commission, 116
agriculture: aid for, 152; cooperative
    arrangements for, 93, 97, 136; eco-
    nomic structure of, 87; productivity
    in, 53–54
Ahdut Ha'avodah (Unity of Labor):
    and access to jobs and services, 67,
    236n22; and the Alliance, 157, 158;
    and break with Mapam, 4, 6, 28, 169;
    cultural activities of, 38; divisions in,
    147; in elections to Knesset, 122–23;
    and entry into government, 148;
    and ethnic voters, 119, 120, 122–23;
    founding of, 27; in labor move-
    ment, 229n2; mass party structure
    of, 31; membership in, 69; position
    on Arab question, 32; relation-
    ship with Mapai, 152, 154; support
    for, 70; urban activists in, 123; and
    wage freeze, 155. *See also* Alignment
    (HaMa'arakh); cultural front; eco-
    nomic inequality
Ahdut Ha'avodah–Poalei Tzion (Unity
    of Labor–Workers of Zion), 27
Akraba farmland incident, 113–14, 137
Al Hamishmar: coverage of riots, 151;
    criticism of, 213; debate about
    Alignment in, 183–84; debate about

Soviet Union in, 182–83; debate on
    automation in, 134, 135; in expansion
    of culture, 210–11; *Hotam*'s merger
    with, 212; leadership's control over,
    191, 214; on *The Me Nobody Knows*,
    206; on New Left, 139; and shift away
    from indoctrination, 181–82
Alignment (HaMa'arakh): Ahdut
    Ha'avodah and, 142, 147, 157, 158;
    debate on, 177, 190; election results
    for, 1, 126, 142; founding of, 141, 142,
    174, 224; Mapam and, 4, 98, 155–57,
    161–62; opposition to, 159, 221
aliyah (immigration to Israel), 59–60
Allon, Yigal, 76, 123, 133, 141, 146,
    252n16
Aloni, Shulamit, 99–100
American capitalism, 51, 52, 61, 87
American Jewish community: Israe-
    lis' cultivation of, 60–61; Mapam's
    relations with, 58; support from, 58,
    59–60, 77
Americans for Progressive Israel, 61
American youth movements, 59–60
Amit, Meir, 213, 246n24
Amit, Ya'akov, 182, 212
Amitai, Yossi, 211, 212, 251n3
Among Young People (no author men-
    tioned), 202
Am Oved (Working People), 37

Chizik, Moshe, 193, 194
Churchills (band), 203, 209
class consciousness, 196
class differences: in economic equality, 75, 121; in factories, 135; in pay scale changes, 91, 92. *See also* middle class; professional class; working class
class struggle. *See* Marxism
Cohen, Ran, 251n3
Cohn-Bendit, Daniel (Danny the Red), 139
colonialism, 172
commercialization of culture, 166, 181–82, 183, 200, 204
Communist bloc, 1, 40
Communist Manifesto (Marx and Engels), 187
competitiveness: in economy, 91; in kibbutzim, 66, 94, 135; and volleyball, 43, 196, 197, 198–99
consumerism, 62, 63, 133, 165–66, 225
Critical School of Israeli sociology, 7–8, 72, 241n61
cultural autonomy: in counterculture, 215; in media, 215–16; of the press, 210–15; rise of, 200, 203, 215, 225; of Tzavta Tel Aviv, 204–10, 210–16
cultural centers. *See* Tzavta (Circle of Friends)
cultural front: establishment of, 38; expansion of, 165, 210; and expression of opposition views, 200; and ideology, 32; meaning of term, 30, 36; as platform for debate, 168, 210 (*see also Al Hamishmar; Bahativah; Basha'ar; Givat Haviva; Hashavu'a Bakibbutz Ha'artzi; Hedim; Hotam*; "New World Order, A"; Sifriyat Poalim; theory of camps; Tzavta Tel Aviv); and regulation of internal

tensions, 224–25; subversive nature of, 183–84
cultural rebellion, 8
culture as change agent, 166, 216, 218–20, 225
Czechoslovakian–Egyptian arms agreement, 170

Daniel, Eliyahu, 211
Dash (Tnu'a Demokratit LeShinui, or Democratic Movement for Change), 100, 221, 246n24
Davar (Speech) (newspaper), 37, 40, 215
Davar Hashavua (Item of the Week) (magazine), 215
Dayan, Moshe: on Akraba farmland incident, 114; ambitions of, 146; criticism of, 203; efforts to block actions of, 160–61; and government's listening to the public, 117; letter of protest to, 108; and *mamlakhtiyut*, 145–46; in Mapai campaign, 122; opposition to, 160; popularity of, 142
democratic centralism, 28, 102, 182–83
democratization, 98–104, 176, 214, 217
democrats (left wing): and Ahdut Ha'avodah, 147; and criticism of Yom Kippur War, 116; and critiques of Israeli society, 105; ideology of, 127; and labor movement, 101–4, 220–21, 223, 225; and Min Hayesod, 146; and peace treaty, 107–8; and rise of New Left, 104–5; and rise of Yesh, 114–15; and rivalry with sectoralists, 162; and violations of Arabs' basic rights, 108–14
Department of Culture and Propaganda of Hakibbutz Ha'artzi, 43
Dinur, Ben-Zion, 37
discourse culture, 103–4

Germany: personal compensation from, 58–59; as source of equipment and industrial knowledge, 58

Givat Haviva, 43, 44–45, 191–93, 194–96, 214, 261n102

Goldmann, Nahum, 107

Goldschmit, Ze'ev, 184

Group of Eleven (Hug ha-Achad-Asar), 102–3, 138, 189, 245n10

Gush Emunim (Bloc of the Faithful), 118

Hacohen, Eliezer, 135, 188–89, 213

Haganah (self-defense force), 27

Hahug Habein-Kibbutzi (Interkibbutz Circle), 103–4

Hair (musical), 203

Hakibbutz Ha'artzi (Kibbutz Movement): about, 3–4, 231n18; assertion of independence by, 157; conservatism of leadership of, 135–36; and cooperation with other movement organizations, 97–98; ideological authority of, 192; ideological principles of, 32–33; and IDF, 149; membership of, 68–69; as part of labor movement, 229n2; political framework for, 24–27; in protest movement, 105, 115; revolutionary romanticism of, 169; socialist roots of, 168–69; social structure of, 9; Youth Division of, 112, 174, 203. *See also* cultural front; economic prosperity and affluence; Hakibbutz Ha'artzi and Mapam movement; Hashomer Hatza'ir youth movement; historic leadership; ideological collectivism; industrialization; kibbutz ideology; kibbutzim; meshekism; protest movement; theory of camps

Hakibbutz Ha'artzi and Mapam movement: building of, 222; change and crisis in, 4; contradictions in growth and decline of, 5–8; and Hashomer Hatza'ir, 230n13; historic leadership of, 4, 25, 162; and independence of kibbutzim, 85; and opposition to capitalism and imperialism, 58; and position on Arabs, 236n23; power structure and purposes of, 9–10; and role in labor movement crisis, 6–7; scholarship on, 5–7, 231n20; as socialist paradox, 226; socioeconomic development and political crisis of, 9; tensions between reality and utopian ideology of, 34–35; tensions within, 10–11. *See also Al Hamishmar*; cultural front; democrats; Givat Haviva; Hazan, Ya'akov; historic leadership; protest movement; sectoralism; Sifriyat Poalim; sports, support for; theory of camps; Ya'ari, Meir

Hakibbutz Ha'artzi–Hashomer Hatza'ir (Nationwide Kibbutz), 15–16. *See also* Hakibbutz Ha'artzi (Kibbutz Movement); Hashomer Hatza'ir youth movement

Hakibbutz Hameuhad (United Kibbutz): and cooperation in kibbutz movement, 97, 136; cultural activities of, 38; divisions in, 147, 169; factories founded by, 56; founding of, 16; and Hashomer Hatza'ir, 4; and Hehalutz movement, 71; as kibbutz movement, 3, 229n2; leadership of, 26; political party founded by, 27–28; politics of, 17; socialist roots of, 168–69; sports in, 42; and supporters of Ahdut Ha'avodah, 70

Mapam (United Workers Party): about, 3–4, 28; and criticism from government, 110; divisions and contradictory positions in, 120, 147–54, 158–59; election losses of, 28; in elections to Knesset, 4, 28, 98, 102, 130, 148, 152, 155, 158; historic leadership of, 4, 25; independence of, 137, 149, 155, 158, 161–63, 175; institutional structure of, 235n17; and joining government, 4, 156–58; and loss of voters, 224; membership in, 69, 235n21; as opposition party, 4, 154–55; position on Arabs, 32–33, 113; and role as mediator, 22–23; salaried positions in, 236n22; and selection of Executive Committee members, 127–28; support for, 32, 69–70; and tensions with Mapai, 151–52; and urban supporters, 123–24. *See also Al Hamishmar*; Alignment; capitalism; cultural front; democrats; economic inequality; Givat Haviva; Hakibbutz Ha'artzi and Mapam movement; Hazan, Ya'akov; historic leadership; mass party model; Mizrahim; New Left; protest movement; sectoralism; Sifriyat Poalim; sports, support for; theory of camps; Tzavta (Circle of Friends); Ya'ari, Meir
Marcuse, Herbert, 139
Marshall Plan (European Recovery Program), 50
Marxism: and art, 43; criticism of, 181; and ideology of kibbutzim, 39, 40, 168; and ideology of labor movement, 6, 33, 226; and New Left, 202; and Sifriyat Poalim, 181, 194, 214; and theory of camps, 184–85, 187

mass party model: and adaptation to age of affluence, 145; concentric political structure in, 73, 120; description of, 29–30; and economic inequality, 119, 223; in labor parties, 30–31, 222
Matzpen (Compass, the anti-Zionist Israel Socialist Organization), 110, 138–39
Meir, Golda: and Akraba farmland, 114; and Arabs' return to villages, 112; and Ashkenazi's vigil, 117, 118; criticism of, 203; and economic inequality, 82; leadership of, 146–47; occupied territories, peace, and, 147; and Rafiah settlement, 109, 110; and revision of policies and methods, 142; and Yom Kippur War, 116; and youth's protests, 138, 252n16
Menahem, Shimon, 206, 208, 210
Me Nobody Knows, The (musical, trans. Ben-Amotz), 206
Meri (Machane Radicali Israeli, Israeli Radical Wing), 107
meshekism, 192, 195, 198
meshekists: as change agents, 199; and Mapam, 148, 177; origination of term, 245n11; power of, 135, 136; rise of, 93–98; and theory of camps, 188–89
Meshel, Yeruham, 82
middle class: and counterculture, 215; and dependence on labor movement, 85; effect of economic boom on, 79; emergence of, 5, 223; and ideological fervor, 195; politics of, 99–101, 105; Rafi, Mapai, and, 99; rise of, 62–67, 68; sectoral interests of, 127; and unemployment, 76; and younger generation, 172–73

Tal Elmaliach is a Kreitman Postdoctoral Fellow in the Ben-Gurion Institute for the Study of Israel and Zionism. Prior to that, he was an Israel Institute Postdoctoral Fellow for 2015–17 at the Mosse-Weinstein Center for Jewish Studies, University of Wisconsin–Madison. He wrote his doctoral dissertation at Haifa University on the Hashomer Hatza'ir kibbutz movement and the Mapam party in 1956–77.

Haim Watzman is a Jerusalem-based writer and translator. He is the author, most recently, of *Necessary Stories*, a collection of short fiction. His previous books are *Company C: An American's Life as a Citizen-Soldier in Israel* and *A Crack in the Earth: A Journey up Israel's Rift Valley*.